CRITICAL EXPOSITION

OF THE

THIRD CHAPTER

OF

PAUL'S EPISTLE TO THE ROMANS.

A

CRITICAL EXPOSITION

OF THE

THIRD CHAPTER

OF

PAUL'S EPISTLE TO THE ROMANS.

A MONOGRAPH.

By JAMES MORISON, D.D.

WIPF & STOCK · Eugene, Oregon

Wipf and Stock Publishers
199 W 8th Ave, Suite 3
Eugene, OR 97401

A Critical Exposition of the Third Chapter of
Paul's Epistle to the Romans. A Monograph
By Morrison, James
ISBN 13: 978-1-60608-376-5
Publication date 6/18/2009
Previously published by Hamilton, Adams & Co., 1866

PREFACE.

THE following MONOGRAPH on *the Third Chapter of the Epistle to the Romans* is respectfully and diffidently submitted to the judgement of scholarly students of the Bible. It has been a "labour of love" to the author,—a solace to his spirit amid trials which he need not particularize. Retiring from the din and strife and worry of the outer world, he entered, as by an inner gate, into the school of the Prophets and Apostles. It was like a Spiritual University. It was like a home too,—a home for the heart. Having entered, he engaged with ardour in the studies pursued. He found them soothing. He found the teachers inspiring as well inspired. But he felt peculiar attractions drawing him toward Paul. "Quid est enim Paulo rarius?" exclaims Melancthon.* Surely he is a rare man, Paul. He is a rare teacher. "Nothing" is rarer. Mingling freely with the other scholars,—patristic, medieval, modern, and more modern,—whom the author found clustering around this incomparable instructor, he listened eagerly to the divine utterances that fell from his lips. He entered, too, with zest into the discussions of the pupils, when, in their respective groups, they ventilated among themselves the import of the Master's utterances. In these scholastic exercises,—prosecuted without noise and wrangling,—he

* Declamatiunculae duae in Divi Pauli Doctrinam, *p.* 2, ed. 1522.

found inexpressible delight. The following Monograph is the result of a little portion of his investigations and reflections.

The *Third Chapter of the Epistle to the Romans* has, from a very early period of the Christian era, been *a special study to Paul's students.* It has been regarded,—and with great justice,—as of very peculiar significance in relation to some of the most important doctrines of theology. As regards more particularly the vital doctrine of *justification by faith*, it is, perhaps, the principal *locus classicus* that is to be found in the Bible. At that part of the Chapter in which we find the culminating point of the Apostle's exhibition of this great and favourite theme, Luther, in a marginal note attached to his German translation, arrests the attention of the reader, saying:—"*Take heed to what is here said.—It is the central and most important passage of the Epistle, and indeed of the entire Scripture.*" * Calvin coincided with Luther in opinion. "*There is probably,*" he remarks, "*no passage in the whole Bible of greater significance as regards the justifying righteousness of God.*" † Corresponding opinions are expressed by multitudes of other theologians and critics whose judgements are entitled to consideration. ‡

It is hence the case that, if there be, in an exposition of *the Third Chapter of the Epistle to the Romans*, anything approximating to a thorough investigation of the broader

* Merke dies.—Ist das Hauptstück und der Mittelplatz dieser Epistel und der ganzen Schrift.

† "Nullus est forte in tota Scriptura insignior locus ad vim istius justitiae illustrandam." His French expression is,—"Il n'y a pas paraventure en toute l'Escriture un plus excellent passage, pour exprimer la grande efficace et la vertu magnifique de ceste justice."

‡ See an ample list of quotations, inclusive of those from Luther and Calvin, at pp. 269—272 of the present volume.

aspects as well as of the minuter elements of the Apostle's teaching, there will be the realization of theological results of no inconsiderable magnitude and moment. The mind will most probably acquire a very definite conception of that "article of a standing or a falling church,"—*justification by faith without works.* Such other articles, too, as are inseparably connected with that doctrine,—the articles which refer to man's need of a gratuitous method of justification, and to God's provision of propitiation as the ground or "meritorious cause" of gracious justification, will probably be apprehended, and, to a certain extent, even comprehended. In this *Third Chapter of Romans* the Apostle portrays, in a most elaborate manner, man's need of gratuitous justification. He likewise exhibits, in some most weighty and far-reaching observations, the necessity of propitiation, and its relation to justification. He says something, too, of very great significance regarding *redemption* and the *pretermission* (as well as the *remission*) of sins.

All these subjects are carefully considered, from a critical and exegetical point of view, in the following Monograph; and there has been at least an honest effort to look at them, and to see them, in that clearest of all lights,—the light which the Apostle's own phraseology, when fairly and adequately analyzed and understood, is fitted to shed upon them.

The author has had in view at once the permanent interests of Biblical Exegesis, and the present phases of some great theological controversies. He has the conviction that it is matter of special moment that the minds of theological inquirers in general, and of theological controvertists in particular, should be recalled, at frequently recurring intervals, to the calm investigation of the biblical ideas *as they lie in continuity on the page of inspiration.* If such investigation does not exhaust,—as it does not,—the possibilities of doctrinal analysis and synthesis; if it leaves indeterminate,—as it does,—the measure of vital elasticity, as regards form, of which the essential realities of theology and religion are susceptible in thought;—it shows nevertheless,—at least when conducted with sufficient freedom from sectarian prepossession, and with adequate literary skill and scientific intuition,—what were the actual representations of things which were evolved in the minds of the inspired writers. When these actual representations are actually ascertained, a touchstone is got hold of, that is of inestimable value for testing the legitimacy of the theological conceptions which are either already current in the churches, or which are pushing their way into public notice, and seeking or demanding ecclesiastical recognition. The farther, undoubtedly, that any doctrines diverge in form from the forms that are explicitly exhibited on the pages of the Book, the less is the likelihood of their resolvability, in substrate, into the biblical forms; and the farther, consequently, must they be removed, so far as real authority is concerned, from the sphere of men's consciences. The more unwieldy, too, must they be in the matter of adaptability for exerting a wholesome ethical influence on men's hearts and lives.

It is presumed that scholars will perceive that—whatever may be the value of the theological results arrived at in the following Monograph—the critical researches are the author's own. The learned will be able, by the simplest application of their diacritical tests, to determine that he has not dealt in second-hand references. He trusts to the generosity of his readers to pardon such errata of inadvertence as are incident to works of the kind.

As the Work was intended to be a somewhat thorough and fundamental *expiscation* of the Apostle's teachings in the Chapter, the author has aimed at furnishing his readers with something like a free-and-easy history of the interpretation that has been given to the various expressions of the Apostle. He could easily, of course, have pursued another plan. He could easily have confined himself to the exhibition and confirmation of his own particular views. But it was a different ideal of exposition on which he wished to work. He assumed that his readers would really feel no particular interest in finding out *his* particular standpoint. He felt, himself, a genuine interest in going round among the various standpoints that have been occupied by other earnest thinkers,—the thinkers who have respectively endeavoured, in the spirit of loyal pupils, to catch and exhibit the Pauline shades of thought. He hence occupied himself, for his special purpose in this Monograph, in stepping upon these various standpoints, and looking at every subject in succession from those peculiar angles of vision that were determined by the relative peculiarity of the standpoints occupied. He has not grudged this labour; but, on the contrary, he has taken pleasure in it, under the conviction that, if one be able, with steady head, *sich zu orientiren* amid a multiplicity of standpoints, he is all the more likely to get deliverance from crotchets, partialities, and ideal pets, and to acquire breadth and manysidedness of conception. The author hopes, too, that it may not be uninteresting to younger theologians to be introduced into the company, —no inconsiderable circle,—of the chief Expositors of the Epistle, patristic, medieval, and modern.

While, in the following pages, there are numerous quotations from foreign expositors, these are nevertheless almost always rendered, either literally or freely, into English. And the original quotations themselves, as well as Hebrew phrases, and the Apostle's own Greek expressions, are in general so interwoven in parentheses that the thread of English composition runs on continuously. It is hence the case that even such readers as cannot make free use of foreign languages will, in all ordinary cases, be able to follow the line of exposition without any very serious "let or hindrance." The author does not think that it is needful, in such expositions, to throw all kinds of observations and quotations *chaotically into a heap.* Neither can he see any good reason for banishing from the domain of scientific exegesis concinnity of logical thought and the graces of tolerably well-sustained and classic composition. Neither does he know of any valid reason why biblical exposition, as such, should be made to run in any of the peculiar ruts,—grammatical, logical, theological, historical, or practical,—that have been the favourite lines of any of his distinguished predecessors.

No special *Prolegomena* are required. They merge themselves in the general *Prolegomena* that belong to the Epistle as a whole. It would hence be out of place to disintegrate the literature and literary history of the Chapter from the literary history and the literature of the entire Epistle.

FLORENTINE BANK HOUSE,
GLASGOW, *Oct. 1, 1866.*

ORIGINAL TEXT OF ROMANS III.

(*THE AUTHOR'S RECENSION.*)

1 [1]Τί οὖν τὸ περισσὸν τοῦ Ἰουδαίου; ἢ τίς ἡ ὠφέλεια τῆς
2 περιτομῆς; [2]Πολὺ κατὰ πάντα τρόπον. Πρῶτον μὲν γὰρ,
3 ὅτι ἐπιστεύθησαν τὰ λόγια τοῦ θεοῦ. [3]Τί γὰρ εἰ ἠπίστησάν τινες; Μὴ ἡ ἀπιστία αὐτῶν τὴν πίστιν τοῦ θεοῦ
4 καταργήσει; [4]Μὴ γένοιτο. Γινέσθω δὲ ὁ θεὸς ἀληθής,
πᾶς δὲ ἄνθρωπος ψεύστης, καθὼς γέγραπται, Ὅπως ἂν
δικαιωθῇς ἐν τοῖς λόγοις σου, καὶ νικήσῃς ἐν τῷ
5 κρίνεσθαί σε. [5]Εἰ δὲ ἡ ἀδικία ἡμῶν θεοῦ δικαιοσύνην
συνίστησιν, τί ἐροῦμεν; Μὴ ἄδικος ὁ θεὸς, ὁ ἐπιφέρων τὴν
6 ὀργήν;—κατὰ ἄνθρωπον λέγω. [6]Μὴ γένοιτο· ἐπεὶ πῶς
7 κρινεῖ ὁ θεὸς τὸν κόσμον; [7]Εἰ γὰρ ἡ ἀλήθεια τοῦ θεοῦ ἐν
τῷ ἐμῷ ψεύσματι ἐπερίσσευσεν εἰς τὴν δόξαν αὐτοῦ, τί ἔτι
8 κἀγὼ ὡς ἁμαρτωλὸς κρίνομαι; [8]καὶ μὴ—καθὼς βλασφημούμεθα καὶ καθώς φασίν τινες ἡμᾶς λέγειν ὅτι—ποιήσωμεν
τὰ κακὰ ἵνα ἔλθῃ τὰ ἀγαθά;—ὧν τὸ κρίμα ἔνδικόν
ἐστιν.

9 [9]Τί οὖν; Προεχόμεθα; Οὐ πάντως· προῃτιασάμεθα γὰρ
Ἰουδαίους τε καὶ Ἕλληνας πάντας ὑφ' ἁμαρτίαν εἶναι·
10 [10]καθὼς γέγραπται ὅτι οὐκ ἔστιν δίκαιος, οὐδε εἷς·
11 [11]οὐκ ἔστιν ὁ συνιῶν· οὐκ ἔστιν ὁ ἐκζητῶν τὸν
12 θεόν. [12]Πάντες ἐξέκλιναν· ἅμα ἠχρεώθησαν·
οὐκ ἔστιν ποιῶν χρηστότητα, οὐκ ἔστιν ἕως ἑνός.
13 [13]Τάφος ἀνεῳγμένος ὁ λάρυγξ αὐτῶν· ταῖς γλώσσαις αὐτῶν ἐδολιοῦσαν. Ἰὸς ἀσπίδων ὑπὸ τὰ

14 χείλη αὐτῶν. 14 Ὧν τὸ στόμα ἀρᾶς καὶ πικρίας
15 γέμει. 15 Ὀξεῖς οἱ πόδες αὐτῶν ἐκχέαι αἷμα·
16 16 σύντριμμα καὶ ταλαιπωρία ἐν ταῖς ὁδοῖς αὐτῶν·
17, 17 καὶ ὁδὸν εἰρήνης οὐκ ἔγνωσαν. 18 Οὐκ ἔστιν
18 φόβος θεοῦ ἀπέναντι τῶν ὀφθαλμῶν αὐτῶν.
19 19 Οἴδαμεν δὲ ὅτι ὅσα ὁ νόμος λέγει, τοῖς ἐν τῷ νόμῳ
λαλεῖ, ἵνα πᾶν στόμα φραγῇ, καὶ ὑπόδικος γένηται πᾶς ὁ
20 κόσμος τῷ θεῷ· 20 διότι ἐξ ἔργων νόμου οὐ δικαιωθήσεται
πᾶσα σὰρξ ἐνώπιον αὐτοῦ· διὰ γὰρ νόμου ἐπίγνωσις ἁμαρτίας.

21 21 Νυνὶ δὲ χωρὶς νόμου δικαιοσύνη θεοῦ πεφανέρωται,
22 μαρτυρουμένη ὑπὸ τοῦ νόμου καὶ τῶν προφητῶν, 22 δικαιοσύνη δὲ θεοῦ διὰ πίστεως Ἰησοῦ Χριστοῦ, εἰς πάντας, καὶ
23 ἐπὶ πάντας τοὺς πιστεύοντας· οὐ γάρ διαστολή· 23 πάντες
24 γὰρ ἥμαρτον, καὶ ὑστεροῦνται τῆς δόξης τοῦ θεοῦ, 24 δικαιούμενοι δωρεὰν τῇ αὐτοῦ χάριτι διὰ τῆς ἀπολυτρώσεως τῆς
25 ἐν Χριστῷ Ἰησοῦ, 25 ὃν προέθετο ὁ θεὸς ἱλαστήριον, διὰ
πίστεως ἐν τῷ αὐτοῦ αἵματι, εἰς ἔνδειξιν τῆς δικαιοσύνης
αὐτοῦ διὰ τὴν πάρεσιν τῶν προγεγονότων ἁμαρτημάτων
26 26 ἐν τῇ ἀνοχῇ τοῦ θεοῦ, πρὸς τὴν ἔνδειξιν τῆς δικαιοσύνης
αὐτοῦ ἐν τῷ νῦν καιρῷ, εἰς τὸ εἶναι αὐτὸν δίκαιον καὶ δικαιοῦντα τὸν ἐκ πίστεως Ἰησοῦ.

27 27 Ποῦ οὖν ἡ καύχησις; Ἐξεκλείσθη. Διὰ ποίου νόμου;
Τῶν ἔργων; Οὐχί· ἀλλὰ διὰ νόμου πίστεως.
28 28 Λογιζόμεθα οὖν δικαιοῦσθαι πίστει ἄνθρωπον χωρὶς
ἔργων νόμου.
29 29 Ἢ Ἰουδαίων ὁ θεὸς μονον; Οὐχι δὲ καὶ ἐθνων; Ναὶ
30 καὶ ἐθνων· 30 ἐπείπερ εἷς ὁ θεὸς ὃς δικαιώσει περιτομὴν ’κ
πίστεως, καὶ ἀκροβυστίαν διὰ τῆς πίστεως.
31 31 Νόμον οὖν καταργοῦμεν διὰ τῆς πίστεως; Μὴ γένοιτο·
ἀλλὰ νόμον ἱστάνομεν.

TRANSLATION OF ROMANS III.

ENGLISH AUTHORIZED VERSION.

(Paragraph I.)

1 WHAT advantage then hath the Jew? or what profit *is there* of circumcision?

2 Much every way: chiefly, because that unto them were committed the oracles of God.

3 For what if some did not believe? shall their unbelief make the faith of God without effect?

4 God forbid: yea, let God be true, but every man a liar; as it is written, That thou mightest be justified in thy sayings, and mightest overcome when thou art judged.

5 But if our unrighteousness commend the righteousness of God, what shall we say? *Is* God unrighteous who taketh vengeance? (I speak as a man)

6 God forbid: for then how shall God judge the world?

7 For if the truth of God hath more abounded through my lie unto his glory; why yet am I also judged as a sinner?

AUTHOR'S REVISED VERSION.

1 [1]WHAT then is the preeminence of the Jew? or what
the advantage of circumci-
2 sion? [2]Much in every respect.' For, in the first place,
they were intrusted with the
3 oracles of God. [3]For what
although some believed not?
Shall their unbelief make the
faithfulness of God to fail?
4 [4]Far be it! Let God on
the contrary turn out to be
true, but every man a liar,
as it has been written, **That
thou mightest be justified in
thy words, and overcome when
thou enterest into judgement.**
5 [5]But if our unrighteousness
sets off God's righteousness,
what shall we say? Is God
unrighteous, who inflicteth
wrath?—I speak after the
6 manner of man. [6]Far be
it! Since how shall God
7 judge the world? [7]For if
the trueness of God superabounded through my lie, unto
his glory, why notwithstanding am even I judged as a

AUTHORIZED VERSION.

8 And not *rather*, (as we be slanderously reported, and as some affirm that we say,) Let us do evil, that good may come? whose damnation is just.

REVISED VERSION.

8 sinner? [8] and (why) might we
not—as we are slandered and
as some allege that we say
that we might—do evil that
good might come?—whose
judgement is just.

(Paragraph II.)

AUTHORIZED VERSION.

9 What then? are we better *than they?* No, in no wise: for we have before proved both Jews and Gentiles, that they are all under sin;

10 As it is written, There is none righteous, no, not one:

11 There is none that understandeth, there is none that seeketh after God.

12 They are all gone out of the way, they are together become unprofitable; there is none that doeth good, no, not one.

13 Their throat *is* an open sepulchre; with their tongues they have used deceit; the poison of asps *is* under their lips:

14 Whose mouth *is* full of cursing and bitterness:

15 Their feet *are* swift to shed blood:

16 Destruction and misery *are* in their ways:

17 And the way of peace have they not known:

18 There is no fear of God before their eyes.

19 Now we know that what things soever the law saith, it saith to them who are under the law: that every mouth may be

REVISED VERSION.

9 [9] WHAT then? Do we
put forth pleas in our own
behalf? No certainly; for we
before impeached both Jews
and Greeks of being all under
10 sin:—[10] as it has been written, **There is none righteous,**
11 **not even one:** [11] **there is none**
who understandeth: there is
none who is seeking out God.
12 [12] **All turned aside: together**
they became corrupt: there is
none doing goodness; there is
13 **not so much as one.** [13] **Their**
throat is a sepulchre opened:
with their tongues they were
using deceit. Asps' venom is un-
14 **der their lips.** [14] **Whose mouth**
is full of cursing and bitter-
15 **ness.** [15] **Their feet are swift**
16 **to shed blood:** [16] **destruction**
and misery are in their ways:
17 [17] **and the way of peace they**
18 **did not know.** [18] **There is not**
the fear of God before their eyes.
19 [19] But we know that whatsoever things the law saith,
it speaketh to them who are
in (the sphere of) the law,
that every mouth might be
stopped, and all the world
become liable to pay pen-

AUTHORIZED VERSION.

stopped, and all the world may become guilty before God.

20 Therefore by the deeds of the law there shall no flesh be justified in his sight: for by the law *is* the knowledge of sin.

REVISED VERSION.

20 alty to God; [20] because by
works of law shall nobody
be justified before him: for
through law is knowledge
of sin.

(Paragraph III.)

21 But now the righteousness of God without the law is manifested, being witnessed by the law and the prophets;

22 Even the righteousness of God *which is* by faith of Jesus Christ unto all and upon all them that believe: for there is no difference:

23 For all have sinned, and come short of the glory of God;

24 Being justified freely by his grace through the redemption that is in Christ Jesus:

25 Whom God hath set forth *to be* a propitiation through faith in his blood, to declare his righteousness for the remission of sins that are past, through the forbearance of God;

26 To declare, *I say*, at this time his righteousness: that he might be just, and the justifier of him which believeth in Jesus.

21 [21] BUT now without law
God's righteousness has been
manifested, being attested
by the law and the prophets,
22 [22] even God's righteousness
through faith in Jesus Christ,
unto all, and upon all the
believing; for there is no
23 difference: [23] for all sinned,
and are fallen short of the
24 glory of God, [24] being justi-
tified freely by his grace,
through the redemption
which is in Christ Jesus,
25 [25] whom God set (publicly)
forth (as) propitiatory,—
(available) through faith in
his blood,—for demonstration
of his righteousness, because
of the pretermission of the
26 sins of former times [26] in the
forbearance of God,—in order
to the demonstration of his
righteousness in the present
time, that he may be righteous even in justifying him
who is of faith in Jesus.

(Paragraph IV.)

27 Where *is* boasting then? It is excluded. By what law?

27 [27] WHERE then is the glorying? Shut out. By what

AUTHORIZED VERSION.

of works? Nay: but by the law of faith.

28 Therefore we conclude that a man is justified by faith without the deeds of the law.

29 *Is he* the God of the Jews only? *is he* not also of the Gentiles? Yes, of the Gentiles also:

30 Seeing *it is* one God, which shall justify the circumcision by faith, and uncircumcision through faith.

31 Do we then make void the law through faith? God forbid: yea, we establish the law.

REVISED VERSION.

kind of a law? Of works?
Nay, but by the law of faith.
28 [28] We reckon, then, that
a man is justified by faith
without works of law.
29 [29] Is God (the God) of
Jews only? Is he not, on
the contrary, (the God) of
Gentiles also? Yes, of Gen-
30 tiles also; [30] seeing it is one
God who shall justify circumcision by faith, and uncircumcision through faith.
31 [31] Do we then abolish
law through faith? Far be
it! On the contrary, we
establish law.

RELATION OF ROMANS III TO THE CONTENTS OF THE EPISTLE IN GENERAL.

THE Third Chapter of the Epistle to the Romans is *a wheel within a wheel.* This is just what might have been expected, when we consider that the entire Epistle, of which it is an integrant part, is a marvellous pile of finely adjusted intervolutions of theological argument and religious exhortation. It is a magnificent specimen of complexity and unity combined.

The situation of Chapter III,—relatively to the complicated mass of the Epistle in general,—is in the special department of theological argumentation, (Chapters I—XI), as distinguished from the special department of religious exhortation, (Chapters XII—XVI). And if we partition off the special department of theological argumentation into sections, we find that Chapter III occupies the centre of that great and important section, (Chapters I—V), which treats of *justification,* as distinguished from that other great and important section, (Chapters VI—VIII), which treats of *sanctification.*

In the first twenty verses of the Chapter, the argumentation is linked on to that portion of the Apostle's discussion in which he shows that *all men need some gracious method of justification,*—Chapter I 18—Chapter III 20. In the remaining verses,—21 to 31,—it is linked on to that other side of the Apostle's discussion on this topic,—its glory-side,—in which he shows that there is, available to all men, *a gracious method of justification, through a righteousness provided by God Himself,*—Chapter III 21—Chapter IV. The meridian line that divides these two hemispheres of argumentation runs between verses 20 and 21. In what lies on the one side of this line, the Apostle shows that Jews, privileged though they had been, as compared with Gentiles, are nevertheless unrighteous, and therefore *need some gracious method of justification.* In what lies on the other side of the line, he shows that, both for Jews and Gentiles, without distinction, and notwithstanding their sins, *justification is a grand possibility.* It is a possibility *through the righteousness of God—the Propitiation of Christ.*

ANALYSIS OF ROMANS III.

The Third Chapter of Romans is quadripartite in its structure. In the first part,—verses 1st—8th,—the Apostle meets an objection, that might be suggested by his remarks at the conclusion of Chapter II in reference to the true Jew and the true circumcision. In the second part,—verses 9th—20th,—he establishes the fact of the unrighteousness of both Jews and Gentiles, and their consequent need of justification by grace. In the third part,—verses 21st—26th,—he exhibits the gracious method of justification which God has devised, and which is equally available to Jews and Gentiles. In the fourth and last part,—verses 27th—31st,—he jubilantly crowns his exhibition of the gracious plan of justification with a wreath, or cluster, of doctrinal corollaries,—each of momentous moral significance.

The discussion in the first two sections of the Chapter, —verses 1st—8th, 9th—20th,—is a pendant on the great discussion which is prosecuted throughout the Second Chapter of the Epistle,—and which has for its aim the establishment of the fact that the Jews, just as truly as the Gentiles, need a gracious method of justification. The evangelical exhibitions of the other two sections of the Chapter,—verses 21st—26th, 27th—31st,—connect themselves, evolutionally, with the theme of the whole Epistle, as announced, in brief, in the 16th and 17th verses of Chapter I.

A TABLE OF REFERENCE

TO A FEW OF THE MORE SALIENT TOPICS CRITICALLY AND EXEGETICALLY ELUCIDATED IN THE FOLLOWING MONOGRAPH.

THE SUM OF

ROMANS, CHAPTER III.

INCLYTA JUDÆÆ QUAMVIS SIT GLORIA GENTIS,
CRIMINIBUS PŒNAS COMMERUERE TAMEN:
NON ETENIM PROSUNT DIVINÆ DOGMATA LEGIS;
SOLA JUVAT MISEROS GRATIA LÆTA DEI.

RODOLPHUS GUALTHERUS
(*Argumenta*).

"Et amanda et magnificanda est Grammatica enarratio vocabulorum, quorum usus est in praecipuis locis doctrinae cœlestis. Ecclesia enim interpretatione sua non gignit nova dogmata; sed quæ tradita et patefacta sunt voce divina, scrutatur, discit, et accipit."—Chemnitius.

(*De Justificatione*, Cap. iii.)

THE THIRD CHAPTER

OF

THE EPISTLE TO THE ROMANS.

VERSE 1.—*Τί οὖν τὸ περισσὸν τοῦ Ἰουδαίου; ἢ τίς ἡ ὠφέλεια τῆς περιτομῆς;*

English Authorized Version. *What advantage then hath the Jew? or what profit* is there *of circumcision?*

Revised Version. *What then* is *the preeminence of the Jew? or what the advantage of circumcision?*

§ 1. Koppe thinks that the new chapter should not have commenced here. (*Male hic novi capitis initium constituitur.*) De Brais, long before, had expressed a similar opinion. These critics would undoubtedly be right in their idea, if we were to suppose that the division of the Epistle into chapters must represent the partition of its contents into exceedingly distinct sections. There is no such partition: and, probably, Hugo de Sancto Caro did not aim at very great precision in the way of effecting a correspondence between his capitular divisions and the logical groupings of the inspired text. His aim was, predominantly, one of convenience for purposes of reference.

§ 2. This first verse consists of two affiliated interrogations,—the second echoing the first, but substituting a particular, instead of a general, idea:—*What then* is *the preeminence of the Jew? or what the advantage of circumcision?* In the interrogations there is doubtless the embodiment of thoughts which would be regarded by the Apostle as probable objections to the doctrine, which, toward the conclusion of the second chapter, he had been engaged in inculcating. And thus, in proposing the interrogations, he wisely anticipates the objections to his doctrine, which some of his readers might be disposed to start. By anticipating them, he gets the opportunity of meeting and removing them.

In this anticipation, however, of possible and probable objections, the Apostle does not formally summon an objector into the arena of dispute; and consequently he does not formally transfer to the objector's mouth the queries which he proposes. Ewbank puts the case far too artificially when he says,—"Here a Jewish objector starts up, and interrupts the argument." Taylor commits a still greater exaggeration, when he says of the Apostle,—"Here he "seasonably introduces a dialogue between himself and "the Jew, which," he adds, "would amuse, and, at the same "time, instruct the latter, and possibly cool his resentment: "especially as the Apostle's answer to the first question is "much in his favour." Taylor accordingly supposes,—and he is followed by Macknight, Adam Clarke, and others,—that it is a Jew who speaks in verses 1, 3, 5, 7, and the 1st clause of verse 9, while the Apostle, as he imagines, replies in verses 2, 4, 6, 8, and the 2nd clause of verse 9. Others arrange the dialogue in a somewhat different manner. Some, for instance, suppose that it is the Apostle who speaks in verse 1, and a Jew who replies in verses 2 and 3: the Apostle is supposed to speak again in verse 4, the Jew in verse 5, and the Apostle again in verse 6, &c. Heumann supposes that the dialogue extends to the close of verse 22.—With respect to the first verse of the chapter, in particular, many critics, in addition to those already specified, have regarded it as spoken in the person of a Jewish objector, as, for example, Pelagius (*ex persona Judæi interrogantis dicitur*), Hunnius, Oertel, Walford. But it is far more in harmony with the Apostle's standpoint to suppose, with Origen, that he anticipatingly proposes the interrogations to himself, (*occurrens, proponit sibi ipsi*). "He proposes to himself an objection," says Œcumenius, (ἀντιτίθησιν ἑαυτῷ). "He proposes these things to himself by way of objection," says the scholiast in Matthæi, (αὐτὸς ἑαυτῷ ταῦτα ἀντιτίθησι). The best modern critics, such as de Wette, Fritzsche, Meyer, Philippi, Tholuck (in his 4th and 5th editions), Oltramare, are of the same opinion. There is no need for a formal refutation of the notion of Seb. Schmidt,—adopted by Ch. Schmid,—that the interrogations are proposed in the person of a Gentile zealot, who felt that he could not let the opportunity pass of glorying over the Jew, and asking exultingly, "What then is the superiority of the Jew? and what the advantage of circumcision?" There is nothing whatever to indicate the intrusion of such an exultatory element.

§ 3. *What then is the preeminence—the prerogative—of the Jew?* (Τί οὖν τὸ περισσὸν τοῦ Ιουδαίου;) The illative particle *then* (οὖν) connects the interrogation with the concluding statements of the preceding chapter. It is in these statements that we find the originating occasion of the interrogation. It is as if the Apostle were to say,—*But if indeed it be the case that it is* **the inward Jew** *who is* **the true Jew,** *and* **the inward Circumcision** *which is* **the true Circumcision**;—*if it be the case that* **the outward Uncircumcision** *of the Gentiles, who keep the statutes of the law, shall be counted to them* **for Circumcision,** *and that they shall condemn the outwardly circumcised transgressors of the law;—if all this be the case, then the question may be forcing itself upon the minds of not a few,—What is the prerogative of the (ethnological) Jew?—What is the superior condition of the (ethnological) Jew?—Wherein consists the peculiar privilege or preeminence which we must ascribe to the (ethnological) Jew?* The expression, which, with Calvin, Er. Schmid, H. A. Schott (in his 3rd and 4th editions), and others, we may freely render *prerogative,* (τὸ περισσόν), means *surplus:—What is the surplus of the Jew?* that is, *What is the surplus of privilege* *which belongs to the Jew?* (Compare the Hebrew, יֶתֶר, יִתְרוֹ, יוֹתֵר) The whole expression is well rendered by the Vulgate,—"What therefore is there over and above to the Jew?" (*Quid ergo amplius Judaeo est?*) It is translated in the Rhemes,—"What preeminence then hath the Jew?" Tyndale gives it,—"What preferment then hath the Jew?" The Eng. Geneva better, "What is then the preferment of the Jew?" Not so happily Coverdale, "What furtheraunce then have the Jewes?" Erasmus's version is, "What therefore hath the Jew in which he excels?" (*Quid igitur habet in quo praecellat Judaeus?*) Melancthon's, "In what therefore does the Jew excel?" (*Qua igitur re antecellit Judaeus?*)

Knight translates the interrogation thus,—"What advantage, or use, then, was there of the Jew?"—that is —"What was the advantage of their calling?"—"What was the use of separating them at all as a nation from the mass of mankind?" He supposes that the question "points to the object of the calling of the Jews, in connection with God's intentions towards mankind, and as introductory to the proclamation of the Gospel; and not with reference to the advantage of their calling to the Jews themselves." He adds,—"St. Chrysostom, Theophylact, Œcumenius, and Melancthon, are, I think, the only commentators who at all adopt this interpretation." But not one of these commentators really adopts his interpretation: although Chrysostom and Melancthon run up the Apostle's query, very naturally, into this,—*What reason had God for conferring peculiarities of prerogative upon the Jews, if these peculiarities involved after all no real privilege?* Theophylact echoes Chrysostom. But Knight misquotes Œcumenius for Theodoret, *who is quoted by Œcumenius.* And he did not know that many other expositors express exactly the same ideas, as those quoted by him from Chrysostom and Melancthon; as, for example, Musculus, Gualther, Grotius, Spener, Klee, Rückert, Gilpin. It ill became one who knew nothing of the host of German critics, and nothing of the Dutch and French, and but little even of others, whether ancient, medieval, or modern, to say that he thinks the four expositors, whom he names, stand alone in their interpretation. His view, moreover, of the interpretation of his four precursors, and thus his view of the import of the Apostle's interrogation, is inconsistent with the possibilities of the inspired phraseology. The expression which we have freely rendered, *preeminence* or *prerogative,* (τὸ περισσόν), cannot possibly mean "advantage *or use.*" It brings into view, as we have seen, the idea of *surplus,* or *relative abundance.* It may denote *relative advantage;* but it cannot denote *use.*

§ 4. *or what the advantage of circumcision?* (ἢ τίς ἡ ὠφέλεια τῆς περιτομῆς;)—*or what is the benefit of that ceremonial circumcision which is so distinguishing a characteristic of the (ethnological) Jew?*—The Apostle subjoins to his first and chief interrogation this second and subordinate one in reference to circumcision, because circumcision was regarded as the principal badge of outward Judaism, and because he had occasion to specify it, in a prominent manner, in verses 25—29 of the preceding chapter. "Circumcision," says he, "verily profiteth (ὠφελεῖ), if thou keep the law." (ver. 25.) It is no doubt, however, singled out and signalised *representatively* in the interrogation before us. It is as if the Apostle had said,—*What is the benefit accruing to the Jews from all the peculiarities, which constitute them a separated people?*

VERSE 2. Πολὺ κατὰ πάντα τρόπον. Πρῶτον μὲν γὰρ ὅτι ἐπιστεύθησαν τὰ λόγια τοῦ θεοῦ.

Engl. Auth. Vers. *Much every way: chiefly, because that unto them were committed the oracles of God.*

Revised Version. *Much in every respect. For, in the first place, they were intrusted with the oracles of God.*

§ 1. The Apostle answers his own questions thus:—*Much in every respect,* (Πολὺ κατὰ πάντα τρόπον). The gender of the adjective translated *much* is neuter, (πολύ), and some expositors, such as Meyer and van Hengel, suppose that, as such, it refers indifferently to the two objects, which are queried in the preceding verse,—that is, both to *the surplus of privilege* belonging to the Jew, and to *the benefit* of ceremonial circumcision. Erasmus, on the other hand, conjectured—(*inaniter et intempestive*,—Este)—that the word should be written, not as neuter, but as feminine (πολλή); supposing that its reference is exclusively to the second interrogation,—"What is the benefit (ἡ ὠφέλεια) of circumcision?" In this conjecture he had been anticipated by at least one unimportant manuscript, viz. 120; and he has been followed by several of the obscurer editors of the text. In Bebelius's edition, for example, of 1535, and in Platter's of 1540, and in the Froschouiana edition of 1547, we read πολλή. According to Calvin, the second interrogation of the foregoing verse explains the meaning of the first: and thus, in substantial agreement with the exegesis of Erasmus, he supposes that in the answer, "much in every respect," there is a predominating reference to the advantage of circumcision. A wider view, however, of the Apostle's reference is requisite. The neuter gender of the adjective (πολύ) naturally leads the thought back to the neuter word in the first interrogation, (τὸ περισσόν), *the surplus* (*of privilege*). And when the Apostle proceeds to disintegrate the "much," and to say "for, in the first place, *they* were intrusted with the oracles of God," we see that his mind was thinking rather of *the Jews*, in their personality, than of their ceremonial *circumcision*. And thus,—as in relation to the 29th verse of the preceding chapter,—we may legitimately conclude that the idea of the second clause, concerning circumcision, becomes merged in the idea of the first, concerning the circumcised Jew. And hence the answer to the second query is implicitly involved in the explicit answer to the first:—*The surplus of privilege belonging to the Jew—the preeminence of the Jew—is much.*

When the Apostle says that the Jew's surplus of privilege is "much *in every respect*" (κατὰ πάντα τρόπον), his language should not be measured off as by a precisely scientific foot-rule, and hence pronounced to be a "hyperbolical" way of denoting "in many respects," (*hyperbolisch, in vielfacher Rücksicht*,-Reiche). Neither has the expression,—as Day, followed by Haldane, supposes,—"no other efficacy than to make a strong asseveration or affirmation, as if he should say, *very much*." Neither does it mean "certainly very much," or, "without doubt much;"—though such is the interpretation of Luther (*zwar fast viel*), and Tyndale (*surely very moche*), and Calvin (*omnino multa*); of Castellio too (*multa omnino*); of Koppe also (*multum omnino*), and Zinzendorf (*gewiss in vielen dingen*), and Flatt (*allerdings haben sie viele Vorzüge*), and indeed many others,—more especially of the older critics. The expression employed by the Apostle, though idiomatically susceptible, in certain cases, of this translation, is yet far more commonly used in its simple and obvious sense. (See Wetstein and Raphel.) It is just the opposite of "in no respect," (κατ' οὐδένα τρόπον, 2 Macc. xi. 31; Polyb. *Hist.* iv. 84. 8). And there is no reason for departing, in the case before us, from the natural interpretation. The surplus of privileges enjoyed by the Jews, in relation to things moral, spiritual, and eternal, over and above the privileges enjoyed by the Gentiles, was assuredly, and without any exaggeration, "much *in every respect*,"—"much," that is to say, "*in every view of the case that can be rationally taken*." If, for example, we consider the Jews as susceptible of blissful influence, in a hereditary manner, from the sires of their race, we see that they were highly exalted in privilege; for "theirs were the patriarchal fathers,"—Abraham, Isaac, and Jacob. (Rom. ix. 5.) If we consider them as susceptible of blissful influence from ordinances of religion, eminently significant and sublimely typical, we see again that they were peculiarly exalted in privilege, for their ritual of religious "service" (their λατρεία) was incomparably superior to that of all surrounding peoples. (Rom. ix. 4.) If we consider them as susceptible of blissful influence from a legislative code of preeminent moral purity, we see again that they were peculiarly privileged, for the core of their whole legislative system was a singularly pure and complete edition of the moral law. (Rom. ix. 4.) If we consider them as susceptible of blissful influence from the zealous ministrations of faithful, uncorrupted, and incorruptible instructors and reformers, we see again that they were singularly privileged in having had among them a succession of holy and devoted prophets, "who spake as they were moved by the Holy Ghost." If we consider them as susceptible of blissful influence from a very special divine providence guiding them, restraining them, constraining them, hedging them round and round in the way of shutting them off from evil, and in the way of shutting them up to good, surely we must see again that their surplus of privilege was very great. And if we consider it a means of peculiarly blissful influence to have a high ideal presented to the mind, and a lofty aspiration stirred within the heart; then in the exhibition of the Messiah to come, as the "Seed" *par excellence*, that was germinally enclosed in their distinctively Abrahamic "seed," —in this exhibition, as forming indeed the very central element of the Jewish peculiarities, we see that the Jews enjoyed a privilege that was altogether unrivalled and inestimable. In short, view the subject as we may, "the surplus of privilege belonging to the Jews" is,—both *intensively* and *extensively*, as logicians speak,—"much *in every respect*." They possessed, as Grotius remarks, far greater facilities, than the Gentiles, for attaining that inward piety, without which neither Gentile nor Jew can be fit to be an heir of unending glory. (*Eadem in utroque pietas apud Deum valet; sed ut ad eam perveniat, Israelita sive circumcisus aliquis faciliores habet aditus.*)

§ 2. *For, first, they were intrusted with the oracles of God*, (Πρῶτον μὲν γὰρ ὅτι ἐπιστεύθησαν τὰ λόγια τοῦ θεοῦ). There is considerable difficulty in determining whether the ratiocinative particle *for* (γάρ),—strangely called an *illative* by Turner,—really belongs to the text, or is a spurious addition. Lachmann has dismissed it. It is wanting in B D E G; and in the Peshito, Italic, and Vulgate versions, and hence too in Pelagius and Ambrosiaster; and also in Chrysostom's text. Fritzsche suspects that it is apocryphal, and has enclosed it within brackets. Rückert too (2nd ed.) and Tholuck (5th ed.) hold it for suspected. Burton too suspects it. And Oltramare rejects it. On the other hand, it is found in ℵ A K L, and in the Philoxenian Syriac, and in Theodoret, Theophylact, and Œcumenius. And it is retained by Griesbach, Scholz, and Tischendorf. It would certainly appear to be more difficult to account for its deliberate intrusion into the text, than for its unintentional omission, or even its deliberate extrusion, (for it might seem to some to embarrass somewhat the subsequent ὅτι): and hence we are disposed to regard it as belonging to the autograph of the Apostle's epistle. *For, first.*—It is as if the Apostle had said, *I may well use the word* **much**; *the surplus of privilege enjoyed by the Jews is indeed* **much**; *for, first, they were intrusted with the oracles of God.*

(*a.*) The import of the word *first* (πρῶτον) has been considerably disputed. It is regarded by some as an adjective, and as having the signification of *principal* or *chief.* This is the view that is taken by Abelard, Beza, Rollock, Wolf, Heumann, Michaelis, Bolten, Flatt, Stuart, Greve, &c. These expositors supply the substantive verb, to fill up the construction. They are fairly represented by Beza, who translated the clause thus :—"For the principal *is this,* that they were intrusted with the oracles of God," (*primarium enim illud est quod eis credita sunt eloquia Dei*). It is, however, an objection to this interpretation, that it does not vindicate the preceding affirmation,—"much, in every respect." We do not prove anything to be "much," far less to be "much in every way," when we merely adduce its "principal" ingredient. That which is *little* may have its principal ingredient, as well as that which is *much.* The subject, moreover, of which the quality of "principal" would be predicated, could not, according to this interpretation, be some disintegrated ingredient of the *much surplus of privilege* enjoyed by the Jews. It would require, according to the grammatical interrelations of the passage, to be *the entire surplus itself.* But in that case there would be no room left for any secondary ingredients of prerogative. We must then abandon this interpretation of the word *first.*

Fritzsche, Rückert, van Hengel, T. Schott, &c., agree with the critics whose opinion we have just been considering, in regarding the word as an adjective: but they think that it means *first* in the order of enumeration, not *chief* in the order of importance. It is obvious, however, that similar objections lie against this interpretation; and more particularly does its incongruity appear, when we consider that the subject, which would be qualified by the adjectival term *first*, must, on the assumption of the correctness of the interpretation, be *the whole surplus of privilege* belonging to the Jews. But if *the whole surplus* be *first* in the order of enumeration, what part of it will remain over to be second?

There can be little doubt that we should dismiss the idea that *first* is an adjective. It is manifestly an adverb; and has been so regarded by the majority of critics. This majority, however, divides itself into two distinct classes. The one, represented by le Fèvre, Calvin, Este, Vitringa, Koppe, Ernesti, regard the adverb as used qualitatively, meaning *chiefly*, or, as Vater gives it, " before all other things," (*ante omnia alia*). To this class the authors of the English Geneva version (*chieflye*), and the French Geneva (*sur tout*), and our English authorized version, belong. Apparently, too, Theodoret, (*μεγίστη γὰρ αὕτη τιμή*). The other class,—embracing Erasmus, Luther, Piscator, Grotius, Cocceius, Boysen, de Wette, Meyer, Baumgarten-Crusius, Hodge, Krehl, Maier, Ewald, &c.,—regard the adverb as used quantitatively, having its common signification, *firstly*, or, *in the first place*, and indicating an order of enumeration. This latter class would doubtless have swallowed up the greater proportion of the former, had it not been the case that in the Apostle's discourse there is no prosecution of the enumeration. (There is no δεύτερον δέ or ἔπειτα δέ, or any similar expression.) And men who think and feel reverently on the subject of inspiration, shrink and feel repelled when the idea is thrust in upon them by such expositors as Fritzsche, that, in the ardour of composition, the Apostle forgot to finish his discourse in the way that, at the outset, he had intended. It is certainly, to say the least of it, quite unnecessary to assume such forgetfulness. It is enough to know that the Apostle was not punctilious in the matter of rhetorical composition. He made no pretension to "wisdom of words." And, wielding as he did a foreign language, we need not marvel that his extraordinary vehemence of feeling broke loose from some of the more symmetrical forms of discourse. It is an objection to the interpretation of le Fèvre, and Calvin, and their followers, that the particle (μέν) associated with this adverb, naturally leads the mind to look out for other particulars, (which might be introduced by the correlative δέ). It is thus the case, as Piscator technically remarks, that it is impossible to avoid the admission that there is an *anantapodoton*. The Apostle's expression certainly imports, as says Cocceius, "that there are other prerogatives." And these other privileges must have actually streamed out into view before the Apostle's thoughts, while he dictated the word *first*. The enumeration in chapter ix. 4, 5, is evidence that his mind was full on the subject. But certainly we need not suppose, with Grotius, that the Apostle, as it were, deliberately suspends, till he reaches that advanced portion of his discussion, the specification of the remaining list of advantages. (*Sermonem autem hunc hic non consummat apostolus, sed differt in cap.* ix. 4.) This would be to turn the whole intervening part of the epistle into an immense parenthesis. And yet Hammond did not hesitate to gulp such an idea:—"An objection," he says, "here diverted the Apostle's purpose for many chapters together, not permitting him to return from that digression till chapter ix., where he falls again to the same matter, and enumerates the remainder of those privileges." This is outré. But we may imagine that the real state of the Apostle's thoughts might be thus represented:—*I may well aver that the surplus of privilege belonging to the Jew is much in every respect; for, in the first place,—and I need not at present stop to specify the other particulars,—they were intrusted with the oracles of God.*

(*b.*) In the original there is a demonstrative particle (ὅτι) standing before the verb *intrusted* (ἐπιστεύθησαν):—"*that* they were intrusted." It may be advantageously omitted in English translation. But it is to be accounted for, by supposing that the fulness of the Apostle's expression would have been something like the following:—*for, in the first place, it is a privilege* that *they were intrusted with the oracles of God,* (πρῶτον μὲν γὰρ περισσόν τι ἐστίν ὅτι κ. τ. λ., or, πρῶτον μὲν γὰρ περισσεύουσιν ὅτι κ. τ. λ.).

It would appear that this demonstrative particle (ὅτι) was either omitted in some ancient copies of the text, or was overlooked by some ancient expositors, so that the word *first* (which was sometimes freely changed into a plural adjective, πρῶτοι,) was construed with the verb *intrusted:*—*for they first were intrusted with the oracles of God,*—the Jews first, and Christians afterwards. This, if we may judge from Rufinus's translation, was the interpretation of Origen: and, singular to relate, it has been adopted and defended by Seb. Schmidt. It cannot, however, be considered for a moment as a probable interpretation, unless we either obliterate the demonstrative particle, or make, according to the suggestion of Hombergk, a "trajection" of it to the commencement of the clause, (ὅτι γὰρ πρῶτον μέν, &c.),—a pair of alternatives, for either of which we have no valid authority whatever.

(*c.*) The expression which we have rendered, *they were intrusted with the oracles of God,* (ἐπιστεύθησαν τὰ λόγια τοῦ θεοῦ), is susceptible of a different construction. The word *oracles* may be regarded as the nominative to the verb; and the whole clause may be rendered thus,—*the oracles of God were believed.* This interpretation is mentioned by Chrysostom, as one that was approved of by some, at or before his time. And Melville hesitates to reject it. Heinfetter gives it. But, as Chrysostom correctly remarks, the context does not admit of it, (ἀλλὰ τὸ ἑξῆς οὐκ ἀφίησι τοῦτο νομίζεσθαι).

Koppe adopts the same principle of construction, though he does not attach to the verb the same signification. He would translate the clause thus,—*the promises of God were confirmed to them;* that is,—as he explains,—The Jews, as distinguished from the Gentiles, *had reliable promises of God.* The ingenious critic invented a meaning for the verb. And, in appealing to the Septuagint version of Ps. xcii. 5, and 1 Kings viii. 21, in support of the translation, he actually confounded a totally different verb (ἐπιστώθησαν), with that which is employed by the apostle (ἐπιστεύθησαν). And yet de Dieu, trusting to the use of the word in 2 Thess. i. 10, gave the same interpretation to the clausule, and was, indeed, the means, direct or indirect, of misleading Koppe. Cramer too was similarly misled. Hombergk also was so far misled, as to think that the expression *might* be thus interpreted (*non absurde*). And good honest Gottfried Wichmann contends strongly for the translation. So too D. G. Herzog. Wakefield too. And Jones assumes it on the authority of Wakefield. But nothing is more certain than that the verb, if not translated *were believed,* must be rendered *were intrusted.*

But while the verb must be rendered *were intrusted,* it must not be supposed that the clause might, so far as structure is concerned, be literally translated, *the oracles of God were intrusted* (*to them*). On the contrary, the usage of the verb demonstrates, that the word *oracles* is in the accusative ;—the nominative to the verb being the unexpressed pronoun, which would have been in the dative, had the verb been used in the active voice. The verb (πιστεύω), when used transitively in reference to a twofold object (πιστεύω τινί τι) means *to intrust, to confide, to commit to the custody of.* And when it is employed in the passive, under the same rubric of signification, the object intrusted is not expressed in the nominative (πιστεύεται τινί τι),—as le Fèvre assumed, and as Philippi seems to think it sometimes is, and as the second corrector of the *Codex Boernerianus,* or the Manuscript G, assumed,—but it is specified in the accusative (πιστεύεταί τις τι). The Apostle, then, means,—*they* (*i. e.* the Jews) *were intrusted,*—or, as Brown of Wamphray expresses it, *were concredited,—with the oracles of God.* (Compare Gal. ii. 7 ; 1 Cor. ix. 17 ; 1 Thess. ii. 4 ; 1 Tim. i. 11 ; Tit. i. 3.) The Apostle, it will be noted, says *they*, in the plural, though referring to "the Jew" spoken of in the singular, in the first verse. He expands, that is to say, into its natural numerical plurality, the collective unity which was representatively embodied in his former expression:—just as in 1 Tim. ii. 15, he says, "notwithstanding *she* (ἡ γυνή) shall be saved in child-bearing, if *they* (αἱ γυναῖκες) continue in faith."

(*d.*) The Jews "were intrusted with *the oracles of God*," (τὰ λόγια τοῦ Θεοῦ). Beza dislikes the word *oracles*, on account of its heathenish associations; and he disuses it in all his editions, after that of 1556, (substituting *eloquia*, the Vulgate rendering, for *oracula*, the translation of Erasmus). *Oracles* is undoubtedly, nevertheless, the best translation by far, which can be given to the term. And heathenism has no more right to the exclusive use of the word, than to the exclusive use of such other terms as *temple, priest, prophet, God.* The true God has spoken. And as his utterances are responsive to the irrepressible moral longings, and questionings, and aspirations of man, they are emphatically *oracular revelations.* They are *oracles.* The original term (λόγιον) is a diminutive from a word of much wider conventional reference, meaning *a saying*, (λόγος). And there is thus, in its very idiosyncrasy or make, an intimation of the *pithy condensation*, and consequent *pregnancy of import*, which were frequent characteristics of oracular utterances in general, and which are, preeminently, features of the infallible and all-important oracles of Jehovah.

Both in classical and in Biblical Greek the word (λόγια) is set apart to designate *divine utterances.* There is nothing, indeed, in its etymology to produce this circumscription of reference. But usage has ordained it. The term occurs in only other three passages of the New Testament, viz. Acts vii. 38; Heb. v. 12; 1 Pet. iv. 11. And in all of these, as well as in the one before us, there is an exclusive reference to *the utterances of God.* It occurs frequently in the Septuagint, and more especially in the 119th Psalm, (= אִמְרָה); and, in every instance, it designates, not the sayings of men, but the "spekyngis," as Wycliffe here translates it, of God. There is but one apparent exception to this rule. In Ps. xix. 15 (14), the term thus occurs:—"let the words of my mouth, (τὰ λόγια τοῦ στόματός μου, = אִמְרֵי־פִי, from אָמַר), and the meditation of my heart, be acceptable in thy sight, O Lord, my Strength and my Redeemer." But even here the term may be fitly regarded as having its otherwise invariable reference. The Septuagint translator looked upon the sacred writer as giving utterance, in his psalm,—*the words of his mouth,*—to diviner thoughts than his own, to the thoughts of God Himself. He regarded him as "moved" in what he said "by the Holy Ghost." (Hesychius *represents the conventional usage of the term, both in sacred and in classical writings, when he explains it thus;*—λόγια, θέσφατα, μαντεύματα, φυτεύματα [προφητεύματα,-Palmer and Suicer], φῆμαι, χρησμοί. Suidas,—*copying almost verbatim from the scholiast on* Thucydides ii. 8,—*draws a distinction between* λόγια *and the last of its synonyms as given by* Hesychius, viz. χρησμοί,—*the former being represented as denoting* oracles in prose, *whereas* χρησμοί, *it is said, properly means* oracles in verse. Λόγια, τὰ παρὰ θεοῦ λεγόμενα καταλογάδην· χρησμοὶ δὲ, οἵτινες ἐμμέτρως λέγονται θεοφορουμένων τῶν λεγόντων. Beza *indorses this distinction. And it may have been, to some partial extent, realized. But certainly, as* Alberti *and others have remarked, it does not rule the usage. See* Wetstein *also. The two terms are, indeed, often interchangeably employed, as by* Chrysostom, *for example, in his Commentary on the very passage before us. They correspond to* **dictiones** *and* **responsa**, *as well as to* **oracula**, *in Latin.*)

As to the reference of the term in the passage before us, there has been, on the whole, considerable unanimity among expositors. It is often explained as meaning *the Scriptures.* But the word, of course, is not absolutely identical with the word *Scriptures*, or the expression *Holy Scriptures.* There is no reference in it to writing; although undoubtedly the particular *oracles* intended were, as a matter of fact, committed to writing, and constituted the *Holy Scriptures.* It was, too, as written oracles that they were committed to the custody of the Jews. Still, it is the *oracles* themselves that are referred to in the Apostle's expression,—the *oracles, as oracles,* not *as writings.* It would be unadvisable, therefore, to translate the expression with Drysén, *the divine Scriptures* (*de Guddomliga skrifterna.—På detta ställe menas i min tanke sjelfva skrifterna, som innehöllo dessa orakel*). But Calvin went farther wrong in considering the reference of the word. He says, "by *oracles* is meant *the covenant* which was divinely revealed to Abraham and his posterity, and afterwards recorded and explained in *the Law and the Prophets,*" (*oracula vocat foedus quod Abrahæ primo, ejusque posteris divinitus revelatum, postea Lege et Prophetiis consignatum ac explicatum fuit*). This is not only too arbitrary, it is also too narrow an interpretation. The word might indeed denote the various *revelations* of the covenant. But assuredly it cannot mean *the covenant* itself. And yet Beza not only adopts Calvin's notion. He gives it an additional squeeze, and turns it still more awry. He represents the word as meaning *the legal covenant* (*legale foedus*), as distinguished from *the Gospel;*—at which subject, he says, the Apostle has not yet arrived, (*de evangelio nondum disserens*).—These are freaks of exegesis.

Theodoret was more successful. He identifies the term with the word *law* (νόμος);—apparently understanding by *law,* the whole supernatural Revelation of God, as distinguished from the Revelation which is made in nature. If this was really his meaning, he hit upon the Apostle's idea. Chrysostom, before him, gives the same explanation,—*law.* So Œcumenius, (ἐνεχειρίσθησαν τὸν νόμον· οὗτος γὰρ τὰ λόγια τοῦ θεοῦ). So Theophylact and Ambrosiaster.

The interpretation of Luther is less ambiguous, though his translation is circumlocutionary. He renders the phrase, "what God has spoken" (*was Gott geredet hat*). Emser and Dietenberger give the same translation. So Coverdale, "what God spake." Piscator renders it, "God's word" (*Gottes Wort*). So Tyndale, *the worde of God;*—Heumann also and Matthias. The plural form of the same version is given in Cranmer's Bible, and in the Rhemes, *the wordes of God;* in the Dutch versions, too, old and new, (*de woorden*

Gods); and also in Calvin's French version of 1556, (*les parolles de Dieu*); and in the Peshito, (ܡ̈ܠܘܗܝ ܕܐܠܗܐ). Johan Hollybushe, in the English version of 1538, printed by Nicolson,—the duplicate of Myles Coverdale's Paris edition of the same year, printed by Regnault,—renders the expression, rather grotesquely, *the speeches of God.* Count Zinzendorf, on the other hand, translates the phrase freely, and in the singular number, "the divine revelation" (*die göttliche Offenbarung*),—a translation adopted by Michaelis. The English Geneva gives the word *oracles,* putting in the margin, *or words.* Martin retains *oracles,* and explains the term as meaning *the writings of the Old Testament,* (*c'est à dire, les Ecritures de l'Ancien Testament*). Este agrees with Martin, and, in very explicit terms, explains the word as comprehending all the contents of Scripture. (*In sacris literis vox extenditur ad omne Dei verbum hominibus traditum, cujusmodi est universa Scriptura sacra, sive prophetica, sive historica, seu quaecunque alia.*) Este is undoubtedly right; and with him agree Sadolet (*oracula Dei sunt quaecunque ad docendum, regendum, et, maximarum rerum promissionibus, confirmandum populum Israeliticum, a Deo prolata sunt*); Vitringa too (*door dese woorden Gods in dese plaatse, de gansche openbaringe van sijne wille moet verstaan worden*), and Calov, Seb. Schmidt, Day, Turretin, Wolf, Böhme, Rosenmüller, de Wette, Hodge, Glöckler, Umbreit, Olshausen, Oltramare, Philippi, T. Schott, &c. The expression, as used by the Apostle, is general and indefinite; and there is no good reason for restricting its import to any particular or specific ingredients of the revelation contained in "the volume of the book." It would be wrong, very wrong, we presume, to suppose, with Semler, that the reference is exclusively to *the Decalogue.* It would also, we apprehend, be wrong to suppose, with Mehring, that the word simply means "prophecies" (*Weissagungen*). Oracles in general were, no doubt, from the nature of the circumstances that almost always led to consultation, predictive. But prediction, nevertheless, is not their differentiating essence. Neither would we regard the term, with perhaps Photius, and, at all events, with Vatable, Bugenhagen, de Paris, Koppe, Kistemaker, Reiche, Lossius, Köllner, Fritzsche, Maier, Baumgarten-Crusius, Krehl, Jatho, &c., as simply denoting *promises.* And yet, that the Apostle had a very special reference to the divine promises seems to be indisputable, (see ver. 3rd), and has been perceived by the great majority of expositors, such as,—in addition to those just mentioned,—Zuingli, Melancthon, Bullinger, Aretius, Melville, Hunnius, Rollock, Grotius, Day, Böhme, Drysén, Flatt, Klee, Glöckler, Rückert, Meyer, Oltramare, Haldane, &c. The "oracles of God," indeed, as contained in "the volume of the book," are preeminently characterized by promises. Their essence consists of promises. It is the alpha and omega of the oracles of the Old Testament,—to which, of course, the Apostle exclusively referred,—to promise "the Christ," and light and life and bliss in him. It is the alpha and omega of the oracles of the New Testament,—which are but the complement and completion of the Old,—to promise pardon, justification, glorification, in one word, eternal life or salvation, along with peace, joy, hope, consolation, sustentation, and holiness to all who are willing to avail themselves of "the Christ" who had been "promised to the fathers." The "oracles of God," viewed broadly and as a whole, are God's communications of mercy to men, considered as sinners. And from the necessity of the case, such communications must very largely partake of a promissory element. They must be of the nature of promises which either already are, or which yet shall be, "yea and amen in Jesus Christ." All the other details of the oracles must necessarily be subsidiary and subministrant. (*Hic observabis totam legem, et literam veteris Testamenti, editam esse potissimum propter revelandas promissiones de Christo,*-Melancthon, *Annot.*)

When it is said that the Jews *were intrusted* with these oracles, the expression, as Erasmus noted, indicates that it was not for their own benefit alone that the oracles were given to them. The revelation with which they were blessed was intended for wider dissemination. It was a boon for universal man. And they were therefore trustees, for a season, for the behoof of the human race. Nevertheless, they were not simply Depositaries in behalf of others,—or *Capsarii nostri*, as Augustin playfully calls them (*Enarr. in Ps.* xl. 14),—or "our Librarians" (*Librarii nostri*), as the same Father elsewhere designates them, (*Enarr. in Ps.* lvi. 9). They were not even simply "*God's* library-keepers," as Trapp expresses it. They themselves were heirs of the blessing which was confided to their charge. The revelation, with all its gracious and glorious promises, was a divine message to themselves. And in the possession of it, they enjoyed for themselves an inestimable privilege. It was the Gospel in anticipation. It was the verbal word, mirroring the personal Word. It was the impersonal word of eternal life, mirroring Him who is, preeminently, at once the personal Word of God and the Eternal Life of man. It was the glad tidings of salvation through the atonement that was to be. It was all this,—*with an additament*, the additament, namely, of an assurance to the Jews, that, in consequence of the peculiarly intimate relation which the future Messiah was to sustain to their race they would meanwhile be distinguishingly blessed in the enjoyment of anticipative spiritual advantages, and eventually exalted into the dignity of being the almoners of God,—the dispensers of some of the richest elements of his bounty, to the world at large. They would hence be emphatically,—in virtue of such prerogatives,—God's favoured people,—his national "son," as well as his national "servant,"—his "peculiar people." In addition to the fundamental promises, relating to the provision of mercy made for men, as men, the *oracles* of the Old Testament are, as a matter of fact, bestrewed, from beginning to ending, with gems of exceeding great and precious promises relating to the provision of favour made for the Jews, as Jews. GOD "SHEWED HIS WORD (*K'ri*, דבריו, HIS WORDS, HIS ORACLES) UNTO JACOB; HIS STATUTES AND HIS JUDGEMENTS UNTO ISRAEL. HE HATH NOT DEALT SO WITH ANY NATION; AND AS FOR HIS JUDGEMENTS, THEY (THE NATIONS IN GENERAL) HAVE NOT KNOWN THEM."

VER. 3. Τί γὰρ εἰ ἠπίστησάν τινες; Μὴ ἡ ἀπιστία αὐτῶν τὴν πίστιν τοῦ θεοῦ καταργήσει;

Eng. Auth. Vers. *For what if some did not believe? shall their unbelief make the faith of God without effect?*

Revised Version. *For what although some believed not? shall their unbelief make the faithfulness of God to fail?*

§ 1. The Apostle, instead of enumerating other privileges enjoyed by the Jews, proceeds, in the most energetic and semi-dramatic manner, to vindicate his first specification of prerogative. Hence he employs the ratiocinative particle *for* (γάρ). It is as if he had said,—*I am justified in specifying the possession of the oracles of God as a high privilege of the Jews,*—**for**, *whatsoever may be the actual treatment which these oracles have received at the hands of my countrymen, the possession of them is nevertheless, when intrinsically considered, an inestimable boon.* This vindicatory relation of the verse to what goes immediately before, seems abundantly evident; and when Hodge (*ed.* 1864) imagines that, instead of establishing such a connection, the Apostle takes into consideration an objection to his doctrine that runs out abreast with the one that is referred to in verse 1st, his interpretation is at once entirely arbitrary and extremely violent.

§ 2. *For what if some believed not?* or, *For what if some had no faith?* (Τί γὰρ εἰ ἠπίστησάν τινες;) Taylor of Norwich, and a large proportion of modern critics, place the interrogation after the first two words, and thus split up the clause into two:—*For what? if some believed not, &c.* Griesbach ultimately approved of this interpunction: and so do Knapp, Tittmann, Hahn, Vater, Muralto, Alford, and Tischendorf. Fritzsche contends for it. Erasmus's editions, on the other hand, postpone the interrogation to the close of the clause. They were followed by the Stephanic editions; and by Beza in his various editions; and by the Elzevir editions. Bengel approves; and Scholz; and so does Lachmann. The Peshito translator had been of the same opinion; and the older critics in general. So, too, Hilarion, in his modern Greek version, (*Corfu*, 1827, Καὶ ἂν ἀπίστησαν τινὲς, τί;) We are disposed to think that it is not a matter of much moment whether of the two methods of interpunction be accepted. It is but a little difference in pause while pronouncing the words. But, with van Hengel, we prefer to keep the whole clause as a unit:—*For what if some believed not?* And, unlike van Hengel, we would, with Henry Stephens and Lachmann, throw out even the comma which Erasmus and Robert Stephens inserted after the first two words.

The expression is evidently elliptical. And the ellipsis may be variously supplied. Luther, for instance, supplies it thus,—"What is involved?" (*was liegt daran?*): and Piscator thus,—"what shall we say?" (ἐροῦμεν;): Fritzsche thus,—"how stands the case?" (τί γάρ ἐστιν;—*denn was giebts?—denn wie liegt die Sache?*): Oltramare thus,—"What have you to reply?" (*qu' avez-vous à redire?*) It is evidently in some such way that we are to fill up mentally the abrupt breviloquence of the Apostle:—*For what signifies it, if it be the case,—as it is,—that some disbelieved?* (*Significat, nullius esse ponderis, hac phrasi,* τί γὰρ, *sc.* ἐστί.-Bos, *Ellipses, p.* 421, *ed.* 1762.)

As already remarked,—(see ver. 1),—some critics, such as Taylor and Macknight, suppose that the words of this verse are not spoken by the Apostle in his own person. They imagine that the paragraph is a dialogue,—a dialectical debate; and that in this verse it is a Jewish objector who speaks. These expositors are shut up to regard the ratiocinative participle *for* (γάρ) as used in an idiomatic manner, with almost every element of its original ratiocinative force merged into latency. Taylor translates it *and;* Macknight, *but.* And Macknight is constrained, moreover, to give an unnatural import to the interrogative particle (μή) which introduces the succeeding clausule. Instead of translating the clausule thus,—*shall their unbelief make inefficient the faithfulness of God?* he translates it thus, "will *not* their unbelief destroy the faithfulness of God?" Both of these disadvantages are avoided, and the additional disadvantage, moreover, of imagining a formal dialogue, without any formal indication of its introduction,—when we take the words in their natural and unconstrained import, and suppose that they are used by the Apostle, as speaking in his own person, to confirm what he had alleged in the preceding verse.

At the same time, it is not to be doubted that the Apostle's confirmatory remark is given in the particular prophylactic form in which it occurs, and in its peculiarly militant attitude, because it was designed to anticipate an objection which he was aware would be readily started in some Jewish minds. He knew that some would be disposed to say, as it were;—*But if, Paul, we be so bad as you represent us;—if we be such unbelievers as you persist in making us out to be;—if, as according to your doctrine, we have not believed in the great evangelical revelation contained in the Bible;—of what real benefit have the oracles been to us?—wherein consists the high privilege of being their depositaries?* Such we may conceive to have been the state of mind which the Apostle had in view when he appended to the asseveration of the preceding verse the confirmatory remarks of this.

It has been disputed whether it is the idea of *unbelief, non-belief, no-faith*, or the idea of *unfaithfulness*, which is the characteristic notion of the verb (ἠπίστησαν). A considerable number of critics would translate the clause thus,—"For what if some were *unfaithful?*"—that is, says Alford, "*unfaithful to the covenant*, the very condition of which was to walk in the ways of the Lord and observe his statutes." Alford follows de Wette. And of the same opinion, as to the translation of the term, are Beza (*in the later editions of his New Testament*), Piscator (*in his Latin version and Notes*), Er. Schmid, le Cene, Zachariä, Koppe, Köllner (*substantially*), Matthias, Mehring, Lange. The same interpretation is given by a large number of our English expositors,—in addition to Alford,—such as Sclater, Wells, Taylor, Belsham, Heberden, Stack, Cox, Terrot, Stuart, Hodge, Sumner, Bosanquet, Purdue, Conybeare, Wordsworth,

Vaughan, Colenso, Webster and Wilkinson, Shepherd, &c. Rückert, in his first edition, supported,—though obviously in a labouring manner, indicating the consciousness of difficulty,—the same rendering. Reiche seeks to combine the two translations, (*vielleicht vereinigt das Wort beide Begriffe*). And, although de Wette has no decisive ground for adducing Theodoret, Œcumenius and Theophylact as of coincident opinion, it is manifest that some of the ancients had espoused the view, for the Alexandrian manuscript (A) substitutes the verb, which properly means *were disobedient* (ἠπείθησαν), for the verb which the Apostle actually employs. The critics who support the translation, *were unfaithful*, rely upon the harmonious relation of that version to the subsequent expression, "the *faithfulness* of God." But there can be no doubt that the translation is unwarrantable. For, (1), the verb in every other passage in which it occurs in the New Testament means *to be destitute of faith.* See Mark xvi. 11, 16; Luke xxiv. 11, 41; Acts xxviii. 24; and 2 Tim. ii. 13 is no exception. (2), The cognate noun (ἀπιστία) means invariably *want of faith.* See, besides the other passages, the places in which it is used by our Apostle, Rom. iv. 20; xi. 20, 23; 1 Tim. i. 13. (3), The cognate adjective (ἄπιστος) means invariably, as used by our Apostle, *without faith.* See 1 Cor. vi. 6; vii. 12, 13, 14, 15; x. 27; xiv. 22, 23, 24; 2 Cor. iv. 4; vi. 14, 15; 1 Tim. v. 8: Tit. i. 15. (4), If the expression in the preceding verse, "the oracles of God," means, not "the covenant of God," but the promissory and evangelical revelation of God, that is, the Sum of the Bible, as it manifestly does, then it is far more natural to refer to the unbelief or non-faith, than to the faithlessness, of the Jews in relation to these oracles. In an important sense they were *faithful to their trust.* They faithfully preserved the oracles. But they did not exercise faith in that which is their grand evangelical import. And, (5), when the Apostle asks, "shall their ἀπιστία make void the *faithfulness* of God?" it is natural to suppose that God's faithfulness is referred to in relation to the promissory element of the oracles of God, and that consequently the ἀπιστία refers to the same promissory element, and is non-faith, or unbelief, in relation to the great evangelical blessings exhibited in the volume of the book, as these blessings are summed up in "the Christ of God." To object, with Beza and Alford, that it would be out of place to suppose that the Apostle is speaking, at this stage of his epistle, "of faith or want of faith," is to forget that he is composing an epistle, free and easy in its interrelations—and not a stiff, formal, dialectical dissertation. It is to forget, moreover, that in the passage before us, he is making a detour from the straight line of his argument, for the purpose of meeting, and setting aside such irruptive objections as he deemed it right to anticipate. And it is, moreover, to forget that it is impossible to understand aright such portions of the preceding context as chapter ii. 4; chapter ii. 13—16; and chapter ii. 28, 29, except in the light that emanates from the assumption of *faith in the Gospel of God's grace.* It is satisfactory, therefore, to find that the great body of enlightened critics support the translation which we have given to the verb:—"For what if some *had no faith?*" It is the translation of the Vulgate (*non crediderunt*), and of Luther (*nicht glauben*), Œcolampad, Calvin (*fuerunt increduli; n'ont point creu*), Castellio (*diffiderunt*), Diodati (*sono stati increduli*), the Dutch versions, old and new, Grotius, Day, Este (*incrediderunt*), Seb. Schmidt; Tholuck too, and Schrader, Fritzsche, Rückert (2nd *edit.*), Meyer, Baumgarten-Crusius, Olshausen; Krehl also, and van Hengel, Philippi, Jowett, Mac-Evilly, Oltramare, &c.

The Apostle says, "what if *some* (τινές) had no faith?" The distinction is not between *some* and *many*, but between *some* and *all.* For even *many* are only *some*, if they be not *all.* The Apostle might have said *many* (πολλοί),—a more sweeping word, which both Photius and Œcumenius insensibly substitute, in the course of their expositions; for the Apostle's more generous term. But he was accustomed to speak graciously, says Grotius. (*Ita solet* χαριεντίζειν). When it was not needful for the attainment of high moral ends to exhibit the whole unpleasant reality, the Apostle took pleasure in drawing a veil over multitudinous defalcations. Comp. chap. xi. 17; 1 Cor. x. 7. And as, in the present case, his argument neither demanded nor declined the more unwelcome term, he contented himself with saying *some.* It is "a species of reticence," says Calvin. It is "a euphemism," says Bengel. But when the latter of these distinguished critics insinuates, in addition, that there is a streak of contempt in the expression, we are not prepared to indorse his reading of the Apostle's thoughts. (*Atque infideles, quamvis multi, habentur ut* **quidam** *indefinite; quod non valde sub censum veniant.*) Philippi, however, catches up the idea, and blows it into most inflated proportions. "The host of the unbelieving appears," he says, "over against the truthfulness of the divine word, as a little contemptible handful." (*Der Wahrhaftigkeit des göttlichen Wortes gegenüber erscheint die Schaar der Ungläubigen als ein kleiner, verächtlicher Haufe.*) Lange seems charmed with this inflation. (*Der Gewissheit der Erfüllung der göttlichen Verheissung gegenüber ist auch die Masse des abfälligen Volks nur ein armer Haufe von Einzelnen.*) But this is, we conceive, an entire misapprehension of the Apostle's attitude. He was not speaking in the character of a rhetorician, or of a rhetorical chronicler, but in the character of an earnest logician. And he simply employs an expression which intimates that *there were some who believed,* as well as *some who believed not.* The relative numerical proportions of the classes did not affect the case he was handling. He might, indeed, if he had chosen, have taken another,—a historic standpoint, and have said, "For what although *the great masses* believed not?" Or, he might have occupied a still higher standpoint, and have said, "For what although *not one had* believed?" For, as Theodoret puts the case, "although all men had proved ungrateful, their ingratitude would not have lessened in the least the glory of God," (κἄν γὰρ ἅπαντες οἱ ἄνθρωποι περὶ αὐτον ἀχάριστοι γένωνται, οὐκ ἐλαττώσει τοῦ θεοῦ τὴν δόξαν ἡ τούτων ἀχαριστία.) And although all men had proved to be unbelieving, their want of faith would not, in the least, have evacuated or diminished or dimmed the faithfulness of God. What God had unconditionally promised, that he would unconditionally fulfil: and what was promised only conditionally would wait, with untarnished honour, for its fulfilment on the forthcoming of the condition. For although, as Œcumenius remarks, "men should not have been willing (to do *their* part), it would still be true that God did the part that devolved upon him," (εἰ γὰρ καὶ αὐτοὶ οὐκ ἠβουλήθησαν, ὁ μέντοι θεὸς τὸ αὐτοῦ πεποίηκεν).

It has been queried, whether, when the Apostle says, *what if some believed not?* he referred exclusively to the spiritual history of the Jews in times then past, or exclusively to their spiritual characteristics in the time then present;—whether, in other words, he referred to their prevailing unbelief under the entire currency of the Old Testament economy, as Philippi, for example, supposes, or, as Locke and Meyer, on the other hand, suppose, to their general rejection of the Messiah after the Messiah's appearance. The tense of the verb employed by the Apostle shows, as it appears to us, that the lines of his thought were running in the plane of the past,—that plane of things which covered the entire period when the Jews, as distinguished from the Gentiles, *were intrusted with the oracles of God*. But, logically, his reference was not confined to this plane. His eye swept, indeed, over the past ages; but it ranged downward through these ages till it rested on what had been, and was still, transpiring, since "the fulness of the time" had arrived, and since that illustrious Personage had appeared, in whom the precious promises of God were "yea and amen," and who, in his own grand personality, is the Consummation and the Sum of the oracles of God. *What matters it*, says the Apostle, *though some believed not?*—that is—*What matters it though many, in the bygone ages have lived and died without faith in the true Import of the oracles of God, and thus without faith in the Great Propitiator?—And what matters it, though many of their descendants, now living, are walking in their footsteps, and have refused to believe that which is the very Sum and Substance of their own precious Scriptures?—What signifies all this, so far as the question of prerogative is concerned?*

Van Hengel imagines that when the Apostle says *some*, he leaves out of view for the moment the special case of the Jews, and means *some men* (*indefinitely*). Jones goes farther, and imagines that there is a special reference, not to Jews, but to *Gentile unbelievers*. Yet nothing, surely, can be more obvious to the unprepossessed reader, than that the Apostle is speaking of the Jews alone. It would, however, be erring in the direction of the contrary extreme, to imagine, narrowingly and most capriciously, with Bahrdt, that the reference is confined to the Jewish *leaders* and *priests*. All such imaginations are the vagaries of exegesis.

§ 3. *Shall their non-faith make the faithfulness of God to fail?* (μὴ ἡ ἀπιστία αὐτῶν τὴν πίστιν τοῦ θεοῦ καταργήσει;) The expression which, with our *Auth. Eng. Vers.*, we render *the faithfulness of God*, (τὴν πίστιν τοῦ θεοῦ), has, by some critics, been regarded as meaning *faith in God*. They have regarded, that is to say, the genitive case of the word *God* as being *the genitive of the object*, rather than *the genitive of the subject*. Paulus took this view, (*uberzeugungstreue Anderer gegen die Gottheit*). So did Schrader, (*Glauben an Gott*). So did Abelard, (*fidem Dei, id est, per quam Deo crediderunt*). So too Bugenhagen, (*fides Dei ea est qua Deo credimus*). Aquinas hesitated; and also Dionysius à Ryckel; and so did Doddridge, who says, "This is an "ambiguous expression, and may either signify the *fidelity of* "*God*, or that *faith of ours* which God has pointed out as the "way of obtaining justification and life: the senses run at "last into each other:—I have included both." But, (1), the antithesis of the expression to the preceding one, "their non-faith" (ἡ ἀπιστία αὐτῶν); (2), the purport of the reply to the query, in ver. 4, "let God turn out to be true;" and, (3), the import of the parallel expression in ver. 5, "the righteousness of God;"—all these relations of the phrase conspire to make it certain that the genitive *of God* is to be understood subjectively, and that the whole phrase therefore means *the good faith*, or *faithfulness, of God*. "God *is* faithful" (πιστός). "Even though we refuse to have faith in him, yet he abideth *faithful,*" (2 Tim. ii. 13,—εἰ ἀπιστοῦμεν, ἐκεῖνος πιστὸς μένει). By a natural oscillation of import, the word (πίστις), which generally signifies, in the New Testament, *faith* or *belief,* occasionally denotes its counterpart,—that *good faith* or *faithfulness* which elicits reciprocating *belief* or *faith.* (See Gal. v. 22; 2 Tim. ii. 22; Tit. ii. 10; &c.: and comp. on chap. i. 17.) In the passage before us, it evidently has reference to the faithfulness of God in fulfilling those precious evangelical promises regarding the Saviour and salvation, which are the prominent feature and the culminating point of the "oracles of God." (*Sumitur enim hic fides pro fide qua fiunt dicta,*–Cajetan.) Photius (in Œcumen.) explains correctly, on the whole, the phrase as meaning "the faithfulness, truth, and immutability of the divine promises," (τὸ πιστὸν τῶν ὑποσχέσεων αὐτοῦ, τὸ ἀληθὲς, τὸ ἀμετάθετον). It thus follows, from the nature of the case, that the Apostle's query is substantially equivalent to this,—*Shall their unbelief nullify the fact of their high privilege? shall it make that special prerogative unreal which was conferred on them, when they were set apart as the peculiar Messianic people, and, as such, were intrusted with the oracles of God?* Their prerogative *was* an inestimable blessing,—abuse it as they might. It would be philologically outré, were we, with Seb. Schmidt, to regard the word *faith* as meaning, objectively, on the one hand, the object of justifying faith, and metonymically, on the other, that *gratuitous mercy of God,* in which men, needing justification, ought to have faith.

The interrogation,—*Shall their unbelief overturn the faithfulness of God?*—is of such a nature, phraseologically considered,—(as is indicated by the particle μή),—that a negative answer is anticipated. ("*Est,*" says Pareus, "*interrogatio negantis.*"—"*Neque enim,*" says Franke "*unquam quisquam particula μή in interrogando sic usus est, ut rem affirmari voluerit.*"–*De particulis negantibus* Com. I. p. 18.) We find, accordingly, a negative answer in the following verse. In concurrence with this negative answer Calvin supposed that the faithfulness of God was not neutralized by the unbelief of some of the Jews, because there was a secretly elected Israel within the ethnological Israel, in whose blessed experience the promises were realized. Lange's notion is somewhat similar. (*Also weist der Apostel den Gedanken ab, als ob die τινὲς die πίστις Gottes aufheben* (sic), *also auch die Verwirklichung des ewigen Gnadenbundes in dem Kerne Israels und in einem neutestamentlichen Gottesvolke vereiteln könnten.*) But such an idea is a superaddition to the Apostle's thought,—a superfœtation. The *oracles* to which reference is made were, as we have seen, the sum and substance of the entire moral revelation of God. And, as that revelation was addressed to all the Jews indifferently, and exhibited mercy to the people as a people, and to all the units composing the people, without distinction or exception, its possession was a veritable and inestimable privilege to all, whether they believed or not in the real Import of the Oracles. God was faithful to the people as a people, and to all the individual units who composed the whole, whether they chose to avail themselves of his faithfulness or not. They were blessed in having the Oracles, and in possessing the multitudinous concomitant advantages attached to the Oracles, whether they improved their high privilege, or not. (*Valet canon respectu, tam promissionum absolutârum, quam hypotheticarum seu conditionalium. Neutro modo infidelitas hominum fidem Dei cassam reddere potest,*-Varenius.) The exposition of Pareus is an advance on that of Calvin. He brings into view the condition of *faith*, on which the personal enjoyment of the chief blessings exhibited and promised in the Oracles is suspended. When this faith was withheld, the blessings referred to could not be enjoyed; and yet the faithfulness of God in (conditionally) promising them, and in (unconditionally) promising the propitiatory ground on which they rested, is unimpeached and unimpeachable. (Pareus, indeed,—faithful adherent, as he was, of Calvin's theological system,—puts it somewhat too strongly,—*Omnes promissiones tam legis quam evangelii annexam habent conditionem.*)

The verb (καταργήσει) which the Apostle employs interrogatively,—and which we may freely translate, *shall it undo?—shall it overturn?—shall it make to fail?*—originally means *shall it make inert* or *idle?* (See on verse 31.) It is rather too interpretatively rendered in our Auth. Eng. Version, and in the English Geneva, and by Tyndale, *shall it make without effect?* The interpretation assumed in such a translation,—that substantially of Calvin,—is too narrow. The word rather means *to make inefficient*, than *to make without effect.* It negatives the idea of *agency* or *operation*, rather than the idea of *result* or *effect.* It is one of the Apostle's favourite terms; though his application of it is so varied that it is difficult to give it anything like a uniform translation in English. It is rendered *destroy* in Rom. vi. 6; 1 Cor. vi. 13; Heb. ii. 14; *bring to nought* in 1 Cor. i. 28; *do away* in 1 Cor. xiii. 10, &c.; *put away* in 1 Cor. xiii. 11; *put down* in 1 Cor. xv. 24; *make void* in Rom. iii. 31; *abolish* in 2 Cor. iii. 13; Eph. ii. 15; 2 Tim. i. 10. Any of these translations,—though all of them are free,—would suffice in the passage before us:—"Shall their unbelief *do away,—put away,—put down,—bring to nought,—make void,—destroy,—abolish* the faithfulness of God?" (ἀποπαύω,–Suidas.) The temporal force of the verb does not, exactly, merge and lose itself, as some suppose, in the kindred idea of *possibility;*—although undoubtedly the future phase of the temporal import must be regarded as specified representatively. The meaning is not, exactly,—*Is it possible for the unbelief of some of the Jews to nullify the faithfulness of God?* The idea is more concrete:—*Has God's faithfulness been nullified? is it nullified? will it ever be?* The Apostle wisely devolves, however, on the future tense the function of representing the two other phases of time;—because, in the case supposed, the natural sequence of the events is such that the action of God must be viewed as *succeeding* the action of men. It must, that is to say, be viewed as *future* in relation to the action of men. God's unfaithfulness to his promises, if supposed at all, must be supposed as occurring *subsequently* to the unbelief of the men who are regarded as interested in these promises.

VER. 4. Μὴ γένοιτο. Γινέσθω δὲ ὁ θεὸς ἀληθής, πᾶς δὲ ἄνθρωπος ψεύστης· καθὼς γέγραπται, Ὅπως ἂν δικαιωθῇς ἐν τοῖς λόγοις σου, καὶ νικήσῃς ἐν τῷ κρίνεσθαί σε.

Eng. Auth. Vers. *God forbid: yea, let God be true, but every man a liar; as it is written, That thou mightest be justified in thy sayings, and mightest overcome when thou art judged.*

Revised Version. *Far be it. Let God, on the contrary, turn out to be true, but every man a liar; as it has been written, That thou mightest be justified in thy words, and overcome when thou enterest into judgement.*

§ 1. *Far be it!* (Μὴ γένοιτο). The Apostle repels, with vehemence, the idea that the faithfulness of God is made to fail by the unbelief of men. The expression which he employs is a kind of idiomatic exclamation, which is as idiomatically rendered in our *Auth. Eng. Trans.*, and in most of the English Translations which preceded it,—as, for instance, in Purvey's Revision of Wycliffe, in Tyndale, in the Geneva and the Rhemes,—"God forbid." Literally it means,—not, as Robinson renders it, *let it not happen*, but,—*let it not be:* for the verb is in the past; and when *coming-to-pass* actually *comes to pass*,—when it *has come to pass*, it *is*. The expression was not uncommon in the later Greek. It is found frequently, for example, in Arrian. It corresponds to the Latin *absit*, which is the translation of the Vulgate. It is rendered by Luther, "Das sey ferne,"—*That be far.* Piscator, Bengel, Heumann, Schrader, van Ess give the same translation. So did Wycliffe, *Fer be it.* De Saci renders it, "Non certes,"—*No truly.* Castellio (= Chateillon), more musically, "Nenni-da." Calvin, "Ia (*ultimately* ainsi) n' adviene." A considerable number of our English translators, such as Mace, Taylor, Wakefield, Newcome, Scarlett, Cox, Turnbull, render it, "by no means,"—a rather feeble version. The phrase corresponds to the Hebrew word חָלִילָה, which means *profane!*

and which is rendered in the Septuagint, sometimes by μὴ γένοιτο, *may it not be!*—sometimes by μηδαμῶς, *by no means!*—sometimes by μὴ εἴη, *may it not be!*—and sometimes by ἵλεως, *(God) be merciful to us (and prevent)*! This last expression is used in Matt. xvi. 22; where it is rendered, *be it far*. It corresponds to the common expression in Syriac, ܚܣ, which is used by the Peshito translator in the passage before us. The Apostle's phrase is used by him chiefly in this epistle to the Romans, in which it occurs ten times. It occurs thrice in the Epistle to the Galatians (ii. 17; iii. 21; vi. 14): and once in 1 Corinthians, (vi. 15). It is found nowhere else in his writings. In the whole of the rest of the New Testament it is found only in Luke xx. 16. It indicates a feeling of strong antagonism and aversion. (*Est valde aversantis*, says Grotius: *est abominantis sermo*, says Erasmus.) It is as if it were said, *Away with the thought!*—*Avaunt!* De Paris explains it as meaning here, *To say so would be a blasphemy.* Our idiomatic English translation, *God forbid!* is, in some cases, rather inapplicable, as, for instance, when the address is either directly *to God* (Gen. xviii. 25), or very directly *of God* (Job xxxiv. 10, and here Rom. iii. 3), or *by God* (1 Sam. ii. 30). But it is not seriously objectionable, as Thomson and others suppose, on the ground of the introduction of the word *God:* for the original expression embodies a desire, which, when uttered by such a man as the Apostle, may be legitimately regarded as, in all ordinary cases, rising up to God, and as thus involving what is tantamount to a prayer.

§ 2. *Let God, on the contrary, turn out to be true, but every man a liar*, (γινέσθω δὲ ὁ θεὸς ἀληθής, πᾶς δὲ ἄνθρωπος ψεύστης,). The introductory particle (δέ), which we have somewhat freely translated, *on the contrary*, indicates a swing, on the part of the Apostle's mind, toward the antithesis of the idea, which is eschewed in the preceding exclamation. We would have translated the particle, *but*, had it not been for its repetition in the following clause,—"*but* every man a liar."

Let God turn out to be true, or, more literally still, *Let God become true.* The employment of the verb *to become*, (γίνομαι), as distinguished from the verb *to be*, (εἰμί), has occasioned perplexity to some critics, expositors, and translators. The expression seems to have appeared to some of the old Greeks themselves inappropriate; and hence, instead of γινέσθω,—"let God *become* true," we read in L, and in Chrysostom, γενέσθω, and in G, ἔστω,—"let God *be* true." The Vulgate, again, and the Peshito cut the knot of the apparent difficulty by extreme freedom of translation. They render the phrase, "God *is* true," (*est autem Deus verax:* "forsoth God is trewe *or sothfast*,"—Wycliffe:—ܐܝܬܘܗܝ ܕܝܢ ܐܠܗܐ ܫܪܝܪܐ *for God is true*). In another direction, again, Ch. F. Schmid, uses equal liberty. He says that γινέσθω is used for ἔσται, and thus he translates the clause, "God *will be* true." He agrees with Bengel in supposing that there is a reference to what will be "in judgement;" although Bengel does not agree with him in rendering the verb as if it were future. He renders it *fiat*,—"may he become." Zinzendorf, however, renders it "will be," (*Gott wird wahrhaftig seyn*). Jo. C. Herzog (*De interpunctionum positu in Ep. ad Romanos*) seeks to escape the difficulty by another expedient. He would punctuate and explain the Apostle's statement thus:—"Let this Old Testament testimony become verified, viz. God is true, and every man a liar," (*Hoc fieri debet:—Deus in veritate sua est idem, homo vero omnis fraudes excogitat*). Koppe gives a similar explanation. He interprets the statement thus:—"Rather let it be held that God is faithful, though every man should be faithless," (γινέσθω δέ *interpunctione sejunxi a seqq*). It was substantially the same view that was taken of the construction by Luther himself:—"Rather let it remain that God be true, and all men false," (*es bleibe vielmehr also, dass Gott sey wahrhaftig, und alle Menschen falsch*). So too Coverdale,—"Let it rather be thus, that God is true, and all men lyers." Seb. Schmidt approves of the rendering. So does Lange. De Paris took a similar view, (*Reconnoissons au contraire pour une vérité incontestable, Grec* γινέσθω, **sit**, *que Dieu* *est véritable dans ses promesses, est la vérité même).*—Such a construction, however, is far too artificial; though it does not, it is true, pervert the substantial idea of the Apostle.

The Apostle's expression, *let God become true,* does not intimate or insinuate that God has, in times past, been untrue. Everything the reverse. The word *become* is used, not so much objectively in relation to God himself, as subjectively in relation to the minds of men. It is only in the sphere of men's apprehensions of things that the Apostle's wish can eventuate and realize itself. God, indeed, may "turn out to be true" in a *semi-objective* way, as the wheel of events turns round. His predictions become verified; and the principles of his procedure become justified. His words *turn out to be true,* and he himself, consequently, as the utterer of the words, is *found to be true.* He is *found,* viz., by his observant moral creatures. He *becomes,* viz., to the judgement of such of his moral creatures as judge aright. The Apostle's expression, therefore, must be understood logically;—(*non in se, sed in hominum opinione.*–Mussus.) It is thus that Theophylact explains it,—*Let God be shown or demonstrated to be true,* (*τὸ δὲ, γινέσθω ὁ θεὸς ἀληθὴς, ἀντὶ τοῦ, φανερούσθω, ἀποδεικνύσθω*). The worthy father, indeed, puts it perhaps,—at least so far as pure exegesis is concerned,—rather too strongly. Matthias improves the form of representation,—"Let God become true in our eyes,"—"Let him be acknowledged to be true," (*ergänze 'in unseren Augen.'—Γινέσθω in logischen, nicht in realen Sinne steht, synonym mit ὁμολογείσθω*). Photius comes very near the mark by simply supplying the personal pronoun, "Let God become true *to you*" (*γινέσθω ὑμῖν, in Œcum.*).

We have said that the Apostle's language is to be interpreted in a *logical* sense:—*logical,* we mean of course, as distinguished from *real;* not *logical,* as distinguished from *rhetorical.* The phraseology is eminently rhetorical. It is the lively utterance of strong, impulsive, devotional feeling, rather than the measured diction of philosophical ratiocination. Hence it takes the shape of an ardent aspiration or desire, instead of a calm and deliberate affirmation. But if we abstract this accidental shape or form from the substance of the thought which was lying in the depth of the Apostle's mind, we may express his idea in some such way as the Vulgate or Syriac translator has done, or as Conybeare does, "*Yea, be sure that God is true.*" And since God is "true," it follows that he will "faithfully" fulfil what he promises in his oracles. (*Deus inconcusse servat quae pollicetur.*–Zuingli.) He has ever been, and he will ever be faithful to his evangelical promises.

When the Apostle ascribes *truth* to God, he uses the word, not in a narrow or very sharply defined acceptation. Certainly, he does not simply mean that God will be found to be *true*, in the sense of accurately representing realities in his thoughts or in his words. Aquinas, indeed, with characteristic scholasticism, assumes that the reference is to the divine *intellect*, which, unlike the human intellect, is the archetypal cause and measure of things, so that things are true and real in the proportion of the conformity which they bear to the divine ideas. The divine intellect is thus in itself infinitely true. (*Secundum seipsum est indeficientur verax, et unaquæque res est vera inquantum ei conformatur.*) But the Apostle uses the word in its moral significance. God ever has been, and is, and ever will be *true* in his relation to his great evangelical promises. He is *faithful* in this respect. And doubtless he is thus *faithful* and *true* because he is *true*, throughout, in all the voluntary outgoings, immanent and transient, of his activity. They are all harmonious with the dictates of his infinite reason and his infinite conscience. They are all right and righteous. Thus the *truth* or *truthfulness* of God, as referred to in verses 4 and 7, is coincident, in the Apostle's mind, with his *faithfulness* as specified in verse 3rd, and with his *righteousness* as specified in verse 5th.

When the Apostle adds, *but every man a liar*, (πᾶς δὲ ἄνθρωπος ψεύστης), there can be no doubt that Rückert is right in regarding the addition as being, so far as the Apostle's main object is concerned, unessential (*unwesent-*

lich). The statement is thrown in by the way, and serves the purpose of a foil,—giving contrastive intensity to the statement regarding the truthfulness of God. Thus it is in reality, *though not in form*, a hypothetical additament:—"let God turn out true, *even though every man should turn out a liar*." It is not unlikely, indeed, that the idea of Koppe and van Hengel is correct, that the whole proposition, with the mutual antithesis of the two clauses which constitute it, was a kind of gnome, or proverbial expression, circulating, with more or less of currency, among the people. And hence we cannot think, with Meyer and Fritzsche, that the clause, *but every man a liar*, was specially intended, by the advance of the word *every* on the word *some*, to amplify the supposition contained in the preceding verse, *what if some believed not?* Still less is it, as Augustin and many of the subsequent critics, who took the Vulgate for their text, supposed, a positive affirmation that "every man *is*—as a matter of fact—a liar." The verb of the preceding clause (γινέσθω) is undoubtedly to be carried forward to this:—"but *let* every man *become* a liar." And the substrate of the idea intended is obviously this:—"Let God turn out true, but every man a liar,—*if that should be necessary to secure the truthfulness of God, which, however, it happily is not.—Be sure that God is true, even though every man should prove to be a liar.*

There is, indeed, a sense in which "every man *is a liar*." He will fail us in the time of our greatest need, if we trust to him entirely, to the neglect of God. He will "fail," we say; for see Isai. lviii. 11, (יְכַזְּבוּ). And in another and more active sense every fallen man may be said to be *a liar*:—he is not, out and out, true to every dictate of his conscience. He is not, in every respect, true to his God, true to his fellow-men, true even to himself. He is not absolutely faithful throughout. There is not an absolute harmony between the acts of his will and the dictates of his conscience or reason. And it was doubtless when the Psalmist was taking one or other of these views of human nature, that he said "in his haste," or, *in his agitation*, "all men are liars," or, as it is in the Septuagint "every man (is) a liar," (πᾶς ἄνθρωπος ψεύστης), —Ps. cxvi. 11. It is impossible to determine whether or not the Apostle was mentally referring to this exclamation of the Psalmist. And, whether he was or not, it is manifest, from the relation of the clause to the preceding one, as a subordinate antithetic additament, and from the necessity of carrying forward the imperative verb γινέσθω, "but *let* every man *become* a liar," that the Apostle was not intending a categorical affirmation of the actual untruthfulness, unfaithfulness, or unrighteousness, of every human being. Still less was he intending to assert that every man, or that any man, is, in everything which he says and does, untruthful and unrighteous. Hence we need not start the question, with Origen, Whether, if every man be a liar, Paul and the Psalmist themselves were not liars; and liars, too, when they said that *every man is a liar*. Neither need we try to answer this question, with the hyper-ingenuity of Origen, by appealing to John x. 34, 35, "Jesus answered them, Is it "not written in your law, I said, *Ye are gods?* If he "called them *gods*, unto whom the word of God came, "and the scripture cannot be broken," &c. "The word of God," says Origen, "came to David and Paul;" and therefore "they were *not men, but gods*," (*sine dubio non erant homines, sed dei*); and thus they were not liars when they said that *every man is a liar*. Nor need we start Augustin's question. The martyrs, he said, were called martyrs because they died for the witness which they bore to the truth. But how, he asks, can we be warranted to regard them as having borne witness to the truth, if the Scripture itself be true, which says that *every man is a liar*. If the martyrs, he argues, were not liars, we seem to make the Scripture to lie; and if they were liars, then they were not witnesses for the truth. He tells us that he will labour (*laborabimus*) to solve the difficulty. And, after ringing abundant changes upon escaping from a lie on the right hand, or a lie on the left, he finds an end to his labour, and a key to the mystery, in the words of our Lord,—"When they deliver you up, take no thought how or what ye shall speak, for it shall be given you in that same hour what ye shall speak; *for it is not ye that speak, but the Spirit of your Father which speaketh in you.*" Lo, here, exclaims the delighted casuist, is the reason why the martyrs were not liars in their testimony:—*it was not they who spake, it was the Holy Spirit.* (*Ecce quare veraces fuerunt; quia non ipsi loquebantur, sed Spiritus Domini.*—**Sermo**, *328, in Natali Martyrum.*) But the difficulty, though thus adroitly and edifyingly got rid of, in the particular case of the martyrs, went forth at large, and roamed far and wide through the ages. It met Abelard in a peculiar way:—Since, says he, it is true that *every man is a liar*, what are we to think of *the man Christ Jesus?* Was it possible for him to lie? He was too reverent to ask, Was he a liar? On such a subject the subtle Doctor had to pick his steps with carefulness; for the cry of heresy might have burst out on the right hand or on the left. So he made, in true schoolman-style, a *distinction*, and determined that the manhood of Christ, considered *simpliciter*, laboured under no impossibility of lying or otherwise sinning, else he would have been destitute of free-will, (*libero videtur privatus arbitrio, et necessitate potius quam voluntate peccatum cavere*); but when we think of the natures of Christ in their union, or *compliciter* as we might say, we must come, he admits, to the conclusion that he was absolutely impeccable.—Jerome took a different way of getting out of the difficulty, the way of a grammarian. The words *all* and *every*, he says, do not always denote absolute universality (*non ad universitatem referunt*), and the real meaning of the declaration, "Every man is a liar," is, he thinks, "*a great part* of men are liars." (**Omnes** *sic accipiendi sunt, quod* **magna pars** *hominum mentiatur.*—**Com.** *in Eph.* i. 22, 23.) Pelagius agreed with Jerome. The word "every," he says, is used for "the greater part," (*hic* **omnes** *pro* **maxima parte** *dicit*). —But all these exegetical expedients, from Origen's onward, are merely ingenious efforts to cook, for our digestion, theological chickens which have never been hatched, and which have not even existed in embryo within the egg. The Apostle is not categorically asserting that *every man is a liar*, and *a liar too in every thing he says.* There is not, as Krehl remarks, the least approach to hyperbole in his idea. The man, Krehl justly adds, who agrees not with the Apostle in his feeling and conviction, is yet far from the true knowledge of God. (*Es ist keinesweges eine Hyperbel; nein,—der Mensch, der nicht dieselbe Empfindung und Ueberzeugung hat, ist von der wahren Gotteserkenntniss noch fern.*) He who has just views of God as the "All in all," *will heartily desire that he should ever turn out true, even although all mankind, if this should be necessary to establish his truthfulness, should prove to be false.* God's *truthfulness* in his declarations, and especially in the fulfilment of his precious promises,—in other words, his *faithfulness* (πίστις,–ver. 3), or, to go out wider still, his *righteousness* (δικαιοσύνη,–ver. 5),—is the ground on which the hopes of the human world, and indeed of the whole moral universe, repose.

§ 3. The Apostle confirms his own aspiration, or asseveration, regarding the truthfulness of God, by a quotation from the Old Testament Scriptures:—*As it has been written, That thou mightest be justified in thy words, and overcome when thou enterest into judgement,* (καθὼς γέγραπτει, Ὅπως ἂν δικαιωθῇς ἐν τοῖς λόγοις σου, καὶ νικήσῃς ἐν τῷ κρίνεσθαί σε.) The introductory expression, *as it has been written,* (καθὼς γέγραπται), is admirably rendered by Luther, *as it stands written,* (*wie geschrieben steht*). It is not so literally reproduced in our various English versions;—*as it is written.* The passage quoted occurs in the penitential psalm which David wrote "when Nathan the prophet came unto him, after he had gone in to Bathsheba,"–Psalm li. It is the latter part of ver. 4 (Hebrew, v. 6) which is referred to. But it may be well to quote the preceding verses. "1. Have mercy upon me, O God, "according to thy lovingkindness; according unto the "multitude of thy tender mercies blot out my transgres-

"sions. 2. Wash me throughly from mine iniquity, and "cleanse me from my sin. 3. For I acknowledge my "transgressions; and my sin is ever before me. 4. Against "thee, thee only, have I sinned, and done this evil in thy "sight: *that thou mightest be justified when thou speakest,* "and *be clear when thou judgest,*" (לְמַעַן תִּצְדַּק בְּדָבְרֶךָ תִּזְכֶּה בְשָׁפְטֶךָ).

The Apostle's quotation differs slightly from the literal import of the Hebrew terms: but it is a precise transcription of the Septuagint version. And it is only in form, not in substance, that the Septuagint version, when correctly understood, varies from the original. The expression, *that thou mightest be justified,* (ὅπως ἂν δικαιωθῇς), might have been translated, *that thou mightest be righteous,* (לְמַעַן תִּצְדַּק). But this could only mean, *that thou mightest be made out to be righteous,* that is, *that thou mightest be justified.* The expression, *when thou speakest,* or, *in thy speaking,* (literally, ἐν τῷ λέγειν σε), is really equivalent to, *in thy words,* (ἐν τοῖς λόγοις σου), and, so far as Greek is concerned, it is more idiomatically rendered as the Septuagint translator and the Apostle give it. The conjecture of Drusius, that the Septuagint translator read בִּדְבָרֶךָ, (or rather, as we presume, בִּדְבָרֶיךָ), is unnecessary; although, at the same time, it is to be borne in mind that this is the only passage in which the kal of the verb occurs, except in the participle. The expression, again, *be clear,* (תִּזְכֶּה), is, in substance, represented by the Greek idiomatic word *overcome,* (νικήσῃς), when that word is applied to the successful party in a judicial cause. (*Verbum Hebraeum et Graecum non reapse, sed literis, diversum est,*–Surenhusius.) He who overcomes, if he be the defendant in the case, is *cleared,* and is presumed to be *clear.* He is *legally clear.* The party thus cleared, or he who gains the suit, whether defendant or prosecutor, was said to *overcome* (νικᾷν, *vincere*). See Elsner and Wetstein, *in loc.* Hence in Rabbinic Hebrew the verb is freely used, in the sense of the Hebrew צָדַק, as meaning *to be righteous, to be made out to be righteous, to be justified.* (See Buxtorf, *in voc.*) And in Syriac the word–ܙܟܐ–though retaining abundant remnants of its original signification, *to be pure,* is currently employed to mean *to get the victory, to conquer, to overcome.* (See Castell and Schaaf, *in voc.*) The only remaining expression is that which is rendered in the psalm, *when thou judgest,* (בְּשָׁפְטֶךָ, literally ἐν τῷ κρίνειν σε), but which is rendered in our authorized English version of the Septuagint translation, as given by the Apostle (ἐν τῷ κρίνεσθαί σε), "when thou art judged." It is manifest that our translators had regarded the word employed in the Septuagint as being in the passive voice. And in this opinion they are supported by the Vulgate (*cum judicaris*); also, apparently, by the Peshito (ܡܐ ܕܕܐܢܝܢ ܠܟ—*when they judge thee*); as well as by Erasmus, Luther, Calvin, Camerarius, and many other distinguished critics, inclusive, in more modern times, of Bos, Elsner, Wetstein, Koppe, Böhme, Reiche, Rückert, de Wette, Alford, Maier, Mehring, Lange, &c. Calvin says,—"Although the verb κρίνεσθαι can be taken either actively or passively, I nevertheless do not doubt that the Greek translators, contrary to the mind of the prophet (*praeter mentem prophetae*), rendered it passively." Beza, however, on *re*consideration, differed in this matter from his illustrious predecessor. We say, *reconsideration*; for, in the 1st edition of his Translation of the New Testament with Notes (1556), he took Calvin's view, (*quando de te fit judicium*). In all his other editions he maintains that the word is used in the middle voice, and has the identical signification which attaches to the active. Calvin and he, we apprehend, are both wrong: Calvin wholly; and Beza partially Beza is wrong in so far as he identified the signification of the verb in its middle and in its active voice. There is no such identity. The verb in the middle voice does not mean precisely what it means in the active; though Piscator, Pareus, and the authors of the new Dutch version (*wanneer Gij oordeelt*), agree with Beza in attributing such a signification to it. (See Dresigius, *de verbis mediis,* ii. 11; and especially Kuster, *de verb. med.* ii. 6.) And yet it has a modified *active* import. It means *to litigate, to enter a case at law, to go to law* (*with any one*), *to contend* (*with any one*), *to enter into judgement.* (See Hesychius,—κρινώμεθα, ἀντὶ τοῦ μαχώ-

μεθα ἢ διαλεγώμεθα.) The verb is used in this acceptation in Matt. v. 40, "if any one *will sue thee at the law,*" (θέλοντί σοι κριθῆναι); 1 Cor. vi. 6, "brother *goeth to law* with brother," (ἀδελφὸς μετὰ ἀδελφοῦ κρίνεται); see also 1 Cor. vi. 1. In the Septuagint, from which the Apostle quotes, this medial use of the word is frequent; sometimes with a more or less strictly judicial reference, and sometimes without it (as meaning *to contend* extrajudicially). See Gen. xxvi. 21; Judg. viii. 1; xxi. 22; Job ix. 3; xiii. 19; xxxi. 13; Eccles. vi. 10; Isai. xliii. 26; l. 8; Jer. ii. 9; ii. 35; xxv. 31; Hos. ii. 2; Mic. vi. 1. In some of these passages the corresponding verb in Hebrew is שָׁפַט; in one (Eccles. vi. 10) it is דִּין; and in the most, רִיב.

If we assume that the verb is used medially in Ps. li. 4, then the ideas expressed by the original Hebrew, and by the Septuagint version, are thoroughly harmonious and almost coincident. For it is substantially one thing for God *to be clear when he judges* sinners, and *to overcome when he contends, or enters into judgement,* with them. There is only an unessential variation in the standpoint from which his relationship is contemplated. In the one case he is contemplated as acting the part of a judge; in the other he is considered as acting the part of a prosecutor. In the one case he passes sentence against; in the other he pleads against. But in both relationships he is sure to be equally right in the utterances to which he gives expression. And his utterances, moreover, will, in either case, be in substance identical. There would be little wonder, therefore, if the Septuagint translator should freely substitute the expression, *that thou mightest overcome when thou enterest into judgement,* for the expression, *that thou mightest be pure when thou judgest,* (especially if the phrase καθαρὸς γένῃ ἐν τῷ κρίνειν σε might appear to be unidiomatic to Greek ears; and if to say, on the other hand, νικήσῃς ἐν τῷ κρίνειν σε, would be to confound the respective relationships of *prosecutor* and *judge*). We are disposed, then, to come to the conclusion that the Septuagint translator used the verb in its medial acceptation: and thus we would regard the original Hebrew and the Septuagintal Greek as substantially accordant. Of the same opinion, apparently, was Photius, (ἵνα νικήσῃ, εἰς κρίσιν τοῖς ἀνθρώποις καταστάς, *ut vincat, ubi cum hominibus in judicium congreditur*). And of modern expositors the following approve:—Drusius, Hammond, Whitby, Bengel, Tholuck (in his 1st, 2nd, 3rd, and 5th editions, though in his 4th he took the word to be passive), Meyer (in his 3rd and 4th editions, though he confounds the functions of prosecutor and judge; in his 1st and 2nd editions he maintained that the verb is passive), Philippi, van Hengel, Ewald, Matthias, &c. Fritzsche says that he is at a loss to determine which of the two interpretations he should prefer. Wordsworth too must have been at a loss, for he leaps over the expression without touching it at all. Reithmayr acknowledges that "the medial form gives a good sense." And Klee inclines to it. It seems certainly better to take this view of the meaning of the Septuagint translation,—a meaning so harmonious with the Hebrew phrase and with the scope of the passage in the psalm,—than to hold, with Rückert, that "the Alexandrian translator had made a mistake," which the Apostle adopts; or to maintain, with Taylor, that the Apostle quotes the faulty translation, not so much to adopt it, as merely to refer to the passage of Scripture. Taylor adds,—but we think very unwarrantably,—"when the Hebrew and Greek differ, I cannot find the Apostles ever argue from the Greek. It is upon this ground," he continues, "that, for my own part, I pay no regard to the words of the Septuagint, as quoted in the New Testament: the Hebrew is my standard, because I am persuaded it was so to the Apostles."

The passage which the Apostle quotes may be considered both in its relation to its original context in the Psalm, and in its relation to its context in the Apostle's discussion.

And, *firstly*, as regards the Psalm:—The teleological form of the expression,—"*that*," or, "*in order that* (לְמַעַן = ὅπως ἄν) *thou mightest be justified* when thou speakest, and be clear when thou judgest,"—has occasioned much diversity of opinion regarding the logical antecedent on which the clause is dependent. Hitzig, indeed, says nothing on the subject; and Maurer says nothing definite. Hupfeld, on the other hand, says much, but would not press a very definitive determination of the relationship. Of those who have definitive opinions, (1.) Some suppose that the antecedent is to be found in the second verse of the Psalm,—"wash me throughly from mine iniquity, and cleanse me from my sin,—*that thou mayest be justified,* &c." This is the opinion of Munster, Vatable, Ferrand, de Saci, Day, &c. (2.) Others suppose that the antecedent is to be found in the third verse,—"For *I acknowledge* my transgressions; and my sin *is ever before me ;*—against thee, thee only have I sinned, and done this evil in thy sight;—*I make this acknowledgement or confession* that thou mayest be justified when thou speakest, and be clear when thou judgest." Of this opinion, substantially, are Tremellius and Junius, Pareus, Taylor, Michaelis, Fritzsche, &c. (3.) Some, again, imagine that the Psalmist's idea is,—"Against thee, thee only have I sinned, and done this evil in thy sight, *and this thou hast permitted or decreed,* that thou mightest be justified, &c." Of this opinion are Abelard, Zuingli, Sclater, Brentano, Hengstenberg (*under a modification*), Alexander, &c. (4.) While others still, such as Chrysostom, Theodoret, Dionysius à Ryckel, Campensis, Calvin, Mussus, Geier, Moller, Amyraut, Green, Venema, Dathe, Phillips, &c., give to the conjunction an ecbatic or consecutive instead of a telic or causative import, and understand the Psalmist as saying, "against thee, thee only have I sinned, and done this evil in thy sight, *so that thou art righteous* in what thou sayest, &c." This last device, though regarded by Hupfeld as practically admissible, amounts, we should imagine, to a sacrifice of philology to theology. The preceding or third interpretation intrudes, on merely theological grounds, a supplementary idea, which, to say the least of it, is certainly not expressed by the Psalmist, and which must remain, therefore, so far as the Psalmist's language is concerned, entirely conjectural. The first interpretation, on the other hand, involves the unnatural assumption of a very long parenthesis: and it necessitates, moreover, the idea that when it is said "that thou mayest be justified in thy *words*," the reference is to *promises;* as also that the last clause of the verse should be understood passively, "and overcome when *thou art judged*." It remains, thus, that we accept the second interpretation as expressive of the Psalmist's mind. The Psalm is penitential. The element of confession pervades it. There is explicit expression given to this element in verse 3,—the central verse, as Thrupp remarks, of the first strophe, *vv.* 1–5,—"for I acknowledge my transgressions; and my sin is ever before me." And when the Psalmist continues, in ver. 4, to say, "to thee, thee only, have I sinned, and done that which is evil in thy sight," his words prolong the confessional element, *and are, indeed, a confession.* He had injured man, it is true;—grievously;—atrociously. He had been most cruel and most selfish. But "sin," as sin, *can be relative to God only.* The most regardless self-indulgence and the most atrocious cruelty could never be "sin," *except in relation to the will of God.* Suppose that there were no will on the part of God in the matter, *and there never could be sin.* It was in relation to God, then,—to God only,—that the Psalmist had sinned. But he *had* thus sinned. He had done "what was *evil in God's sight*," (for the expression *in thy sight* is to be connected, not with the verb *I have done*, but with the expression *what is evil*). He made this confession. And he made it "in order that God might be justified (in men's minds) in speaking against the guilty monarch,—that He might be clear (in the apprehensions of men) in passing judicial sentence," as when He said, "Now therefore the sword shall never depart from thine house,"—"behold I will raise up evil against thee out of thine own house." (2 Sam. xii. 10, 11.) It thus follows that the words quoted by the Apostle express the Psalmist's desire that God should be regarded by men as right, entirely right, in what he says. The Psalmist was not solicitous about the opinions which men might entertain regarding himself. It was his great desire that they should have high ideas of the righteousness of God,—that they should, amid all circumstances and eventualities, vindicate God as one who is infinitely "true" to all his claims,—to all that He ought to do and to be.

When we turn now to the quotation, as it lies in the Apostle's text, we see at once its relevancy to the Apostle's aim. He had said, *Let God be acknowledged as true, though every man should be regarded as a liar.* And thus, when he adds, *as it has been written, That thou mightest be justified in thy words, and overcome when thou enterest into judgement,* he, as it were, says:—"I may well exclaim, *Let God be acknowledged to be true,* "*though every man should be regarded as a liar;* I am "but echoing, in such an exclamation, the sentiment of "King David, who was forward to condemn himself in "what he had done, that he might vindicate God in "what He had said; and who, accordingly, made public "confession of his guilt, *in order that God might be* "*justified in the words* (*which he had uttered against him*), "*and might overcome* (*in all men's estimation*) *when he* "*entered into judgement* (*with him*)." Rückert says that the quotation contains no proof at all of God's truthfulness. (*Einen Beweis für Gottes Wahrhaftigkeit enthält die Stelle gar nicht.*) But if we take an enlarged conception of what is involved in *God's truthfulness,*—as we are bound to do when we consider the parallel words *faithfulness* and *righteousness* in verses 3d and 5th,—the statement of David assuredly proves, (1), that he was profoundly persuaded that *God was to be entirely depended upon in all that he said,* whatever might be the nature of his utterances, and their bearing upon men's state and prospects; and, (2), that he was most desirous that *men in general should agree with himself* in his view of the character of God. But these ideas are entirely and to a nicety coincident with the Apostle's own, when he exclaims, *Let God be acknowledged as true, though every man should be regarded as a liar.* It was surely rash in Rückert to "enter into judgement" with Paul in such a matter. He must certainly, when Enlightened Candour sits on the bench, come out of court "overcome."

The conclusion of the whole matter is, that it must

be the case that *God has ever been, and is, and ever will be, faithful and true in all that he says and promises in his lively* **oracles**. And therefore no unbelief of the Jews, in reference to the evangelical contents of these **oracles**, can ever militate against the asseveration, *That it is a very great privilege and prerogative to be intrusted with them.*

VER. 5. Εἰ δὲ ἡ ἀδικία ἡμῶν Θεοῦ δικαιοσύνην συνίστησιν, τί ἐροῦμεν; Μὴ ἄδικος ὁ Θεὸς ὁ ἐπιφέρων τὴν ὀργήν; κατὰ ἄνθρωπον λέγω.

Eng. Auth. Vers. *But if our unrighteousness commend the righteousness of God, what shall we say?* Is *God unrighteous, who taketh vengeance? (I speak as a man.)*

Revised Version. *But if our unrighteousness sets off God's righteousness, what shall we say? Is God unrighteous who inflicteth wrath? I speak after the manner of man.*

§. 1. The Apostle, instead of now proceeding to detail other ingredients of the high prerogative enjoyed by the Jews, runs out still farther on that defensive line of things, along which he had travelled in verses 3rd and 4th. He extends his *detour*, or *digressiuncule*—as Bullinger styles it. He anticipates *an objection to his justification* of the privilege which he had specified in the latter part of verse 2nd. "Note," says Mussus, "the adversative *But;—But if these things be true, lo a difficulty!*" (*Notate dictionem adversativum,* Sed, *vel* Autem :–*Si autem haec vera sunt, ecce difficultas.*)

§ 2. *But if our unrighteousness sets off God's righteousness,* (εἰ δὲ ἡ ἀδικία ἡμῶν Θεοῦ δικαιοσύνην συνίστησιν). The verb (συνίστησιν), which we have rendered *sets off*, originally means *to place together,* and is used with very various references. Sometimes *persons* are *placed together*, that the one may be introduced to the other. In such cases the one is often *commended* to the other. And this word *commend* is the translation which is most frequently given to the term in our Authorized English Version. See Rom. v. 8; xvi. 1; 2 Cor. iv. 2; x. 18; xii. 11. Compare 2 Cor. iii. 1; v. 12; x. 12.—But *things*, as well as persons, may be *placed together*. And when they are thus brought into contiguity, it often happens that one appears to advantage by the side of another, in virtue of the influence of contrast. It is *set off*. It is made more striking and conspicuous. This is the meaning of the term in the passage before us. It is translated, indeed, "commends" (*commendat*) by the Vulgate; and by Wycliffe, Castellio, and Beza, and in the Eng. Geneva, and our Auth. Eng. Vers. A modification of the same rendering,—"recommends,"—is given by Martin, Wynne, Belsham, &c.; as also in some of the Revisions of the French Geneva, (see, for instance, the Brussels ed. of 1616; and the Amsterdam ed. of 1710). Luther's translation is similar, *preiset*. It is reproduced by Coverdale, "prayseth." It is retained by Bengel. It is certainly much superior to Tyndale's version, "makes more excellent." It is given in a modified form in the French Geneva of 1562, as also in Calvin's French Translation,—"makes to be praised" (*fait que soit louee*). But neither *praiseth*, nor *makes to be praised*, nor *recommends*, nor *commends*, is an altogether satisfactory rendering for the passage before us. Still less satisfactory is the translation of Erasmus,—"confirms" (*stabilit ac confirmat fulcitque*),—although it is certainly the case that things are often *placed together*, that one, or other, or all of them may be *supported*, or *established* and *confirmed*. Erasmus's version was given, long before his day, by the Syriac translator (ܡܩܝܡ); and it is reproduced by Turnbull, Conybeare, and *The Five Clergymen*;—as also by Worsley, Macknight, Göschen, and Rilliet. Cooper renders the word, analogously,—*proves*. A much better rendering is that of Mace, Wakefield and Walford,—*displays*. Vaughan intensifies it unnecessarily,—"displays strongly." The version of the Bishop's Bible lies on the same line of representation,—"setteth foorth." (Grotius's explanation of the word is felicitous and elegant, *spectabiliorem facit.* So is Abelard's, *maxime laudabilem ostendit.* So, indeed, is Stolz's translation,—*in's Licht sezt;* and van Ess's,—*an's Licht bringt.*) The real idea is,—*sets off.*

The Apostle's expression, introduced, as it is, with the hypothetical particle *if,* is tantamount to a concession. And hence it is better to translate the verb, *sets off,* in the indicative, than *set off,* in the subjunctive. If the word *commend* should be chosen for the translation, it ought rather to be *commends,* than, as in our Auth. Eng. Vers. and in Wycliffe, *commend.* The meaning of the Apostle is, —"if,—*as I admit to be the case,*—the righteousness of God is actually set off by our unrighteousness."

In introducing such a concession, the Apostle intends to meet and thrust aside an objection, which might be apt, in view of what is said in the preceding verse, to spring up in some Jewish minds. The objection might be represented thus:—"If God remains faithful to all "his promises, true *to* all his declarations,—true *in* them "all,—howsoever unbelieving and rebellious we may be: "if He is always victorious, and justified, or made out to "be right and righteous, howsoever unfaithfully and falsely "and wickedly we may act: then, as our unrighteousness "really serves to set off to advantage His righteousness, "would it not be too bad if He were to punish us for the "advantage which he gets? Our unrighteousness is a "useful foil to his righteousness:—why should He then "make us suffer for it?"

This objection assumes, in the Apostle's view of it, a peculiar phraseological shape, in virtue of the word for *justified,* or, *made out to be righteous,* (δικαιωθῇς), which occurs in the passage that is quoted, in the preceding verse, from the 51st Psalm. It is hence that we are to account for the employment of the expression, *God's righteousness* (θεοῦ δικαιοσύνην), rather than the expression, *God's truthfulness,* or *God's faithfulness.*

As to the expression, "*our* unrighteousness,"—the pronoun *our* has no relation, as Meyer and Philippi seem to think, to the statement, *every man a liar.* And hence it is not, with Seb. Schmidt, Fritzsche, Baumgarten-Crusius, and van Hengel, to be interpreted as embracing, within the sweep of its reference, *men in general.* Neither are we to rush to the other extreme, and, with Wetstein, interpret the plural as standing for the singular, "if *my* unrighteousness," (*si hoc ipsum, quod* **ego** *gentibus iniquior sum*). Neither has the Apostle vaulted into the standpoint of heathens; as Thomson imagines. The reference, as was seen clearly by Grotius, Bengel, Koppe, Reiche, de Wette, Oltramare, is to the Jews exclusively. It is to them that the Apostle is referring, at once in the preceding context, and in that which comes after, (see ver. 9). He has been stripping the unbelieving Jews of their high assumptions; and he had found, we presume, in the course of his actual contact with them, that, when thus stripped, they felt as if they were spiritually flayed, and were ready, in their soreness, to give utterance to the most irreverent and outrageous apologies for their state. It is to be borne in mind, nevertheless, that such irreverent recklessness is no peculiarity of Jews; and that consequently the Apostle's words, when viewed apart from their strict contextual relations, are applicable to individuals of all peoples and climes.

The Apostle, associates himself, for a moment, with his unbelieving countrymen, and says "our," because he was viewing the subject in hand, not so much historically, according to actual facts, as hypothetically and logically. He was treating it as a general principle. And yet, for aught that any one can tell, he might be all the more readily led to employ the plural pronoun, as his memory might instinctively and instantaneously suggest to him, that once he himself was exactly in the position in which the great body of his countrymen continued to be.

The expression, "our *unrighteousness*" (ἡ ἀδικία ἡμῶν), is put in contrast to the antithetic expression, "God's *righteousness.*" The word *unrighteousness* is generic. But it was undoubtedly intended, though maintaining its general import, to be a designation of something specific. The reference is to the *unbelief* (ἀπιστία) spoken of in ver. 3rd. That unbelief was not only unbelief; it was also *unrighteousness.*

The contrasted expression, *God's righteousness* (θεοῦ δικαιοσύνην), is, in like manner, and notwithstanding its generic import, employed with a specific reference. It refers to that phase of God's righteousness which is spoken of in the 3rd verse,—that phase of his righteousness which is realized in his *faithfulness* to the promissory element of his Oracles. When Ch. F. Schmid, Rosenmüller, and Brentano translate the word, *benignity,* they are not only wrong in their interpretation of the term; they also confound the office of interpretation with the office of translation. And when the two former critics aver, in addition, that Chrysostom and Theodoret ascribe the same import to the term, their averment is unwarranted by the words of the fathers appealed to. Mace commits a similar mistake in criticism and interpretation, when he translates the word, *veracity.* And when Seb. Schmidt, Whitby, Doddridge, Adam, Turner (in the main), and van Hengel suppose that *the righteousness of God* which is referred to, is the same that is spoken of in chap. i. 17 as "revealed in the Gospel,"—constituting that Gospel "the power of God unto salvation,"—they lose sight of the relation of the expression to δικαιωθῇς in the preceding verse,—"that thou mightest be made out to be *righteous.*" They overlook, moreover, the parallelism of the word with the term *faithfulness* in ver. 3rd, and the terms *truth* and *trueness* in verses 4th and 7th.

§ 3. *what shall we say?* (τί ἐροῦμεν;) This is an expression that indicates a brief voluntary pause in thought. In using it, the Apostle seems to have stopped for a moment, that he might reweigh the idea or expression which was rushing forward for utterance. It is fitted to lead the reader to collect himself; while it makes him feel his inquisitiveness whetted, and also brings him abreast with the Apostle in the conscious exercise of the logical faculty. It is worthy of being noted, that the expression occurs only, so far as the New Testament is concerned, in the epistle to the Romans. But there it occurs frequently. See,—besides chap. iv. 1,—chap. vi. 1; vii. 7; viii. 31; ix. 14, 30. It is used, with great effect, in meeting erroneous notions or objections, as here, and in chaps. iv. 1; vi. 1; vii. 7; ix. 14.

§ 4. *is God unrighteous, who inflicteth wrath?* (μὴ ἄδικος ὁ θεὸς, ὁ ἐπιφέρων τὴν ὀργήν;) A considerable number of critics, — misunderstanding the Apostle's real relation to the objection introduced,—render the interrogative particle μή by the Latin *nonne*,—"*is not* God unrighteous, who inflicteth wrath?" Grotius gives this rendering; and he has been followed by Day, Locke, Wells, Taylor, Mace, Knatchbull, Boysen, Macknight, and Ch. F. Schmid; by Reiche too; and even by Rückert and Philippi; and by Jowett and Oltramare; by Shepherd also. Matthias says that it is exceedingly difficult (*überaus schwierig*) to account for the μή, which leads us to anticipate a negative answer to the query. The difficulty grew upon him; so that, in the 2nd edition of his Exposition, after weighing anxiously the whole case, he supposes that there must be a predominant leaning toward an affirmative reply, and yet, at the same time, a slight doubt in the direction of the contrary, (*einem leisen zweifel hinsichtlich ihrer Verneinung*). We are surprised at all this. It looks like critical licentiousness. We see not the slightest need for assuming a departure from the regular import of this particle. ("*Qualem*," says Hoogeveen, "*particulae* μή *impetum notare deprehendimus in dehortantibus, prohibentibus, deprecantibus, et aversantibus; similem etiam observamus in sciscitantibus, sed illis, qui rem, quasi ignari, alium rogant, cum ipsi de contrario satis sint certi*."–*De Partic.*, xxvii. 4.—"*Tenendum est enim*," says Franke, "*in hoc genere loquendi* μή *ad metum sive opinionem alius personae, quam quæ indicativo indicata est, referri*."–*De Partic. Negantibus*, i. 16.) The question proposed by the Apostle is put from his own standpoint, although it embodies the objection of his unbelieving and recalcitrating countrymen. Being put from his own standpoint, and thus proposing the objection, not directly, but indirectly, it naturally carries in its bosom the prophecy of his reply. De Wette, therefore, along with Meyer, Tholuck, Mehring, and van Hengel, have done well in retaining, in their translations of the interrogation, the usual and natural force of the particle, as affording a prognostication of a negative reply.

When it is asked, "is he *unrighteous?*" (ἄδικος), the word *unrighteous* drops all reference to the specific phases of *unrighteousness* and *righteousness* which are covertly referred to in the preceding part of the verse. It is employed in its purely generic import:—*Is God acting in a way that is inconsistent with perfect rectitude?*

The appended clausule, *who bringeth on wrath, who inflicteth wrath,* (ὁ ἐπιφέρων τὴν ὀργήν), is rather misconceived by some translators. Mace, for example, translates it, "to inflict punishment,"—"is it not injustice in God *to inflict punishment?*"—Conybeare similarly renders it, "in sending the punishment;"—Wakefield and Belsham, "for inflicting punishment;"—Walford, "if he inflict punishment;"—Turnbull, "when he inflicts punishment;"—Knight, "inflicting wrath;"—old Myles Coverdale, "that he is angrie therefore." (*Many of the German translators give corresponding versions. Thus Luther, "dass er darüber zürnet": —Emser and Dietenberger, "dass er darüber erzörnet":—Piscator, "dass er den Zorn über sie bringt":—Heumann, "dass er über uns zürnet":—Zinzendorf, "dass er strafft": —Michaelis, "wenn er Strafen übt":—van Ess, "wenn er straft":—Stolz, "wenn er Strafe auferlegt": &c.*) In all these translations the force of the article before the participle is not adequately represented; although there is in some of them a nearer approximation than in others to the fulness of the import of the original. The idiom cannot be precisely reproduced in the English language. Our substitution of the *relative* with the *indicative*, for the *article* with the *participle*, brings us as near, as the conventionalisms of our language will admit, to the force of the original,—*who inflicteth wrath.* A matter of fact is asserted. *It is the case that God inflicts wrath for unrighteousness.* The Apostle makes the assertion; for it is, as we have said, from the standpoint of his own subjectivity that he gives utterance to the objection of his unbelieving countrymen. (Bengel's translation, so far as the power of the article is concerned, is right, *der den zorn auf* uns *wirft.* So was Felbinger's before him, *der den zorn über* uns *bringet.*)

Matthias supposes that in this expression, *who inflicteth wrath*, there is a retrospective reference to what is said in ch. i. 18,—"*The wrath of God is revealed from heaven against all ungodliness and unrighteousness of men,* who hold the truth in unrighteousness." It may be so: though we discern no evidence of the retrospection. In that asseveration the Apostle had special reference to God's relation to Gentiles: whereas in this he has reference to his relation to Jews. And the attribution to God of the characteristic which is embodied in the clause before us, was so much in harmony with common conviction and consent, that there seems to be no occasion for supposing a specific retrogression in thought to what was expressed in that initial part of the epistle. There is not the same objection to the idea of Baumgarten-Crusius and others, that there is a reference to what is said in chap. ii. 5-9; in which passage there is distinct mention made of that wrath of God which is impending over impenitent Jews. But whether there was actual conscious reflection, on the part of the Apostle, upon what is there said, it seems impossible to determine. The article which stands in the original before the word *wrath* (τὴν ὀργήν) has no bearing on the question. It cannot, however, be fitly reproduced in English. The idiom of our language, so far from demanding it, rather rejects it. We cannot, with propriety, say, in such a connection as is before us, "who inflicteth *the* wrath." And yet the Greek expression is eminently significant. Fritzsche represents the idea thus,—"who inflicteth *the wrath of which every one is aware,—the wrath to come,*" (*iram nemini ignotam, h. e., poenas quas futuras esse scimus: Mat.* iii. 7.). This is, no doubt, substantially the correct idea. It might, under a slight variation of aspect, be represented thus, "who inflicteth *the wrath which is generally recognized as the desert of unrighteousness.*" The Five Clergymen, and Worsley before them, as also Matthias and others, translate the clause, "who inflicteth *his* wrath." The Peshito, indeed, had given the same version (ܪܘܓܙܗ,) though it is possible that the translator had found in his copy of the original, as in א, the superaddition of the pronoun (τὴν ὀργὴν αὐτοῦ). The translation of the Greek article by the possessive pronoun, is not, in our opinion, a felicity in this instance. For while the article may be often regarded as, in various respects, tantamount to a weak possessive pronoun, (*steht er oft als schwächeres Possessiv,*–Krüger, *Gr. Sprachlehre,* 50. 2. 2), yet here it has a far more decided emphasis,—although that emphasis is incapable of reproduction in our English idiom.

In place of the word *wrath,* many critics have substituted the term *punishment,* as a translation of the Greek expression. Beza, for example; who not only makes the substitution in his version, but also criticises the Vulgate and Erasmus for abiding by the word *wrath,*—which, says he, seems more obscure (*quod videtur obscurius*). It is nevertheless the only correct rendering. The other is interpretational. It intrudes the function of exegesis into the function of translation. And it robs us, moreover, of that exceedingly important representation of things, so harmonious with the great realities of the Divine Nature, which exhibits a certain emotional aversion of the Infinite Mind, as comprehending or evolving the fundamental element of the wo with which sin deserves to be visited. The translation of our English Authorized Version, found also in the English Geneva of 1557, and introduced by Tyndale,—"who taketh *vengeance,*" is an unnecessary departure from literality. The subsequent Geneva version follows Beza, and renders the clause, "which punisheth."

It still remains to be mentioned that the expression, *who inflicteth wrath,* is slightly elliptical: although it may be advantageously left to every reader's mind to supply the complement. Luther supplies it thus,—"that he is angry *on account of it*," (*das er darüber zürnet*). So Piscator. Felbinger and Bengel, again, supply the personal objects on whom the wrath is assumed to terminate:—"who inflicteth wrath *upon us*," (ἡμῖν, or ἐφ' ἡμᾶς). If we were to abandon the natural indeterminateness of the original, we should certainly approve of the supplement of Felbinger and Bengel.

§ 5. *I speak after the manner of man*, (κατὰ ἄνθρωπον λέγω). A large proportion of expositors regard these words as an avowal, on the part of the Apostle, that in proposing the question contained in the preceding part of the verse, he was not giving utterance to his own ideas. Taylor paraphrases the expression thus:—"here I represent the reasoning of an unbelieving Jew." Theodoret's explication is tantamount:—"it is not I who say these things; I have but adduced the reasonings of others," (οὐ γὰρ ἐγώ, φησι, ταῦτα λέγω, ἀλλὰ τοὺς τῶν ἄλλων τέθεικα λογισμούς). Wetstein's is similar:—"I speak as men are wont, who, as by an innate vice, endeavour to roll off from themselves all blame, and cast it on another," (*Loquor, ut solent homines, qui, insito quasi vitio, culpam omnem a se amoliri, et in alium conjicere conantur*). Bengel, in his usual condensed manner, represents the same idea thus:—"a man might thus humanly think," (*homo humanitus posset sic cogitare*).

Some suppose, in addition, that the expression is designed to indicate that the Apostle felt shocked in his spirit at the idea to which he gave utterance. Such is the opinion of Day, de Wette, Tholuck, Vaughan, &c. And there is no doubt that the idea would be shocking to his feelings; more especially when it presented itself in the form in which an actual objector would propose it;—"is *not* God unjust?" Still, there is no evidence that the parenthetical clause was inserted for the purpose of giving relief to such a perturbation of feeling. And in the other passages in which the expression occurs there is no indication that it was employed in consequence of realizing a relation of shockingness in the idea expressed. See 1 Cor. ix. 8; Gal. iii. 15; and compare Rom. vi. 19.

Those critics are undoubtedly right, who recognize in the expression a latent antithesis,—an antithesis between such modes of conception and speech as are common among men, and such as would, in a higher plane of things, be intrinsically worthy of the august subjects referred to or described. The Apostle was conscious that, in his thoughts, he was accustomed to rise reverentially toward spiritual heights. Like a spiritual skylark, it was his delight to soar, in spirit, into heaven. He mounted to the neighbourhood of divinity. And there, as at the Fountain-head of truth, he drank in, with eager recipiency, the thoughts of God. He seemed to hear and understand unutterable things. When he descended and mingled with his fellow-men, it was that he might communicate to them the mind of God, "not in the words which man's wisdom teacheth, but which the Holy Ghost teacheth," (1 Cor. ii. 13). There was thus much of the divine in the Apostle's utterances. (He spake κατὰ θεόν.) But still, "because of the weakness of man's flesh" (Rom. vi. 19), he had to blend, with what was divine, not a little of what was human. The two elements, indeed, were absolutely requisite. In his own receptivity, and in the receptivity of those to whom he spake, and in the imperfect plasticity of the human language which he wielded, at once in thinking and in speaking, the human was inevitable. And thus the divine was laid, as it were, under a disadvantage. It could not be revealed in its own absolute splendour and glory. And at certain stages of the impenetration of the human by the divine, the Apostle felt, more keenly than at others, the inadequacy of the susceptibility of the human. Hence he had to condescend to illustrations, and other modes of phraseology, which were the best, indeed, in the circumstances, but which he could not but intensely feel to be intrinsically imperfect and inadequate. (*Comp.* Gal. iii. 15; and Rom. vi. 19. *See also* 1 Cor. ix. 8. *Such passages as* 1 Cor iii. 3; xv. 32, *belong to another circle of things, as not being connected with modes of speech.*) It is in the consciousness of such a feeling that he says here,—*I speak after the manner of man*, (*more humano loquor*), that is, "When I ask the question, *Is God unjust who inflicteth* "*wrath?* I am deeply conscious that I am using language "which is intrinsically improper when applied to God. "But, in condescension to human weakness, I transfer to "Him language which it is customary for men to employ "when referring to human relationships." Le Cene, though by no means reaching the fulness of the idea, was yet on the line of the right notion when he translated the expression, "I speak popularly" (*Je parle populairement*). Hilarion was more felicitous, (ἀνθρωπίνως λαλῶ). It is, of course, as Fritzsche perceived, the application of the term *unjust* to God which led the Apostle to speak apologizingly. His idea might be otherwise exhibited, though with a defalcation of energy:—"Is God, who inflicteth wrath, unjust (*so to speak*)?"—"unjust, (*if I might venture to employ such a term*)?"—"unjust, (*pardon the inappropriate word as applied to God, for really, after all, I cannot, in human speech, find a more suitable term*)?"

It is said in Origen's Commentaries, as translated by Rufinus, that in some copies of the text there was a variation of reading, affecting this clause:—"is God unjust, who inflicteth wrath *upon men?*" (κατὰ ἀνθρώπων,—instead of κατὰ ἄνθρωπον,—with the omission of λέγω). But as there is no remnant of the variation in existing manuscripts or versions, we may conclude that it rested on no solid foundation.

Paulus reads the expression interrogatively, (*Sage etwa auch Ich, was in diesem Sinn manche Menschen hierüber sagen?*) But the interrogation destroys the parenthetical relation of the remark, and would consequently interpose a barrier between the direct relation of the rejoinder in ver. 6, to the query in the preceding part of ver. 5.

There are many other vagaries of interpretation proposed by critics, more distinguished for ingenuity than judgement, on which it would be in vain to waste time in the way of formal refutation. Such is, for example, Jones's notion, who supposes that there is a reference in the preceding context to the authors of the Sibylline Oracles, and to the measures adopted against them by the Emperor Tiberius; and who interprets the parenthetical clause thus: —"I speak in respect to (the punishment inflicted by) a man, namely Tiberius."

An idea has been entertained by some that the expression has a prospective, instead of a retrospective, reference: —that it looks to what is to be said in ver. 6, rather than to what has been said in the preceding part of ver. 5. We shall consider this opinion in our remarks on ver. 6. But it may be noticed, meanwhile, that a considerable number of critics—inclusive, for instance, of Belsham and Mac-Evilly,—although not entertaining this opinion concerning the internal relation of the expression, have yet externally transferred it to the commencement of ver. 6. Such a transference, however, is an unhappy interference with Robert Stephens's versiculation.

VER. 6. Μὴ γένοιτο· ἐπεὶ πῶς κρινεῖ ὁ Θεὸς τὸν κόσμον;

Engl. Auth. Vers. *God forbid: for then how shall God judge the world?*

Revised Version. *Far be it. Since how shall God judge the world?*

§ 1. Theophylact supposes that it is the contents of this verse in reference to which the Apostle says, at the close of the preceding, *I speak after the manner of man.* That statement, he says, "has this sense:—*I make reply in behalf of God, in such a way as it is competent for man to plead; for God has doubtless secret reasons for his actions, transcending human reasonings, and not needing human apologies*," (τὸ δὲ, κατὰ ἄνθρωπον λέγω, τοιοῦτον ἔχει νοῦν· ἐγὼ μὲν, φησι, τοιαῦτα ἀπολογοῦμαι ὑπὲρ τοῦ Θεοῦ, κατὰ ἀνθρώπινον λογισμὸν, τουτέστιν, ὡς ἔνι δυνατὸν ἀνθρώπῳ λογίζεσθαι δικαιολόγῳ. Ἐπεὶ ὅσα ποιεῖ ὁ Θεὸς, ἔχει τινὰς ἀποῤῥήτους λόγους, καὶ ὑπὲρ τοὺς ἀνθρωπίνους λογισμούς ἐστί, μὴ δεόμενα τῆς παρ' ἡμῶν ἀπολογίας). But we do not see that the argumentation of the 6th verse requires any special apology. Rückert, indeed, affirms that it is "weak, very weak," (*das diese Argumentation schwach, sehr schwach sey, ist zuzugestehn*); but Rückert was fond, even to the length of "very weakness," of finding flaws and failings in the Apostle; and he misunderstands, moreover, in the case before us, the point of the inspired man's argumentation. This we shall see in course. It is another objection to Theophylact's interpretation, that the expression, *I speak after the manner of man*, stands before the exclamation, *Far be it!* as well as before the argument, "*since how shall God judge the world?*" And assuredly there was no special necessity for the Apostle apologizing for his own earnest repudiation of a reflection upon the moral character of the Infinite One, our Father. In short, if Theophylact's idea had been correct, we should certainly have expected the clause to have been introduced at the close of the 6th, rather than at the close of the 5th verse.

Theodor Schott takes substantially the same view with Theophylact. He thinks that the statement, *I speak after the manner of man*, is prefixed by the Apostle to the contents of the sixth verse, to indicate that the objection referred to in the preceding verse can be sufficiently met and obviated,—without any appeal to Holy Scripture or history,—by an argument which the human understanding is perfectly competent to draw immediately from the nature of the case. (*Jenem Schluss des natürlichen menschlichen Verstandes tritt er eben auch mit einem Schluss entgegen, der nicht aus heiliger Schrift oder Geschichte entnommen, sondern aus der unmittelbar einleuchtenden Natur der Sache, so wie Menschen eben schliessen, gezogen ist.*) But the position of the statement,—as a kind of *avant-coureur* remark,—is unaccountable on this hypothesis,—coming, more especially, as it does, even before the introductory exclamation. And then, besides, it is really not the case that the argument is remarkable, either in its essence or in its accidents, for any particular infusion of a human element of things, as distinguished from what is biblical or divine.

Mehring, too, contends for the prospective reference of the clause. But he differs from Theophylact and T. Schott in his view of the aim of the Apostle. He imagines that the import of verses 5th and 6th is the following:—"But "if our unrighteousness sets out the righteousness of God, "what shall we say? Is God unjust who inflicteth wrath? "that is, Is God, who inflicteth wrath, *so unjust as to* "*condemn me, whose unrighteousness sets off to advantage* "*his righteousness?*—That,—(I speak not my own senti-"ments),—be far from God! for how then will he judge the "world?" (*Gott ist doch nicht ungerecht, welcher das Straf-gericht verhängt, dass er auch mich richten wird? d. h. würde es wohl mit seiner Gerechtigkeit übereinstimmen, wenn er in diesem Falle auch* **mich** *verurtheilte?*) He thinks, in other words, that the contents of verse 6, instead of being the Apostle's refutation of a blasphemous objection to his reasoning, such as is generally supposed to be referred to in verse 5, is an objector's vindication of the idea, that *God will not punish his unrighteousness, if it sets off to advantage the divine righteousness.* The interpretation, though an ingenious expedient for relieving the succeeding verse of the difficulties which are supposed to beset it, is an evident reversal of the Apostle's idea. For when the Apostle asks, *Is God unjust who inflicteth wrath?* the internal nature, as well as the external relations of the query, make it manifest that the idea, at bottom, is this,—*It is not unjust in God to inflict wrath upon those whose unrighteousness illustrates by contrast, and thus magnifies, his own righteousness.*

There is no good reason, then, for coming to the conclusion that the closing clause of the preceding verse has any other reference than what is retrospective.

§ 2. *Far be it!* (Μὴ γένοιτο), that is, *Far from us be the thought that the wrath-inflicting God would be unjust in inflicting wrath upon the unbelieving Jews, although, by their unrighteousness, they give occasion for the display of his own righteousness.* (*Procul avertat Deus hanc cogitationem a piis animis.*–Erasmus.) See on the phrase, *Far be it,* ver. 4. Count Zinzendorf translates it here, "O no," (*O nein*). Bugenhagen's explanation is,—"It is a blasphemy." It is of moment to notice that it is not simply and abstractly the idea which forms the conclusion of the objector's implied syllogism,—the idea, *that God is unjust,*—which the Apostle repels with detestation. It is this conclusion in its relation to the conceded hypothetical premiss, *if God punish the unrighteous who display his righteousness.* And hence it was natural in the Greek expositors to show that the unrighteous are not the true and proper *Causes* of God's glory or righteousness or justification or victory. If they were, it would be difficult to vindicate the justice of God in punishing them. But they merely afford *incidental occasion* for the display of the intrinsically glorious attributes of the divine nature. (Οὐκέτι αἴτιος αὐτῷ τῆς νίκης γέγονας,–Chrysostom.—Οὐκ εἰσὶν οἱ ἁμαρτάνοντες, οὔτε νίκης, οὔτε τῆς ἀληθείας, οὔτε τῆς δικαιοσύνης, αἴτιοι,–Photius *in* Œcum.—Δῆλον ὅτι οὐχ' ἡμεῖς αὐτῷ τῆς ἀληθείας καὶ τῆς δικαιοσύνης αἴτιοι, ἀλλ' αὐτὸς ἑαυτῷ,–Ditto.—Τὴν πρόφασιν τῆς νίκης παρέσχομεν.–Œcum.)

§ 3. *Since how shall God judge the world?* (ἐπεὶ πῶς κρινεῖ ὁ θεὸς τὸν κόσμον;) The conjunction (ἐπεί), which we have simply rendered *since,* means, when exegetically considered, *since, if that be the case,*—*since, if so;* that is, *since, if it be the case that it is unrighteous in God to inflict wrath upon those whose unrighteousness sets off his righteousness.* The supplementary idea is not inherent in the word, but is derived from the logical relation of the clauses. It is expressed, however, in our authorized English version, "for *then,*"—a translation which came down from Tyndale. Wycliffe renders the term similarly, "ellis" (else); and the Vulgate, "otherwise" (*alioquin*). So Luther and Bengel (*sonst*). In our *Authorized Version* the term is rendered "otherwise" in Rom. xi. 6, 22; Heb. ix. 17; and "else" in 1 Cor. vii. 14; xv. 29. It is, however, as a general rule, inexpedient to render a translation more explicit or determinate than the original.

By the expression *the world* (τὸν κόσμον) some critics understand *the heathen-world, the Gentiles.* This is the opinion of Cocceius, who seems to have been the father of the notion. Wittich, de Brais, Venema, accepted the idea. Vitringa gave in his cordial adhesion, (*Ik ben van de waarheit deser verklaringe ten eenemaal overtuigt*). Reiche strenuously contended for the interpretation; as did Koppe before him, who says, indeed, that it must be accepted, if we would not utterly destroy the whole force of the apostle's argument, (*nisi efficere velis vertendo et interpretando, ut omnis argumenti vis prorsus pereat*). Olshausen, too, contends for it. And it has, besides, been approved of by Ernesti, Cramer, Stolz, Drysén (*det öfriga menniskoslägtet*), Böckel, Schrader, &c. Limborch also would be willing to accept it. But it is questionable whether the term *world* is ever used as sharply and precisely equivalent to *the Gentile-world.* Olshausen says that "the context imperatively requires this signification in Rom. xi. 12 and 1 Cor. i. 21." But even in these passages the word rather denotes, indefinitely, *the world of mankind in general,* which no doubt consists, in the main, of Gentile peoples. And, whatever may be the possible limitations of the term in certain relationships, there is, assuredly, no logical or exegetical necessity for assuming these limitations in the case before us. The Apostle has represented in the preceding chapter the universal reference of the final judgement. And it was not disputed by the Jews that all men would ultimately stand before the judgement-seat of God, to have their everlasting award judicially determined. The Apostle, therefore, assumes that the certainty of the general judgement was admitted. He regards the admission as common ground, on which he and his theological antagonists could meet, and from which, therefore, it was legitimate, as *ex concesso,* to derive the material of an argument.

His argument is sufficiently obvious, though it has been strangely missed by many both of the ancient and of the modern expositors. It has been supposed, for example, by Origen, Theophylact, Aquinas, de Lyra, Cajetan, Paciuchelli, Hemming, as well as by Day, Este, Doddridge, Heumann, Klee, Köllner, and even Meyer, Rückert, Jowett, and Colenso, that the Apostle simply means that God could not be the judge of the world if he were an unjust being; for a judge should be just, and an infinitely perfect judge will be just. It was because Rückert imagined that this was the Apostle's idea, that he pronounced the argumentation to be "weak, very weak." And a man who had none of Rückert's deficiency of reverence for the Apostle, Sclater, said of the confutation,—"the manner of answer *may in logic seem absurd;* but it is, in Christianity, the best that can be shaped to deniers of principles." He had evidently thought the reasoning, when logically viewed, to be "weak." Glöckler, too, says that the apostle's question, *as thus understood*, "may be good enough for children, who cannot reason, but certainly not for such kind of people as those to whom the epistle was addressed," (*diese Frage passt einerseits nur für Kinder, welche die Begriffe noch nicht recht zusammenfügen können, nicht aber für solche Leute, an welche dieser Brief geschrieben ist*). Even Calvin is perplexed, and admits that the Apostle "does not wholly clear away the calumny, but only replies to this effect, that the objection is absurd," (*neque enim penitus calumniam diluit, sed tantum respondet, absurdum illud esse, quod objicitur*). And, as it were to supplement the Apostle's omission, he says, (in the language of old Rosdell's translation,)—"If thou doest desire a directe refutation, whereby such blasphemous speeches may be quenched, understande it thus, That this cometh not to passe throughe the nature of unrighteousnesse, that the righteousnesse of God should appeare the more thereby: but our wickednesse is so overcome of the goodnesse of God that it is rather converted into another ende, then it doth tende unto," (*quodsi directam refutationem cupis, qua ejusmodi sacrilegia compescantur, sic accipe: Non hoc fieri injustitiæ natura, ut Dei justitia magis eluceat, sed Dei bonitate superari nostram malitiam, ut in diversum potius, quam tendat, finem convertatur*). But this supplement to the apostle's argument is altogether unnecessary; and all low or painful ideas of the irrelevancy of the reasoning take flight as soon as the real nature of the argumentation is apprehended. It is admirably exhibited by Haldane:—"If the objections were well founded, "it would entirely divest God of the character of judge of "the world. The reason of this is manifest, for there is no "sin that any man can commit, which does not exalt some "perfection of God, in the way of contrast. If, then, it be "concluded that because unrighteousness in man illustrates "the righteousness of God, God is unrighteous when he "taketh vengeance, it must be farther said, that there is no "sin that God can justly punish: whence it follows that "God cannot any longer be the judge of the world. The "objection, then, is such that, were it admitted, all the "religion in the world would at once be annihilated. For "the sin of the world, for which men will be everlastingly "punished, will no doubt be made to manifest God's glory. "Such is the force of the apostle's reply." Bengel gives the idea in one short remark, appended to his German translation:—"*the world;*—which is full of unrighteousness, and thus sets off the righteousness of God." The Apostle appeals to a general principle which was acknowledged by those who, in their own particular case, pleaded for exemption. He, as it were, reminds them, that, just as it is true that they were part and parcel of "the world,"—which they admitted was to be judged according to real character and not according to incidental and undesigned consequences of conduct,—so it is true that they could have no just reason to expect that they would be exempted from punishment, if their character were bad, although by the side of it the character of God should appear to be surpassingly glorious. It is of course assumed, when it is said, "*how shall God judge the world?*" that, taking the actual moral condition of the world into account, the judicial sentence passed, on the great day of assize, must, in very many cases, be condemnatory.

Glöckler,—to avoid apostolic childishness of argumentation,—supposes that the emphasis of the question rests on the word *how* (πῶς):—"for *how* (i.e., *in what manner, quasi* τίνι τρόπῳ) will God judge the world?" And he imagines, therefore, though he does not formally admit, a consequent aposiopesis in the discourse. The Apostle's argument, as he understands it, might be represented thus:—"*For* **in what manner** *will God judge the world? Manifestly* **in this manner;** *—Every man's destiny shall be awarded to him, not according to the incidental and undesigned consequences of his actions, but according to their essential and intrinsic moral quality.*" The substantive result of this explanation is coincident with the interpretation already given. But it is an objection to the explanation itself, that it throws into aposiopesis the whole force of the argument. It divests, moreover, the particle *how* of its dialectical force,—a force which leads us to expect that the word introduces a logical difficulty, which is presumed to be insurmountable on the hypothesis implied in the preceding interrogation. And then, thirdly, it assumes that the conjunction *since* is used by the Apostle as simply equivalent to the usual ratiocinative particle *for* (γάρ),—a usage of the word which would be entirely unprecedented in the Apostle's writings. Compare Rom. xi. 6, 22; 1 Cor. v. 10; vii. 14; xiv. 12, 16; xv. 29; 2 Cor. xi. 18; xiii. 3;—these are all the passages in which the conjunction occurs.

Some critics assign to the future verb, "since how *shall he judge?*" (κρινεῖ),—its idiomatic import of *moral possibility:* —"since how *could he judge?*" Of this opinion are Heumann, Oertel, de Wette, Oltramare, Matthias, &c. Calvin had evidently taken the same view; and hence he does not restrict the "judgement" spoken of, to the general judgement to come. Luther, too, translates the clause thus:—"Otherwise how *could* God judge the world?" (*Wie könnte sonst Gott die Welt richten?*) It is not a matter of much moment whether we adopt such an idea of the import of the verb, or retain its simple reference to futurity. The notions of futurity and possibility naturally interlace, in such a case as this. But as the reference is doubtless to a strictly future event,—the final judgement,—we agree with Meyer in thinking that there is no reason why we should depart from the common import of the tense, so far at least as translation is concerned.

VER. 7. Εἰ γὰρ ἡ ἀλήθεια τοῦ Θεοῦ ἐν τῷ ἐμῷ ψεύσματι ἐπερίσσευσεν εἰς τὴν δόξαν αὐτοῦ, τί ἔτι κἀγὼ ὡς ἁμαρτωλὸς κρίνομαι;

Eng. Auth. Vers. *For if the truth of God hath more abounded through my lie unto his glory: why yet am I also judged as a sinner?*

Revised Version. *For if the trueness of God superabounded through my lie to his glory, why notwithstanding am even I judged as a sinner?*

§ 1. The relation of this verse to the preceding context has been the subject of considerable dispute; and Conybeare represents the whole passage as "most difficult." Grotius says that the 6th verse, along with the last clause of the 5th, *I speak after the manner of man*, should be regarded as parenthetical; and he thus maintains that the query of the 7th verse follows up continuatively the query of the 5th. Calvin was of the same opinion. He says, "I do not doubt that the Apostle, in advancing this objec-" tion also, is personating the ungodly. For it is, as it" were, the explanation of the preceding one; and it would" have been joined to it, had not the Apostle, moved by the" dishonour (done to God), broken off in the middle of what" he was saying," (*Non dubito, quin haec quoque objectio in persona impiorum proferatur. Est enim velut exegesis superioris; et connectenda fuerat, nisi Apostolus, indignitate permotus,* (incorrectly translated by Owen, *moved with indignation;* and correspondingly by Krummacher and Bender *aus Unwillen*), *medium sermonem abrupisset*). Theophylact took the same view, (καὶ πάλιν τὸ αὐτὸ ἐπαναλαμβάνει, διὰ τὸ σαφέστερον αὐτὸ ποιῆσαι). So too did Willet, Day, Turretin, Locke; Bengel also, and Wolf, and Taylor, and many others of the older expositors; as also, of more modern critics, Bahrdt, Rückert, Köllner, Tholuck, Philippi, Vaughan, Jowett, &c. Bahrdt, in his Translation, actually transposes verses 6, 7, putting verse 7 before verse 6. Ver. 7, says Vaughan, is a "repetition, in the form of a more direct objection, of the difficulty raised in ver. 5, and already partially answered." Moses Stuart is of the same opinion, and rather arbitrarily translates the ratiocinative particle (γάρ) at the commencement of the verse, *still*:—"still, if the truth of God hath abounded more unto his glory on account of my false dealing." It is an insuperable objection to this theory of the connection, that verse 6 has really nothing in it of a parenthetical nature. And exegesis must be reduced to extremity before it can allow that the particle *for*, at the beginning of verse 7, overleaps, in its reference, the whole of that immediately preceding verse. We may conclude, then, that the verse contains what is intended either to establish or to illustrate the argument of verse 6. Zuingli, with fine exegetical tact, remarks, that it is subjoined to verse 6 as a sort of additional or appended apodosis,—a *prosapodosis*. (*Subjiciuntur quasi prosapodosis haec illius quod supra dixit, Quare Deus possit judicare mundum; et hoc cognoscitur ex conjunctione rationali, etenim*, εἰ γάρ, *nam si.*)

§ 2. *For if the trueness of God superabounded by my lie to his glory,* (Εἰ γὰρ ἡ ἀλήθεια τοῦ θεοῦ ἐν τῷ ἐμῷ ψεύσματι ἐπερίσσευσεν εἰς τὴν δόξαν αὐτοῦ), *why nevertheless am even I judged as a sinner?* (τί ἔτι κἀγὼ ὡς ἁμαρτωλὸς κρίνομαι;) The following remarks may suffice for exposition:—

1. The connection of the contents of the verse with what goes before, as indicated by the ratiocinative particle *for* (γάρ), may be represented thus;—"I have asked, *how shall* "*God judge the world?* The question is emphatically to "the point, on the hypothesis that it would be unjust in "him to punish our unrighteousness, if it sets off his "righteousness:—*for if the trueness of God superabounded*, "&c." The statement, however, thus introduced, is only *analytically demonstrative.* It is explanatory. (The γάρ is thus γάρ *illustrantis et confirmantis.*)

2. The Alexandrian MS. reads "*but* if" (εἰ δέ), instead of "*for* if" (εἰ γάρ). So does the Sinaitic MS.,—though Scrivener, in his collation, has overlooked the fact. The

author or authors of the reading had apparently, like Calvin, Grotius, Philippi, and others, failed to discern the connection of the contents of the verse with ver. 6th; and, supposing that the Apostle was returning to the strain of ver. 5th, had concluded that the text was corrupt, and conjecturally sought to bring it into harmony with the assumed theory of connection.

3. The expression, *ἡ ἀλήθεια τοῦ θεοῦ*, is to be understood, not objectively, but subjectively. It denotes *the trueness of God*,—that element of his moral character in virtue of which he is *true* to all the promises of his grace, as well as to all the other claims of his infinite reason and infinite conscience. The phrase is used by the Apostle with an evident reference to what is said in ver. 4th, "Let God turn out *true* (ἀληθής), though every man should prove a liar:" and thus the attributive runs parallel with the word *faithfulness* (πίστις) in ver. 3rd, and with the word *righteousness* (δικαιοσύνη) in ver. 5th. It is better, therefore, that it be translated *trueness*, or *truthfulness*, than rendered *truth*. And while, at this stage of the Apostle's reasoning, and more especially after his use of the generic term *righteousness* in ver. 5th, the word is not, perhaps, to be rigidly and absolutely restricted to God's truthfulness in regard to his gracious utterances in the lively Oracles; still, there cannot be a doubt that it is with a principal reference to his *trueness* in relation to the indications, promises, and protestations of his grace that the term is employed. This is evident from the obvious scope of the whole paragraph, verses 1—8, and the designed return of thought to what is stated in ver. 4th.

4. When it is said, "for if the trueness of God *superabounded*" (ἐπερίσσευσεν), the verb is in the aorist, because the Apostle is thinking proleptically of *what is past* relatively to the *judging*, of which he speaks in the apodosis of the sentence. He had already referred to the final judgement of the world. His present statement is an analytical confirmation of the argument involved in that reference. And thus, in imagination, he goes forward to that day of grand assize; and thence looking backward,

he says, "for if the trueness of God *superabounded* (viz., during the period of my terrestrial probation) to his glory, through my lie, &c." When the Apostle ascribes to the occasion of his lie, a *superabounding* of the trueness of God, he does not refer, of course, to any intrinsic increase of the subjective moral excellence of God. The notion of such an increase would be utterly inconsistent with the inspired man's conceptions of the infinite perfection and independence of God. The overplus referred to is entirely relative to the apprehensions of men and other intelligent creatures. It is *logical*, not *real: objective* relatively to God,—not *subjective:* but *subjective* relatively to men and angels. The representation is thus identical with what is contained in the expression, in ver. 4th, "let God *become* true." Tyndale's translation, therefore, though not literal, is exegetically correct:—"Yf the veritie of God *appere moare excellent* thorow my lye." De Saci's is correspondent,—"si par mon infidelité la fidelité de Dieu *a éclaté davantage.*"

5. The expression, *to his glory* (εἰς τὴν δόξαν αὐτοῦ), evidently means, *to the furtherance of his glory.* And the *glory* referred to must be his *relative glory*, or rather, *his intrinsic glory relatively viewed*,—his intrinsic glory, as relatively apprehensible and realizable by men and other intelligent creatures. Luther, Tyndale, Piscator, Morus, and others, render the word *praise.* But this is to change the standpoint of view; and to confound, moreover, the function of exegete with that of translator.

6. The words, *through my lie* (ἐν τῷ ἐμῷ ψεύσματι), literally mean, *in* (*the sphere of*) *my lie.* The term for *lie* used by the Apostle is very rarely found in Greek writers, and is condemned by Thomas Magister, (ψεῦδος λέγε, οὐ ψεῦσμα). It occurs nowhere else in the New Testament. It is not found in the Septuagint. It is used, however, by Symmachus, Aquila, and Theodotion, (see Montfaucon's *Lexicon Græc.*), and it is found not only in Aristides, as indicated by Thomas Magister, but also occasionally in Lucian, and elsewhere. It has descended into current use in modern Greek. The *lie* referred to is something

in antithesis of the *trueness* ascribed to God. And, as it reflects back through verse 4th on verse 3rd, it doubtless denotes that particular phase of *untrueness or unfaithfulness to the claims of conscience and of God* which realizes itself in relation to the dispensation of grace, and the proffer of salvation through Christ the Saviour. Such *untrueness* is *unbelief* (ἀπιστία). He who believes not in God's grace, God's propitious mercy, God's gospel, not only treats God as if he were false,—"making him a liar" (ψεύστην), 1 John v. 10,—he is also himself a "liar." He is not only in contradiction with God, with whom alone the truth lies; he is inexcusably and wilfully in contradiction. He chooses to disobey the divine dictates, which come to him either directly through his conscience, or at least abreast with it. Instead of responsively saying *Yea* to God, as God reveals Himself in propitiousness, he says *Nay*. And his *Nay* is a *lie*.

7. The expression, "*if* the trueness of God superabounded to his glory by my lie," contains an obvious assumption or concession; which, however, is pronounced by Moses Stuart to be false. He says,—"The nice observer of idiom will note that the *conditional* sentence here, beginning with εἰ, has an aor. indic. (ἐπερίσσευσε) in it, and therefore indicates that the speaker here states a case which he did not believe could take place." (Com. *in loc.*) And this, Mr Stuart's observation, has been quoted with approbation by Knight as if it contained an important truth, and were an evidence of nice observation of Greek idioms. It involves, however, a total inversion of the apostle's idea; for, as in v. 5, he makes what is *tantamount to a concession* in what he conditionally utters. (*Dass* εἰ *ist hier particula concessionis*,-Rambach). And whosoever considers the mutually illustrative character of contraries, must concede that God's trueness is increasingly realized when put in contrast with man's falseness. That the use of εἰ, moreover, with an *aorist indicative*, does not, of itself, in any way, or to any degree, denote or suggest improbability of occurrence, is evident from innumerable instances. See, for example, in New Testament usage, John xiii. 32, "*if God was glorified in him*, (εἰ ὁ θεὸς ἐδοξάσθη

ἐν αὐτῷ), God shall also glorify him in himself":—Rom. xv. 27, "*if the Gentiles were made partakers of their spiritual things,* (εἰ τοῖς πνευματικοῖς αὐτῶν ἐκοινώνησαν τὰ ἔθνη), their duty is also to minister unto them in carnal things":—1 John iv. 11, "*if God so loved us,* (εἰ οὕτως ὁ θεὸς ἠγάπησεν ἡμᾶς), we ought also to love one another." M. Stuart had quite misapprehended at once the philosophy and the philology of conditional sentences. So far as the mere conditional particle, in its relation to the indicative of the aorist, is concerned, there is no indication whatever of the inherent probability or improbability of the fact assumed. (Εἰ *legitur, secundo,* says C. Ab. Wahl, *ea ratione, qua sumimus fieri aliquid, sed utrum possit fieri vel futurum sit, nec ne, nihil curantes. Construitur in talibus cum indicativo omnium temporum.*–Comment. *de particulae* εἰ *apud N. T. scriptores usu et potestate. p.* 12. See also *p.* 16.)

8. It has been asked whose person it is which the Apostle assumes when he says, "for if the trueness of God superabounded through *my* lie to his glory." The critics who regard verse 6th as actually or substantially parenthetical, and who thus suppose either a continuation of the strain of verse 5th, or a return to it, think, in general, that the Apostle speaks in the person of an unbelieving Jew. Those, again, who suppose that by the word *world,* at the close of verse 6th, is meant *the heathen-world,* generally think that he speaks in the person of a heathen. "The heathen," says Reiche, "is introduced as speaking," (*Der Heide wird redend eingeführt*). The same was the opinion of Rosenmüller ultimately, (*Paulus in persona pagani hominis loquitur*). Koppe, Whitby, Flatt, Thomson, Olshausen, &c., coincide. And in general they interpret the word *lie,* as meaning *idolatry* or *idol ;* and *trueness* as meaning *the true attributes of God* (Vitringa), or *the true majesty of God* (Koppe), or *the true religion* (Reiche). But as we found that the *world* referred to is not simply *the heathens* or *Gentiles,* this interpretation of the Apostle's impersonation is without foundation. There is, however, an element in it which is right. There *is* a reference to the word "world." And the apostle is evidently speaking just as *an individual representative*

of the world at large. We do not think, indeed, with van Hengel — though with him both Wittich and Vitringa would agree—that the sentence might have run thus :—" for if the trueness of God superabounded through *the world's* lie to his glory, why yet is *the world* judged as sinful ?" for the Apostle's argument does not require him to assume that the whole world is false, or unbelieving. It only requires him to hold that some (or many) in it are of this character. When he makes reference to the final judgement, it is to the judgement as it shall actually be, when there shall take place a separation between the actually justified (the believing) and the actually condemned (the impenitent). The Apostle, then, when he says, " in the sphere of *my* lie," personates for the moment any given individual of the world who may be found, on the final day, on the left hand of the Judge. He (thus *μετασχηματίζει*, 1 Cor. iv. 6, and) as it were says ;— " I may well ask the question, — **How shall God, on the " principles referred to, judge the world ?** For, to descend " to particulars, let me represent the case of an indi- " vidual belonging to the vast class of the unbelieving and " ungodly. Any such individual might say, *if the trueness " of God superabounded to his glory through my lie, why " still am even I judged as a sinner ?*"

9. In the expression, *why still ?* (*τί ἔτι*), or *why yet ?* or *why nevertheless ?* or *why notwithstanding ?* the adverb points to the fact of the superabounding of the trueness of God, to His glory, through the lie of the person condemned. For " the holiness of the divinity," as Chalmers expresses it, " has blazed forth, as it were, into brighter conspicuousness on the dark ground of human guilt and human turpitude." Sharpe ignores altogether the interrogative element in the expression, and renders the entire clausule thus,—*why, I am yet judged as a sinner.* But this is really, though in things small, to ignore the part of Hamlet in Hamlet's play. It is to ignore, moreover, the force of the Greek *τί*.

10. In the expression, *am even I judged as a sinner ?* the phrase *even I* (*κἀγώ*) is rendered by many *I too,* and interpreted, according to the theory taken of the whole verse, either *I as well as the Gentile,* or *I as well as the Jew.* But

since the Apostle is dramatically personating neither the Jew as the Jew, nor even the Gentile as the Gentile, but an individual, taken as it were at random from the mass of the world, the καί, in conjunction with ἐγώ, simply intensifies the idea which lies on the line of the adverb *still* (ἔτι), and gathers up into the pronoun the full peculiarity that attaches to the Being who personally occasions the superabounding of the divine truthfulness and glory. The phrase is rendered *even I*, by both Meyer and Tholuck, as also by Baumgarten-Crusius. The rendering seems to be the best of which the phrase is susceptible; although it is, perhaps, a trifle too strong. No account is taken at all of the καί, by Beza, Heumann, the Five Clergymen, &c. "Abundat," says Beza; and he actually finds fault with the Vulgate and Erasmus for translating the phrase "et ego."

11. "Why notwithstanding *am even I judged as a sinner?*" The verb is in the present, (κρίνομαι), because the Apostle has, in a sort of dramatic way, sisted himself anticipatively before the great white throne, and heard, in his assumed character of one of the mass of unbelievers, his sentence of condemnation pronounced. The verb has its natural and simple meaning, *am I judged?* but the nature of the case, as indicated by the connected phrase *as a sinner*, and more remotely by the expression "in the element of *my lie*," demonstrates that the judgement referred to is condemnatory: *why am I condemned in judgement?* When Fritzsche supposes that the condemnation referred to emanates from men (*cur adhuc ab hominibus culper?*); and Sclater, that it emanates from both "God and man," they entirely overlook the relation of the argument to the "judgement" spoken of in verse 6th. The word *sinner* (ἁμαρτωλός) is used, as the nature of the case indicates, and as is remarked by Zachariä, as well as by others, in its intensified acceptation, as the antithesis of *saint* or *believer*. (Comp. chap. ii., 12.)

12. In order to understand the force of the Apostle's argument, it is necessary to carry out of verses 5th and 6th the hypothetical assumption of the abhorred idea expressed in the interrogation, "is God unjust who inflicteth wrath?"

The reasoning of the 7th verse might, then, be represented thus:—" My question—*How shall God judge the world?*— " cannot be answered on such principles. For,—to assume for " the moment the person of one of the unbelieving mass of " the world,—I am warranted in asking another question; " and I may make bold to ask it, in the confidence that it " cannot be answered. It is this,—If the trueness of God " hath superabounded to His glory through my lie, why not- " withstanding am even I,—*if it be unjust in God to punish* " *those who are the occasion of setting off his righteousness* " *and glory*,—why, I say, am even I judged as a sinner?" The argument, though apagogical, is unanswerable, resting, as it does, on the common ground which was occupied at once by the Apostle himself and by the unbelieving Jew, whose objection he was combating. They both admitted, and indeed contended, that *God will judge the world.* And with the help of that one admission, the Apostle has successfully, as Oltramare expresses it, " put the Jew in contradiction with himself," (*Il met ainsi le Juif en contradiction avec lui-même*). He has thus most effectually gained his point, and triumphed in his argument. But he proceeds to rivet his reasoning in the verse that follows.

VER. 8. Καὶ μὴ—καθὼς βλασφημούμεθα καὶ καθώς φασίν τινες ἡμᾶς λέγειν ὅτι—ποιήσωμεν τὰ κακὰ ἵνα ἔλθῃ τὰ ἀγαθά; ὧν τὸ κρίμα ἔνδικόν ἐστιν.

Eng. Auth. Vers. *And not* rather, (*as we be slanderously reported, and as some affirm that we say,*) *Let us do evil, that good may come? whose damnation is just.*

Revised Version. *And* (*why*) *might we not—as we be slandered and as some allege that we say that we might— do evil that good might come?—whose judgement is just.*

§ 1. This verse has occasioned to expositors still greater perplexity than the preceding. And many have been the expedients devised for extracting its genuine import. "I know," says Benecke, "of no satisfactory attempt to elucidate the construction." (*Ich gestehe dass alle mir bekannt gewordenen Versuche die Construction zu erklären mir nicht genügen.*) "This passage seems to me," says Cognatus, "to be one of those to which Peter refers as *hard to be understood.*" (*Videtur et hic sermo obscurus, et ex his de quibus Petrus ait,* **obscura inveniri in epistolis Pauli, et difficilia ad intelligendum.**) And yet, after one has got to understand clearly the extrinsic relations and intrinsic import of the preceding verse, there is no reason why there should be the least despair of reaching a correct apprehension of the peculiarity and meaning of this. The *Auth. Eng. Version,* however, is a tanglement.

Vater takes a rather singular view. He regards the sentence as abruptly broken off after the introductory conjunction *and* (καί), and he looks upon what follows as a prohibitory silencing of the remark that was about to be made. He supposes that it is an objector to the Apostle's doctrine who is represented as speaking in the preceding verse. This objector, he imagines, after saying—"if the trueness of God superabounded to his glory through my lie, why yet am even I judged as a sinner?" wished to proceed to something else; and hence he commenced with "and." But before he brings out his blasphemous idea, the Apostle, as Vater supposes, breaks in and says, "Let us not—(as we be blasphemed, and as some affirm that we say)—do evil, that good may come." (τί ἔτι κἀγὼ, ὡς ἁμαρτωλὸς, κρίνομαι; καὶ . . . . Μὴ (καθὼς βλασφημούμεθα, καὶ καθώς φασίν τινες ἡμᾶς λέγειν· ὅτι) ποιήσωμεν, κ. τ. λ.) This rather violent expedient for introducing order into the Apostle's phraseology proceeds on the erroneous assumption that the preceding verse contains, not the apagogical reasoning of the Apostle in reply to an odious objection, but the argumentation of the supposed objector himself.

Other critics, agreeing with Vater in regarding the statement which follows the introductory conjunction *and* as deprecatory and not interrogatory, take other ways of elucidating the construction. Cocceius, for example, would supplement the expression thus,—"and *let it* not *be,*—as we be blasphemed, and as some affirm that we say—that we should do evil, that good may come," (καὶ μὴ εἴη or γένοιτο, κ. τ. λ. —ὅτι ποιήσωμεν κ. τ. λ.). D. G. Herzog proposes the same supplement. Turner, too, suggests a similar device, (καὶ μὴ ἔστω). But, besides other objections to these supplements, it is fatal to the principle on which they proceed, as expedients,—and also to Sharpe's translation, *and by no means let us do, &c.,*—that they do not account for the initial conjunction, which evidently hooks on, to what goes before, some remark, tending *in the same dialectical direction.* On this account we must likewise reject the supplement of Baumgarten-Crusius,—"And *let us* not *say or think*—as we be blasphemed, and as some affirm that we say—that we might do evil, that good may come," (*ist aus dem folgenden* λέγειν *zu verstehen* λέγωμεν *oder* λέξομεν *oder* ἐροῦμεν. *Lasst uns ja nicht sagen oder denken, &c.*) Wolle's expedient, too, is, for the same, as well as for other reasons, inadmissible. He would put a colon after the *not* (μή) which follows the introductory *and* (καί), and substituting *but* for *and,* he would interpret the whole verse thus :—*But no:—(as we be blasphemed, and as some affirm that we say)—because we should thus be doing evil, that good might come, of which sort of persons the condemnation is just.* (*De Parenthesi Sacra,* pp. 42-44.)

We must, indeed, hold it as unquestionable that the language which follows the conjunction is not deprecative, but interrogative. Almost all good critics acknowledge this. And some, such as Bengel (ultimately), Fritzsche, Meyer, Philippi, van Hengel, putting only a comma at the close of verse 7, postpone the point of interrogation till they reach the words "that good might come," (ἵνα ἔλθῃ τὰ ἀγαθά). Matthias does not even interpose a comma. It is perhaps better, however, with Lachmann and Tischendorf, to repeat the point of interrogation, inasmuch as the clauses, though running on in one line, are so far distinct that the Apostle makes a transition in the second from the singular to the plural. Wave of interrogation succeeds wave; and the second wave spreads out wider than the first.

Of those who have perceived that the interrogation of the preceding verse carries itself forward into this, some have proposed to supplement the statement thus:—"and *shall we say,*—as we are blasphemed, and as some affirm that we say, —that we might do evil, that good may come?" (καὶ μὴ ἐροῦμεν κ. τ. λ.) This is the view of Wittich, Moses Stuart, Benecke, &c. They regard the particle (μή) which comes after the initial conjunction as having a simply interrogative import (*num*). A much larger proportion of critics, however, suppose that the particle has its usual negative import: and, while they would supply the same or some equivalent verb,—*shall we say?* or, *do we say?* or, *should we say?*—they would also carry forward, out of the query at the close of verse 7th, the interrogative "why" (τί):—"and *why should we* not *say,*—as we are blasphemed, and as some give out that we say—Let us do evil, that good may come?" (καὶ τί μὴ ἐροῦμεν, or λέξωμεν, or λέγομεν, κ. τ. λ.) This is, in substance, the view of Erasmus (*cur non potius ita cogitamus*), Calvin (*cur non potius dicitur*), Limborch (*cur non dicimus*), and Wolf, who adopted it from Limborch, and, rejoicing over it, says, that, according to it, "the Pauline discourse runs most beautifully," (*hac ratione oratio Paulina bellissime procedit*). It is also adopted by Rollock, Hammond, Natalis, Wells, Taylor, Doddridge, Macknight (*why not add?*); as likewise by Koppe, Wakefield, Belsham, Boysen; and by Walford, Peile, Conybeare, Vaughan, &c. Van Hengel acquiesces in the view; only, instead of a plural verb, he would supply a singular, (καὶ τί μὴ λέγω κ. τ. λ.). Turretin and Morus approximate to the same interpretation: only, instead of carrying forward the interrogative "why" (τί) from the preceding verse, they unwarrantably regard the particle (μή), succeeding the initial conjunction, as equivalent to the Latin *nonne:*—"might we not say?" or "should we not rather say?" (*nonne dicere possumus?*–Morus: *nonne potius dicendum esset?*–Turretin). But there is assuredly the appearance of what is unnatural in deriving, for the main proposition, a supplemental word (*shall we say,* λέξωμεν, λέγομεν, or λέγω, &c.) from a proposition which must be regarded as either actually or virtually parenthetical, —"as we are blasphemed, and as some allege that we *say.*" We cannot, then, adopt any phasis of this interpretation.

Matthias takes a peculiar view. He supposes that if the Apostle had carried out the structure of his sentence, as he began it in the 7th verse, it would have run thus:— "why, notwithstanding, am even I judged as a sinner, and not (i. e., *and not rather*, *und nicht vielmehr*) as having done good?" (καὶ μὴ ὡς ποιήσας τὰ ἀγαθά;) He supposes, however, that before the Apostle had time to complete his sentence, the idea rushed into his mind that he himself and his fellow-christians were slanderously accused of holding that evil may be done in order that good may ensue; and hence he ruptures the structure which he had commenced, and lets his sentence go, anacoluthically, thus:—"why notwithstanding am even I judged as a sinner, and not rather according to what we are blasphemed, and according to what some affirm that we say, namely, according to that—*Let us do evil, in order that good may come?*" (*was werde auch ich dann noch wie ein Sünder gerichtet und nicht vielmehr nach dem wir verlästert werden und nach dem Etliche sagen, dass wir sprächen, nämlich danach: "Lasset uns Böses thun, damit Gutes komme?*") It is an objection to this interpretation, that it leaves the construction exceedingly perplexed. It is another objection, that if we suppose that the suppressed antithesis to the expression, *as a sinner* (ὡς ἁμαρτωλός), is simply, *and not as having done good,* (καὶ μὴ ὡς ποιήσας τὰ ἀγαθά), we do not furnish a sufficiently full idea to suggest the Apostle's quotation of the calumny, "*let us do evil,* that good may come;" whereas, if we suppose that the suppressed antithesis is, *and not as having done evil, that good may come,* (καὶ μὴ ὡς ποιήσας τὰ κακὰ ἵνα ἔλθῃ τὰ ἀγαθά), we destroy the reality of the antithesis assumed; for *to be a sinner,* and *to do evil, that good may come,* are, though not identical statements, yet parallel to one another. It is a third objection to Matthias's construction, that it would have required the objective negative (οὐ), instead of the subjective (μή), after the initial conjunction.

To pass over other anomalous attempts to explicate the Apostle's phraseology, such as Herzog's ποιήσω μέν, instead of ποιήσωμεν, &c., we may simply say that by far the easiest, by far the most natural, and by far the most effective disentanglement of the interrogative sentence, is, just to carry forward mentally the *why* (τί) of the preceding query, and to regard the verb (ποιήσωμεν), which we translate "we might do," as *the angular point in which two distinct lines of thought meet and blend*,—a primary and interrogative line, and a subordinate and affirmative line. Thus,—"why still am even I judged as a sinner? and *why might we not*—as we be slandered, and as some give out that we say that *we might*—*do* evil that good may come?" (τί ἔτι κἀγὼ ὡς ἁμαρτωλὸς κρίνομαι; καὶ μὴ—καθὼς βλασφημούμεθα καὶ καθώς φασίν τινες ἡμᾶς λέγειν ὅτι—ποιήσωμεν τὰ κακὰ ἵνα ἔλθῃ τὰ ἀγαθά;) In English, if we would remove the appearance of anacoluth, we must repeat the verb, or at all events its auxiliary. But this is a necessity arising from the peculiarity of our English tongue. In Greek there is no auxiliary required; and the one word represents, with perfect propriety, the two modifications of idea, interrogatory and non-interrogatory, with which the two lines of thought are respectively wound up. There is a peculiarity of structure indeed. There is a kind of grammatical perturbation. The verb must be understood both interrogatively and non-interrogatively. But this is no violent anacoluth. There is merely the suspension, for a moment, of an incomplete line of thought, until another is picked up, and carried forward convergingly to the point at which the first was left, and in which, as in an angle, both meet and blend. So far as the Greek is concerned, the construction may be indicated by a double *pause*, or by what is tantamount to a double hyphen or *dash:* or, if brackets be employed, the second should not be put before ὅτι, as has been done by R. Stephens (*eds.* 1550 and 1551), Beza, the Elzevirs, Wetstein, Griesbach, Knapp, Scholz, &c., but, as Vater has it, after it.

The ὅτι has been generally regarded as merely recitative, introducing what follows in the direct form of speech,—the *oratio recta.* In that case the particle would not bear to be translated in English, and the verb following it would require to be translated *let us do.* The entire statement would then need to be rendered in English thus, —and why *might we not do*—as we be slandered, and as some allege that we say *Let us do*—evil, that good might come?" It is far more likely, however, that the particle is to be regarded as introducing, in indirect form,—in *oratio obliqua,*—the statement alleged to be made. In that case it would require to be rendered *that,* and the verb must then be translated *we might do:*—"and why *might we not*—as we be slandered, and as some allege that we say *that we might*—*do* evil, that good may come?" This is undoubtedly the more likely resolution of the Apostle's expression; as is evident, partly, from the fact that it demands a much smaller amount of grammatical perturbation than must be assumed on the other hypothesis, and, partly, from the consideration that it is more likely that slanderers would represent the Apostle and his compeers as maintaining, by dogmatical involution of ideas, *that they might do evil, that good might come,* than as actually stirring up each other, in a directly hortatory way, saying to one another, *Let us do evil, that good may come.* If this conception of the particle be correct, then the only difference in the relations of the verb to the two lines of thought consists in this:—that in the one case there is amalgamated with its import an element of interrogation, in the other, there is amalgamated an element of affirmation.

This method of enucleating the construction is, in substance, that of Luther, Beza, Melville, Pareus, and Bengel; of Worsley also, and of Drysén, Reiche, Lossius, and Winer; of Rückert too, and Fritzsche, Meyer, Philippi, Mehring; and, among English expositors, of Purdue, Mac-Evilly, Ornsby, Jowett, &c. We say, in substance; for there is considerable diversity in minute details of views, and more especially as to the amount of grammatical perturbation which has been occasioned by the *attractive* influence of the intervening proposition, *as we be slandered, and as some give out that we say that*, (καθὼς βλασφημούμεθα καὶ καθώς φασίν τινες ἡμᾶς λέγειν ὅτι). Luther translates thus,—*und nicht vielmehr also thun, wie wir gelästert werden, und wie etliche sprechen, dass wir sagen sollen: Lasset uns Uebels thun, auf dass Gutes daraus komme?* His translation is fairly reproduced by Coverdale thus,—"and not rather to "do thus (as we are evell spoken of, and as some reporte "that we shulde saye), Let us do evell, that good maye "come thereof." Beza says that he perceives no ellipsis, (*neque hic quicquam subaudio*): only he would regard the clause, *as we be slandered, and as some affirm that we say*, as parenthetical. Melville, on the other hand, perceives no parenthesis, but admits an ellipsis, (*est igitur ellipsis sine ulla parenthesi legenda*). He would explain thus,—*and shall we not do evil, that good may come, as we be slandered, and as some affirm that we say, Let us do evil, that good may come?* Pareus, again, discards the idea of ellipsis, and takes Beza's view. Bengel holds an ellipsis, and supplies it thus,—*and why do I not so, as, &c.*, (subaud. **sic facio**), or, *and should it not be*, (und solls nicht seyn?). Reiche says that the first two words of the verse (καὶ μή) stand anacoluthically; (but he supplies from the connection ποιήσωμεν or ποιῶμεν). Winer says (iii. 66, 5), that "the Apostle had intended to make ποιεῖν (ποιήσωμεν?) κακά dependent on καὶ μή, but, on account of the parenthesis, appended it to λέγειν in *oratio recta*." Rückert says that without ὅτι there would have been a parenthesis, but as ὅτι is introduced, there is no parenthesis, but an anacoluth, arising out of attraction, (*ohne ὅτι hätten wir eine Parenthese, jezt aber keine, sonder ein Anacoluth, aus Attraction entstanden*). Had it not, however, been for the intervening remark, which would otherwise have been a parenthesis, he thinks that the Apostle would have employed the singular number of the verb;—*and why should I not do evil, &c.?* Fritzsche thinks that the Apostle would in all likelihood have used the plural verb, but yet with a singular reference; and he supposes that, had not the clause, *as we be slandered, &c.*, suggested itself to the

Apostle's mind, he would have said, *and why do I not do evil, &c.?* or, *and why may I not do evil, &c.?* (καὶ τί μὴ ποιοῦμεν τὰ κακὰ κ. τ. λ.—*Utrum* καὶ τί μὴ ποιοῦμεν τὰ κακά **et cur non improbe ago,** *an* καὶ τί μὴ ποιῶμεν τὰ κακά, **et cur non improbe agam,** *Paulus dicere constituerit, de eo cum nemine ambigam.*) Meyer, while recognizing the interblending of two constructions, holds that there is neither parenthesis nor ellipsis, (*Grade wegen dieser Verschmelzung ist aber weder etwas zu parenthesiren, noch hinzuzudenken*).

Grotius *felt* apparently that the words should be understood in some such way as that indicated; but, not perceiving how to reach the goal he wished, he fancied that μὴ ὅτι stand for ὅτι μή, which he strangely supposes mean, or may mean, *why not?* Yet Vitringa takes up and repeats his notion. Wall improves on it,—saying, "the sense would guide one to read καὶ τὶ μή; *and why not?*" Glöckler attempts to reach the same result by a more circuitous route, and thus by an arbitrary supplement. He would supplement the Apostle's expression thus:—"and why is it not so, as we be slandered, &c.?" (*Construirt aber muss werden,* καὶ τί μή ἐστιν οὕτως, καθώς κ. τ. λ.) Estius, with several others, hesitates between the two constructions, *why do I not rather* **say,** *&c.,* and, *why do we not rather* **do,** *&c.* Oltramare, without carrying forward the interrogative *why,* would render the verse thus:—"and —(as some persons who calumniate us, give out that we say)—shall we not do evil, that good may come?" (*et —comme quelques personnes qui nous calomnient, nous prêtent de le dire—ne ferous-nous pas le mal afin qu'il en arrive du bien?*) But such a translation proceeds on a misapprehension of the natural import of the particle μή,— as much so almost, though in another direction, as that of le Févre, who regarded the particle as an objective negative, and rendered the expression, "and it is not the case, &c." (*et non est ut, &c.*)

§ 2. *as we be slandered* (καθὼς βλασφημούμεθα), that is, *as we be calumniously reported to do.* The expression is brachylogical.—(Fritzsche, Rückert, Tholuck, Krehl, and

Mehring would supply ποιεῖν after βλασφημούμεθα. But such an immediate complement seems, to say the least of it, to be of doubtful propriety. The idea is exegetically correct. But the grammatical construction is questionable.)—The Apostle speaks in the plural number,—re-entering, as it were, insensibly, into the consciousness of his union, not with the circle of the Jews, as Michaelis supposed, but with that extending circle of kindred spirits, Jews and Gentiles, who looked at the way of salvation from the same standpoint with himself. The impersonation which he assumed when he said, *why am I judged?* is thus only momentary. But the course of the argument does not deviate. For it is logically a matter of indifference whether the queries proposed in verses 7th and 8th be regarded as the utterances of a *representative individual* belonging to the world of mankind at large, or of a *representative party of individuals.*

§ 3. *and as some allege that we say,* (καὶ καθώς φασίν τινες ἡμᾶς λέγειν). Some would blend this clause with the former, so as to bring out, as the import of both, the following complex idea,—*as some blasphemingly give out that we say,* (καθὼς βλασφημοῦντες φασίν τινες ἡμᾶς λέγειν). This is the idea of van Hengel and Matthias, as also, substantially, of Reiche. But the Apostle seems to be careful to cause the clauses to bifurcate ;—"*as* we be slandered, *and as* some affirm that we say." And doubtless he refers to two distinct allegations which had obtained more or less currency regarding himself and his Christian brethren. The one was a charge against their conduct : the other was a charge in reference to their doctrine. They were, (1), calumniously reported to *do* evil, that good might come ; and, (2), they were represented as, directly or indirectly, *maintaining* that it was a right thing, in certain circumstances at least, to do as they were reported to do.

It is in vain to ask for very definite answers to the questions, Who were the calumniators? and, What was the occasion of the calumnies? As to the former question, Locke says, "It is past doubt that these were the Jews." And many critics coincide in his opinion. Theophylact, on the other hand, says it was the Greeks, (καὶ γὰρ οἱ Ἕλληνες, ἀκούσαντες τοῦ Παύλου λέγοντος, ὅτι ὅπου ἐπλεόνασεν ἡ ἁμαρτία, ὑπερεπερίσσευσεν ἡ χάρις, ἐκωμῴδουν τοῦτο, καὶ ἔλεγον, ὅτι οἱ Χριστιανοὶ λέγουσι, ποιήσωμεν τὰ κακὰ ἵνα ἔλθῃ τὰ ἀγαθά). The opinion of Locke is probably correct in the main ; and yet there is no reason for supposing that it was the Jews alone who took up and rung changes on the calumnies. As to the occasion of the calumnies, it may perhaps have been partly biographical and historical ; but doubtless it would be principally doctrinal. When the Apostle burst through the shackles of Judaism, and associated freely with the Gentiles, and not only ate with them, but dissuaded them from judaising ; he might, by some of his wondering countrymen, be honoured for his motives, while yet they would call in question, not only the propriety, but also the morality of his procedure. They might not unlikely say of him, *He is doing evil, that good may come.* But when he enunciated boldly his great doctrine of justification, " by faith without works," it is probable that the hue and cry would be raised by his theological opponents, *He is disparaging good works,—He is teaching that they are of no value, and that, as the more that sin abounds, grace will much more abound, the more we sin the better.* It is natural to suppose that, as the hearts of men are somewhat alike in all ages, there would be, on the part of unindoctrinated Jews and others, a misrepresentation of Paul's idea, somewhat similar to the caricature of the Protestant doctrine of justification, which has been more or less current among Roman Catholics and others, ever since the time of the Reformation. (*Quod Paulo contigit, hodie quoque his contingit, qui gratiam et misericordiam dei per Christum extollunt,*-Zuingli ;—*Quod autem Paulo contigit, id hodie omnibus fere syncerae gratiae praedicatoribus usuvenit.*-Bullinger). To this caricature, indeed, and reproach, some handle was sometimes given by unguarded and imprudent expressions on the part of Luther and others.

§ 4. *we might do evil things, that good things might*

come (ποιήσωμεν τὰ κακὰ ἵνα ἔλθῃ τὰ ἀγαθά). A Jesuitical principle, ultimately subversive of all moral distinctions, and thus, too, of the foundation of confidence between man and man. It is a principle to be abhorred. It is, says Bullinger, "a nefarious dogma" (*nepharium dogma*). And yet, when aesthetically veiled, and allowed to bear in its hand an immediate bribe, it too frequently receives entertainment, where better things might have been expected. Sometimes it is even unblushingly avowed as a legitimate rule of action. (*Solche plumpe horrible Raisonneurs giebts unter den Menschen, und findet man noch oft solche Raisonnemens bey den Christen.*–Rambach). It is, however, its contradictory,—*We must* **not** *do evil that good may come*, that is one of the chief moral condiments of the incorruptibility of churches and states. (*Famageratissima verba*, **non sunt facienda mala ut veniant bona**.–Paciuchelli). Noble are the words of Cardinal Cajetan,—"Take note, noviciate, that according to sound and true doctrine, sins must never be chosen as means to any end whatsoever.—And, thou learned reader, take thou note, that since the avoiding of a worse evil is a kind of good, it must be a principle with us, never to do a lesser (moral) evil in order to avoid a greater." (*Intellige, novicie, quod secundum sanam veramque doctrinam, peccata non sunt eligenda ut media ad quemcunque bonum finem.—Adverte et tu, erudite lector, quod quia vitatio mali pejoris est quoddam bonum, eadem doctrina qua horremus facere mala ut eveniant bona, eadem horrere debemus facere mala ut evitemur pejora.*)

When the Apostle runs out his argument thus:—*why yet am even I judged as a sinner? and why should we not do evil things, that good things may come?*—his second as well as his first question draws its logical force from the "nefarious" hypothetical assumption which he is engaged in carrying out into absurdity, namely, That it would be unjust in God to punish the unrighteousness in men which sets off his righteousness. If this were unjust, then there would be no solid reason why men should not do every sort of moral evil, that God's moral goodness might be contrastingly displayed. The idea, says Calvin, is an "impious cavillation" (*impia cavillatio*). It is further, as Pareus observes, a *fallacia accidentis*. It assumes a *non-causa pro causa*. For God's moral goodness does not require men's moral evil for its display. Although, instead of being put into the shade, it is brought out into relief when placed side by side with men's moral evil, yet no thanks to men for the foil. They do not cause, they merely give unwitting, unwilling, and unintended occasion to the lustre.

§ 5. *whose judgement is just*, (ὧν τὸ κρίμα ἔνδικόν ἐστιν), *whose judgement is* ἐν δίκῃ, *in harmony with right*. The word *judgement* (κρίμα), though strictly denoting only *a judicial sentence* is generally used in the New Testament with the subsumption of *an adverse decision*. (See chap. ii. 1, 2.) This subsumed idea attaching to the term may not improbably have arisen from the fact, that, in consequence of the abounding of moral evil, the great majority of legal decisions are actually adverse to the parties summoned into court. This is true of human courts in general; and it is true too,—emphatically so,—in reference to the divine tribunal. The term is frequently translated, in our Authorized Version, *condemnation* and *damnation*. See Luke xxiii. 40; xxiv. 20; 1 Cor. xi. 34; 1 Tim. iii. 6; Jas. iii. 1; Jude 4; Mat. xxiii. 14 (13); Mark xii. 40; Luke xx. 47; Rom. xiii. 2; 1 Cor. xi. 29; 1 Tim. v. 12; and also the passage before us, "whose *damnation* is just." The same translation is given by Wycliffe, (*whos dampnacioun is just*); by Tyndale, too, and in the Geneva. It is the reproduction of the Vulgate, (*quorum damnatio justa est*). Mace, Wynne, Worsley, Wakefield, Newcome, Cox, Sharpe, and other English translators, render the word *condemnation*. And this, undoubtedly, is the meaning of the term. The *judgement*, or *doom*, or *judicial sentence*, is supposed to be condemnatory. (Indeed, Theophylact, in his Commentary, substitutes, when quoting the passage, the word κατάκριμα for κρίμα,—ὧν τὸ κατάκριμα ἔνδικόν ἐστι.) Nevertheless, the English word *judgement* is the exact equivalent of the Greek term; and Turnbull, certainly, goes altogether out of the orbit of a translator when he renders the term *punishment*.

It has been disputed, who are the parties referred to, when it said "*whose* judgement is right." Many critics assume that it is they who calumniated the character and the doctrine of the Christians. This is the opinion of Theodoret and Grotius, the latter of whom supposes that in the Apostle's expression there is a latent prediction of the destruction of the Jewish city and temple, and the dispersion of the Jewish people, (*Latenter prædicit hîc Paulus urbis et Templi excidium et populi dissipationem*). It is also the opinion of Abelard, de Lyra, Pareus; and of Day, Locke, Whitby, le Cene; as also of Tholuck, Baumgarten-Crusius, Sumner, Wardlaw, Mehring. But it certainly better accords, (1), with the moral earnestness of the Apostle's spirit; (2), with the fact that the reference to the slanderers of the Christians is only incidental and quasi-parenthetical; and, (3), with our ideas of what is congruous in order to wind up the Apostle's argumentation in opposition to the wicked principle referred to in ver. 5th, and brought out in the query,—*Is God unjust who bringeth wrath upon the unrighteousness which sets off his righteousness?* —it is more congruous to suppose that the Apostle's concluding statement refers to *those who do evil, that good may come.* And this is the opinion of Aquinas, Cajetan, Este, Bengel; and likewise of de Wette, Fritzsche, Meyer; of Hodge, too, and Haldane; and Oltramare, Philippi, Krehl, Alford, and others. There is not, indeed, so far as the preceding words are concerned, a precise or sharply defined personal antecedent, grammatically considered, to which the relative can refer. But the Apostle was not fastidious in the structure of his sentences. And the relative, though thus floating somewhat loosely in relation to the preceding part of the verse, is clearly equivalent to some such expression as this,—"*of all persons who act on the principle referred to,* the condemnation is right."

Heumann takes a strange view of this closing clause. He regards the word *judgement* as used extrajudicially, and as referring, not to what objectively terminates on the parties referred to by the relative, but to what subjectively emanates from them:—*whose judgement* (i. e., *the judgement of which calumniators as to the falsity of the doctrine that evil may be committed for the sake of good to come) is entirely right.* (*Dieser, der Jüden, Urtheil ist ganz recht, spricht Paulus, dass man nemlich nicht dürfe böses thun in der Absicht, dadurch etwas gutes zu erlangen.*) But the customary judicial usage both of the word *judgement* (κρίμα) and of the word *right* (ἔνδικον) stamps this interpretation with the utmost improbability. And, moreover, it is scarcely conceivable that the Apostle would, in bringing such an argument to a close, pause to throw a wreath of laudation upon the judgement of his calumniators, who were also the slanderers, not only of the conduct, but likewise of the principles of all his Brethren in Christ.

D. G. Herzog regards the relative *whose* (ὧν) as neuter, referring it to the *evil things* spoken of:—*the condemnation of which evil things is right.* The interpretation involves, theologically, on the one hand, an intolerable truism, and, philologically, on the other, an intolerable capriciousness as regards the determination of the relative's antecedent.

§ 6. In some of the more dogmatic *Commentaries*, as in Willet's for example, and in that of Pareus, the theological bearing of the Jesuitical principle condemned by the Apostle is discussed. Willet asks;—"whether God do not evil, that good may come thereof, in reprobating (viz., unconditionally) the vessels of wrath, to show his power?" Such is his question. It is pertinent. But he certainly fails to clear, *in the light of his peculiar theology*, the character of God. He says that the action referred to is not evil: (1.) "Because it is God's will, which is always just and holy:" (2.) Because "that which tendeth to God's glory cannot be evil:" (3.) Because "that which is lawfully done cannot be evil." "God," he adds, "in rejecting some, doth that which he may do by lawful right, to dispose of his own as it pleaseth him; as no man can reprove the potter in making some vessels of honour, some of dishonour, of the same piece of clay." (4.) "But," continues he, "seeing in the end God's rejecting and reprobating of some, viz., such as by their sins deserved eternal death, appeareth to be most just, it must needs also be good, for that which is just is good." In the last of these reasons the critic reverses his own theory of unconditional reprobation. And in the former three he only echoingly reiterates the idea, that the Jesuitical principle may be to God, though not to man, a legitimate and right glorious rule of conduct. Pareus, a short time before Willet, had trodden exactly the same round of apologetic thought; and thus, so far as we can judge, Feurborn is correct when he contends that the great theologian of Heidelberg has violated the Apostle's axiom. His whole reasoning seems simply to amount to this, *that God is an infinite Jesuit.*

§ 7. In coming to the conclusion of this verse,—which is in fact the conclusion of one of the subordinate paragraphs of the chapter,—Theodoret pauses, winds up the first *Tome of his Commentary*, and says, "here we would unbend a little, and pray the Lord that we may thoroughly understand the meaning of the Apostolical doctrine; for, assuredly, he who says, **Ask, and ye shall receive; Seek, and ye shall find; Knock, and it shall be opened unto you,** will give." (*ἡμεῖς δὲ ἐνταῦθα τὴν ἑρμηνείαν στήσαντες, καὶ τὸν νοῦν διαναπαύσαντες, τὸν δεδωκότα στόμα ἀνθρώπῳ, καὶ ποιήσαντα δύσκωφον καὶ κωφὸν, ἀνυμνήσωμεν, καὶ τῆς ἀποστολικῆς διδασκαλίας τὸν νοῦν καταμαθεῖν ἱκετεύσωμεν. δώσει γὰρ πάντως ὁ εἰπὼν, αἰτεῖτε κ. τ. λ.*) Surely it is not unbecoming or unbefitting that the modern critic should go and do likewise.

VER 9. Τί *οὖν*; Προεχόμεθα; Οὐ *πάντως· προῃτιασάμεθα γὰρ* Ἰουδαίους *τε καὶ* Ἕλληνας *πάντας ὑφ' ἁμαρτίαν εἶναι.*

Eng. Auth. Vers. *What then? are we better than they? No, in no wise: for we have before proved both Jews and Gentiles, that they are all under sin;*

Revised Version. *What then? Do we put forth pleas in*

our own behalf? No, certainly: for we before impeached both Jews and Greeks of being all under sin;

§ 1. In reference to this verse, as to those which immediately precede, there has been diversity and conflict of opinion among expositors. The dissidence, indeed,—relatively to that on the other verses,—has been peculiarly great. It centres in the interpretation of the verb (προεχόμεθα), which is translated in our authorized English version, *are we better (than they)?* Even in ancient times this verb seems to have occasioned no little difficulty. Hence the readings of the MSS. are far from being uniform. Neither are those readings harmonious which are imbedded in the old expositors, and indicated in the ancient versions. The dissonance of readings is so great, and the apparent difficulty of reaching the Apostle's idea so formidable, that van Hengel, after a most scholarly investigation of the passage, and of the history of its interpretation, gives way to despair. He declares his conviction that the text, as generally presented, is corrupt; and he avows that it is quite beyond his ability to suggest its rectification. (*Oratio mihi laborare videtur mendo librariorum: hoc autem quo modo tollendum sit, acutiores viri judicent.*) We believe, however, with Fritzsche, that a minute and comprehensive examination of all the variations of the text, and the circumstantialities connected with these variations, will conduct us to the conclusion, not only that the received reading is to be preferred to all the others, but also that it is perfectly free from corruption. (*Dubitari non potest, quin hic versus sine ullo mendo sit.*—Fritzsche.)

§ 2. Instead of τί οὖν; προεχόμεθα; οὐ πάντως· D* and G read τί οὖν προκατέχομεν περισσόν; and omit οὐ πάντως. Chrysostom, in explaining the passage, does not cite the words; but he quotes them at the commencement of his 8th *Homily*, in explaining the 1st and 2nd verses of chap. iv.; and he there cites them according to the reading of D* and G. Theodoret reads the passage in the same way, with the exception that he gives the simple verb κατέχομεν instead of the compound *προκατέχομεν*. Severus gives the same reading with Theodoret. The Italic version (as exhibited in manuscripts d. e. g.) seems to have been made from the same reading, (*quid ergo tenemus amplius?*) This version is given, moreover, in Rufinus's translation of Origen. It is given also in some of the MSS. of Ambrosiaster. The Peshito version seems to correspond. If not made from Theodoret's reading, it must, we should suppose, have been based on an interpretation of *προεχόμεθα* that made it equivalent to *κατέχομεν περισσόν*. It omits *οὐ πάντως*. ܡܢܐ ܗܟܝܠ ܐܬܝܬܪܢ ܝܬܝܪܐ—*what superiority then do we possess?*—infelicitously rendered by Etheridge, *what then, have we attained excellence?*

E, again, reads the clause thus,—*τί οὖν προκατεχόμεθα*, and adds *οὐ πάντως*. This varies from the received text only to the extent of introducing *κατά* into the verb, apparently compounding between the two readings *προεχόμεθα* and *κατέχομεν*.

A and L give the received text, with the exception of having the verb in the subjunctive, *προεχώμεθα*. Suidas must have had this reading in his codex, for, with obvious reference to the passage before us, he gives the word thus in his *Lexicon*, *προεχώμεθα, ὑποβαλλώμεθα, ἢ προβαλλώμεθα*. Valckenaer deemed the reading correct; apparently conjecturing it indeed, at least in the first instance, on internal grounds. (*Schol. in Luc.* xx. 47; comp. *Schediasma* in loc.)

א and B give the *Received Text* complete: and no doubt correctly. For, by assuming it as the original reading, we can account for all the divergencies as its mere deflected radiations. The reading of A and L—*προεχώμεθα*—may have been a mere slip, arising from indistinct pronunciation on the part of a reader, or from indistinct hearing on the part of a writer; or it may have been a conjectural emendation on some such grounds as approved themselves to Valckenaer. *Προκατέχομεν* again would appear to have been a conjectural emendation on the part of some one who found it difficult to explain *προεχόμεθα*. *Κατέχομεν περισσόν* would appear to have been a gloss explaining *προκατέχομεν*, and reflecting back on verse 1st. And when either the one reading or the other was adopted, οὐ πάντως required to be struck out, as being an obvious superfluity and impertinence. Starting from any of the readings, besides that of ℵ B and the *Received Text*, it is difficult to account for the divergencies. Starting from the *Received Text*, we can see into the genesis of all the variations.

§ 3. *What then? Do we defend ourselves?—Do we screen ourselves?* that is, *Do I, as a Jew, stand on the defensive in relation to the Jews?—do I, in maintaining the fact of their prerogative and preeminence, screen them in relation to the charge of unrighteousness?—Do I put forward pleas in their behalf?*—It is thus that we would render and interpret the first three words of the verse, (τί οὖν; προεχόμεθα;)

The matter of difficulty, and the matter of moment, is to determine the import of the verb (προεχόμεθα).

The great body of expositors, both ancient and modern, have supposed that it must mean, *do we excel?* This is the translation of the Vulgate (*præcellimus eos?*). It is adopted and approved of by Erasmus (who gives as a synonym *praestamus?*). Le Fevre, Calvin, Beza, and Grotius, accord. Luther's version is similar, *Have we an advantage?* (*Haben wir einen Vortheil*). The Dutch versions, old and new, correspond, (old, *Hebben wij voordeel?*—new, *Zijn wij uitnemender?*). Tyndale's is analogous, *Are we better than they?*—a translation which has descended into our Authorized Version. It corresponds with Erasmus's paraphrase,—*Num potiores sumus?* The English Geneva version is, *Are we more excellent?* The French Geneva is identical (*Sommes nous plus excellens?*) It is Calvin's version. Diodati's corresponds, (*Habbiamo noi qualche eccellenza?*).—It is, however, an insuperable objection to this interpretation of the verb, that it is absolutely without precedent. The verb in the active voice, (προέχειν) does mean, in the neuter branch of its import, *to excel.* But *it has no such import in the middle voice.* The most learned of those who contend for the interpretation make the admission. (*Die Sprache steht insofern entgegen, als uns nicht nur jedes Beispiel eines ähnlichen Gebrauches fehlt, sondern auch die Medialform für diese Bedeutung der innern Wahrscheinlichkeit entbehrt.*–Rückert.) The meaning attached to the term is thus a mere invention, springing out of a supposed exegetical necessity. Grotius, feeling that he should say something in defence of it, says that the middle is used Attically for the active. Wittich and Boysen,—though as out of their own cathedra,—echo his affirmation. In the scholia of Œcumenius the active voice is again and again quietly substituted for the middle. And the mass of the modern critics who support the interpretation vindicate themselves by saying that the exigency of the passage demands the attribution to the middle of the signification of the active. See Köllner, de Wette, Schrader, Rückert (*second edit.*), Baumgarten-Crusius, Oltramare, Maier, Philippi, Hodge, Jowett, Wordsworth, &c.

But there is another objection to this interpretation. *It seems to be out of joint with the context.* For, *in the first place,* if the reference of the term were to privilege, *do we excel (in privilege)*? and if, as is generally assumed by the expositors who contend for the interpretation, the question be proposed in the name of the Jews, then it seems to be a strange question, after what has been asked and answered in verses 1st and 2nd,—" What then is the superiority of the Jew? or what the advantage of circumcision? *Much in every respect.*" In this 9th verse the Apostle answers his question by an expression, (οὐ πάντως), which must either mean, *no, certainly,* or *not at all,* or *not in all respects.* But if, *in the second place,* it be assumed, as is generally the case, that the question has—as might be expected, it is contended, from the middle voice—(see Oltramare, Jatho, Lange, &c.)—a reference to what is subjective, or to character,—*do we excel (in character)*?—then there was really no occasion for the question on the one hand, and there is no answer to it on the other, or, at least, no vindication of the answer. (1), There was no occasion for the question:—for, from the Apostle's standpoint, in relation to the universal necessity of seeking justification by faith, it was a matter of no significance whether the Jews in general were better in character than the Gentiles in general, or whether the reverse were the case. The necessity of seeking justification by means of faith does not spring from any "bad preeminence" in sinfulness. It springs from the mere fact of sinfulness, without having any respect whatsoever to the question of degrees. Then, (2), even although there had been occasion for proposing the question, yet the Apostle,—in his answer in verses 10-19, does not, as a matter of fact, show that the Jews in general were on an equality, as to amount of wickedness, with the Gentiles in general. He only shows, *without instituting any comparison between the two classes,* that they were all exceedingly sinful. Moreover, it is difficult to see the connection of the question with what goes before. When the Apostle says, *what then?* the *then* seems to intimate that he is looking back over the ground which he had just been traversing. And when he adds, *do we excel (in character)*? we should have expected that something or other in what precedes was fitted to suggest the question. But there is certainly nothing in verses 3—8 that seems to prompt such a query. And if it be supposed,—as it is by Melancthon, Calvin, Bengel, and others,—that the Apostle returns from his digression in verses 3—8 to the subject which is introduced in verse 1st, then we still fail to find anything to suggest the question, when we assume that it refers to character, rather than to privilege, to that which is subjective rather than to that which is objective. If we should imagine, on the other hand, that the question refers to privilege rather than to character, we are confounded by the collision of the answers which are given by the Apostle in the two places respectively. We must, then, abandon that interpretation of the verb which would make it mean, *do we excel?*

Some would understand the word as being in the passive voice, and would translate it, *are we excelled?* This interpretation is suggested in one of Œcumenius's scholia, (ἡμεῖς προελήφθημεν;). It was revived by Cocceius, (*superamur?*). It is propounded again by Wetstein, (who quotes in support of it Plutarch, on *The Contradictions of the Stoics, p.* 1038, *ed.* 1599), οὕτω τοῖς ἀγαθοῖς πᾶσι ταῦτα προσήκει, κατ' οὐδὲν προεχομένοις ὑπὸ τοῦ Διός, *so these things*—viz., self-complacency and self-applause—*are becoming in all the good, who are in no wise excelled by Jupiter.* It is adopted by Cramer and Michaelis; by Matthias too; and by Mehring also. Rückert, in his first edition, gave in his adhesion to it; but in his second he surrendered it as untenable. It is tenable, indeed, so far as regards the philology of the word. But it seems to be untenable so far as the exegesis of the passage is concerned. In Œcumenius the question is supposed to be proposed by a Gentile in relation to the Jews. A similar opinion is expressed by Cocceius, (*ita erit questio gentium*). It is contended for by Mehring. But there is certainly nothing in the context to warrant the intrusion of such a questioner. The other patrons of the translation regard the question as proposed by the Jews in relation to the Gentiles. (*Si vera sunt, quae dicis, gravius nos peccamus, quam gentes aliae, iisque pejores sumus; illaene ergo nobis praestant, populo Dei electo?*–Wetstein.) And the answer (οὐ πάντως) is supposed to be, either, *not at all*, or, *not altogether.* But there is really no such distinct antithesis, in verses 3—8, between the Jews and the Gentiles, as to warrant the supposition that the latter were very prominently before the Apostle's mind when he commenced the 9th verse. And if we suppose that he was bridging over the space covered by verses 3—8, and returning to the subject-matter of verses 1 and 2, then, if the question, *are we excelled?* refers to privilege, it has been answered already in verse 2nd. But if it refer to character, it has really no relation to verses 1 and 2. Besides, if it refer to character, as Wetstein supposes, there is,—as Rückert acknowledges,—(1), no occasion in all that goes before for proposing it. The Apostle had never said anything that was fitted to suggest that the Gentiles in general are less sinful than the Jews in general. And, (2), there is nothing in what comes after to show that the Jews in general were either superior, or equal, in character, to the Gentiles. The question, then,—*are we Jews excelled* (*by the Gentiles*)?—seems to be altogether out of place in such a discussion as the Apostle has on hand.

Some other critics, believing, with those of the last class, that the verb is in the passive, and yet not approving of the interpretation, *are we excelled?*—have rendered the word, in a manner which brings out almost the opposite pole of idea, *are we preferred?* Cocceius propounded this interpretation, as an alternative, in his *Commentary;* and he had, at an earlier period, decided for it in his *Diagrammata.* Reiche, in his *Exposition,* repropounded the interpretation, without any reference to Cocceius; and he explained in accordance with it the passage which Wetstein adduced from Plutarch. Moses Stuart, too, gives the same interpretation (and borrowed, in his second edition, Reiche's blunder in reference to the meaning of the term in Plutarch). Olshausen also accepted it. So has Vaughan, and, after him, as is his wont, Colenso. But, in his *Critical Commentary,* Reiche has withdrawn his imprimatur from the interpretation, and acknowledges that there are no examples found of such a use of the word. The reason for the withdrawal is a good one. And there is this other good reason for it in addition,—though it is an exegetical one. The answer to the query, as the query was originally given by Reiche,—and before him by Cocceius,—and whether the answer be *no certainly,* or *not at all,* or *not altogether,*—is to all appearance at variance with ver. 2nd, in which it is said that the preference given to the Jews was "much *in every respect.*" In verses 10—19, moreover, the Apostle does not proceed to show, as we should have expected if Reiche's original hypothesis had been correct, that no preference is accorded to the Jews. He merely adduces passages to prove that they are exceedingly sinful. This interpretation too, then, must be renounced.

One other interpretation of the disputed word,—though branching out into a variety of developments,—remains: and the Apostle's real idea must, we apprehend, be found in one of its phases. This interpretation proceeds on the assumption that the verb is in *the middle voice,* and has, as distinguished from its use in the active voice on the one hand, and its use in the passive on the other, a proper medial import.

This medial import was originally exceedingly simple,—*to have or to hold* (something) *before oneself.* See Homer,

Iliad, xvii. 354, 355,—*and they who stood around Patroclus were protected on every side with shields, and* **held** *their spears* **before them,** i. e., **before themselves,** (πρὸ δὲ δούρατ' ἔχοντο). See also Hom. *Od.* iii. 8,—*and* **they had before them,** i. e., **before themselves,** *nine bulls for each bench of five hundred men,* (καὶ προὔχοντο ἑκάστοθι ἐννέα ταύρους). See also Aristophanes, *Nubes*, 1388,—*and taking thee* (a child) *in my hands, I would carry thee out of doors, and* **hold** *thee* **before me,** (κἀγὼ λαβὼν θύραζε ἐξέφερον ἄν, καὶ προὐσχόμην σε).—Such then,—*to hold before oneself,*—was the primary import of this verb in the middle voice.

Closely allied to the idea of *holding* (something) *before oneself,* is the idea of *holding forth* something *for oneself,* or, *in one's own behalf.* And hence a second stage in the development of the meaning of the word, as may be noticed in that variety of the term, προΐσχομαι. See, for example, Thucydides, iii. 58,—*ye received us when we had voluntarily submitted, and* **were holding out** *our hands,* (viz., for mercy to ourselves); *and it is a rule with the Greeks not to slay such,* (ὅτι ἑκόντας τε ἐλάβετε, καὶ χεῖρας προϊσχομένους,—ὁ δὲ νόμος τοῖς Ἕλλησι μὴ κτείνειν τούτους). See also Thucyd. iii. 66, where the same expression occurs. The hands were held out, *in the behalf of those who held them out.* The action was *a dumb pleading in behalf of oneself.* It indicated a desire that the stroke of vengeance should be arrested. The word προέχομαι hence, and προΐσχομαι, came to be used when other things besides hands were put forth in self-defence. Words, and the things represented by words, may be thus put forth. Hence Thucydides says, i. 140,—*Let none of you think that we shall go to war for a trifle, if we do not rescind the decree concerning the Megareans,—which* (rescission) *in particular* **they hold forth** *would arrest the war,* (ὅπερ μάλιστα προὔχονται, εἰ καθαιρεθείη, μὴ ἂν γίγνεσθαι τὸν πόλεμον). The Lacedemonians *held forth for themselves,—on their side of the case,*—and *in defence of the attitude which they had assumed,*—that the abrogation by the Athenians of the decree concerning the Megareans would cut off occasion for going to war. This was their *plea.* The scholiast explains προὔχονται here by προβάλλονται, and Thomas Magister gives the same explanation. He says, οὐ μόνον προΐσχω καὶ προΐσχομαι, τὸ προβάλλομαι, ἀλλὰ καὶ προέχομαι. He then quotes a passage of Sophocles, to be afterwards adduced; and adds this passage of Thucydides. Suidas quotes the same passage, and explains the word by προβάλλονται, προτείνουσι. In his third Book, 68th chapter, Thucydides speaks again of the conditions, *which before the siege the Lacedemonians* **proposed,** or **held forth,** *to the Platæans, that they should be neutral,* (ἃ πρὸ τοῦ περιτειχίζεσθαι προΐσχοντο αὐτοῖς κοινοὺς εἶναι κ. τ. ἑξῆς). The *proposal* was that which the Lacedemonians *put forth on their part,* and thus, in a manner, *in their own cause,* and *for their own advantage.* It was what they pleaded for. (In this passage, too, the scholiast explains προΐσχοντο by προεβάλλοντο.) So in Book iv. 87, we read again,—from the mouth of Brasides the Lacedemonian,—εἰ δ' ἐμοῦ ταῦτα προϊσχομένου, *but if when* **I propose** *these things,* that is, *when I, on my side of the case, propose these things.* Brasides, in making the proposal, was pleading the cause of his own people, the Lacedemonians. The idea of *putting forth as a plea* is involved. This same idea is very strikingly involved in an expression of Sophocles, —referred to by Thomas Magister,—*Antig.* 80. Ismene had urged that it would be madness to attempt the burial of their brother's corpse, against the will of the citizens; and the chafed Antigone replies,—(σὺ μὲν τάδ' ἂν προὔχοι'· ἐγὼ δὲ δὴ τάφον | χώσουσ' ἀδελφῷ φιλτάτῳ πορεύσομαι,)— *you may, if you will,* **bring forward** *these things* **as a plea,** —(**you may plead** *these things* **in defence of yourself** *if you please,*—**you may excuse yourself** *with these things as you please*),—*but I assuredly shall go and bury my darling brother:* (*du magst das vorschützen,*-Schneider). — In all these passages we see the proper medial import of the verb. It means *to hold* (something) *before oneself,*—*to put forth* (something) *for oneself,*—*to put forth* (something) *as a plea in one's own behalf.* Hesychius,—as well as the scholiast on Thucydides, and Thomas Magister,—explains the word by προβάλλομαι. With undoubted reference to the passage before us, he says, προεχόμεθα, προβαλλόμεθα. And on προβάλλομαι the idea is very emphatically impressed of *throwing forward* (something) *on one's own part, by way of defence,* and, in the case of judicial defence, or of moral defence in general, *by way of plea.* Such a *defence,* whether material, or juridical, or logical, was a πρόβλημα.

This proper medial import of the verb is, under one phase or another, attached to it, in the passage before us, by Valckenaer, and Venema; by Ernesti too, and Morus, Koppe, Jaspis, D. G. Herzog; and by Wahl, and Glöckler (*in the end*), and Benecke, Fritzsche, Meyer, Hofmann (*Schriftbeweis,* i. 443); by Krehl too, and Naebe, Reiche (*ultimately*), and Ewald, Theodor Schott, Rilliet, &c. It is said by Fritzsche, Reiche, and others, that Henry August Schott is also a patron of the medial interpretation of the verb. And it is true that at one time he was. In the 1st edition of his *New Testament* (1805) his translation of the verb was, "Have we an excuse?" (*suppetitne nobis excusatio?*) This version he repeated in the 1809 issue; and again in the revised edition of 1811. But in the 3rd and greatly re-revised edition of 1825,—published long before Fritzsche's *Commentary,* or Reiche's *Exposition,*—Schott renounced the medial rendering, and translated the word, "Do we excel (the Gentiles)?" (*Praestamusne gentilibus?*) And this rendering is retained in the final edition.

Some of the critics named,—such as Koppe and Ewald,—divide the entire verse into two interrogative clauses, and drop from the second the ratiocinative particle *for* (γάρ):—"What shall we then allege as an excuse? Have we not proved already that all the Jews, as well as the Gentiles, are under sin?" (*Was sollen wir nun vorschützen? Bewiesen wir nicht überhaupt schon voraus dass Judäer sowohl als Griechen unter Sünde seien?*-Ewald.) But, besides other objections to this mode of construing the verse, it is an insuperable obstacle to its admission, that it ignores, and must ignore, the particle *for*:—(*ejecto* γάρ *post* προητιασάμεθα.-Koppe. He renders the second clause thus, *Nonne omnino supra declaravi et demonstravi Judaeos omnes non minus poenis divinis esse obnoxios, quam Ethnicos?*) Ernesti agrees with Koppe and Ewald in throwing the first three words into an interrogative clause,—"What pretext—what excuse—shall we then employ?" (*Was wollen wir also vorwenden?*),—but, as he apparently leaves the remainder of the verse as it stands in the *Received Text*, the single query into which he gathers the first three words would have required to have been followed by the adjectival expression, *none assuredly*, (οὐδὲν πάντως), instead of the adverbial one, *no certainly*, or, *not at all*, (οὐ πάντως). Jaspis took the same view of the construction as Ernesti:—(*quanam igitur excusatione uti possumus?*) So Herzog;—but certainly not Meyer and Fritzsche, as is alleged by *The Five Clergymen*. Hofmann, however, and Theodor Schott take the same view, (*womit decken wir uns also?*–Hofmann.—*Was halten denn wir vor uns zum Schutz?*–Schott). Hofmann would represent the relation of the query to the following adverbial negation thus,—"With what do we then defend ourselves? We do not defend ourselves at all." Theodor Schott's idea is an echo of Hofmann's, (*Paulus kann um so leichter mit einem blossem* οὐ πάντως *antworten, als diese Worte eigentlich gar nicht Antwort sind, sondern mehr nur eine zu der schon in der Frage selbst als einer rhetorischen liegenden Verneinung hinzutretende Bekräftigung*). But such an expedient in interpretation,—doing such violence to the natural inter-relations of clauses,—is utterly inadmissible, except at least as the very last resort. Valckenaer's interpretation so far corresponds with that of Ernesti, Jaspis, Hofmann, and Schott; but by throwing the verb into the subjunctive, (προεχώμεθα), he introduces still greater difficulty into the succeeding clause, in as much as we should have expected,—even if the adverb, instead of the adjective, were admissible,—that the subjective negative (μή) would have been employed, instead of the objective (οὐ).

Morus translates the expression,—"Have we a pretext?" (*num praetextus nobis est?*). Fritzsche's version still more exactly represents the force or energy that is expressed by the verb,—"Do we use a pretext?" (*utimurne praetextu*), that is, "Do we look about for excuses for our sins?" (*circumspicimusne peccatorum excusationes?*). Krehl accords with Fritzsche. Reiche supposes that the Apostle, though using the plural number, is speaking strictly in his own individual person, but speaking nevertheless of his action in reference to his countrymen,—"Do I throw a shield (over the sins of the Jews)?" (*Num peccatis Judæorum clypeum quasi praetendo?—num ea excuso?—num Judæorum patronum ago?*) Benecke's version is,—"Have we a defence?" (*Haben wir noch einen Vorwand?*) Meyer's corresponds, (*Haben wir vorschutz?*) But in his 4th edition he has very decidedly improved the form of his translation, (*Schützen wir vor?*).—Amid all this variety, there is loyalty to the medial import of the verb. And this loyalty is something of moment;—more especially when we take into consideration that some of the critics specified sit on the very highest bench of scholarship.

We have expressed our strong dissent from those who combine the two interrogations into one,—*What do we put forward then as a plea?* The adverbial negative expression (οὐ πάντως) which succeeds, is, as we have said, inconsistent with the coalition. And yet there is a reason why so many distinguished critics have proposed the amalgamation. Without it the verb is used *absolutely*. And such an absolute use of the word has been thought by them to be unlikely. But we see not why it should be viewed with philological suspicion. It is true, indeed, that in the comparatively limited number of passages in which the word is found in the middle voice, it is, as a matter of fact, almost always construed with the accusative of the object, or objects, *held forth*. Nevertheless, there is nothing in the nature of the word to render its use in an *absolute* way, an *a priori* improbability. And it is noticeable that the kindred word προβάλλομαι, which is so often employed by the old scholiasts and lexicographers to explain προέχομαι, is, in well-accredited cases, used absolutely. It is so, in reference to physical self-defence, in Demosthenes, for instance, 1*st Philip.* 51, when, in describing the *unscientific* way in which barbarians fight pugilistically, he says of "one of them," that προβάλλεσθαι δ' ἢ βλέπειν ἐναντίον οὔτ' οἶδεν οὔτ' ἐθέλει, *he has neither skill nor will* **to defend**

himself, (**to forefend himself,** viz., by proper fencing), *or to look his antagonist steadily in the face* (viz., so as to watch the eyes, and thus anticipate the movements of the hands). Xenophon, in his *Cyropaedia*, ii. 3. 10, uses the word in the same manner,—καὶ ἐγώ, ἔφη, ἐκ παιδίου εὐθὺς μὲν προβάλλεσθαι ἠπιστάμην πρὸ τούτου ὅτῳ ᾤμην πληγήσεσθαι,—*and I, said he, understood from a child how* **to put myself** *at once* **in a self-defending attitude—to fence**—*before any one from whom I anticipated a blow.* He acquired this "accomplishment" without training, he says. For, adds he, "so far from being trained to it, I was even punished, εἰ προβαλοίμην, *if I fenced.*" The absolute use, then, of προβάλλομαι is indisputable,—*to throw forward* (the hands or something else) *in self-defence.* And it seems to us that it is probable that προέχομαι is used similarly by Herodotus, ii. 42, where, in reference to the Egyptian ram-headed *Noum* (*Num* or *Chnum*) whom he designates *Jupiter*, he says that the Thebans allege "that Hercules (Hermes) wished exceedingly to see Jupiter, who, however, was unwilling to show himself; but that at length, on Hercules insisting, τὸν Δία μηχανήσασθαι, κριὸν ἐκδείραντα, προέχεσθαί τε τὴν κεφαλὴν ἀποταμόντα τοῦ κριοῦ, καὶ, ἐνδύντα τὸ νάκος, οὕτω οἱ ἑωυτὸν ἐπιδέξαι, *Jupiter contrived, having flayed a ram, both* **to screen himself,**—*having cut off the head of the ram* (and no doubt put it on, like a helmet),—*and, having enveloped himself in the skin, thus to show himself to him.* But, whatever may be made of this passage of Herodotus,* there can be no reasonable room for

* The passage,—assuming the correctness of the text,—is somewhat involved, interpret it as we may. It has puzzled considerably commentators and translators. The following are some of the English versions, which have been given to it :—

"*At last, Jupiter, yielding to his importunity, contrived this artifice :—Having separated the head from the body of a ram, and flayed the whole carcase, he put on the skin with the wool, and in that form showed himself to Hercules.*" Littlebury

"*In consequence of his repeated importunity, the god, in compliance, used the following artifice :—he cut off the head of a ram, and, covering himself with the skin, showed himself in that form to Hercules.*" Beloe

"*At last, in consequence of the earnest entreaties of Hercules, Jupiter made use of the following artifice :—having skinned a ram, and cut off the*

doubting that the word is used absolutely by the Apostle Paul in the passage before us, and that it means, *Do we put forth pleas in self-defence?* that is, *Do we defend ourselves (before the tribunal of God)?—Do we stand on the defensive (as regards our title to glory, honour, and immortality)?—Do we bring forward a plea in bar of a condemnatory sentence?—Do I, a Jew, bring forth a plea in behalf of the Jews?—Do we,* in this way, *screen ourselves?*

head, he placed it before him, and covering himself with the fleece, showed himself in that manner to him." Laurent

"*At length, as Hercules persisted in his endeavours, Jupiter adopted the following device:—flaying a ram, he put the horned scalp of the head he had severed on his own, and clothed himself with the fleece; thus attired he showed himself.*" Isaac Taylor

"*At length, when Hercules persisted, Jove hit on a device—to flay a ram, and, cutting off the head, hold the head before him, and cover himself with the fleece. In this guise he showed himself to Hercules.*"

Rawlinson

None of these translations are quite satisfactory. Littlebury and Beloe,—perplexed no doubt by the word,—take no account of it whatsoever. Laurent,—overlooking its dependence, as an infinitive, on μηχανήσασθαι, and the co-relative dependence of the succeeding ἑωυτὸν ἐπιδέξαι,—supposed that the word means that Jupiter *held* (*the head of the ram*) *before him.* Rawlinson,—though seeing the dependence of the first infinitive, at least, on μηχανήσασθαι, nevertheless took Laurent's view of its import. So did Schweighaeuser. So did Larcher. And yet the Egyptian god, to whom Herodotus is referring, is *ram-headed.* He does not merely *hold the head of a ram before him;* he *has it on him,* as if it were his own head. Isaac Taylor understood this, and, feeling persuaded that Herodotus could not be making any discordant representation, he has expressed the idea in his translation. But he has dexterously avoided, nevertheless, any reference to προέχεσθαι. He did not see the relation to μηχανήσασθαι of the two co-relative infinitives. But yet nothing seems more certain than that Baehr is right in affirming the conjoint dependence of these two infinitives, (*equidem infinitivos sequentes ab ipso verbo* μηχανήσασθαι *pendere dixerim*). Krüger, too, distinctly perceived the dependence of προέχεσθαι, (-μηχανήσασθαι προέχεσθαι *habe das Mittel, den Ausweg, ergriffen sich vorzuhalten*); but he missed the real import of the word. Herodotus and Paul mutually illustrate one another. Jupiter really *screened himself.* He *defended himself* (from the gaze of the too prying Hercules) by *having and holding before himself,* **all round and round his imperial head,** *the corresponding parts that constituted the head of the ram.* And yet *he showed himself,* in a sense,—enveloped and screened in the fleece of the ram.

We shall now pass on to consider the component parts of the verse in detail:—

§ 4. *What then?* (Τί οὖν;) In the *scholia* of Œcumenius there is hesitation expressed whether these words should be regarded as a distinct interrogation, or as welded with the following verb into one query. We have seen that not a few modern critics have adopted the welding plan,—reading the words in continuance,—ἐν συνεπείᾳ, as it is expressed by Œcumenius. And we might add to those already mentioned, Mace, Bolten, Heberden, Cox, Peile, &c. The fact, however, that the answer is adverbial, *not at all*, or *not altogether*, or *no certainly*, (οὐ πάντως), and not adjectival, *none at all*, (οὐδὲν πάντως), is, as we have intimated, decisive reason for the division of the introductory words into two distinct questions. The question, *What then?* is elliptical, and may be supplemented thus, *What is the case then?* (Τί οὖν ἐστίν; see Acts xxi. 22; 1 Cor. xiv. 15, 26), or, as Luther gives it, *What shall we say then?* (τί οὖν ἐροῦμεν;—see Rom. iv. 1; vi. 1; ix. 14, 30). The expression indicates a pause in the Apostle's reasoning, during which he, as it were, gathers himself up for a new start; while he is careful, at the same time, to quicken the intelligence of his readers into sympathy with himself, so as to carry them along with him. *What then?—How stands the case* (viz., *with us Jews*)? The particle *then* (οὖν) most naturally refers to the preceding paragraph (verses 1—8) as a whole; so that the mind is carried back, in its review, to the main idea of the paragraph,—namely, that the advantage possessed by the Jew, in his peculiar relations and institutions, is *much in every respect.*—"*What then?*" It is as if the Apostle were to say,—*Since it is the case that the prerogatives of the Jew, whatever use or abuse may be made of them, are much in every respect, what then?*

§ 5. *Do we bring forward pleas in behalf of ourselves?* i. e., *in bar of a sentence of condemnation against ourselves,* (προεχόμεθα;). The Apostle, in his pause, has re-entered into intercommunion of consciousness with his countrymen in general. In the preceding verse, in which he says, "as *we* be blasphemed," he was realizing his union, not, as Michaelis supposes, with his fellow-countrymen in general, but with his fellow-Christians in particular. In the 7th verse, again, in which he says, "why yet am even I judged as a sinner?" —he was throwing himself, in consciousness, into the far larger community of the mass of the human world, *why am even I, as a unit of the world at large, yet judged as a sinner?* But in the 5th verse he had, as now again in the 9th, identified himself, for logical purposes, with the mass of his countrymen, even although profoundly realizing their opposition to the Gospel of Christ,—"if *our* unrighteousness sets off the righteousness of God, (as it really does), what shall we say?" The Apostle, thus, in his large-heartedness and many-sidedness, finds, as it were, numerous doors in his own spirit which he can successively open, and out of which his sympathies can go, now toward his fellow-Christians of the Gentiles, now towards his fellow-Christians of the Jews, now toward all his fellow-Christians, whether Gentiles or Jews, now toward the mass of his countrymen, though, in general, unbelieving, and now toward the mass of his fellow-men at large. The rapidity with which he opens door after door in his spirit, and, communicating outward for a moment, shuts them again, sometimes occasions to the expositor a little difficulty in determining the specific attitude and direction of his consciousness. The lambent flame of his ardent spirit turns, flickeringly and rapidly, hither and thither. But in such a case as the present, the connection seems to make it evident that he is speaking, not, as Theodor Schott supposes, in the name of men in general, (*wir Menschen alle*), but in the name of Jews in general. He speaks in their name, and yet, as in verse 5th, he gives utterance rather to his own conception of the state of their case, than to theirs. He realizes, in consciousness, his union with the Jews in general; but he looks at their position from his own particular standpoint, and in his own peculiar light. And hence in asking, *Do we, in maintaining that the prerogative of the Jews is much in every respect, bring forth a plea for the justification of our moral state, and in defence of our right to everlasting life and glory in the kingdom of heaven?*—in asking this question, and in answering it as he does, (οὐ πάντως), he does not mean that there would be none among his countrymen who would be ready to defend themselves in judgement. He means that when he himself speaks in reference to them, and as far as possible in their behalf, and as one of them, he will not, and does not, and cannot, speak in the way of defence. He cannot plead, *Not Guilty.* He was profoundly convinced that guilt was attaching to himself for his own unrighteousness. And he was equally sure that it was attaching to all his countrymen, for theirs. Such is the significance of the Apostle's identification of himself with the mass of his countrymen when he says "we." We do not recognize in the fact,—with Calvin,—any evidence of what may strictly be called "a holy artifice," (*sanctum artificium*). We recognize, on the other hand, a perfectly unartificial simplicity of spontaneous intercommunion and sympathy.

§ 6. *No, certainly,* (οὐ πάντως). Such, perhaps, may be as good a translation as is practicable of the original expression. The negative adverb,—the *no,*—should be betoned in reading, so that the voice, after pausing upon it, may add, in an under-tone, and subordinately, the universal adverb, as an additament that is expressly intended to confirm the negation :—*No,—by all means no.* (See *Winer,* iii. 61, 4 f.) There is thus a shade of difference between the expression and our more peremptory negation, *not at all;* although the phrases are in some respects analogous. Οὐχ ὅλως and οὐ πάνυ are more precisely coincident with our *not at all,* or with the French *point du tout.* There is reason, indeed, to believe that the Apostle, reversing the order of the words, would have said πάντως οὐ, had he intended to bring out the precise idea which is indicated conventionally by our expression, *not at all,* or *by no means.* (See 1 Cor. xvi. 12; Hom. *Il.* viii. 450, &c.) Beza has put a comma between the adverbs, inasmuch as he looks upon them as transposed. Piscator follows in his wake. They render the expression, "by no means," (*nullo modo*). The version of the Vulgate corresponds, (*nequaquam*). Theophylact's explanation is identical, (οὐ πάντως, ἀντὶ οὐδαμῶς). Tyndale's version, followed by the Geneva and our Authorized English Version, is consentaneous:—*no, in no wyse.* But such a meaning of the two adverbs, when they are closely welded together, and in the order in which they stand in our text, is, to say the least of it, uncommon. (See, especially, Mehring, *in loc.*) The passages cited in support of it by Fritzsche, Meyer, Reiche, and others, are not quite decisive. (The passage from Theognis, 305, οἱ κακοὶ οὐ πάντως κακοὶ ἐκ γαστρὸς γεγόνασιν, seems simply to mean, "the evil were not, certainly, evil from birth:" and the passage from the Epistle to Diognetus, 9, οὐ πάντως ἐφηδόμενος τοῖς ἁμαρτήμασιν ἡμῶν, ἀλλ' ἀνεχόμενος, while undoubtedly susceptible of the translation, *by no means rejoicing in our sins,* may with equal propriety be rendered, **not, certainly, rejoicing** *over our sins, but enduring them.* The οὐ should be closely connected with the participle ἐφηδόμενος.) It is, at all events, the case, that in the overwhelming majority of instances in which the adverbs are welded together, in the order in which they stand before us, they mean, *not altogether, not wholly, not in every respect.* In other words, the negative qualifies and limits the universal: the universal does not (as in πάντως οὐ, and οὐ πάνυ, and οὐχ' ὅλως) explain and intensify the negative, by opening up, as it were, an unlimited field for the scope of the negation. This meaning of *not altogether* is apparently attached to the phrase in 1 Cor. v. 10,—the only other passage in the New Testament in which the combination occurs. The passage, at all events, cannot admit the translation, *not at all.* And in the passage before us, the translation, *not altogether, not in all respects,* has been given to the phrase by Grotius, Wetstein, Whitby, Wittich; Morus too, and Flatt; Köllner, also, and van Hengel, Matthias, Umbreit, Mehring, &c. But this rendering is, of course, inconsistent with the correct interpretation of the preceding verb.

§ 7. *For we before impeached both Jews and Greeks of*

being all under sin, (προῃτιασάμεθα γὰρ Ἰουδαίους τε καὶ Ἕλληνας πάντας ὑφ' ἁμαρτίαν εἶναι). This clause exhibits the reason, or at least a reason, why the Apostle, as a representative of the Jews, did not, and would not, and could not, put in pleas for them. It would be utter inconsistency to attempt any such defence: for he had in the preceding part of this very epistle,—namely, in chap. i. 18—32, and in chap. ii. 1—29,—"impeached both Jews and Gentiles of being all under sin," and maintained that they were *without excuse*, (ἀναπολόγητοι). See chap. i. 20; ii. 1. The *we*, involved in the verb, is of course *the Apostle himself*. The use of the plural in such a relationship as this, is, in his case, an instinct of modesty. He partially merges out of view his individuality. See chap. i. 5.

Erasmus Schmid takes a peculiar view of the verb, which we have rendered, *we before impeached*, (προῃτιασάμεθα). He regards it as being in the passive;—*We have been already impeached*, namely, *by the law*, (*jam ante-accusati sumus per legem*): and he adds that he will not criticise, because he does not understand, Beza's translation, *ante criminati sumus*, (*we before impeached*). Good Homer, we presume, had been nodding.

Instead of the compound verb, "we *before* accused," (προῃτιασάμεθα), the MSS. D* and G read, *we impeached*, (ᾐτιασάμεθα). The Vulgate version corresponds, (*causati sumus*); and so the Italic, as represented in the MSS. d. e. g. Mill approves of the reading (*Proleg.* 450), and imagines that some scholiast had added the preposition *before* (πρό) to make the reference to the preceding part of the epistle more express. But, as the variation occurs in those codices which present the most corrupt reading of the preceding clause of the verse, we think that the other critical editors have done wisely in dissenting from the opinion of Mill, and retaining the compound verb.

The word is translated in our Authorized Version, *we have before proved*. Tyndale, followed by the Geneva, had given a similar translation, *we have already proved*. Luther's version had led the way, "we have proved above," (*wir haben droben bewiesen*). Wycliffe's was similar,—*we have schewid by skile.* Göschen's translation corresponds, (*antea enim probavimus*). The Peshito is analogous, *we have before determined*, or *decided*, as both Etheridge and Murdock translate the term, or *concluded*, as Reusch renders it. (ܩܪܡܢ ܓܝܪ ܦܣܩܢ). Dionsyius à Ryckel's version corresponds, (*rationabilitur declaravimus*). But such a way of rendering the word is aside from the precise idea of the original. For the reference is not to logical demonstration, but to forensic accusation. Calvin noticed this, (*verbum* αἰτιᾶσθαι, *quod hic usurpat Paulus, proprie est judiciale: ideoque reddere placuit* **Constituimus**). And Grotius, too, caught the true idea, (*accusationem praestruximus*). So did Vitringa, (*Paulus moeste hier gelijk als een seeker Landsfiscaal of Procureur aangemerkt worden, welke alle menschen voor de rechterstoel Gods daagt, en haar proces maakt, en over wandevoir of eenige misdaad beschuldigt*). So did Bengel, (*Paulus agit, cap.* 1 *et* 2, *tanquam severus Procurator justitiæ divinæ*). So de Paris, (*C'est un terme de plaidoirie*). The simple verb properly means *to charge as being the cause* (*the* αἰτία) *of some evil*, that is, *to accuse, to impeach, to criminate.* The term, as Day remarks, "is a law term, and is usually said of those which are accusers, who accuse or charge the defendant with what they have to say against him." (Hesychius, hence, says, αἰτιᾶται, μέμφεται.)

The verb has for its objects (and governed in the accussative case) the words *both the Jews and the Greeks*, (Ἰουδαίους τε καὶ Ἕλληνας), or, as the Peshito characteristically renders it, *both the Jews and the Aramaeans;* that is, *both the Jews and the Gentiles.* See chap. i. 16; ii. 9, 10; &c. There has been much discussion about the import of the connective particles (τε καί), and whether the clause should be rendered *the Jews as well as the Greeks*, or, *not only the Jews, but also the Greeks.* Mehring contends for the former; Matthias for the latter. But a more comprehensive view will lead to the conclusion that the expression is absolutely identical neither with the one translation nor with the other, (see Acts xv. 9; Rom. x. 12; Heb. xi. 32; &c.); though, of course, it is here, when exegetically viewed, coincident with the former. Compare Rom. i. 14; 1 Cor. i. 2; Acts v. 14; viii. 12; ix. 6; xiv. 5; &c. It simply means *both Jews and Greeks.*

The appended clause, *of being all under sin,* (πάντας ὑφ' ἁμαρτίαν εἶναι), is epexegetical, and expressive of the matter of the impeachment. The word *all* (πάντας) is the subject of the epexegetical clause, and, in the Greek, is the accusative before the infinitive:—*that all are under sin.* It gathers up into unity, and spreads out into universality, the contents of the two preceding words, *Jews* and *Greeks.* The Apostle had impeached the two classes indifferently, and all in the two classes, of being *under sin.* The expression, *under sin,* (ὑφ' ἁμαρτίαν), is pictorially significant. By a natural personification,—specially familiar to the mind of our Apostle,—sin is represented as being the lord of the sinner. For the moment that a man commits sin he makes a slave of himself, and is liable for ever afterwards, unless divine mercy interpose, to be under the lash of retribution. In this respect, all men indifferently, whether Jews or Gentiles, are, as the Gospel finds them, *under sin;* for, as Adam correctly remarks, "being *under sin,* and being *condemned,* are equivalent." Thus the phrase, *to be under sin,* is not, as Fritzsche would have it, absolutely identical with *to be sinners,* (*idem valet quod* ἁμαρτωλὸν εἶναι *sive* ἁμαρτάνειν. Cajetan justly remarks, *significantius dicit* **sub peccato esse,** *et non dicit* **peccatores esse** *aut* **peccasse**). Neither does it mean, as Grotius supposes, "to be addicted to peculiarly heinous vices," (*significat, gravibus vitiis addictos esse*). And hence also the word *all* is not, as the same great critic and Rosenmüller suppose, to be interpreted as meaning *the greater part,* (*de plerisque*). Neither is it, as Oltramare will have it, to be interpreted of "the ideal persons, the categories, to wit, of Jews and Gentiles," (*les personnes idéales, les catégories Juifs et Païens*); but doubtless of the real, unabstracted individuals who are objectively referred to when we subjectively classify into categories the responsible members of the human family.

VER. 10. καθὼς γέγραπται ὅτι οὐκ ἔστιν δίκαιος, οὐδὲ εἷς·

Eng. Auth. Vers. *As it is written, There is none righteous, no, not one:*

Revised Version. *As it has been written, There is none righteous, not even one:*

§ 1. *As it has been written,* (καθὼς γέγραπται). The Apostle having mentioned that he had "impeached both Jews and Gentiles of being *all* under sin," adduces documentary evidence of the legitimacy of his impeachment. He appeals to *the Volume of the book,—the Law and the Testimony,—the Old Testament Scriptures;* and shows that his accusation was in perfect accordance with what stood written in the record. "And hence," as Calvin remarks, "ministers of the Gospel may learn what is their duty. For if Paul is careful to assert no doctrine, without immediately confirming it out of Scripture, much less should the attempt be made by those who have no other commission than to proclaim the Gospel, which they have received through the hands of Paul and of others." (*Atque hinc discant ecclesiastici doctores, quale suum sit officium. Nam si nullum dogma hic asserit Paulus, quod non Scripturae certo oraculo simul confirmet, multo minus illud ipsum tentandum est iis, quibus nihil aliud est mandatum, quam ut evangelium praedicent, quod per Pauli et aliorum manus acceperunt.*) This remark of Calvin is but the condensation of a similar remark by Origen.

§ 2. The Apostle strings together into a cluster a variety of detached Old Testament statements, which bear, more or less directly, upon his process of impeachment. The cluster embraces verses 10—18. It was the custom of Jewish Rabbis to form such clusters of quotations:—(see Surenhusius, βίβλος καταλλαγῆς, *thesis* 7, *de Modis*):—and the same custom, we presume, will prevail more or less among all who have occasion to make appeal to documents of authority.

§ 3. The passages adduced are, as we shall find, generally quoted from the Septuagint version. But they are not slavishly or strictly transcribed. They are given in a free and easy manner; and bear marks, in the forms they assume, of the plastic energy of the mind through which they passed. The substance of thought is invariably given, as the Apostle found it on the ancient page; but the shaping of the substance is, in some cases, considerably modified during the process of transmission.

§ 4. There is an appreciable method in the arrangement of the quotations. They are grouped. In verses 10—12 the universality of sin is affirmed, and some of its universal characteristics pointed out. In verses 13, 14, certain prevalent phases of sin are, representatively, specified:—namely, social transgressions in words. In verses 15—17 certain other prevalent phases of sin are, also representatively, specified: — namely, social transgressions in those works which may be distinguished from words. In verse 18 a general and God-ward phase of sin is exhibited,—a phase which consists in a moral privation, and which may be regarded as being, to a great extent, the source of the social sins in words and works which are specified in verses 13—17.

§ 5. Howard Hinton—carrying out into exaggeration an idea of Taylor—supposes that the whole paragraph which contains the quotations,—namely, verses 10—18,—is displaced, and should have been introduced after the 24th verse of the second chapter. He thinks that in its present position it is "irrelevant;" but that, nevertheless, it was the Apostle himself who stuck it in at the wrong place. He supposes that the inspired writer was going to quote the passages, immediately after verse 24 of chap. ii., "but from the actual quotation, something in the course of his thoughts at the moment turned him aside." Hence in this critic's translation of the epistle, *the passage is transposed to the situation which, as he conceived, it should have originally occupied.* This is indeed to turn the epistle into a nose of wax. But the critical libertinism of the worthy commentator is baseless. It rests upon a threefold misunderstanding,—a misunderstanding, (1), of the reference of chap. ii. 24; (2), of the import of chap. iii. 9; and, (3), of the contextual exigencies and congruities of both of these passages.

§ 6. It is noteworthy that the entire cluster of quotations contained in verses 10—18 is found, just as the Apostle gives it, in the 14th Psalm,—as the Psalm stands in the common editions of the Vulgate, and in some editions of the Septuagint, and in the Roman, Arabic, Ethiopic, and English Psalters. It is incorporated in the Vatican MS. of the Septuagint, though omitted in the Alexandrian. (Jowett incorrectly says that it is "in the Alexandrian MS.") It is not found in the Chaldee Paraphrase, nor in the Syriac version. Origen was aware that it was a compilation from various parts of Scripture. Some of the older advocates of the superiority of the Vulgate version to the Hebrew text (Comp. Ferrandus, &c.) contend that the Hebrew text of the Psalm,—which does not contain verses 13—18 of the Epistle, —is mutilated. But this idea has been for long abandoned by all competent Roman Catholic critics, such as Dionysius à Ryckel, Cajetan, Este, Natalis, Klee, Reithmayr, Maier, Bisping, &c. It was some ignoramus, says Cardinal Cajetan, who attached the cluster of passages to the 14th Psalm, (*sed ignorans nescio quis adjunxit haec psalmo decimoquarto*). Jerome, in his preface to the 16th Book of his *Commentary on Isaiah*, speaks in a similar manner,—characterizing the patching of the Psalm as the work of those who did not understand the Apostle's method of interweaving his Old Testament testimonies, (*qui artem contexendarum inter se Scripturarum Apostoli nesciebant*). He admits, however, that when the fact of the discrepancy between the Hebrew Psalm and the Septuagint version then in use, was first pointed out to him by his favourite pupil, Eustochium, the daughter of the noble Paula, he felt stunned as if he had been struck by the hand of a powerful boxer, (*quasi a fortissimo pugile percussus essem, coepi tacitus aestuare, et stuporem mentis vultus pallore signare*). The passages, in detail, are actually found elsewhere; though not all in the Psalms (as Shepherd alleges).

§ 7. *There is none righteous, not even one,* (ὅτι οὐκ ἔστιν δίκαιος, οὐδὲ εἷς :—*there is not a righteous* (*person*), *not one:* —*a righteous* (*person*) *is not, not even one.* Wycliffe's version is, *there is not ony man just.*—We cannot reproduce, to an absolute nicety, in our English idiom, the precise phase of the original.

The introductory particle (ὅτι) is untranslatable in English, if the quotation, as is most probable, be given in the direct form. In that case the particle is merely *recitative,* (see ver. 8th), and performs the function of a verbal finger-post, —pointing forward to what is to come. It somewhat corresponds, as Philippi remarks, to the quotational colon in German (:). The analogy, at least, holds good so far as the relation to the eye is concerned. But the Greek has the advantage in being equally serviceable to the ear. When Philippi compares it, still further, to our modern *inverted commas,* he unduly stretches his comparison; for the *inverted commas* mark off the ending as well as the beginning of quotations. (*Die Conjunktion* ὅτι *dient zur Anführung, etwa wie unser Colon oder Anführungszeichen.*) The particle is omitted altogether in Chrysostom's text, and in many of the cursive manuscripts. And Mill has condemned it, (ὅτι *perperam insertum est,* Proleg. 1204). But doubtless the great critic judged injudiciously. And when he appeals to the Syriac version in support of his judgement, he mistakes: for the analogue of the demonstrative is found there (ܕ); as also in the Vulgate (*quia*); and the particle itself is found in the great manuscriptural authorities.

Some expositors, however, have supposed that the words, *There is none righteous, not even one,* are not a quotation at all, but are intended to be the Apostle's own summation of the quotations which follow in verses 11—18, and thus of the teaching of the Old Testament Scriptures in general, in reference to the moral state of men. They would consequently regard the introductory particle as having its ordinary demonstrative import:—"As it is written *that there is not a righteous person, not one.*" This is the view that is taken by Calvin, and Brown of Wamphray; by Koppe too, and by Köllner, and Fritzsche; by Hurgronje too, (*De membrorum concinnitate in Pauli ad Rom. epist.*), and by Oltramare; and partially by Klee. Tholuck, too, supported it in his 1st, 2d, and 3d editions; but he subsequently renounced it. It is improbable; inasmuch as the words, *there is not a righteous person, not one,* correspond as nearly and literally to the conclusion of verse 1st of Psalm xiv. as the words of the 11th verse correspond to the 2d verse of the Psalm. It is probable, therefore, that the Apostle was giving a free rendering of the concluding clause of the 1st verse of the Psalm :—*there is none that doeth good.* It is noticeable, moreover, that when the formula, *as it stands written,* (καθὼς γέγραπται), is, in other passages, *prefixed* by the Apostle to any remark, that remark is invariably a quotation in the direct form. (In Rom. ii. 24, the formula is *postfixed;* and there is, besides, no ὅτι. The two passages are in no wise analogous cases.) Oltramare admits the universality of the rule; but says that in no case but the one before us is the formula succeeded by the demonstrative conjunction (ὅτι), and that hence an exception to the general rule is intended. He is mistaken, however, in his statement of facts, for the demonstrative conjunction does follow the formula in Rom. iv. 17; viii. 36. We seem shut up, then, to regard the words succeeding the demonstrative particle as a direct quotation.

Cocceius supposed that the quotation was taken from Eccles. vii. 20,—"There is not a righteous man upon earth, that doeth good, and sinneth not," (ἄνθρωπος οὐκ ἔστι δίκαιος ἐν τῇ γῇ, ὃς ποιήσει ἀγαθὸν καὶ οὐχ' ἁμαρτήσεται). Vitringa adopted Cocceius's opinion. So Wittich. Mussus had had the same idea: and also Cajetan. But the purely subordinate relation of the first clause of the affirmation in Ecclesiastes to the last,—"who will do good and will not sin" (אֲשֶׁר יַעֲשֶׂה־טּוֹב וְלֹא יֶחֱטָא)—makes it utterly improbable that the Apostle's mind could be referring to it. There is no good reason for doubting that the general opinion of expositors, both ancient and modern, is correct,—that the Apostle is quoting from the first verse of the 14th Psalm.

The passage, as it stands in the psalm, is simply, *there is none that doeth good*, (אֵין עֹשֵׂה־טוֹב). But it is rendered, with reduplicating emphasis, in the Septuagint, *there is none that doeth goodness, there is not so much as one*, (οὐκ ἔστι ποιῶν χρηστότητα, οὐκ ἔστιν ἕως ἑνός). The reduplicative element may probably have been suggested by the third verse, which is quoted by the Apostle in his 12th verse. It is, however, an element that concerns, not the substance, but merely the form of the statement; and hence the Apostle was thoroughly justified in adopting it. He nevertheless abbreviates it, (οὐδὲ εἷς). And instead of that specific aspect of *righteousness*, which is exhibited in *doing goodness*, he generalizes the expression, though he retains the exact essence of idea, and says, *there is none righteous.*

We need not here analyze the 14th Psalm as a whole. Neither need we investigate its aim as a whole. Nor need we speculate as to the occasion of its composition. Nor need we consider why it is repeated, with minute variations, in Psalm liii., (which is regarded by Thrupp as the original copy). These matters belong to the expositor of the Psalms. It suffices for us that the quotation made by the Apostle in this and the two succeeding verses is emphatically to the point. Grotius holds, indeed, that the asseveration, *there is none righteous, no, not one*, is "hyperbolical." And many critics are puzzled with the expression. D. G. Herzog imagines that David is speaking of his enemies alone. Origen supposes that the expression is used comparatively: *compared with God, for example, none is righteous.* Day has recourse to a *mystical*, as distinguished from the *historical*, sense of the words. Belsham suggests that "possibly the Psalmist had too bad an opinion" of the persons whom he describes! De Saci, on the other hand, not content with the natural comprehensiveness of the phraseology, insists on jumping into the unoccupied space beyond, and maintains that there is an intentional description even of *the infant who has just been born*, (**il n'y en a pas un seul,** *non pas même l'enfant qui ne fait que de naître*). But we see no necessity for either leaping into Charybdis or dashing upon Scylla. As we discover no reference to infants on the one hand, so we discover no hyperbole on the other. The Apostle's standpoint, while he was engaged in echoing the Psalmist's affirmations, seems sufficiently obvious. *Every man living needs the Gospel;* for, *apart from the influence of the Gospel, every man living is sinful.* No man living is, in his moral character, in all its inward, outward, and upward relations, what he ought to have been: that is to say, *he is not righteous.*

VER. 11. *οὐκ ἔστιν ὁ συνιῶν· οὐκ ἔστιν ὁ ἐκζητῶν τὸν Θεόν.*

Eng. Auth. Vers. *There is none that understandeth, there is none that seeketh after God.*

Revised Version. *there is none who understandeth: there is none who is seeking out God.*

§ 1. *there is none who is understanding,* (**οὐκ ἔστιν ὁ συνιῶν**) :—literally, *the understanding* (*man*) *is not,* that is, *the understanding man is not to be found.* Wycliffe gives it, —"Ther is not a man undirstondinge." From the standing-point both of the Psalmist and of the Apostle, and indeed of all the Biblical writers, every man is *deficient in understanding* (ἀσύνετος—see Rom. i. 21, 31) who does not apply his intelligence to the things which concern his relations to God;—so as to be guided aright in his conduct in reference to God. "The fear of the Lord is the beginning of knowledge" (Prov. i. 7) and "of *wisdom,*" (Prov. ix. 10). All the finite objects on which the intelligence may terminate are but intended to be the rounds of a ladder by which the mind may mount up to God. He who does not mount by means of these objects, *does not understand, is not wise.* He has not grasped the realities of things, in their true relations. He does not construe aright the lesson which is spread out before him. (*La terre* *est pleine de personnes habiles dans toutes les sciences, et dans tous les arts; de Philosophes, d' Orateurs, &c. Cependant parmi tant de personnes intelligentes aux yeux des hommes, Dieu ne voit que des aveugles, des insensés, des gens sans lumiere et sans raison; puisqu' ils ne s'occupent point de la seule chose qui leur est absolument nécessaire.*—De Paris.)

The article before the participle is omitted by Lachmann, (οὐκ ἔστιν συνίων). He is supported by A B G. But as it is found in ℵ D E K L, as also in Chrysostom, Theodoret, Theophylact, and Œcumenius; and as, moreover, A introduces it before the participle in the second clause of the verse; and as, besides, its insertion lends a fine emphasis to the quotations; we agree with de Wette, Fritzsche, Scholz, Tischendorf, &c., in approving of its admission. (It may also be noticed that Lachmann accentuates the participle, as from συνίω,—συνίων. Winer agrees,—ii. 14, 3. But almost all other editors accentuate it, as from συνιέω,—συνιῶν. Either accentuation is admissible. See Fritzsche, in loc. Both forms are equivalent to συνιεῖς, from συνίημι. The accentuation which is found in D***, and which is reproduced in Hahn, viz., συνιών, is a blunder, as συνιών is from σύνειμι.)

§ 2. *there is none who is seeking out God,* (οὐκ ἔστιν ὁ ἐκζητῶν τὸν θεόν):—*the diligent seeker for God is not.* The verb is translated *diligently seek,* in Heb. xi. 6; and *carefully seek,* in Heb. xii. 17. (It corresponds to דָּרַשׁ in Hebrew, and also to בִּקֵּשׁ.) The employment of the verb, in relation to God as its object, proceeds on the assumption that God cannot "by searching," be fully "found out." He stretches out illimitably before the investigating mind; and therefore may be more and more discovered in his essential perfections and infinitely complicated relations. He is sought out, progressively and continuously, of all who realize the true end of human life. But there are none except those whose hearts are touched more or less powerfully by the Gospel of God's grace, who thus know themselves, and understand the *whys* and *wherefores* of their being;—and there are consequently none, but these exceptional persons, who make it their constant business *to seek out God.*

This second clause of the verse, in virtue of its parallelism with the first, exhibits negatively what it is which constitutes a right condition of the understanding. It is that attitude or exercise of the intelligence which is realized in *seeking out God.*

(Lachmann inserts within brackets the article before the participle,—[ὁ] ἐκζητῶν. The article is omitted in B E, but is found in A as well as in ℵ D E K L. See on the first clause of the verse.)

§ 3. The quotation, as already stated, is taken from Psalm xiv. 2, (= liii. 2): but, like the quotation in the preceding verse, it is given in a free and easy manner, and thus presents, as to its form, a considerable difference from the form which it sustains in the Psalm. Its form in the Psalm is the following:—" The Lord looked down from heaven upon the children of men, to see if there were any that did understand, and seek God," (κύριος ἐκ τοῦ οὐρανοῦ διέκυψεν ἐπὶ τοὺς υἱοὺς τῶν ἀνθρώπων τοῦ ἰδεῖν εἰ ἔστι συνιῶν ἢ ἐκζητῶν τὸν θεόν.—יְהוָה מִשָּׁמַיִם הִשְׁקִיף עַל־בְּנֵי־אָדָם לִרְאוֹת הֲיֵשׁ מַשְׂכִּיל דֹּרֵשׁ אֶת־אֱלֹהִים׃) As, however, the Lord's all-seeing eye discovered no one who was *rightly exercising his understanding, and seeking out God*, the Apostle contents himself with expressing this result :—" there is none who understandeth, there is none who searches out God."

VER. 12. Πάντες ἐξέκλιναν· ἅμα ἠχρεώθησαν· οὐκ ἔστιν ποιῶν χρηστότητα, οὐκ ἔστιν ἕως ἑνός.

Eng. Auth. Vers. *They are all gone out of the way, they are together become unprofitable; there is none that doeth good, no, not one.*

Revised Version. *All turned aside; together they became* *corrupt; there is none doing goodness, there is not so much as one.*

§ 1. This verse is an exact transcript of the Septuagint version of the first clause of Ps. xiv. 3. It repeats, intensifyingly, the idea of the preceding verse;—giving prominence, under a variation of aspect, to the universality of human sinfulness. The Septuagint version is a faithful reflection of the original Hebrew, (הַכֹּל סָר יַחְדָּו נֶאֱלָחוּ אֵין עֹשֵׂה־טוֹב אֵין גַּם־אֶחָד—*The whole have turned aside; they have together become corrupt; there is none doing good; there is not even one.* There seems to be an interesting etymological filament of connection between our English word *whole* and the Hebrew כֹּל, as well as between both and the Greek ὅλος. The substantive use of *whole* is strikingly coincident with כֹּל).

§ 2. *All turned aside*, (πάντες ἐξέκλιναν). The expression is abrupt, and hence the reader is left to supply out of his own resources,—taking, of course, the context into account,—what it is from which the deviation or swerving has been made. "They are all gone *out of the way*," say our English translators: "out *of the right way*," say Maurer, Hupfeld, de Wette, Meyer, &c. (Similarly Zinzendorf, *aus dem Gleisse.*) "Out of *the way of true happiness*," says de Lyra. The Chaldee Paraphrast explains the expression thus,—"all have turned *backward*" (לַאֲחוֹרָא). Geier again, Seb. Schmidt, Rückert, Oltramare, &c., make the supplement thus,—"all have turned aside *from God*." The lines of the two interpretations meet. But the antithesis to the last clause of the preceding verse rather favours, upon the whole, the second of the two views of the relativity. Or, perhaps, we might express it more precisely thus:—"all turned aside *from the way that leads to God,—the way in which God is to be sought and found.*" When Pareus interprets the expression as denoting "apostasy from God, and from his law and worship, *to idolatry*," he unnecessarily narrows the reference, and consequently the application, of the words.

Bengel has a little doctrinal remark in connection with the

verb, "turned aside." "It supposes," he says, "that all were formerly right," (*omnes antea rectos fuisse*). But it would be more precise to say, that the expression only implies that there was a time when all *began to go wrong.* Men were set down by God in such a position *that they should and might have stepped in the right direction.* "Man once stood," says Origen, "in the right way," (*non dicitur declinasse, nisi is, qui aliquando in via recta stetit*). But he "turned aside." The verb used by the Psalmist (סָר) is most frequently rendered *turned aside* in our English version; but also frequently *departed.* When used in reference to moral action, it may denote *the turning aside from evil to good,* as well as *the turning aside from good to evil.* See Ps. xxxiv. 14; xxxvii. 27. Here, of course, it is employed *in malam partem.*

It is to be noticed that, while in the preceding verse the present state of men is described, in this,—so far as the first clause of the verse is concerned,—there is a reference to their past evil actions, as furnishing the natural antecedents of their present character. Whithersoever the all-seeing Eye turned its gaze,—whether to what was still happening in the moral life of men, or to what had happened before,—the scene was equally melancholy; and part sadly corresponded to part.

§ 3. *together they became corrupt,—together they became useless:* (ἅμα ἠχρεώθησαν.) The word *together* (ἅμα) intensifies the adjective *all,* which runs forward in its influence from the preceding clause. (*Ad* ἅμα *e superioribus mente repete* πάντες,–Fritzsche.) *All, in union, became useless: all, as in concert, became useless; all, as it were unanimously, became useless.* Bengel interprets the adverb as meaning, *at one time,* (*uno tempore.* Compare Hesychius, ἐν τῷ αὐτῷ χρόνῳ). But, instead of viewing it in the light of its current classical import, it is better to regard it as the analogue of the corresponding Hebrew word יַחְדָּו—compare יַחַד, *union,* and אֶחָד, *one*). Viewed in this light it is reproduced, almost to a nicety, in our English *together,* (Wycliffe, *to gidere*); which is a much better analogue for the term than the expression *at once.*

The Peshito version connects the adverb with the preceding clause :—"all turned aside together, *and* were reprobated." But the Hebrew parallelism, as well as the Masoretic punctuation, demands that it be connected with the verb that follows.

They became useless, — (ἠχρεώθησαν), — useless, says Pelagius, "for the work for which they were brought into being," (*inutiles ad opus ad quod fuerunt procreati*). "We call that useless," says Thomas Aquinas, "which does not answer its end," (*hoc enim inutile dicimus, quod non sequitur finem suum*). The expression implies that men are created, in order that they may voluntarily devote themselves to certain definite activities, which should all point, in their aim, toward the glory of God. When these activities are perverted, men are so corrupt as to be *useless* in the world, as far, at least, as their voluntary agency is concerned. If they be not absolutely useless, no thanks to them. They are passive in the matter ; and are turned to account only in virtue of the resources of infinite wisdom and power. They are gone to waste. They are like meat or drink that has become rancid or sour,—corrupt. This is the idea that is suggested by the Hebrew word employed by the Psalmist, (נֶאֱלָחוּ); and which is, however, rather strongly translated *filthy* in our English version. (See Job xv. 16, as well as Ps. xiv. 3; liii. 3.)

(Tischendorf in his 1857 edition reads the verb ἠχρεώθησαν, on the authority of A B D G. The same is the reading of א. In his 1849 edition he had read, along with the Textus Receptus, Griesbach, Lachmann, &c., ἠχρειώθησαν.)

4. *there is none doing goodness, there is not so much as one*, (οὐκ ἔστιν ποιῶν χρηστότητα, οὐκ ἔστιν ἕως ἑνός). There is a relation in the original between the *goodness* (χρηστότης) which none is doing, and men's consequent *uselessness* in the universe, (ἀχρεία). That which is really *useful* in the universe is *good*, and nothing else is *good*. But the goodness that is dependent on choice,—as indeed all moral goodness must ultimately be,—is, in its heart or essence, a modification of that "love" which, in the case of moral creatures, is "the

fulfilling of the law." Hence this "goodness" is, in a large acceptation of the term, "kindness,"—the translation which the word receives in Eph. ii. 7; Col. iii. 12; Tit. iii. 4; 2 Cor. vi. 6. See Rom. ii. 4.

The emphatic additament, "There is not so much as one," (οὐκ ἔστιν ἕως ἑνός), is somewhat ambiguous in the Greek, as also in the Latin, (*non est usque ad unum*, translated by Wycliffe, *ther is not til to oon*); and hence Augustin, who was ignorant of Hebrew, supposed that there might be, in the expression, *an exception of one*, namely, Christ, (*iste est melior intellectus, ut nemo intelligatur fecisse bonitaten usque ad Christum.* **Enarr.** in Psalm, in loc.) When Seb. Schmidt says, however, that Beza made the same mistake, he unaccountably errs; for Beza expressly, and in all his editions, points out Augustin's mistake, and adds, "of such moment is it to draw truth from the fountain," (*Tanti est momenti ex fontibus ipsis veritatem haurire*). There is no ambiguity in the Hebrew, (אֵין גַּם־אֶחָד—*there is not even one*).

(It will be noticed that the construction of the clause, οὐκ ἔστιν ποιῶν χρηστότητα, is different from the corresponding clauses of verse 11th. There is no article before the participle, though it is found in ℵ D E. The second οὐκ ἔστιν is omitted by B, and in the Syriac version. These are trifling variations, incident to the imperfections of transcribers.)

VER. 13. Τάφος ἀνεῳγμένος ὁ λάρυγξ αὐτῶν· ταῖς γλώσσαις αὐτῶν ἐδολιοῦσαν. Ἰὸς ἀσπίδων ὑπὸ τὰ χείλη αὐτῶν.

Eng. Auth. Vers. *Their throat is an open sepulchre; with their tongues they have used deceit; the poison of asps is under their lips.*

Revised Version. *Their throat is a sepulchre opened; with their tongues they were using deceit. The poison of asps is under their lips.*

§ 1. The quotation contained in verses 10—12 is the evidence proper which establishes the harmony that subsists between the teaching of the Old Testament Scriptures and the position of the Apostle—*That all men, without exception, are under sin.* The evidence is decisive and cumulative. And, as Jonathan Edwards remarks, "if the words which the Apostle uses do not most fully and determinately signify an universality, no words ever used in the Bible are sufficient to do it." (*Original Sin*, ii. 3, 2.) "If," says Cartwright, "the Prophet and Apostle had laid their heads together, to have found out the most forcible words, and most significative, to shut all men, born of the seed of men, from righteousness, and to shut them under sin, they could not have used more effectual speeches than these." (*Annot. in loc.*) Clause is repetitiously piled upon clause, to the effect that "all have sinned and come short of the glory of God." The passages which are quoted, in continuation, in verses 13—17, are *tacked on* to the quotation from the 14th Psalm; and *not as containing additional Scripture-evidence of the universality of sin*, but as exhibiting, in graphic touches,—and distributively, as Zwinger remarks,—*representative specimens of the very varied forms into which the essential principle of sin has, in its universal range, developed itself.* The reference more particularly is, as Melancthon observed, to breaches of the second table of the law. (*Annot.*)

§ 2. The first two clauses of the 13th verse are quoted verbatim from the Septuagint version of the 9th (10th) verse of the 5th Psalm. The third clause is taken from Psalm cxl. 3 (4), and is likewise an exact transcript of the Septuagint translation.

§ 3. *Their throat is a sepulchre opened,* (τάφος ἀνεῳγμένος ὁ λάρυγξ αὐτῶν);—*their throat is a sepulchre that has been opened,—that is standing open,* (ἀνεῳγμένος). The formal notation of comparison is omitted; but the meaning is, of course, "their throat is *as* a sepulchre standing open." In the expression, *their throat,* (ὁ λάρυγξ αὐτῶν), we are not to look for a precisely definite, and still less for a precisely scientific, reference to the special part of the organism, lying back of the cavity of the mouth, which is appropriated to the production of voice. The Greek word employed is, indeed, the term which is now, in the technical language of anatomists, the designation of that particular portion of the organism by means of which the production of vocal sounds takes place. But in ancient times the *larynx* and *pharynx* were not accurately discriminated. (See Aristot. *Hist. An.* i. 12. 1; iv. 9. 1; *Part. An.* iii. 3. 1; see also Hesychius's *Lex.*, and Suidas. Phavorinus says, λάρυγξ καὶ φάρυγξ ταὐτόν.) Thomas Magister says that it is by the *larynx* that we swallow, and by the *pharynx* that we speak, (ἔστι δὲ φάρυγξ μὲν ἡ τῆς φωνῆς διέξοδος, λάρυγξ δὲ ἡ τῶν σιτίων εἴσοδος). But the author of the *Etymologicum Magnum* reverses the distinction, and affirms that it is by the *larynx* that we speak, and by the *pharynx* that we swallow, (λάρυγξ μὲν, δι' οὗ λαλοῦμεν, καὶ διαπνέομεν, φάρυγξ δὲ, δι' οὗ ἐσθίομεν καὶ πίνομεν). It is well, therefore, that the general word *throat*, which designates the part which contains *both the thoroughfares*, should be retained as the translation of the term employed. Wycliffe gives it; and the subsequent translators wisely repeat it. The Hebrew term used by the Psalmist (גָּרוֹן) is at least as indeterminate as the term employed by the Septuagint translator. (Compare Ezek. xvi. 11; Jer. ii. 25; Ps. cxv. 7; Isa. lviii. 1.) But it certainly embraced, within the indeterminate sweep of its reference, that part of the organism through which we breathe, and speak, and *groan*. And it was because it fitly suggested the organ of voice, that it was employed by the Psalmist in the passage quoted by the Apostle.

When *their throat* is compared to *a sepulchre that has been opened*, or *that is standing open*, the ground of the comparison may be taken in two ways. Pelagius supposed that the reference is to the contaminating influence of the fœtid and pestilential effluvia which issue from opened tombs. (*Fœtore doctrinae suae, et adulatione* (*pestilentia?*) *contaminans et interficiens audientes.*) Origen's idea was kindred; only he thought that the expression is designed to designate the bold impudence of those who make no secret of their impurity, but expose it to view, (*qui immunditias suas et impuritates in propatulo habent*). And the same notion has been attached to the comparison by a large proportion of expositors, such as de Lyra, Bullinger, Hunnius, Vitringa; Seb. Schmidt too, and Spener, Este, Bengel; Stengel also, and Stuart, Haldane, Sumner, Wardlaw, Vaughan, Stephen, D. Brown, &c. But when we consider the context of the psalm from which the quotation is made, and notice that the reference is, most probably, not so much to licentious persons, whose conversation was corrupt and corrupting, as to malignant enemies who thirsted for blood, and therefore counselled death: and when, besides, we take into account the use made of the same simile by Jeremiah (v. 16), in relation to the Chaldeans,—"their quiver is as an open sepulchre," in which there can be no reference to tainting or noisome exhalations; we seem to be shut up to the conclusion that the expression means,—*their throat, like an open sepulchre, is ready to swallow up and devour*. In the use that is made of it,—*as an organ of speech*,—it is a pitfall,—a burial-place. Death and destruction are in it. This is the interpretation of Ambrosiaster, and of Calvin, (*guttur eorum sepulchrum esse apertum, id est, voraginem ad homines perdendos*); of Grotius too, and de Saci; and likewise of Rückert, Fritzsche, Meyer, Köllner, Oltramarc, &c. The character of those persons is pourtrayed, who are ready, in what they say of others, to consign to destruction either their persons, or their prospects, or their peace, or their reputation. They are intent,—for the purpose of gratifying their malignity,—on ingulphing all that is valuable in the objects of their envy or enmity. "Their tongue," as John Trapp expresses it, "is as a rapier to run men thorow with, and their throat a sepulchre to bury them in." The significancy of the comparison is intensified, as in the case of the quiver, by a glancing allusion to the peculiar physical conformation of the object compared to the opened sepulchre. And, as it is the perfect participle which is employed to express the *opened* condition of the sepulchre, (ἀνεῳγμένος), the idea represented is that of a sepulchre which, for the time being, is *standing open*, because it *has been opened.* It is thus quite ready to receive the victims which it may be possible to get consigned to destruction. Such remorseless malignity—in which the insatiable element of a moral charnel-house is realized—is an undoubted and wide-spread feature of the sin that is universal among men.

§ 4. *with their tongues they were using deceit,* (*ταῖς γλώσσαις αὐτῶν ἐδολιοῦσαν*), or, as Wycliffe renders it, "with her tungis thei diden gilyngly, *or trecherously.*" The expression in the Hebrew is, *they smoothed their tongues,* (לְשׁוֹנָם יַחֲלִיקוּן), that is, *they spake smoothly, that they might be successful in beguiling, entrapping, and ingulphing.* They had, as Thomas Aquinas expresses it, one thing in their heart and another thing in their mouth. They intended unkindness, but hypocritically pretended kindness: —a too common manifestation of malignity. (The imperfect tense seems to denote continuance or perseverance in their hypocritical professions: and the form ἐδολιοῦσαν for ἐδολίουν is common in the Septuagint. It was Alexandrian, and also Bœotian.)

§ 5. *Asps' venom (is) under their lips,* (Ἰὸς ἀσπίδων ὑπὸ τὰ χεῖλη αὐτῶν). See Psalm cxl. 3. The reference, in the Psalm, is to "the evil man," and "the violent man,"—"which imagine mischiefs in their heart; continually are they gathered together for war." (See verses 1, 2.) Their aim in what they say and counsel is to inject some idea into the minds of those who have power, that will work to the ruin of the objects of their malice. They wish to poison, and thus to destroy. And, like asps, they carry their poison about with them, *under their lips,* ever ready, as occasion offers, to fasten upon their victim, and to dart into his veins the deadly venom. It is of no moment to determine what kind of viper or serpent is referred to. Our English word *asp* is just the anglicism of the Greek word ἀσπίς. The Hebrew term (עַכְשׁוּב) occurs only in the passage quoted, and is translated *adder* in our

English version. In the passage before us, Wycliffe's version is, "the venym of eddris, *that ben clepid aspis*, is undur her lippis." For *eddris*, Purvey, in his revision substituted *snakis*.

§ 6. It may be observed that in the sins of word, representatively specified in this 13th verse, there is successive reference to three prominent parts of the organism which has to do with speech,—the *throat*, the *tongue*, and the *lips*. In the next verse the entire cavity of the *mouth* is referred to.

VER. 14. Ὧν τὸ στόμα ἀρᾶς καὶ πικρίας γέμει.

Eng. Auth. Vers. *Whose mouth* is *full of cursing and bitterness.*

§ 1. The contents of this verse are a free quotation from the Septuagint version of Psalm x. 7, (ix. 28). In the Psalm there is reference to some haughty man of violence who scrupled not to oppress and destroy the "poor," the "fatherless," and the "innocent." Of this man it is said,—"his mouth is full of cursing, and deceit, and fraud." The Apostle enlarges the reference, by substituting a plural for a singular relative, (ὧν for οὗ), and omits one item from the triplet of wickedness ascribed to the *mouth*. (The clause, as it stands in the Septuagint, is, οὗ ἀρᾶς τὸ στόμα αὐτοῦ γέμει καὶ πικρίας καὶ δόλου.) By *cursing*, we are probably to understand *malignant imprecation*, such as is still so fearfully prevalent in society. And by *bitterness* is probably meant those other outspurtings of hate which so often accompany cursings. Words which are intended to wound and give pain are "amarulent," as Brown of Wamphray calls them,—"words of bitterness." (In the Hebrew text the term translated πικρία is מִרְמוֹת, *deceits*. It is probable that the Septuagint translator had read either מְרֹרוֹת; see Deut. xxxii. 32; or מְרִירוּת; see Ezek. xxi. 6. And, perhaps, it is not very improbable that one or other of these terms was in the autograph of the Psalmist.) When it is said that "the *mouth* is *full* of cursing and bitterness," the description is a vivid representation of what is still lamentably prevalent in, apparently, all lands, and in none, perhaps, more than in our own. There are multitudes who can scarcely "ope their mouth," but "out thereat" fly both *curses* and *bitterness.* There is upon their lips a total inversion of the law of reverence and love.

VER. 15. Ὀξεῖς οἱ πόδες αὐτῶν ἐκχέαι αἷμα·

Eng. Auth. Vers. *Their feet* are *swift to shed blood:*

This is a condensation of the first clause of the 7th verse of Isai. lix.,—"Their feet run to evil, and they make haste to shed innocent blood," (*οἱ δὲ πόδες αὐτῶν ἐπὶ πονηρίαν τρέχουσι, ταχινοὶ ἐκχέαι αἷμα*). There is thus unison in the various members of the body. The *feet* are in league with the *throat* and the *tongue* and the *lips.* All the parts of the living organism are engaged in a confederacy of malignity. Such malignity is the natural development of sin; for holiness is "love." Even when powerful restraints are imposed upon the various outward members, the inward principle, full of machiavellian subtlety, contrives covered and circuitous ways by which it may prosecute the imagined interests of self by means of the sacrifice of the interests or lives of others.

VER. 16. σύντριμμα καὶ ταλαιπωρία ἐν ταῖς ὁδοῖς αὐτῶν·

Eng. Auth. Vers. *Destruction and misery* are *in their ways:*

This is an exact quotation of the last clause of Isai. lix. 7 as it stands in the Septuagint. The words are a free translation of the original Hebrew, (שֹׁד וָשֶׁבֶר בִּמְסִלּוֹתָם), which might be rendered thus,—*desolation and destruction are in their ways.* That is, wherever they go they leave behind them *destruction and desolation*, and consequently *distress and woe.* (שֹׁד is rendered σύντριμμα, *destruction*, not here only, but in Isai. xxii. 4, and lx. 18 also. It is generally, however, rendered ταλαιπωρία, *misery.* And, conversely, שֶׁבֶר is generally rendered σύντριμμα, and only here, and in Isai. lx. 18, and Jer. iv. 20, ταλαιπωρία.)

VER. 17. καὶ ὁδὸν εἰρήνης οὐκ ἔγνωσαν.

Eng. Auth. Vers. *And the way of peace have they not known:*

Revised Version. *and the way of peace they did not know.*

The words of this verse,—translated by Wycliffe, *and thei knewen not the way of pees*,—immediately succeed in Isaiah the words which form the preceding verse of the Apostle's catena. See Isai. lix. 8. The quotation is taken exactly from the Septuagint, as it is exhibited in the Alexandrine MS. (In the Vatican there is this difference, that οἴδασι replaces ἔγνωσαν.) *The way of peace* will simply be *the way in which peace may be maintained and enjoyed*, —*peace*, namely, *between man and man.* The antithesis to what precedes seems to make it certain that this must be the import of the phrase. And Ambrosiaster therefore errs in understanding it as meaning *the way of inward tranquillity, by which the soul ascends to God.* Bahrdt too misses the mark when he thus translates the verse, "No one gives himself any more concern as to the true means of his bliss," (*Keiner bekümmert sich mehr um die wahren Mittel seiner Glückseligkeit*). And when Origen says that "Christ is our peace; and therefore **the way of peace** is **the way of Christ**," (*Pax nostra Christus est: via ergo pacis, via Christi est*), he leaps, so far as mere exegesis is concerned,—though not, indeed, so far as the philosophy of both theology and religion is concerned,—to an extreme.

Abelard followed him. Melancthon takes, however, a far more erratic leap when he says that the meaning of the passage is, "that they who seek to be justified by works never arrive at peace," (*declarat nunquam pervenire ad pacem, qui se operibus justificant.* Annot.) "The way of peace," says Knopken echoingly, "is faith in Christ," (*via pacis est fides in Christum*). Dionysius à Ryckel, on the other hand, is equally extreme in the opposite direction;—"the way of peace," says he, "is good works," (*id est, opera bona*).

The expression, *they did not know*, or, *they knew not*, (οὐκ ἔγνωσαν), represents an instance of culpable ignorance; and it brings into view a state of mind that was chronologically antecedent to the *destruction and misery* which were found in their ways. The way of peace they *did not know*, because they wilfully *took no note of it*. They wilfully took no note of it, most probably because they were determined to continue in the paths in which they were already walking and running. Had they *known the way of peace*, and how desirable and delightful it is *as a way*, those lamentable experiences of *destruction and misery* would not have followed in their wake.

It is thus noteworthy that sin not only separates man from God; it also separates man from man. It breaks up human harmony. It introduces human antagonisms. It tends to the dissolution of society. Were it not that it is checked by gracious influences from above, it would speedily issue in the superinduction of utter moral chaos and desolation.

VER. 18. Οὐκ ἔστιν φόβος θεοῦ ἀπέναντι τῶν ὀφθαλμῶν αὐτῶν.

Eng. Auth. Vers. *There is no fear of God before their eyes:*

Revised Version. *There is not the fear of God before their eyes.*

This expression is quoted from the Septuagint version of

Ps. xxxvi. 1, (xxxv. 2). And it is an exact transcript, with the trifling exception of the plural pronoun *their*, (αὐτῶν), which, for unison's sake, is substituted for the singular *his*, (αὐτοῦ). "The transgression of the wicked," remarks the Psalmist, "saith within my heart, *That there is no fear of God before his eyes.*" The absence of this fear sufficiently accounts for the presence of the outbreaking iniquities which are referred to in the five preceding verses. And the Apostle, in mentioning it, returns, in his omega, to the idea contained in his alpha,—the idea, namely, which is expanded in verses 11—12. The fear of God, as Spener remarks, is the only bridle by which the wild horse of our nature can be restrained and regulated, (*Denn da die Furcht Gottes allein der Zaum wäre, welcher solch ein unbändiges Pferd zurückhalten Könnte, &c.*) "It is a grand and magnificent thing," says Origen, "always to have before the eyes of the heart the fear of God." (*Opus grande est et magnificum semper habere ante oculos cordis timorem Dei.*) Such fear is "the beginning of wisdom;" and it is not far removed from the end of it. There is a fear, indeed, which "hath torment,"—the fear of the lash, the dread foreboding of final woe. It is well when this fear is "cast out," and supplanted by perfect confidence in the propitious favour of God. And it *is* ousted from the soul when the soul is filled with love; and the soul *is* filled with love, when "we have known and believed the love that God hath to us." (1 John iv. 17—19.) Nevertheless, there is always an element of sensitive fear in man's love to God, and in man's love to man. There is a fear of doing anything to offend or to wound. This fear is inseparable from a consciousness of imperfection; and it is at once a self-imposed rein to restrain, and a self-appointed watch to keep guard. When it is said that "there is not the fear of God *before the eyes*," there is objectivity ascribed to a condition which is, psychologically, subjective. But the subjective may become objective when it is made the mark of reflective thought. The wicked not only do not feel, as a general rule, "the fear of God;" they do not even think of it as a feeling which they should cherish. It is not *kept in view* by them as an object to be realized in emotion.

VER. 19. Οἴδαμεν δὲ ὅτι ὅσα ὁ νόμος λέγει τοῖς ἐν τῷ νόμῳ λαλεῖ, ἵνα πᾶν στόμα φραγῇ καὶ ὑπόδικος γένηται πᾶς ὁ κόσμος τῷ Θεῷ,

Eng. Auth. Vers. *Now we know, that what things soever the law saith, it saith to them who are under the law, that every mouth may be stopped, and all the world may become guilty before God.*

Revised Version. *But we know that whatsoever things the law saith, it speaketh to them who are in (the sphere of) the law, that every mouth might be stopped, and all the world become liable to pay penalty to God,*

§ 1. The Apostle has concluded his documentary evidence in support of the charge, which he had brought against all mankind,—Jews as well as Gentiles,—*that they are under sin.* But lest the Jews, as a spiritually conceited people, should attempt to evade the force of the evidence adduced, by shifting the whole burden of it over upon the shoulders of the Gentiles, he adds the words of this verse. He had "much greater trouble," as Calvin remarks, "in subjugating the Jews, than in relation to the Gentiles; for although the former were as really destitute as the latter, of true righteousness, yet they covered themselves with the cloak of God's covenant, as if it were holiness sufficient for them to be separated from the rest of the world by the election of God," (*in quibus subigendis multo plus erat negotii; quod, vera justitia non minus quam Gentes destituti, praetextu foederis Dei se tegebant, acsi hoc illis pro sanctitate sufficeret, Dei electione a reliquo mundo fuisse distinctos*).

§ 2. *But we know,* (Οἴδαμεν δέ). The conjunctive particle (δέ) connects what follows with what goes before, in such a way as to indicate that a new thread of thought is taken up, to be intertwisted with the preceding threads. The particle is left untranslated by Tyndale. It is omitted from the text by Theodoret; and the omission is approved of by Mill, § 929. It is also omitted in the Ethiopic version, and in Matthaei's codex l. It is rendered *now* in our

Authorized English Version. We have certainly no precise analogue for it; but the translation which we have given—the translation of Myles Coverdale, and corresponding to that of the Vulgate (*autem*) and of Luther (*aber*)—is perhaps the best that is attainable.

When the Apostle says, "But *we* know," he seems to be realizing his union with his readers, whosoever these readers might be. He does not refer to himself in particular, as he does, when speaking in the first person plural, in the second member of the 9th verse. Neither does he refer to Christians in particular, as he does, when using the same first person plural, in the 8th verse. Nor does he refer to Jews in particular, as he does, when using the same person, in verses 5th and 9th. His reference is, indefinitely, to all his readers, along with himself—and to all his readers and himself, not as distinguished, in some precise manner, from all other men, but as adequately representing all of mankind who might consider the subject spoken of. Tyndale freely and somewhat picturesquely renders the expression, "ye and we knowe;" Turnbull, still more freely, "it must be acknowledged;" van Hengel, "it is evident" (constat); Cognatus, "no one doubts" (*nemini dubium est*); de Paris, "it is indubitable" (*c'est une chose indubitable*). It is thus the case that the step which the Apostle is about to take in his reasoning is, as Matthias remarks, taken *ex concessis*. His foot is treading on ground which was undisputed and indisputable. "We *know*." The verb denotes a state of subjective certainty, as distinguished from that condition of the understanding which constitutes mere opinion as to what is probable.

§ 3. *that whatsoever things the law saith, it speaks to those who are in the law*, (ὅτι ὅσα ὁ νόμος λέγει, τοῖς ἐν τῷ νόμῳ λαλεῖ). By *the law* here expositors in general, both ancient and modern, understand *the written Revelation as a whole*, that is, *the Old Testament Scriptures*. Their idea is undoubtedly correct. They suppose that the Apostle, while employing the indefinite expression, *whatsoever things* (ὅσα), had nevertheless a special subjacent reference to the quotations contained in verses 10—18;—quotations which are taken, not from the Pentateuch, which was the original *law*, that is, the original *Authoritative Divine Instruction* (ὁ νόμος, הַתּוֹרָה), but from the supplementary and complementary portions of the volume of the Book, *the Psalms and the Prophets.* This is the view of Chrysostom (τὴν παλαιὰν πᾶσαν), Œcumenius, Theophylact. It was evidently the view of Theodoret also, and of Pelagius. Thomas Aquinas, too, had the same idea; and Abelard, and de Lyra. So had Sadolet, Calvin, Beza, Willet, Piscator, Grotius. Day accords,—"the word *law* here signifieth *all the writings of the Old Testament*, and that it doth in relation to the Hebrew word *Thorah.*" The same view is taken by Tholuck, Reiche, Rückert, de Wette, Meyer, Alford, Wordsworth, and, indeed, as we have said, by the great body of modern expositors.

Some, however, dissent. Ammon, for example, maintains that there is no reference to the passages quoted in verses 10—18, but that there is the start of a new train of thought. He interprets *the law* as meaning strictly *the Mosaic law*, that is, *the precepts of the Pentateuch.* Van Hengel takes the same view, substantially, and approves of Muralto indicating in the text that a new paragraph commences with verse 19. Glöckler, too, opposes the idea that there is a reference to the quotations in verses 10—18, and supposes that the word *law* denotes what is strictly *the Mosaic law.* But he contends that verse 19th is to be closely connected with verse 9th, and thinks that the expression, *the law*, refers not so much to *the precepts of the Mosaic law*, or to *what it enjoins*, as to *what it threatens.* (*Besonders wird hierbei auf die Strafe gesehen.*) Wardlaw takes a somewhat similar view. And so do D. Brown and Brandes, who, both of them, like Muralto and Peile (*ultimately*), suppose that a new section begins with verse 19th.

Vaughan, again, admits that there is a reference to the quotations in verses 10—18, but he supposes that the expression, *the law*, denotes "*the Old Testament dispensation itself*, personified as speaking in its Scriptures." And

Matthias, while contending strenuously that there must be a reference to the quotations, takes the word as denoting that aspect of the Old Testament Scriptures which, as distinguished from the divine *promise,* exhibits the divine *law* as the rule of the divine judgement, (νόμος *ist hier das Wort Gottes, insoweit es Gesetz, d. i. Richtschnur des göttlichen Rechtes ist.*) It was by a somewhat similar hermeneutical device that some of the older Lutheran expositors,—represented by Hunnius, Calov, and Seb. Schmidt, —interpreted *the law* as that doctrine of the Scriptures which is the opposite pole of *the Gospel.* (*Lex est doctrina opera praescribens, et peccata arguens.*–S. Schmidt.) And they have supposed that they who are "in the law" are to be regarded as opposed to them who are "in Christ." (*Putamus enim opponi* τὸ *esse in* **lege** τῷ *esse* **in Christo**.–S. Schmidt.)

All these interpretations, however, are unnatural and unfacile. Those of Ammon, van Hengel, Glöckler, Wardlaw, D. Brown, and Brandes, are inconsistent with the obvious textual connection of the 19th verse with the immediately preceding context. Those of Vaughan, Matthias, Hunnius, Calov, and S. Schmidt impose a meaning on the word *law,* which, when the reference to the quotations of verses 10—18 is allowed, is unaccounted for and unaccountable. For the subject-matter of the quotations, is, in the main, didactico-historical, and not specifically legal or dispensational.

Origen took a different view of the Apostle's reference. He maintains that *the law* spoken of is "the law of nature, which is written on the hearts of men;" and "in which," or "under which," all men are, as soon as they arrive at the years of discretion. Olshausen and Oltramare take a similar view : only, they suppose that the reference is not exclusively to *the law of nature,* but equally to *the law of nature* and *the law of Moses,*—the two editions of the one everlasting law which regulates human duty. Peile takes the same view ; and hence he interpolates and translates the Apostle's expression thus,—"*Now—be the Law what it may*—we know that, in all that the Law saith, it is addressing those who live under such law." (*New Transl.,* 1854.) This interpretation, however, of the Apostle's expression, though certainly embodying an important truth, and though wrought out ingeniously, especially by Origen, is, as truly as that of Ammon, van Hengel, Glöckler, &c., inconsistent with the natural relation of the verse to what goes immediately before.

There is no interpretation which is simple, facile, and natural, but that which supposes the word *law* to have the same meaning which it bears in the preceding chapter, in verses 12, 13, 14, 15, 17, 18, 20, 23, 25, 26, 27; and which it also bears in Matt. v. 18; John x. 34; xii. 34; xv. 25; 1 Cor. xiv. 21. In all these passages it means *the Authoritative Written Revelation*, viewed as a whole. And the Apostle, referring to the quotations which he had made in verses 10—18, speaks of them as the *sayings* of *the Old Testament Scriptures*:—"But we know that whatsoever things the law *says*, it speaks to them who are in the law."

The Apostle uses two distinct verbs in the two clausules of his remark,—*says* (λέγει) and *speaks* (λαλεῖ). There is felicity and nicety in the distinction. The former of the two (λέγει) directs attention to the *meaning*, while the latter (λαλεῖ) directs attention to the *utterance*, of what is stated in the Scriptures. In the former there is a special reference to that which is *internal* in *what is spoken;* while in the latter there is a special reference to that which is *external* in *what is said*. What is *said* is addressed to the intelligence, though through the ear: what is *spoken* is addressed to the ear, though for the intelligence. Compare John viii. 43. (Melville explains λαλεῖ thus,—*familialiter et sedulo exponit.*) It is an imperfection in the Vulgate, that it makes no distinction between the two terms: it translates them both "speaks," (*loquitur*). It is an equal imperfection in Beza's version, in all its editions after the first, that he translates them both "says," (*dicit*). In the first edition, that of 1556, he contented himself with the Vulgate translation. Calvin drew the proper distinction in his Latin version, though not in his French, (*quaecunque lex* **dicit,** *iis qui in lege sunt* **loquitur**). So did Bengel, (*was das Gesetz* **saget,** *das* **redet** *es zu denen die im Gesetze* *stehen*). So did Piscator in his German version. And so Zinzendorf and Felbinger. But Luther missed it; and so did Tyndale, and Coverdale, and the English Geneva, and hence also our *Authorized English Version.*

When the Apostle says that "whatsoever things the law says, it speaks to *them who are in the law*," (τοῖς ἐν τῷ νόμῳ), it is unnatural to suppose that the word *law* has a different reference from what it bears in the preceding part of the remark. He manifestly refers to the Jews as such. And he refers to them as living *in the sphere of the written Revelation.* They were *within*, not *without*, that sphere or domain. And hence what was said in the written Revelation was spoken *to them. To them*, it will be noticed, is the Apostle's expression: not *of them*, nor even *for them.* No doubt, what was spoken *to them* would be intended *for them*, and would be calculated and designed to be *beneficial to them*, (it would be *um derer willen.*–Zachariä). Nevertheless the dative is not the *dativus commodi.* It merely indicates the personal objects toward whom the speaking was directed. Whatsoever things the Old Testament Scripture said, these it spake to those who were within its sphere, and not to those who were beyond it. The contents of the Old Testament Bible were addressed *to the Jews; (quibus quidem solum, non de solis, lex loquitur.*–Abelard). And the nature of the case makes it certain that the instruction of these Jews was aimed at in what was spoken to them. This seems to be the sum total of the thought that was present to the Apostle's mind when he made the observation before us. And hence Grotius is wrong when he says that the Apostle's observation, though true as a general rule, was liable to exceptions, as, for example, in those parts of Scripture in which we read of "the burden of Egypt, the burden of Damascus, the burden of Edom, the burden of Nineveh." Even these oracles were recorded in *the Volume of the Book* for the special benefit of the Israelites; and, as thus recorded, were addressed *to them.* Klöter is equally wrong when he translates the Apostle's observation thus,—"but we know that all which the law says, it speaks *in relation to them* who are in the law," (*in*

Bezug auf die, die in Gesetze sind). For, assuredly, there is much in the law which is spoken *in relation to* the Egyptians, the Damascenes, the Edomites, the Ninevites, &c. There is not a little which is spoken *in relation to all mankind.* And in the leading statements found in the quotations in verses 10—18 there is, we may assume, express reference, not merely to the Jews, but to all mankind, and consequently to Gentiles as well as to Jews, but also—and this is at present the matter of primary exegetical moment—to Jews as well as to Gentiles. The Apostle, then, as it were, says:—"We know that the Scriptures of "the Old Testament were addressed *to the Jews.* This "cannot be doubted. They convey, therefore, in all their "contents, instruction intended *for the Jews.* This cannot "be disputed. And as, in the leading statements which "are quoted in verses 10—18, there is *no exception made* "*of the Jews*, when the sinfulness of all men is asserted and "reiterated, it must be the case that reference to them is "expressly involved, and this reference is announced to "them, *that every mouth might be stopped, and the whole* "*world be brought in guilty in relation to God.*"

Count Zinzendorf punctuates and connects the words of the entire clause in a peculiar way. He translates it thus:—"But we know that what the law says to them who are under it, it speaks on this account, that, &c." (*Wir wissen aber, dass, was das Gesetz denen, die drunter seyn, saget, das sprichts darum, damit, &c.*) But such an arrangement fails to give due emphasis to what seems to have been the immediate aim of the Apostle, his aim, namely, to lead the Jews to take note that their character is pourtrayed in the passages which are quoted. It reduces the distinction between the two verbs *says* and *speaks* to no special significance. It seems, moreover, to be at variance with the collocation and natural rhythm of the inspired words. And it rather offensively suggests that the one aim of the divine Spirit in the written Revelation of the Old Testament was "to stop the mouths of men, and to bring in the whole world guilty before God." It is not, then, to be marvelled at that the Count has had, in this theory of construction, but very few followers. Yet of these few Basil Cooper,—though in all likelihood unconsciously,—is one. He translates the clause thus,—"But we know that whatsoever things the Law saith against them that are within the Law, it uttereth to the end that, &c."

§ 4. *that every mouth might be stopped, and all the world become liable to pay penalty to God*, (ἵνα πᾶν στόμα φραγῇ καὶ ὑπόδικος γένηται πᾶς ὁ κόσμος τῷ Θεῷ). It was debated in ancient times,—and the debate has descended to our own day,—whether this clause of the verse expresses *design* or *result*. Haldane affirms that it "must be taken" both ways. But other critics, in general, are not so accommodating. Those who suppose that *design* is expressed have translated it in some such way as we have done. Those who suppose that *result* is denoted would render it thus,—*so that every mouth must be stopped, &c.*, or, *so that every mouth is stopped, &c.* The advocates of *design* hold, in other words, —to the *telic* import of the initial conjunction (ἵνα),—*in order that:* while the advocates of *result* contend that the particle has its *ecbatic* force,—*so that.* Theodoret gave the particle this ecbatic or eventual import. And in modern times it has been maintained by Cognatus, Taylor, Rambach, Heumann, de Paris, Doddridge; and by Koppe, Flatt, Wakefield, Bishop Barrington; as also by Tholuck, Reiche, Benecke; and Geissler, Stengel, Stuart, Bloomfield, Köllner, &c. Reiche expresses himself strongly on the subject, and says that it is "in every point of view absurd to think that the Old Testament has spoken *in order that* every mouth may be stopped," (*ergreifen wir gern—hier die Auskunft, den nach jeder Ansicht und auf jedem Standpunct absurden Gedanken, als habe das A. T. desswegen gesprochen, damit jeder Mund verstumme, vom Worte zu entfernen*). Tholuck, though modifying in his 4th and 5th editions the decisiveness of his 1st, nevertheless says that it would be to handle the words of the Apostle in the spirit of the veriest pedant, if one were to insist that they teach "that he held, as a definite doctrine, that there was in the words of the Old Testament a divine intention to stop every mouth, and thus the mouth of the Jew;" (*es schulmeisterlich pedantisch wäre, anzunehmen, der Ap. habe bei den Worten des alten Bundes mit dogmatischer Bestimmtheit die göttliche Absicht angenommen,—jeden Mund, also auch den des Juden, zu stopfen.*) But though the announcement of such a divine intention was certainly not the prominent aim of the Apostle in the passage before us; and though intention, as a matter of actual fact, often runs coincidently into result; yet we discover no pedantry in holding, what seems perfectly obvious, that the conjunction in question (ἵνα) naturally and conventionally denotes design, and is generally, if not invariably, so used in the diction of Paul. (Even 2 Cor. vii. 9 is no real exception.) And, as regards Reiche's remark, it seems to us to be absurd to allege that it is "in *every* point of view absurd to think that the Old Testament has spoken what it says in order to stop the mouths of sinners." It would be absurd, indeed, to suppose that the Old Testament was given for the exclusive purpose of stopping men's mouths. It would also be absurd to suppose that this purpose was its principal aim. But we see no absurdity in supposing that the divine quiver is filled with a multiplicity of arrowy aims. And if, as a matter of fact, the stopping of men's mouths is effected by the contents of the Old Testament Scriptures, we see no reason for characterizing either with pedantry or with absurdity the supposition that this actual result,—which is not an Evil, but a Good,—was aimed at and designed. Indeed, we shall never be able to form a broad and comprehensive view of the teleology of the Bible, or of the teleology of Providence, if we do not admit that it is one of the divine aims to convict sinners of the exceeding sinfulness of sin in general, and of their own sin in particular. Whatever in the Scriptures is fitted to initiate or to foster and ripen this conviction, was doubtless deposited there, with an intelligent and far-reaching design, by the over-ruling Hand of Him whose Hand and Heart moved the prophets and psalmists of old. If this be admitted, all difficulty in reference to the conjunction vanishes into nonentity; and there is not the slightest occasion for having recourse to any such violent expedient as that of Michaelis, who throws into parenthesis the whole of verses 10—18, along with the first clause of ver. 19th, and thus connects the expression before us, *that every mouth might be stopped, and that all the world might be brought in guilty before God,* with the concluding clause of verse 9th, *we before impeached both Jews and Greeks of being all under sin.* The telic import of the conjunction (ἵνα) is held not only by Michaelis, but by the great body of the most enlightened critics and expositors, and, among those of recent times, by Paulus, Rückert, Glöckler, Schrader; de Wette too, and Olshausen, Meyer, Fritzsche, Oltramare; Krehl also, and Philippi, Alford, Wordsworth, van Hengel, Mehring, &c.

When the Apostle, referring to one of the aims of the Old Testament Scriptures, says, *that every mouth might be stopped,* we are evidently to suppose that, under the general expression, *whatsoever things the law saith,* he has special mental retrospection to such particular things as have been specified in verses 10—18. If the contents of his idea were analytically exhibited, his statement would be tantamount to the following:—"But we know that whatsoever things "the law saith, it speaks to them who are in the law, *and "such things in particular as it says in the passages which "I have quoted in verses 10—18, and in similar passages, "it speaks, that every mouth might be stopped."*

When he refers to *the stopping of the mouth,* the allusion seems to be to the effect of overwhelming evidence upon an accused person in a court of justice. When such evidence is adduced, it often happens that the accused is struck dumb. His conscience silences him. He feels that it would be an utter absurdity and impossibility to say anything in the way of self-justification. "The metaphor," says Calvin, "is taken from courts of law, in which the accused, if he have anything to plead in self-defence, demands leave to speak, that he may clear himself from the things laid to his charge: but if his conscience condemn him, he is silent, and without saying a word, awaits his sentence, being even already condemned by his own silence." (*Metaphora a judiciis petita, ubi reus, si quid habet ad justam defensionem, vices dicendi postulat, ut quae sibi imposita sunt purget: si vero conscientia sua premitur, silet, ac tacitus expectat suam damnationem, suo jam silentio damnatus.*) This is a far more likely interpretation than the notion of Piscator, that there is an allusion to the violent gagging of the condemned, that they might not have an opportunity of uttering their complaints, and thus of inciting the populace. Moses Stuart, however, adopts, in his 2nd edition, Piscator's idea, though not from Piscator. He says,—"The phraseology is borrowed from the custom of gagging criminals, *i. e.*, stopping their mouths in order to prevent apology or outcry from them, when they were led out to execution." He adopted the notion, though without specific acknowledgement, from Gronovius as quoted by Reiche.

But how should "*every* mouth be stopped" by what is written in the law, when the law speaks only to those who are within its sphere? How should the mouth of the Gentile be stopped, as well as the mouth of the Jew? This is the difficulty which Origen started, and which is echoed by Olshausen and Oltramare. It led all three of them to the conclusion that the law referred to by the Apostle cannot be the law of the Old Testament Scriptures. (*Quod si velimus de lege Mosis intelligere,—quomodo consequens videbitur, quod per hanc legem, quae unam tantummodo institutis suis contingit gentem, omne os obstruatur?*—Origen). But there is no real difficulty. The Apostle is not speaking in the precisely jointed terminology of a formal logician. He leaves scope, in what he says, for the analytic and synthetic play of the intelligence of his readers. And his idea seems obvious enough:—"that every mouth might be stopped," that is, *that there may be no exception,* **on the part of the Jews,** *as regards the conviction of sin.* "It is the Jews chiefly who are referred to," says Bengel, correctly, (*Judaei maxime notantur*). But the language does not actually particularize them, that their assent might be won, as it were, before the force of personal prejudice should have time to turn aside their impartial judgement. (The expression, says Chrysostom, ἐκείνους ἐστὶν αἰνιττόμενον, εἰ δὲ μὴ φανερῶς αὐτὸ τέθειται, it is ὥστε μὴ τραχύτερον γενέσθαι τὸν λόγον.) The Apostle, says Matthias, intends his expression to be specifically applied to the Jews, through the strong betoning of the word *every* before the word *mouth.* (*Der Apostel macht—durch die starke Betonung des* πᾶν *vor* στόμα *eine Anwendung auf die Juden.*) He means, says Pelagius, "not of the Gentiles only, but of the Jews also," (*non solum gentium, sed etiam Judaeorum*). The words are employed, as Owen remarks, "not so much to include the Gentiles, as to include the Jews, who thought themselves exempted."

It is added, *and* (*that*) *all the world might become liable to pay penalty to God,* (καὶ ὑπόδικος γένηται πᾶς ὁ κόσμος τῷ θεῷ). It is a clause, repeating, on the principle of parallelism, the idea of the preceding clause: only, according to custom in such cases, the repetition is made under a variation of aspect.

As in the preceding clause, the adjective is to be betoned: —"*all* the world," that is, "all, *not excepting the Jews.*" For it is at them that the Apostle is still specially aiming. And it is to make sure of including them that he uses one of the most comprehensive phrases which it was possible for him to employ. Yet the phrase is not, by one jot, too comprehensive. It has not an element of the hyperbolical in it. All of the human family who have arrived at the age of accountability are guilty. And it is the desire of God that all, without distinction or exception, should feel conscience-stricken and divinely condemned. All ought thus to feel. For in addition to the written law which spake to the Jews, there is, wondrously interblending with it, that other law, unwritten but not unrevealed, of which Origen speaks, of which, too, our own Apostle speaks in chap. ii. 14, 15, and which has been published within the bosom of every man, Gentile as well as Jew. In accordance with this law every man's conscience, armed with the power of a Procurator or Prosecutor, authoritatively accuses him of doing what he ought not to have done, and of leaving undone what he ought to have done. Grotius, assuredly, was labouring under a great mistake when he says that the expression, "all the world," means merely "the greater part of men," (*maxima pars hominum*). And Reiche repeats the error, though under another phase, when he says that the *world* here can only be "the whole of mankind that lived at that time." (*Hier kann der κόσμος nur die ganze damalige Menschheit sein.*) It is another phase of the same error which is committed by Taylor when he says that "the Apostle is here speaking of bodies of people, or of Jews and Gentiles in a *collective* capacity." Moses Stuart, too, seems to be looking at the subject from an unnatural standpoint, when he says that "the argument of Paul extends only to those who are *out of Christ,*" and adds, "it seems to me a wrong view of the Apostle's meaning in verses 10—19 which regards him as labouring to prove directly the universality of men's depravity, merely by the argument which these texts afford." The Apostle, indeed, is not "labouring." Neither is he building up, in a precisely logical way, the doctrine of universal sinfulness. But most assuredly he is, in a free and easy epistolary way, maintaining and establishing and applying the fact of universal sinfulness, that he might thence lay a basis of necessity for that glorious Gospel which brings glad tidings "to every creature," by revealing a Righteousness which is "unto all."

Wycliffe, misled by the peculiarity of the Vulgate version, (*omnis mundus*), gives a strange translation to the expression πᾶς ὁ κόσμος. He renders it "ech world,"—as if he supposed that the Apostle had divided mankind into two worlds, the world of the Jews and the world of the Gentiles. Purvey, in his revision, retains this translation,—"eche world." Oertel, again, following the interpretation of Bahrdt, uses the liberty of translating the expression, "the whole nation," (*die ganze Nation*). But such liberty is downright hermeneutical licentiousness; and was assumed in consequence of a desire to make out that there is nothing in the Old Testament which should give Christians the slightest concern, or which should be regarded by them as in any way regulative of the principles of their procedure.

The whole *world of men*, Gentile as well as Jewish, is, according to the Apostle, *liable to judicial prosecution*, hence *liable to punishment, liable to penalty, liable to pay penalty;—liable to pay penalty to God.* Such is the import of the expression, ὑπόδικος τῷ Θεῷ. It is an expression that has occasioned considerable perplexity to translators and expositors; and, indeed, it is few comparatively who have seized with perfect exactitude, and expressed with clearness and simplicity as well as precision, its import. The adjective employed by the Apostle (ὑπόδικος) is rather unhappily rendered *subditus* in the Vulgate; and hence it is translated *suget* (subject) by Wycliffe; and *subdued*, by Tyndale, and by Coverdale in his *New Testament* of 1538. The English Geneva version,—borrowing from the French Geneva, and ultimately from Calvin's French version,—renders it *culpable*, which is certainly better than the translation of the Vulgate, but still far too feeble. Luther translates it "guilty" (*schuldig*),—an incomparably better version. The translation has been adopted in our *Authorized English Version.* It was approved of by Willet. It is approved of by Turnbull. But old Myles Coverdale, in trying to reproduce it in his *Bible*, "faithfully translated out of *Douche* and Latyn," took hold, as with the left hand, of the somewhat ambiguous word, and rendered it *detter* (debtor),—*detter unto God.* Day renders the expression, *guilty of condemnation before God.* The idea is on the right line, theologically; but the phrase, *guilty of condemnation*, though modelled on the Scripture phrase, *guilty of death*, is not felicitous,—to our modern ears at least. It has been cast, moreover, in the mould of a misconception. God was regarded by Day as the Judge, rather than as the Injured Party, who has become, or who may become, the Prosecutor. Sclater renders the adjective, *impleadable as guilty of transgression*,—a translation much to be preferred to Day's. It is, indeed, admirably exact in some respects, but it is lumbering on the one hand, and incapable of amalgamation, on the other, with the remainder of the Apostle's expression, *to God* (τῷ Θεῷ). The translation of Vorstius, "subject to the judgement of God," (*judicio Dei subjectus*), adroitly winds up within itself the relation of the adjective to the substantive; but it is nevertheless a philological mistake. It veils from view the fact that God is the Injured Party, who either is, or may become the Prosecutor. It has been reproduced, however, by Wakefield and Archbishop Newcome; and it is introduced into the Unitarian *Improved Version.* Conybeare's translation of the entire clause rather intensifies the mistake,—"might be subject*ed* to the judgement of God." That of the *Five Clergymen* is equally at fault,—"may be brought under the judgement of God." It is God's *rights* that are referred to in the Apostle's expression, not his *judgement.*—Hence, as well as for other reasons, Doddridge's version is incorrect, "convicted before God." Doddridge had evidently meditated considerably on the expression; and he conceived that he had mastered it. He says, in a note, in reference to his translation, "so υποδικος τω θεω seems exactly to signify." Cox, as usual, accepts his version. So did Belsham. But, though theologically admissible, it proceeds, philologically, on wrong assumptions, and is far indeed from being an "exact" reproduction of the idea of the original. The phrase, as the Apostle employs it, denotes, in the first place, *liability,*—a notion that is veiled in Doddridge's version; and, in the second place, it certainly does not determinately denote that *judicial conviction* has actually taken place. Budaeus, indeed, in one part of his *Commentaries* (*p.* 126, *ed.* 1548), says that the term is applicable to convicted persons, (*obnoxius è re judicata*). He was not persistent, however, in this idea. (See *p.* 13.) And undoubtedly the word, in current usage, is, as a matter of fact, applied, not to the *judicially convicted,* but to those who are *liable to judicial prosecution, liable to become judicially convicted.* Henry Stephens supposes that it properly describes such as have still their causes *sub judice,* (ὑπόδικος *potius est de quo in judicio agitur, Reus.*–Thesaur. in voc.). Webster and Wilkinson take hold of this idea in their explanation of the passage before us, and give, as one of their two translations of the word, "under process." It is assuredly a better translation than Doddridge's, and than Owen's,—"condemned," (though Theophylact had given, freely, long ago the same interpretation, κατάκριτος, ἀπαῤῥησίαστος). In reality, however, the word, of itself, only determines that the person whom it describes is *exposed to the swoop of justice, and may be compelled, by judicial action, to pay the penalty of his misdemeanour or crime.*

Such being the import of the word, even Bengel's translation of the expression is a long way from the mark,—"subject to God in judgement," (*Gotte im Gericht unterwürfig*). In his *Gnomon*, however, he seizes the right word in Latin, viz., *obnoxius.* (Festus says, *Obnoxius, poenae obligatus ob delictum.*-De Verb. Signif.) Calvin had seized the word before him. And Erasmus before Calvin. And le Fèvre before Erasmus, although he missed nevertheless the correct explanation of the word. Castellio too, with his fine classic taste, could not miss making use of the same word. And it was employed, indeed, in very ancient times. Rufinus mentions it approvingly, and expressly prefers it to the version given in the Vulgate. (See *Origen's Comment.* in loc.) Beza, with his classic aptitudes, retains the word; but, unhappily, he amplifies the expression, making it, "obnoxious to the condemnation of God," (*obnoxius condemnationi Dei*). His idea is, of course, correct, theologically. But the amplification has spoiled the philological interpretation of the phrase. Erasmus Schmid felt inclined to follow in the wake of Beza; but his exegetical instinct led him to hesitate, and hence he leaves it "a moot point" whether the phrase should be translated "obnoxious to condemnation" or "obnoxious to impeachment," (*obnoxius reatui*). The latter interpretation is, of course, greatly preferable to the former. Grotius seized, as with the hand of a master, the real idea of the word, *debitor poenarum.* The world of men is *debitor poenarum;* and it is one of the desires and aims of God to bring every man living to the consciousness of his condition as a *debitor poenarum.* Every man living is, in consequence of his sins, and until he be released by grace, liable *solvere poenas Deo,—persolvere poenas Deo,—dare poenas Deo.* He is liable to be compelled by judicial action to pay penalty to God. (He is, as Bretschneider expresses it in his Lexicon, *Deo satisfactionem debens pro eo quod peccavit.*) He is under obligation, unless mercy interpose, δίκην διδόναι τῷ Θεῷ,—*to give to God, the injured Party, that which is* **right** *in the circumstances of the case,—to give to God that which will satisfy him,—that which will suffice to repair, as far as practicable, the injury done by the transgressions committed.*—Fritzsche caught the idea of the word. He translates it *straffällig* (liable to penalty). The same translation is given by Meyer, Maier, Matthias, Mehring. Reiche's translation is analogous, *der Strafe verfallen.* Olshausen gives what is equivalent, in his *Commentar*, (*der* δίκῃ *verfallen*), although he retrograded in his *Uebersetzung*, (*Gotte unterworfen*). Philippi's translation corresponds, (*strafbar*, *Strafe schuldend*). Theodoret's interpretation is perfect, (ταῖς τιμωρίαις ὑπεύθυνος). Hesychius's explanation,—copied verbatim by Phavorinus,—is almost all that could be desired, (ὑπόδικος,—ὑπεύθυνος, χρεώστης, ἔνοχος δίκης).

So far as the simple adjective is concerned, we might, with Philippi, render it *punishable.* But when we take the Apostle's expression in its entirety, we cannot say, *punishable to God.* And to say, *punishable by God,* is to change, in some respect, the Apostle's standpoint of observation. And it is apt, moreover, to suggest too obtrusively that God is the executioner of his vengeance. The idea is right in itself; but it is not suggested by the Apostle's expression. We are shut up, therefore, to some more circuitous translation. *Liable to punishment from God,* is near the idea. Still nearer, but intolerably operose, is, *liable to punishment in relation to God.* Sharpe's version is too off-hand at the commencement, and altogether aside from the mark at the end,—"open to punishment before God." The translation we have given,—*liable to pay penalty to God,*—seems to meet, as well, perhaps, as may be, all the requirements of the case.

The dative expression, *to God,* (τῷ Θεῷ), is unhappily rendered *before God* in our *Authorized English Version,* and by many other translators,—as we have seen in the course of our remarks on the phrase as a whole. The rendering is defended by Matthias, who thinks, indeed, that the expression belongs equally to both members of the parallelism,—to the clause, *that every mouth might be stopped,* as well as to the clause, *and all the world become liable to punishment.* According, however, to the usage of the language, as the lexicographer Wahl came ultimately to see, it is the party who has the right to be the prosecutor,—the party, in all ordinary cases, to whom the penalty is due, and not the Judge in the cause,—who is specified in the dative case. (Comp. Demosthenes, 518, 3,—ἐὰν δέ τις τούτων τι παραβαίνῃ, ὑπόδικος ἔστω τῷ παθόντι, *let him be liable to pay damages to the injured party.* Plato *de Legib.*, viii., 11, 846,—τῶν διπλασίων ὑπόδικος ἔστω τῷ βλαφθέντι, *let him be liable to pay to the injured party a penalty of twice the amount of the loss sustained.* Note also those somewhat numerous passages in Plato's *de Legibus,* in which the Prosecutor, as representing the injured State, may be "*Whosoever chooses;*" as for example, ix. 9, 868,—ὁ δὲ ἀσεβῶν τε περὶ ταῦτα καὶ ἀπειθῶν ὑπόδικος ἀσεβείας γιγνέσθω τῷ ἐθέλοντι, *let him be liable to whosoever chooses to prosecute him for his impiety* (*liable to pay the penalty of his impiety*). It is thus the case that in the Apostle's representation, God is represented as the injured Party. It is He who has the right to become Prosecutor. He has the right to get *justice* done to him in judgement against the criminal. As for the criminal, the sword of justice is suspended over his head. He is "*under* justice."

It remains to be noticed that when the Apostle says,—"and that all the world *might become* (γένηται) liable to pay penalty to God," he uses the expression *become* in a logical acceptation, as in ver. 4, "let God *become* true." (γένηται *logice zu fassen,*–Meyer: γένηται *logice, damit es erhelle, esse cognoscatur,*–Reiche.) Beza explains it thus,—"may be found to be guilty," (*reus esse comperiatur*). The explanation is good, theologically considered. But when we take the parallelism of the clausules into account, and the relation of the two parallel clausules to the first clause of the verse, the idea of the Apostle would be more accurately represented thus,—"that all the world *might become,*—viz., *in conscious self-conviction*—liable to pay penalty to God,—liable to divine punishment:"—that is, "that all the world might *realize* its liability to the divine wrath which is to come." Mace was not far from the real idea of the Apostle, though he was far enough from a literal translation, when he rendered the words thus,—"that every one may be silenced, and all the world *plead guilty.*"

"Let us," says Melancthon, "fix this universal proposition in our minds, both that we may acknowledge ourselves to be guilty, and that we may, by means of it, resist the fiction of Pelagians, monks, and such like, that man merits forgiveness by his own works, or is righteous by virtue of his own merits." (*Hanc universalem propositionem infigamus animis, et ut nos ipsos reos esse agnoscamus, et ut opponamus eam Pelagianis, et monachis, et similibus, fingentibus hominem mereri remissionem suis operibus, aut justum esse propriis meritis.*—Enarratio. 1556.)

VER. 20. *διότι ἐξ ἔργων νόμου οὐ δικαιωθήσεται πᾶσα σὰρξ ἐνώπιον αὐτοῦ· διὰ γὰρ νόμου ἐπίγνωσις ἁμαρτίας.*

Eng. Auth. Vers. *Therefore by the deeds of the law there shall no flesh be justified in his sight: for by the law is the knowledge of sin.*

Revised Version. *because by works of law shall nobody be justified before him; for through law is knowledge of sin.*

§ 1. The authors of our *English Authorized Version* have undoubtedly erred in rendering the first word of the verse (the conjunction διότι) as if it were a demonstratively illative particle, *therefore.* They followed the Geneva version, which, in its turn, copied Beza, (*propterea*). The same translation is given in the Dutch versions, old and new, and is accepted by Pareus, Hunnius, Vorstius, de Brais, Turretin, Baumgarten; by Morus too, and Macknight, and Rosenmüller; by Belsham also, and Bolten, Schrader, Naebe, Turnbull. It is defended by Willet. Wells, Doddridge, Worsley, and Cox not only adopt it, but make it,—as does Schöttgen, and also Struensee,—the starting-point of a new paragraph in the arrangement of the text. Tholuck, too, "almost prefers" it, (*fast möchten wir* **propterea** *vorziehen*). It is, however, an entirely illegitimate translation; at variance with the otherwise invariable usage of the New Testament writers, and inconsistent with the intrinsic nature and classical import of the word. In every other instance in which it occurs in the New Testament, it is rendered either *for* or *because*, and can bear no other rendering. (It is a contraction of the phrase διὰ τοῦτο ὅτι, *on account of this—that*, and thus means *propterea quod*, *for this reason, that*, that is *because*.) And, although in classical Greek it is sometimes used indirectly as equivalent to *wherefore*, it is *wherefore* as equivalent to *why* or *for what reason*, (δι' ὅ,τι), and not, illatively and absolutely, *for which reason*. Hence the Vulgate correctly renders it here "because," (*quia*): and Oltramare reproduces exactly the idea of the original by translating it *attendu que, vu que, seeing that, since.* The same translation is given by almost all critics. If the question were asked, therefore, *Why is it that the Written Revelation of God speaks what it says in verses* 10—18, *and that too, in order that every mouth might be stopped, and the whole world realize its obnoxiousness to the wrath of God?—why is it divinely desired that the whole world should thus feel?*—the answer is to be found in the words of this 20th verse,—"*because* by the deeds of the law shall no flesh be justified in his sight." (*Patet vers.* 20 *esse aetiologiam precedentis dicti.*-Cocceius.)

§ 2. This statement, *by works of law shall nobody be justified*, is one of the most pregnant utterances and apophthegms of the Apostle. It is, indeed, the immovable substructure, or, as Vitringa expresses it in his Latin dissertation on the verse, "the chief hypothesis" and "primary foundation" on which is erected the grand distinguishing doctrine of the epistle,—*the doctrine*, namely, *of justification and consequent salvation through the righteousness of God, available to men without distinction through faith.* (See Vitringa's *Praecipua Hypothesis, cui Paulus superstruxit praecellentia Religionis Christianae dogmata in Epistola ad Romanos, ex ejusdem illius Epistolae cap.* iii. 20 *producitur, et producta illustratur, inquisito demonstratoque vero sensu sententiae,*—**Ex Operibus legis nullam justificari carnem coram deo.**—*Observationes*, lib. iv., capp. x. xi.) It is assumed by the Apostle that only two ways of justification are possible to such beings as men;—(1), the way *of works of law* (that is, *personal righteousness*), and, (2), the way *of the work of Christ* (that is, *the vicarious righteousness of God*). If, then, justification be unattainable *by the deeds of the law*, it is of vital moment that men betake themselves by faith to that *righteousness of God*, which, being revealed in the Gospel, constitutes it "the power of God unto salvation to every one that believeth." (Rom. i. 16, 17.) It will thus be spiritually remunerative to study, as comprehensively and exactly as practicable, the apophthegm before us.

§ 3. *by works of law*, (ἐξ ἔργων νόμου). It is a matter of little moment whether we render this anarthrous expression anarthrously, or translate it, *by the works of the law.* Our English idiom is susceptible of either alternative. But as it is the word *works* which was intended by the Apostle to be betoned, and not the word *law*, we see a reason why the article was omitted by him from before the latter word, and thence co-relatively omitted from before the word *works.* Our idiom allows of a precise reproduction of the anarthrous peculiarity of the original; and, therefore, it is better to adhere to an anarthrous translation.

The idea of the Apostle, however, is not, "by works of *any* law," as Wakefield supposed. And yet Beza had the same opinion, (*in hoc versiculo appellatione* **legis** *sine articulo, intelligi omnem doctrinam, seu scriptam seu* *non scriptam, quae aliquid aut jubeat aut interdicat*). And so had Macknight, (*law, whether natural or revealed, moral or ceremonial*); and Middleton, (*the works either of the Jewish law or of any other*); and Oltramare, (*loi, ordre quelconque*); and van Hengel, (*legis alicujus*), &c. We might as well suppose that the Apostle, by the anarthrous word *works*, means "*any* works," as that by the anarthrous word *law*, he means "*any* law." For the same reason we must not adopt Belsham's translation, "by the works of *a* law," or Vaughan's, "in consequence of works of *a* law:" for if the anarthrous word *law* is to be rendered "*a* law," there is no reason why the anarthrous word *works* should not be correspondingly rendered "*some* works." In short, the Apostle's expression is anarthrous, because the emphasis is lying, not on the word *law*, but on the word *works*. (See ver. 27; iv. 2—6; xi. 6; Eph. ii. 9; Tit. iii. 5, &c.)

It is because of the existence of this emphasis, in relation to the word *works*, as well as on account of the posteriority in position of the word *law*, in relation to the word *works*, that we must reject the translation which is given to the phrase by Paulus, Benecke, Schrader, &c.,—*law of works*. This translation is an inversion of the Apostle's expression. It turns it unnaturally into a hysteronproteron. And in the interpretation which its patrons give to the expression, viz., *the law that enjoins outward works*, as distinguished from *the law that regulates the inner man—the law of love,*— (*geht deutlich hervor, dass Paulus in unsrer Stelle das Gesetz des Handelns dem Gesetz der Gesinnung, der Liebe, entgegen stellt*,-Benecke),—there is involved the oblivion that, in the two preceding chapters, the Apostle accuses both Gentiles and Jews, not only of externally unholy works, but also of internally unholy choices, acts, or states. (See i. 18, 21, 25, 28; ii. 7, 8, 28, 29; iii. 11, 12, 18.) There is involved, still farther, the oblivion that the law, to which the Apostle refers, has direct reference, in the upwinding of its prohibitions, to inward *concupiscence*, or *inordinate desire*. (See chap. vii. 7.) There is, moreover, this other objection to the interpretation:—it would render the Apostle's argumentation appropriate only to the Jews, or, at all events, to such of mankind as possessed or possess a verbally written Revelation: for the law, written in the heart, which is given to all men, is not simply, or distinctively, *a law of outward works.* And then, besides, the exclusion of no other works than those which are external, from the ground, or meritorious cause of justification, is entirely inconsistent with the Apostle's doctrine.

When, then, the Apostle says, *by works of law,* he really means, so far as regards the substance, though not precisely as regards the form, of his thoughts, "by *the* works of *the* law." And the *law* to which he refers is undoubtedly just the *law* to which he has all along throughout the preceding part of the epistle been referring,—the divine **νόμος**, looked at in the light of the divine תּוֹרָה, or, in other words, that *Moral Revelation,* which is *The Authoritative Instruction of God.* But then it is this *Moral Revelation,* or *Authoritative Instruction of God,* viewed in a particular aspect.

It is obvious that the *Moral Revelation,* or *Authoritative Instruction* of God,—the *law*—may be viewed in a *variety* of aspects. And it is equally obvious to the expositor of the New Testament writings in general, and of the Pauline writings in particular, that, as a matter of fact, it is viewed, πολυτρόπως,—in several very distinct though inter-related respects. Without seeking to specify all the aspects of the word in the Apostle's nomenclature, it is sufficient for the present to say, that (1.) Sometimes it is viewed simply, indefinitely, and generally, as *the divine Authoritative Instruction,—the Revelation of God to men.* (See Rom. ii. 14, 15; &c.) (2.) Sometimes it is viewed more specially as *the divine Authoritative Instruction regarding the duty which is essentially incumbent* **on men as men.** (See Rom. vii. 7; Matt. v. 17; xxii. 36, 40; &c.) (3.) Sometimes it is viewed, also more specially, as *the divine Authoritative Instruction regarding the duty which is incumbent* **on men as sinful men,** *who are, nevertheless, enjoying* **a dispensation of mercy.** (See Rom. ii. 13; &c.) (4.) And sometimes it is viewed, likewise more specially, as *the divine Authoritative Instruction regarding the duty which devolved* **on the Jews**

as Jews, in their special circumstances as members of the provisional terrestrial theocracy, — the great community that enclosed within itself that Seed of the woman and of Abraham, in which all the nations of the earth were and are to be blessed. (See Phil. iii. 6; &c.) The Authoritative Instruction of God contained, as a matter of reality, these various elements and aspects of Revelation. It contained them, both in the original little Volume of the book, the Pentateuch, and in the larger and more developed Volume, which embraced, in addition to the Pentateuch, the superadded (but homogeneous writings which were given by equivalent inspiration. And the word *law,* as might naturally be expected, is sometimes restricted to that which was *the original Revelation in writing,*—the contents of the little Volume, under whatever aspect these contents might be viewed. (See Acts xiii. 15.) And sometimes its reference is extended to the sum total of the Old Testament Scriptures, whatsoever might be the particular aspect of their contents, which might happen to be contemplated. (See John x. 34; &c.)

The Apostle Paul varies frequently, and sometimes suddenly, his standpoint of observation, when speaking of the *law.* In the 19th verse he views it as *the Authoritative Revelation in general,* constituting *the Old Testament Scriptures.* But in this 20th verse he views it in that specific aspect which exhibits *the divine Authoritative Instruction regarding the duty which is essentially incumbent* **on men as men.** He views it as "the law of commandments," which enjoins upon us those outer acts and inner choices and states which lie at the basis, and indeed constitute the essence, of all true religion. In the background, or focal point, of these commandments, he sees the decalogue or duologue, which is often theologically designated, by way of preeminence, *the moral law,* and which commands us *not to covet,* (chap. vii. 7,) and is summed up in one word—*love,* (chap. xiii. 8, 9). We have no reason to believe that the Apostle, in his phraseology or conception, divided off, in an artificial way, or by a sharply defined line, *the moral law* from *the judicial* and *ceremonial.*

But, as there can be no good reason to doubt that he is here viewing the entire law, in that particular element of it which, when seen in its focal point, condenses itself into what is now technically called *the moral law*, the ends of facile exegesis, and at all events of popular exposition, may be usefully subserved by conceding the employment of the expression *the moral law*—as the explication of the import of the word *law* as occurring in the apophthegm, "by works of law shall nobody be justified before God," that is, *by the works of the moral law,—by doing the works prescribed in the moral law,—shall nobody be justified in God's sight.*

Some expositors, indeed, both in ancient and in modern times, have supposed that it is the *ceremonial* element of the law, rather than the *moral*, which is referred to;—that element, namely, of the Authoritative Divine Instruction which exhibited *the duty which was provisionally devolving on the Jews as Jews*, rather than *the duty which is essentially devolving on men as men.* This was the opinion of Theodoret, of Abelard, of Dionysius à Ryckel, of Emser, of Michaelis, of Ammon, &c., though certainly not of Origen, whose name, as is generally and correctly supposed, is mentioned by Calvin as one of the patrons of the notion,* as it had been before him by Emser. But it

* Calvin's expression is somewhat puzzling:—"Opera legis quae dicantur, ambigitur etiam inter eruditos: dum alii ad universae legis observationem extendunt, alii restringunt ad solas ceremonias. Chrysostomum, Originem, et Hieronymum, ut in *priorem* opinionem concederent, movit adjectum legis vocabulum." So the expression stands in the Geneva editions of 1551 and 1565, as well as in the Berlin ed. of 1834, &c. Owen, in his translation, says, "the context clearly shows that *priorem* is a misprint for *posteriorem*." Sibson, as well as Krummacher and Bender, had been of the same opinion; for Sibson renders the word "last;" Krummacher and Bender "letstern." Good old Christopher Rosdell adheres, in his translation, to the Latin text,—"first." Beveridge too adheres to this text; but he supposes that the expression, "in priorem opinionem concederent," means "concede against,"—"unite in opposing the former opinion." It is a most unlikely interpretation. The old French version of the Commentary,—Calvin's own,—determines the right reading and the right interpretation,—"ont este esmeus a suyure la *derniere* opinion," *have been induced to follow the latter opinion.* But still there is an awkwardness; for Chrysostom and Origen do *not* maintain that the law referred to

was judiciously opposed by Augustin, on the ground of what occurs in the second clause of the verse, "for by the law is the knowledge of sin." (*De Spiritu et Littera*, cap. 8.) It is not, assuredly, by the ceremonial law, alone or chiefly, that *the knowledge of sin* is attained. And there is this other good reason to prove that it cannot be the ceremonial element of the law which is referred to:—The Apostle is making a statement which was intended to shut up Gentiles as well as Jews to the righteousness revealed in the Gospel; and we should suppose, therefore, that in the apophthegm before us,—which is his *Praeparatio Evangelica*,—he is opposing the idea that justification is attainable on the ground of obedience to that absolute law of commandments which is revealed in all men's consciences. The Gentiles, as a body, were never under the ceremonial element of the Authoritative Divine Instruction. That element was not revealed to them. It must, then, be the moral element of the law to which the Apostle refers, and this is admitted by the great body of judicious expositors, Roman Catholic as well as Protestant. See Thomas Aquinas, Este, Klee, Stengel, Reithmayr, Maier, Bisping, &c.

But even among those who admit that it is the moral element of the law that is referred to, there are some who contend that the expression, *the works of the law*, means, not *the works prescribed by the law*, but *the works which are performed under the influence of those motives which the law involves, works performed in a legal spirit, performed apart from the gracious influence of the Holy Spirit.* Luther took this view of the expression, (*Des Gesetzes Werk is alles das der Mensch thut oder thun kann am Gesetze, aus seinem freien Willen und eigenen Kräften.*–Vorrede). He thought that the "works of the law" are "sins." (*Ideo*

is *the law of ceremonies.* Chrysostom says nothing on the subject; but passes over the clause altogether; and Origen expressly explains *the law* referred to as meaning *the law of nature.* Pelagius—for it is he whom Calvin means when he says *Jerome*—does make mention of the ceremonies of the Old Testament dispensation. But his note has evidently been tampered with, and is inextricably confused. The grouping of the three authors by Calvin, as if they were united in opinion, is, doubtless, a real mistake.

necesse est opera legis esse peccata. Com. in Gal. ii. 16.) Philippi takes a corresponding view, (*ἔργα νόμου sind nicht sowohl Werke, welche das Gesetz befielt, als vielmehr Werke, wie sie der Mensch auf gesetzlichem Standpunkte vollbringt*). Barclay, of the Society of Friends, contends for a similar view: he says, "there is a great difference between *the works of the law*, and those *of grace*, or *of the Gospel*. The first are excluded; the second not, but are necessary. The first are those which are performed in man's own will, and by his strength, in a conformity to the outward law and letter." (*Apology*, Prop. vii. § 10.) Este accords, (*Notandum est* **opus legis** *bifariam sumi; vel pro opere quod lex prescribit, quale opus vere bonum est,—de quo cap.* ii. **factores legis justificabuntur**; *vel pro opere quod fit ex lege, id est, ex sola legis cognitione, et non ex fide. Quo porteriori modo loquitur hic Paulus de operibus legis, ea nimirum intelligens, quae quis facit sola lege adjutus*). So Ferus (*opera, quae lex vel minis vel promissis extorquet*). So Mussus too, and de Paris; and so, in a sense, Peile,—"works done under felt obligation of law." But this interpretation, besides proceeding on an erroneous view of the fundamental nature of law, in its bearing on created moral agents, and on an equally erroneous view of the relation of divine agency to creature-holiness, a relation that has nothing in it of the arbitrary, and that is by no means merely recuperative, is based on the exegetically untenable idea that it is the word *law* which is to be betoned: whereas it is the word *works*, as is evidenced, not only by other and textual considerations, but also by the fact that the word *law* is dropped altogether in such passages as ver. 27; iv. 2, 6; xi. 6; Tit. iii. 5. Were the interpretations of Luther, Este, Philippi, &c., correct, it would be impossible for any creatures, in any part of God's universe, to be justified, unless grace, founded on propitiation, or otherwise indissolubly connected with it, should assist them.

There is no reasonable ground for doubting that the expression means, (*the*) *works prescribed by* (*the*) *law*, and that the *law* referred to is *the Divine Authoritative Instruction, in relation to its moral element;* so that the works are really, as the old Protestants in general explained them, *good works*, or "works of righteousness," (Tit. iii. 5). The preposition which the Apostle employs, *by*, or *out of*, (ἐκ), refers to the source, or meritorious cause, of justification. The Apostle avers that the meritorious cause of justification is not to be found in such works as are prescribed in the moral law. It is not to be found, he means, in man's own personal righteousness. The reason *why* will appear when we ascertain the import of the second clause of the verse, *for by law is knowledge of sin*.

§ 4. *shall nobody be justified*, (οὐ δικαιωθήσεται πᾶσα σάρξ). There can be little doubt that the Apostle is mentally referring to the second verse of the cxliii. Psalm,—"Enter not into judgement with thy servant; *for in thy sight shall no man living be justified*," (ὅτι οὐ δικαιωθήσεται ἐνώπιόν σου πᾶς ζῶν). If this mental reference be admitted, as it is by almost all expositors, then the interpretation which we have given of the initial conjunction (διότι) is confirmed:—*because that*. The Psalmist's word is equivalent, *for* (ὅτι, = כִּי). The interpretation, also, which we have given to the expression, *works of law*, is confirmed. The Psalmist does not specify a particular kind of works; and the inference, therefore, is natural, that he means that no living man has done *any works* which can be the ground, or meritorious cause, of justification. No living man has so fulfilled that law, which enjoins a lifetime of good works, that he can rationally expect to be justified on the ground of his own personal righteousness. It follows, *in the third place*, that the expression, *no flesh*, (οὐ—πᾶσα σάρξ), which we have rendered idiomatically *nobody*, is equivalent to *no one living*, (לֹא ... כָל־חָי). Not a few expositors, indeed, have supposed that the word *flesh* is intended by the Apostle to be doctrinally suggestive of the reason why no one living shall be justified by deeds of law. The term, it is thought, points to the weak side of man's nature, and to his consequent incompetency to rise up, in the life-work devolving on him, to the high demands of the law. Of those who hold this opinion, some imagine that the term denotes man's moral corruption as well as his weakness. "The Apostle useth this phrase," says Brown of Wamphray, "to show what the condition of all without Christ is, nothing but a lump of flesh and corruption, full of weakness and sinful infirmities, unfit to do anything that is good: and so by this term he shows that he speaks only of man as he is now corrupted since Adam's fall." Of a similar view, although of more or less elasticity or intensity of doctrinal significance, are Origen, Abelard, Bullinger, Musculus, Mussus; Beza too, and de Paris, Rambach, Flatt; and Benecke, and Struensee, and Olshausen; Haldane also, and van Hengel, Ewbank, Matthias, &c. It seems to be more natural, however, to suppose, that the Apostle,—though not improbably alluding glancingly to that peculiarity of our complex nature which renders us specially liable to fall before temptations,—had, on the whole, no very fixed doctrinal design in selecting the expression, *no flesh*. He but availed himself of a common Hebrew idiom, equivalent to *nobody, no human being*. (See Gen. vi. 12; Num. xvi. 22; Ps. lxv. 2; cxlv. 21; Isai. xl. 5, 6; lxvi. 23, 24; Ezek. xxi. 5; Joel ii. 28. Comp. Luke iii. 12; John xvii. 2; Acts ii. 17; 1 Pet. i. 24.) He took the other, and outer, and complemental side of the expression which he employs in chap. ii. 9, "every *soul* of man." This simple view of the phrase is taken by Ambrosiaster, and by Thomas Aquinas, de Lyra, Calvin, Cajetan; Spener too, and S. Schmidt; Grotius also, and Vitringa, Cocceius, Day; Heumann too, and Fritzsche, Köllner, Baumgarten-Crusius, Krehl, &c. Calvin, indeed, rightly remarks that the phrase is peculiarly expressive. And he refers, as Bullinger had done before him, to the distinction which is drawn in Gellius between the word *man* and the word *mortal*. The reference is legitimate: for there is, undoubtedly, a peculiar connotation of idea in saying *every mortal*, or *no mortal*, instead of *every man*, or *no man*. And so, as Ambrosiaster remarked, there is a peculiar connotation of idea in saying *no flesh*, instead of *no man*, or *no living one*. The peculiarities of our incarnate condition and of our carnal susceptibilities are glancingly alluded to. Mace, however, renders the phrase simply *no one;* Wakefield and Newcome, *no man;* Purdue, *no human being;* Turnbull, *no human being whatever;* Peile, *no man living;* Zinzendorf, *no soul;* Michaelis and Oertel, *no mortal.* Wycliffe strangely renders the clause thus,—"*ech fleisch, that is, mankynde,* schal not be justifyed before him." And yet, strange as the version is, Heinfetter follows in his footsteps:—"*every flesh,* i. e., every class of mankind, *shall not be justified in the sight of him.*"

There can be no doubt that Wycliffe is right in connecting the negative adverb, grammatically, with the verb. The Apostle does not mean, "by works of law *not every body* shall be justified." He affirms of "every body" that "he shall *not* be justified by works of law," (ἐξ ἔργων νόμου οὐ δικαιωθήσεται πᾶσα σάρξ). But in our English idiom, as also in the Latin, German, Dutch, French, Italian, &c., it is expedient to combine the negation with the subject of the verb, *no flesh, no body.* We could not with propriety adopt Heberden's translation, and say, "all flesh shall be unjustified."

Shall be justified, (δικαιωθήσεται). The word is used forensically, and means, *shall be made out to be righteous,* that is, **shall be made out to possess that righteousness which entitles to the immunities and privileges of the kingdom of heaven—to the glory and honour which are coupled in the kingdom of heaven with immortality.** Nobody, says the Apostle, shall, in virtue of works of law, reach such righteousness as shall be judged to entitle to everlasting life.

This forensic import of the verb *to justify* (δικαιόω) has been, with more or less exactitude, seized by the great body of Protestant commentators and divines. And, as regards the passage before us, it is conceded by such Roman Catholic expositors as Reithmayr, (*als gerecht anerkannt werden*), and Maier, (*als gerecht gefunden oder anerkannt werden*). But Roman Catholic expositors and divines in general maintain that the word is used, not forensically, but psychologically, or pneumatologically, or ethically, as meaning *to make* (*inherently*) *righteous*. They are accustomed to refer to the etymological import of the term *to justify* (*justificare*)—insisting that it means,—*to make just* or *righteous*, (*justum facere*). And this etymological import of the term they hold to be its meaning in those passages of Scripture which make mention of evangelical justification. But, *in the first place*, there is no evidence that even the Latin word *justificare* primarily meant *to make* (a person) *just* or *righteous*. The term is not found in classical writers; and, apart from its usage among ecclesiastical writers in relation to the doctrine of evangelical justification, there is no evidence that it ever was employed as meaning *to make* (a person) *just* or *righteous*. If the term was a native of the Latin tongue, it is possible that it may have originally meant *to make* (a thing) *right;* just as, in the technical language of printers, the term is employed, like the term *justiren* in German, to denote the rectification, by special device, of such letters, or lines, as would otherwise be disproportionate or deficient in symmetry. But there is certainly not a vestige of evidence that it originally meant *to make a person righteous*. *In the second place*, it is of little theological moment to ascertain the primary or secondary import of the Latin term *to justify*, (*justificare*). Theology has to do with the meaning of the Greek and Hebrew words which are employed in the sacred Scriptures. And if it should turn out to be the case that the Latin word, (*justifico*), instead of being a native or autochthon of the Latin language, is but an immigrant, or import, or the artificially constructed homologue of the Greek word employed in the New Testament, (δικαιόω), then it would be doubly in vain to attempt to give a meaning to the doctrine of justification by means of any supposed peculiarity, etymological or conventional, of the Latin word.

We must turn, then, to the Greek word, (δικαιόω). What does it mean? And, especially, what is its biblical import? In particular, what is its New Testament import?

We shall, by and by, consider the classical usage of the

word. But, as the term occurs with peculiar frequency in the New Testament, and is found in such a variety of relationships, as affords abundant scope for ascertaining, by means of its settings, the import attached to it,—we shall, first of all, consider its employment by the inspired writers.

It is worthy of being noted, at the outset, that the word is used in the New Testament in relation to *persons* only;—so that *persons* only are the objects on which its action terminates. It is twice used, indeed, in relation to *a quality personified,* (Matt. xi. 19; Luke vii. 35). But a quality personified is just a quality popularly regarded, for the time being, *as a person.* In classical Greek the term has, as we shall see, a wider range of application, and is frequently employed in reference to *facts* or *acts* as its objects.

To come, then, to the New Testament usage. There is a large class of passages in which the term is used with precisely the same doctrinal significance as in the passage before us. These passages we shall not at present appeal to, inasmuch as the very object of our inquiry is to ascertain the meaning which the word should be regarded as bearing, in this and in all the other portions of the New Testament in which the doctrine of *justification by faith without the works of the law* is referred to. The contents, indeed, of many of these passages are such, that they would be of moment to determine the signification of the word. Nevertheless, *ex gratia,* we shall refrain from summoning them, meanwhile, into the court of our inquiry, to give their evidence in support of the forensic idea which we have affirmed.

Apart from such passages altogether, there are still abundant instances of the use of the word, to suffice for the determination of its New Testament import, and thus to decide the great controversy regarding *evangelical justification,*—whether it be *forensic,* or *ethical* and *therapeutic.*

"To the law and to the testimony," then, of those portions of the New Testament Scriptures. To begin with our own epistle, the word occurs in chap. ii. 13,—"not the hearers of the law are righteous in the presence of God, *but the doers of the law* **shall be justified,**" that is, *but the doers of the duties inculcated in the divine Authoritative Revelation or Instruction* (*considered as a revelation of mercy to men as sinners*), **shall be judicially made out to be righteous,** (viz., in the day when God shall judge the secrets of men by Jesus Christ, ver. 16). They shall be *judicially made out to be possessed of that righteousness which is evangelical meetness for the enjoyment of the glory and honour of the heavenly kingdom.* Here the term is manifestly used forensically, and not ethically and therapeutically. For, as Augustin himself remarks, *the doers of the law* are,—in virtue of being *the doers of the law,—the* (*inherently*) *righteous,* (*De Spir. et Litt.*, c. xxvi. 45), and it would be strange, and utterly out of place to say that *the* (*inherently*) *righteous shall be made* (*inherently*) *righteous* (in the day of judgement).

The term occurs again, as we have found, in Rom. iii. 4, where it is applied to God, " that *thou mightest be justified* in thy words, and overcome in thy litigation." Here also the term must be used forensically, meaning *that thou mightest be made out to be righteous—that thou mightest be judged to be righteous.* The forum of man's intelligence is referred to. It would be absurd as well as blasphemous to speak of making God inherently righteous, in a moral, metaphysical, or therapeutical sense.

In the other passages of *the epistle to the Romans* in which the word occurs, (viz., iii. 24, 26, 28, 30; iv. 2, 5; v. 1, 9; vi. 7; viii. 30, 33), with perhaps the exception of chap. viii. 30, the term is used with the same reference as in the paragraph before us; and they are therefore, as being equally *sub judice,* passed by meanwhile uninterrogated. If chap. viii. 30 be an exception to this usage of the term, it will fall to be considered as parallel to chap. ii. 13, and must be forensic.

In the theologically affiliated epistle to the Galatians, the term is used only with the same reference as in the paragraph before us,—a reference, direct or indirect, to the great doctrine of *evangelical justification.* See chap. ii.

16, 17; iii. 8, 11, 24; v. 4. We do not therefore cross-question its passages.

In the epistles to the Corinthians the term occurs twice, —1 Cor. iv. 4; vi. 11. In the former of these passages the forensic import is manifest:—"with me it is a small thing that I should be judged of you, or of man's judgement; yea, I judge not mine own self. For though I am not conscious to myself of any delinquency, yet *am I not hereby justified,* (οὐκ ἐν τούτῳ δεδικαίωμαι); but he that judgeth me is the Lord." It is obviously a matter of *judgement* to which the Apostle refers; not a metaphysical or ethical and therapeutical production of righteousness. In chap. vi. 11, again, he says, "but ye are washed, (or rather, *but ye washed yourselves,* ἀπελούσασθε), but ye are sanctified, but *ye are justified,* in the name of the Lord Jesus, and by the Spirit of our God." In this passage too, although it has been surrendered by some Protestant critics to the Roman Catholic interpretation, there is an evident reference to forensic justification. The Apostle had specified certain immoral classes, and said of them, "they shall not inherit the Kingdom of God." (Verses 9th, 10th.) Then he adds, ver. 11th, "and such were some of you." How, then, shall they inherit the Kingdom of God? "Ye washed yourselves: yea, ye were sanctified (by the Spirit of our God); yea, *ye were justified* (in the name of the Lord Jesus)," that is, "yea, ye were *judicially cleared, and acknowledged to be entitled to the privileges of the Kingdom of God,* (namely, on the ground of the evangelical *righteousness of God*)." There is a climax in the expression, not based indeed on the relation of succession in time, for the forensic justification referred to precedes sanctification; but based on the relation of superiority of degree in the particular case referred to, the superiority, namely, of legal title to moral meetness. It is probable that the two-plied expression,—"in the name of the Lord Jesus, and by the Spirit of our God," *folds back upon the two preceding clauses,* on the principle of inverse parallelism, so that the clause "in the name of the Lord Jesus" applies to the expression "but ye were justified," while the clause "and by the Spirit of our God" applies to the preceding expression, "but ye were sanctified." Comp. Rom. ii. 7—10. If we were to suppose that the expression "ye were justified" had reference to the psychologically therapeutical production of inherent righteousness, meaning *ye were made righteous*, there would be tautology in the clausules, and a suppression, moreover, of the highest evidence that the blessings of the Kingdom of God belonged to the Corinthian believers.

The word occurs once in the Epistles to Timothy, and once in the Epistle to Titus. In 1 Tim. iii. 16, we read of him who is the Innermost Essence of the Mystery of Godliness, that he was "manifested in flesh, *justified* in spirit," &c. The expression is susceptible of various interpretations; but it is certainly unnatural to suppose that it means *made* (*inherently*) *righteous in spirit.* It is much more likely to mean, *judged to be righteous in spirit;* for he was "Jesus Christ *the righteous*," and he brought in his mediatorial righteousness as an "everlasting righteousness" for men. It is this "righteousness" which is "revealed in the Gospel," and which constitutes the Gospel —"the power of God unto salvation." (Rom. i. 16, 17.) It has been approved of and accepted by the Father. The passage in Titus is in chap. iii. 7:—"not by works of righteousness which we have done, but according to his mercy he saved us, (*he delivered us*,—non *re*, sed *spe*,—*from the everlasting woe due to us on account of our sins,—such sins as are specified in ver.* 3), by the washing of regeneration, and renewing of the Holy Ghost, (*by making us morally meet for the opposite condition of everlasting glory,—through the influence of the divine Spirit*), which he shed on us abundantly through Jesus Christ our Saviour; that, **being justified,** that is, **being previously justified,** (δικαιωθέντες), by his grace, (*being previously cleared as regards our title to everlasting glory, by his grace*), we should be made heirs of eternal life, according to our hope, (κληρονόμοι γενηθῶμεν κατ' ἐλπίδα ζωῆς αἰωνίου)." While it might be possible to explain the expression here on the Roman Catholic hypothesis, it seems to be far more natural, either to regard it as looking back to the initial forensic justification that preceded the sanctification referred to in the foregoing clauses, or to interpret it as looking forward to that final forensic justification which precedes glorification, and immediately after which, consequently, "the promises,"—*the things promised,*—are "inherited." (See Heb. vi. 12.)

These are all the passages in which the verb is used by our Apostle. But the word is also found in the writings of Matthew, Luke, and James. It occurs, with the personified application already referred to, in Matt. xi. 19,—"But wisdom is *justified* of her children," (καὶ ἐδικαιώθη ἡ σοφία ἀπὸ τῶν τέκνων αὐτῆς), that is, "And the wisdom (of the arrangement) *was vindicated* on the part of her children." It *was judged* to be real. The *judgement* or *vindication* took place in that little court of judgement—that forum in miniature—which is established in every man's consciousness. And thus the justification referred to lay on the line of forensic adjudication. It had nothing in it of the nature of the metaphysical or psychological or therapeutical production of moral rightness, or righteousness. The only other passage in Matthew, in which the term occurs, is chap. xii. 37,—"by thy words shalt thou be *justified*, and by thy words shalt thou be *condemned.*" Here the antithesis to condemnation makes it evident that the term is used forensically.

In the gospel of Luke the word occurs five times. (1.) Chap. vii. 29,—"And all the people that heard him, and the publicans, *justified* God, being baptized with the baptism of John." The term cannot have here a moral or metaphysical meaning. The idea cannot be that the people in general, and the publicans in particular, produced inherent righteousness in God. It is obviously a term of judgement: they *judged* that God had acted right in the mission of John, and they *declared* their judgement. They praised God. (2.) Luke vii. 35,—"Wisdom is *justified* of all her children." The personified application. See on Matt. xi. 19. (3.) Luke x. 29,—"But he, willing to *justify* himself, said unto Jesus, And who is my neighbour?" The expression, evidently, does not mean that the lawyer was wishful to produce inherent righteousness in himself. It means that he desired *to make himself out to be righteous.* The term has a forensical import. It draws at least upon the usage of courts of judicature. (4.) Luke xvi. 15,—"Ye are they which *justify* yourselves before men: but God knoweth your hearts: for that which is highly esteemed among men is abomination in the sight of God." The Pharisees did not produce in themselves, before men, inherent righteousness. They only washed the outside of the platter. They only whitewashed the outside of the sepulchre. They *made themselves out,* before men, *to be righteous;* they proclaimed themselves to be righteous;—while they were abominable in the sight of God. The term draws the whole of its significancy from forensic procedure. (5.) Luke xviii. 14,—"I tell you, this man went down to his house *justified* rather than the other; for every one that exalteth himself shall be abased; and he that humbleth himself shall be exalted." The publican was *judged by God to be righteous, evangelically righteous.* He looked, or bent himself, toward the typical altar and to the Holy of holies, and, in self-abasement and brokenness of spirit, he lifted up his heart toward God. He believed in the inner import of the temple-symbolism; and he showed his faith by his works. The Pharisee, again "trusted in himself that he was *righteous.*" But God *judged the publican to be righteous.* The word is forensic; though it is used more according to the platform of James, than according to the model of Paul.

In the *Acts of the Apostles* the term occurs twice; but both instances are in one verse. Chap. xiii. 39,—"And in him all that believe are *justified* from all things, from which ye could not be *justified* by the law of Moses." In both instances the term is evidently used pregnantly. Believers are *made out to be righteous in Christ,* and are thus *cleared from those penal liabilities,* from which they could not get clearance by the ceremonial ordinances of the law of Moses, inasmuch as they could not, by the mere observance of these ceremonial ordinances, be made out to be righteous. The forensic import of the term is obvious.

The only other passages in the New Testament, in which this term *to justify* is found, occur in the Epistle of James, ii. 21, 24, 25,—"Was not Abraham our father *justified by works*, when he had offered Isaac his son upon the altar?"—"Ye see then how that *by works a man is justified, and not by faith only*:"—"Likewise also was not Rahab the harlot *justified by works*, when she had received the messengers, and had sent them out another way?" It is evident that in these passages the justification referred to, whatever it may be, cannot be the psychologically therapeutical production of inherent righteousness. For such righteousness develops itself from within outward, and not from without inward. A man's inherent righteousness does not grow from the root of outward works. His outward works grow from the root of his inherent righteousness. The works are the fruit, not the root. What then is the import of the term in James? It is forensical, as truly as in Paul. But it lies on the line of things that is indicated in Rom. ii. 13, rather than on the line of things that is indicated in Rom. iii. 20. We take James's meaning to be this,—a man is *made out to be evangelically righteous in character*, that is, a man is *made out to have that personal evangelical righteousness, which is* **meetness** *for the privileges of the kingdom of God*, **by faith and works combined,—by works as the moral complement of faith.** In James's justification there is a reference to the righteousness which is moral *meetness* for the privileges of the kingdom of heaven; in Paul's there is reference to the righteousness which is the legal *title* to these everlasting blessings. In both, however, the justification is judicial or forensical. In neither is it generically metaphysical or psychological, or specifically therapeutical. It is in the forensic idea alone, as exhibiting that which is common to both the Apostles, but which is sufficiently wide to admit of considerable diversity of relationship, that the nexus of conciliation between the two representations of justification is to be found. It is far, we conceive, from being the case, that we are to effect the conciliation of the two apostles by interpreting, with Bishop Bull, Paul's *faith*, in such a way as to make it coincident with James's *faith and works.*

In the *Textus Receptus* of the New Testament, there is another passage in which the verb *to justify* is found, viz., Rev. xxii. 11,—"He that is righteous, *let him be righteous still,*" or, as Wycliffe renders it, "be justified yit," (ὁ δίκαιος δικαιωθήτω ἔτι). And this passage has often been quoted by Roman Catholics to support their favourite interpretation of the term. It is quoted triumphantly by Bellarmin. (*De Justificatione*, lib. ii. cap. 3.) It perplexed Protestants. See, for instance, Chemitz, *De Justificatione,* cap. 3. But it seems to be certain that it is a corrupt reading; and that the true reading of the passage is, "he that is righteous, *let him do righteousness still,*" (δικαιοσύνην ποιησάτο ἔτι). This is supported by ℵ A B, and many other mss., and also by the best codices of the Vulgate, inclusive of the *amiatinus:* and it has been approved of by the chief critical authorities. Bengel, Griesbach, Lachmann, Scholz, and Tischendorf have introduced the reading into the text.

And thus it is evident, from a full induction of particulars regarding the New Testament usage of the term, δικαιόω, that, in approaching the passage before us, and the kindred passages in the Epistles to the Romans and the Galatians, we have every reason to assume that the word should be understood forensically. Were it to be otherwise interpreted, as denoting a psychologically therapeutical production of inherent righteousness, we should be guilty, we presume, of treating the term with hermeneutical violence.

It is true that the forensic acceptation of the term, in relation to the great doctrine of evangelical justification, seems to have been, to a very large extent, lost sight of in post-apostolic times, and down through the ages of the medieval divines and expositors, till the dawn of the Reformation. The fact is one of a multitude, which demonstrates the early and long continued misconception and corruption of Christian doctrine. Darkness succeeded the first marvellous light. Night came after day.

And yet there were stars of brilliancy here and there.

The author, for example, of the *Epistle to Diognetus*, published in the *Works of Justin Martyr*, speaks beautifully and most evangelically of the "sweet interchange" of our "sins" and Christ's "righteousness," in virtue of which "it is possible for us, transgressors and ungodly, to be justified." He says:—"God gave up his own son a "ransom for us, the holy for the unholy, the innocent for "the wicked, the righteous for the unrighteous, the incor-"ruptible for the corruptible, the immortal for the mortal. "For what else could cover our sins, but his righteousness? "In whom was it possible for us, the unholy and ungodly, "to be justified, but in the Son of God alone? Oh sweet "interchange! Oh unsearchable contrivance! Oh unlooked-"for blessings!—that the transgression of many should be "hidden in a righteous One, and that the righteousness of "One should justify many transgressors!" (*αὐτὸς τὸν ἴδιον υἱὸν ἀπέδοτο λύτρον ὑπὲρ ἡμῶν, τὸν ἅγιον ὑπὲρ τῶν ἀνόμων, τὸν ἄκακον ὑπὲρ τῶν κακῶν, τὸν δίκαιον ὑπὲρ τῶν ἀδίκων, τὸν ἄφθαρτον ὑπὲρ τῶν φθαρτῶν, τὸν ἀθάνατον ὑπὲρ τῶν θνητῶν. Τὶ γὰρ ἄλλο τὰς ἁμαρτίας ἡμῶν ἠδυνήθη καλύψαι, ἢ ἐκείνου δικαιοσύνη; Ἐν τίνι δικαιωθῆναι δυνατὸν τοὺς ἀνόμους ἡμᾶς καὶ ἀσεβεῖς, ἢ ἐν μόνῳ τῷ Υἱῷ τοῦ θεοῦ; Ὦ τῆς γλυκείας ἀνταλλαγῆς, ὢ τῆς ἀνεξιχνιάστου δημιουργίας, ὢ τῶν ἀπροσδοκήτων εὐεργεσιῶν· ἵνα ἀνομία μὲν πολλῶν ἐν δικαίῳ ἑνὶ κρυβῇ, δικαιοσύνη δὲ ἑνὸς πολλοὺς ἀνόμους δικαιώσῃ.*—Cap. ix.) This a star-like passage. But it seems to be almost, if not altogether, impossible to find its "fellow" in the writings of the fathers. There are multitudes of passages, indeed, in which the Scripture declaration is echoed and re-echoed that men are *not justified by works of law.* There are also abundant passages in which those other Scripture declarations are echoed and re-echoed, which assert that men are *not justified by works.* "God," says Theophylact,—uttering the sentiments of the entire cloud of patristic witnesses,—"justifies us, *although we have not works*," (*δικαιοῖ γὰρ ἡμᾶς ὁ θεὸς, κἂν μὴ ἔργα ἔχωμεν.*—*Comment.* in Rom. iii. 21). It is constantly recognized, and insisted on all down through the ages, that it is *by faith* that men are justified.

But Origen, for example, surmises that it might have been as legitimately said of *love*, or *piety*, or *mercy*, as of *faith*, that *it is imputed for righteousness.* (*Et forte, sicut de fide dictum est, quia fides reputata est ad justitiam, ita et de caritate dici potest, quia reputata est caritas ad justitiam, aut pietas, aut misericordia.* Com. in Rom. iv. 22.) It would appear, indeed, that both Origen and the fathers in general were deficient in definitely settled and self-consistent views of the meaning of the word, which we render "justify." At times it is explained forensically; though even at these times the explanation is not always given with a decisive hand. (See Origen, for example, in his Com. on Rom. iii. 25, 26, *Deus enim justus est, et justus justificare non poterat injustos: ideo interventum voluit esse propitiatoris, ut per ejus fidem justificarentur, qui per opera propria justificari non poterant.* He says again, on Rom. iii. 27, 28, *Dicit sufficere solius fidei justificationem, ita ut credens quis tantummodo justificetur, etiamsi nihil ab eo operis fuerit expletum.—Fortassis haec aliquis audiens resolvatur, et bene agendi negligentiam capiat, siquidem ad justificandum fides sola sufficiat. Ad quem dicemus, quia post justificationem si injuste quis agat, sine dubio justificationis gratiam sprevit.* Again on Rom. iv. 23—25, he says, *Justificat ergo eos Christus tantummodo, qui novam vitam exemplo resurrectionis ipsius susceperunt, et vetusta injustitiae et iniquitatis indumenta velut causam mortis abjiciunt.*) These quotations are perhaps not thoroughly self-consistent; but they seem to assume a judicial or forensic import of the word *justify.* (Chrysostom too, in explaining Rom. viii. 33, 34, says, Θεὸς ὁ δικαιῶν· τίς ὁ κατακρίνων; —οὐκ εἶπε, θεὸς ὁ ἀφεὶς ἁμαρτήματα, ἀλλ', ὃ πολλῷ μεῖζων ἦν, θεὸς ὁ δικαιῶν. ὅταν γὰρ ἡ τοῦ δικαστοῦ ψῆφος δίκαιον ἀποφήνῃ, καὶ δικαστοῦ τοιούτου, τίνος ἄξιος ὁ κατηγορῶν; Theodoret, also, in his Com. on Rom. viii. 33, 34, explains the expression *God who justifieth* in the same forensic way,—τοῦ θεοῦ δικαίους ἀποφήναντος, τίς κατακρίναι δυνήσεται.) At other times the term seems to be regarded as almost equivalent to *forgive*,—a meaning often loosely attached to the word by Protestant writers, and even sometimes by Calvin. (See *Theodoret, Com. on Rom.* iii. 24,—where, explaining the expression *justified freely by his grace,* &c., he says,—πίστιν γὰρ μόνην εἰςενεγκόντες, τῶν ἁμαρτημάτων τὴν ἄφεσιν ἐδεξάμεθα.) Chrysostom and Theophylact, however, constantly insist that it denotes something which is much greater than forgiveness. It means, they say, *to make righteous.* (See *Chrysost. Homil. on Rom.* iv. 5, when remarking on the expression, *who justifieth the ungodly,* he says, ἐννόησον γὰρ ἡλίκον ἐστὶ πεισθῆναι καὶ πληροφορηθῆναι, ὅτι δύναται ὁ θεὸς τὸν ἐν ἀσεβείᾳ βεβιωτόκα τοῦτον ἐξαίφνης οὐχὶ κολάσεως ἐλευθερῶσαι μόνον, ἀλλὰ καὶ δίκαιον ποιῆσαι, καὶ τῶν ἀθανάτων ἀξιῶσαι τιμῶν. See also his observations on Rom. iv. 2; iv. 25. Theophylact, in his *Com. on Rom.* iv. 25, says on the expression, *who was delivered for our offences, and raised again for our justification,* ἀπέθανεν οὖν καὶ ἀνέστη, ἵνα καὶ ἁμαρτιῶν ἀπαλλάξῃ, καὶ δικαίους ἐργάσηται. Origen, too, sometimes takes this same psychologico-ethical and therapeutical view, as, for example, in his *Com. on Rom.* iv. 1—8, p. 240, ed. Lommatzsch, *quae fides tanta est, ut justificet etiam eum, qui impius fuerit, ut ultra jam non sit impius.* And certainly the idea turns up again and again and again in Augustin. In his treatise, De Spiritu et Litt., c. xxvi. 45, he says, *Quid est enim aliud,* **justificati,** *quam justi facti, ab illo scilicet qui justificat impium, ut ex impio fiat justus?*—Again, in his Enarrat. in Psal. vii. 5, he says, *Cum enim justificetur impius, ex impio fit justus, et ex possessione diaboli migrat in templum Dei.*—In his Tractat. lxxii. in Jo. xiv. 10—14, —he says, *impios justificare, quod ita facit in nobis, ut faciamus et nos.* In his Sermo clxix., c. x. 13, he says,—*Quid est, propter justificationem nostram? Ut justificet nos,—ut justos faciat nos.* In his treatise De Perfectione Just., c. xvii. 38, he expounds the psalmist's words thus, "**Ne intres in judicium cum servo tuo,** *noli me judicare secundum te, qui es sine peccato:* **quia non justificabitur in conspectu tuo omnis vivens**; *quod de hac vita dictum sine difficili quaestione intelligitur; et quod ait,* **non justificabitur,** *ad illam perfectionem justitiae retulit quae in hac vita non est.*" And yet, whatever was Augustin's view of the *word* "justification," he speaks most delightfully of the *thing*, when he represents Christ, for example, as "making our sins his sins, that he might make his righteousness our righteousness,"—*delicta nostra sua delicta fecit, ut justitiam suam nostram justitiam faceret.*-Enarrat, in Ps. xxii. v. 2.)

In such passages as those, which we have just been quoting, the word *justification* is evidently regarded as denoting an ethical and therapeutical change. It is, as Dr. John Owen expresses it, "taken for *justifaction*." (*Doctrine of Justification*, ch. iv.) And thus the fathers referred to, and the others who coincide with them,—including almost the whole galaxy who flourished in the earlier centuries, and the lesser lights who succeeded, and the great schoolmen too,—must be regarded as overlooking to a very large extent the proper forensic import of the term, in its relation to that great evangelical doctrine, which is the alpha, though it is not the omega, of *the Epistle to the Romans.* Faber, in his *Primitive Doctrine of Justification*, has certainly failed to adduce evidence to the contrary. His quotations suffice to show that the fathers maintained that salvation is a matter of grace, bestowed on us through Christ; but they do not prove that the fathers regarded justification as being a divinely forensic transaction, judicially recognizing the reality and validity of a certain relationship to everlasting glory and honour in the divine kingdom, rather than as being a psychologico-therapeutical exertion of divine power changing the moral character of the soul. Suicer, too, has accomplished less (in his *Thesaurus Eccles.* on δικαιόω), in the way of proving that the fathers are patrons of the forensic view, than Bishop O'Brien would seem to attribute to him. (*Attempt to explain the Doct. of Justif.*, p. 388.) The very first passage, which he quotes to show that the fathers are to be regarded as holding the forensic view of justification,—a passage from Justin Martyr's *Dialogue with Trypho*, (p. 267, ed. 1686),—he somewhat misapplies, as is rendered evident by the succeeding clause, which, however, he does not give. In the words quoted, Justin Martyr says, "God holds as righteous and sinless, him who repents of his sins," (θεὸς τὸν μετανοοῦντα ἀπὸ τῶν ἁμαρτημάτων, ὡς δίκαιον καὶ ἀναμάρτητον ἔχει); but he adds,—for he is reproducing the idea enunciated by Ezekiel in the 33d chapter of his prophecies,—"and him who turns from godliness or righteousness to unrighteousness and godlessness, He accounts as a sinner, and unrighteous and ungodly," (καὶ τὸν ἀπὸ εὐσεβείας ἢ δικαιοπραξίας μετατιθέμενον ἐπὶ ἀδικίαν καὶ ἀθεότητα, ὡς ἁμαρτωλὸν καὶ ἄδικον καὶ ἀσεβῆ ἐπίσταται). The reference of the passage is to *the effect of ultimate character within the period of probation.* He who deliberately ends his period of probation holily, will be treated by God as if he had been always holy. He who deliberately ends it unholily, will be treated by God as if he had always been unholy. As the tree falls, so shall it lie. The great mediatorial realities, which have to do with justification, are implied, indeed, in this divine treatment. But neither they, nor the justification which is based upon them, are directly described or referred to in the passage quoted. There is, as we shall see in course, *a philological reason* to account for the imperfect notions which the Greek and Latin Fathers entertained on the meaning of the word *justify.*

The council of Trent, as might have been expected, did not recognize *justification* as being *a forensic transaction.* They held it to be, either wholly or partially, *the sanctification of the inner man.* (*Non est sola peccatorum remissio sed et sanctificatio et renovatio interioris hominis per voluntariam susceptionem gratiae et donorum, unde homo ex injusto fit justus, et ex inimico amicus, ut sit heres secundum spem vitae aeternae, &c.*" Sess. vi., c. 7.) The *justice* or *righteousness*, from which *justification* takes its denomination, they held to be inherent, originating indeed in the grace of God, infused by that grace, and sustained by that grace, but at the same time so chosen by the human will, as to be really *the righteousness of man*, as well as *the righteousness of God.* (*Neque propria nostra justitia, tanquam ex nobis propria statuitur; neque ignoratur aut repudiatur justitia Dei. Quae enim justitia nostra dicitur, quia per eam nobis inhaerentem justificamur; illa eadem Dei est, quia a Deo nobis infunditur per Christi meritum.* Sess. vi., c. 16.) This is, substantially, the doctrine of Augustin.

And even within the circle of Protestantism, the same view, in the main, of justification,—"justification by *infusion*," or some corresponding modality, as distinguished from what Pemble calls "justification by *apology*" (*Treatise of Justif.*, Sect. 1, ch. 1), or *justification in virtue of imputation*,—has been occasionally advocated. It was advocated by And. Osiander among the Lutheran theologians,—though under a peculiar phase,—the phase of *inhabitation* rather than of *infusion*. For once, at least, Melancthon himself, as is remarked by Winzer, (*De vocab.* δίκαιος, δικαιοσύνη *et* δικαιοῦν *in Paulli ad Romanos epistola*, p. xiii.), was unwarily betrayed into the same notion. ("*Hactenus satis copiose ostendimus,—quod sola fide justificemur, hoc est, ex injustis* **justi efficiamur** *seu* **regeneremur.**"–Apolog. Conf., p. 82.) It was also advocated by Grotius. (*Prolegomena in Romanos.*) It was contended for by Ro. Barclay, of the Society of Friends. (*Apology, Prop.* vii.) It was strenuously maintained by Alex. Knox, of the Church of England, who had for his friend and theological pupil, Bishop Jebb. (*Remains:—Treatise on Justif.*) And it has been upheld by a variety of other individuals, as well as by entire mystic sects.

Notwithstanding, however, these dissentient voices within the sphere of Protestantism; and notwithstanding the fact that the sum total of consistent Roman Catholic theologians are consentient with the Protestant dissentients; and notwithstanding, too, that the Roman Catholic doctrine, as developed and determined by the Council of Trent, is but the completed reproduction of the prevailing views that floated down through the patristic cycles, and the succeeding ages of the schools; notwithstanding these incidents in the history of the tentative exegesis of Christian truth, it is evident, from the particulars of the New Testament usage, regarding the word *to justify*, (δικαιόω),—as these particulars have been already exhibited,—that we are not only warranted, but hermeneutically bound, to approach the great doctrine of evangelical justification with the proleptic conviction that the word employed should most probably be regarded as having a judicial or forensic sense, and not as referring to a psychological and therapeutical change of character. This conviction will become deepened, when we have considered the classical usage of the term.

The classical usage of δικαιόω is far from being coincident, in detail, with the usage of the term in the New Testament. Nevertheless, the *tout ensemble* of classical and biblical usage is, as a philological phenomenon, a unity of symmetrical phraseological development: and we shall not find it difficult to account for the specific divergence of import, which is characteristic of the New Testament.

The verb is a denominative. It is derived from its homogeneous adjective, (δίκαιος); and, in virtue of its terminative (in—όω), belongs to a class of verbs, which, though not invariably denoting the making of a thing into that which the primitive words signify, (see λουτρόω, μαστιγόω, &c.), yet are generally factitive in import,—factitive in the sense indicated. (See δουλόω, δηλόω, πληρόω, τελειόω, τυφλόω, φανερόω, &c.) Hence we may reasonably conclude that *to make right*, or *to right*, was the primitive meaning of the verb.

Both *things* and *persons*, however, may be *made right*, or *righted*, in different ways. They may be *made right*, or *righted*, intrinsically, or extrinsically; absolutely, or relatively; in the contents, or in the circumstantialities, of their being; in themselves, or in the minds of those who have to do with them. It is questionable whether there be any instance extant, in any classic writer, in which δικαιόω means *to make* (*intrinsically*) *right* or *righteous*. Rauwenhoff asserts that there is none. (*Disquisitio de* δικαιώσει, p. 8.) It is, however, an interesting fact, that there is in the Alexandrian version of the Hebrew Bible,—the Septuagint,—one instance of this, the primitive import of the verb. It occurs in Psalm lxxiii. 13. In the 12th verse the Psalmist says,—"Behold, these are the ungodly, who prosper in the world; they increase in riches." Then he adds in the 13th verse,—"Verily, I have *cleansed my heart* in vain, and washed my hands in innocency." (ἐδικαίωσα τὴν καρδίαν μου = זִכִּיתִי לְבָבִי.) The meaning of the Greek version of the Psalmist's expression,—as is evidenced at once by the Hebrew phrase, by the parallelism of the clauses, and by the nature of the case spoken of,—is, *I made right my heart*, i. e. *I cultivated rightness and righteousness of heart.* This, however, is the one solitary instance in the Septuagint in which the word is unquestionably used as meaning *to make* (*intrinsically*) *right or righteous.* And it will be noted that the object of the verb is not *a person*, but *a thing* (the heart). It would seem to be the case that no decisive instance of the same usage of the word has been found in any classical author. The only passage known,—apparently,—that can be considered as exemplifying the same import of the word, is a curious and obscure fragment of Pindar,—often quoted, *partially*, by ancient Greek writers. The passage took hold of the minds of some of the great thinkers, in consequence of containing a peculiar representation of *law.* Law is represented as the Supreme Sovereign, *the king of all mortals and immortals*, (Νόμος ὁ πάντων βασιλεὺς θνατῶν τε καὶ ἀθανάτων). The passage is adduced by Callicles in Plato's Gorgias, and is cunningly wielded by him in opposition to the moral philosophy of Socrates, and in defence of the idea that *might constitutes right.* He does not profess, it must be noted, to quote the words with perfect accuracy. He allows that he could not charge his memory with the *ipsissima verba*, (λέγει οὕτω πως, τὸ γὰρ ᾆσμα οὐκ ἐπίσταμαι). But he gives the passage as follows:—Νόμος ὁ πάντων βασιλεὺς θνατῶν τε καὶ ἀθανάτων, ἄγει δικαιῶν τὸ βιαιότατον ὑπερτάτᾳ χερί· τεκμαίρομαι ἔργοισιν Ἡρακλέος, ἐπεὶ ἀπριάτας—. Vict. Cousin's translation of what is thus ascribed to "Law, king of all mortals and immortals," is as follows:—"Elle traîne après elle la violence d'une main puissante, *et elle la legitime.* J'en juge par les action d'Hercule, qui, sans les avoir achetés—." Boeckh gives the sense thus:—"Fatalis lex etiam vim maximam affert, *eamque justam efficit*, quum humana ratione sit injusta." Pindar, according to this reading of his words, is entirely of one mind with Callicles; and hence Socrates opposes both in one breath; and Aristides, in his Oration περὶ ῥητορικῆς, 89, launches out into an elaborate refutation of the poet's idea. The reasoning of Aristides is, in many respects, truly admirable. But we are disposed to think with Reiske, (see *Dindorf's Aristides*, ad. loc.), that Callicles cunningly and sophistically misapplied and misquoted Pindar. Whether, indeed, it be the case that we have, near the close of the 1st Book of the *Stromata* of Clemens Alexandrinus, as Reiske thinks, the full and correct passage of Pindar,—(he reads ὁδοὺς βιαιότητος ἐλέγχει παιδείᾳ νόμος, ὁ πάντων βασιλεὺς κ. τ. ἑξῆς, instead of ὁδοὺς βιότητος ἐλέγχει παιδεία. Νόμος ὁ πάντων κ. τ. ἑξῆς, and he renders δικαιῶν, *punishing,—punit vel ulciscitur violentiam eminentissima manu*),—we feel satisfied that Callicles *quibbled* with the word δικαιῶν, attributing to it, in order to serve his sophistical end, not its Pindaric and conventional import, but its purely etymological signification. For, certainly, it is exceedingly unlikely that the poet should give expression to such an inverted transcendentalism of speculation as Callicles ascribes to him,—a transcendentalism that is not only of the descending order, but that also involves, in its descent, its own logical annihilation, inasmuch as it merges the notion of *right* as distinguished from *might*, and thus overturns the assumed supremacy of *law*, as distinguished from other forces, impersonated and impersonal. Pindar's real idea, according to Reiske, was the following:—"*Law, the king of mortals and immortals, controls violence, even when in the extreme* (τὸ βιαιότατον),*—controls it in the way of bringing sooner or later upon it, with overmastering hand, the punishment which is its due.*" It is right, however, to acknowledge that a cloud of uncertainty, yet unpenetrated, rests over the entire Pindaric fragment. Apart altogether from the admission of Callicles, that perhaps he did not quote the words with perfect accuracy, there is doubt regarding the identity of the words which Callicles really gave. (In some editions the text runs thus,—ἄγει βιαίως τὸ δικαιότατον κ. τ. ἑξῆς.) And hence we must just leave the passage, feeling absolutely assured of little regarding it that could help us to determine the import of δικαιόω.

In all the ordinary cases, in which the word is used by the classical writers regarding *things* or *acts*, as distinguished from *persons*, it has a meaning that lies on a judicial, forensic, or quasi-forensic line,—the line of *making right in one's judgement*, that is, of *judging to be right.* Thus, in Thucydides, ii. 6, we read of the Athenians "*judging it right* to do retaliatingly to the Lacedemonians what the Lacedemonians had done to them," (δικαιοῦντες τοῖς αὐτοῖς ἀμύνεσθαι οἷσπερ καὶ οἱ Λακεδαιμόνιοι ὑπῆρξαν. The scholiast explains δικαιοῦντες by δίκαιον κρίνοντες). So again, in Book ii. 61, Pericles says that "men *judge it right* equally to blame him who softly yields the glory that belongs to him, and to hate him who impudently arrogates a glory that is not his due," (ἐν ἴσῳ γὰρ οἱ ἄνθρωποι δικαιοῦσι τῆς τε ὑπαρχούσης δόξης αἰτιᾶσθαι ὅστις μαλακίᾳ ἐλλείπει, καὶ τῆς μὴ προσηκούσης μισεῖν τὸν θρασύτητι ὀρεγόμενον). See also Thucyd., iv. 64; vi. 89; vii. 68; as likewise ii. 71; v. 105. In all these passages the judicial import of the word,—*judicial* so far as *the private forum* of *the human judgement* is concerned,—is indisputable;—although, in some of them, the idea of *judging to be right* may appropriately shape itself into such diverse expressions as *decide, allow, require*, &c. In the same author, again,—in Book iv. 122,—the word means *to judge to be the case*, rather than *to judge to be right*, (εἶχε δὲ καὶ ἡ ἀλήθεια περὶ τῆς ἀποστάσεως μᾶλλον ἢ οἱ Αθηναῖοι ἐδικαιοῦν). And in v. 26, it means simply *to judge*, (καὶ τὴν διὰ μέσου ξύμβασιν εἴτις μὴ ἀξιώσαι πόλεμον νομίζειν, οὐκ ὀρθῶς δικαιώσει,—"and if any one should think that the intervening time should not be reckoned to the period of the war, *he would not judge* correctly"). In these latter instances, the judicial element in the word's import has become so dominant, that the etymological idea of *right* is almost entirely merged. Such is Thucydides's use of the word, as applied to *things* and *acts*. His employment of the term is a fair representation of its general usage throughout the classics. We need not, for proof, go into multiplied details. Let it suffice to refer to Herodotus, i. 133, "they *judge it right* to have their table more plentifully furnished than on other days," (ἐν ταύτῃ δὲ πλέω δαῖτα τῶν ἄλλων δικαιεῦσι προτίθεσθαι). The same use of the term is very frequent in Herodotus. It latterly descended into ecclesiastical Greek. The word came to be employed in reference to what was *judged right* or *decided upon* in ecclesiastical councils; as, for instance, in such expressions as this,—"it has been judged right by the holy synod," (ὑπὸ τῆς ἁγίας συνόδου δεδικαίωται). In its meaning of *judging (a thing) to be right*, Justin Martyr,—as a fair representation of the ecclesiastical writers,—affords a beautiful instance in his *Cohortatio ad Graecos*, p. 11, ed. 1686,—"when *he judged it right* that the multitude of the Hebrews should return to their own country," (ὁπηνίκα ἀπὸ τῆς Αἰγύπτου τὸ τῶν Ἑβραίων πλῆθος ἐπὶ τὴν οἰκείαν χώραν ἐπανελθεῖν ἐδικαίωσε).

When the word is applied to *persons* in the classics, its import is still predominantly judicial, or forensic, or quasi-forensic. It never means, apparently, *to make right (intrinsically, or metaphysically, or psychologically, or therapeutically)*. It means *to right* one *in some extrinsic and relative manner*. Aristotle, indeed, in his *Nicomachean Ethics*, (v. 9), uses it in an extra-judicial sense, as meaning *to treat (one) rightly* or *justly*. He employs it in antithesis to ἀδικέω *to injure (one), to wrong (one), to treat (one) unjustly*. And in discussing the relation of *will* to the *wronging of persons*, or, *the treatment of them unjustly*, he says:—"it is not the same *to do unjust things*, and *to treat unjustly;* neither is it the same *to suffer unjust things*, and *to be treated unjustly:* and a like distinction is to be made as to *acting justly*, and *being treated justly*, for it is impossible to be treated unjustly, if there be no one who treats unjustly, or *to be treated justly* if there be no one who treats justly," (ὁμοίως δε καὶ ἐπὶ τοῦ δικαιοπραγεῖν καὶ δικαιοῦσθαι· ἀδύνατον γὰρ ἀδικεῖσθαι, μὴ ἀδικοῦντος· ἢ δικαιοῦσθαι, μὴ δικαιοπραγοῦντος). In this use of the word by Aristotle there is no reference to *intrinsic righting*—or *making (one) inherently right, metaphysically, psychologically, or therapeutically.* The *righting* referred to is extrinsic and relative. The term, as used by other classical writers, has, so far as appears, invariably,—when applied to persons,—an import that is, at least, equally *extrinsic.* It seems to denote, prevailingly, if not uniformly, that *relative righting* which is realized in a judicial, forensic, or quasi-forensic way. In the celebrated, but extremely obscure, passage of the *Agamemnon* of Aeschylus, 391—393, the word,—however perplexed the construction of the sentence as a whole may be, and whatever may be the difficulty of giving an adequate translation to the term,—must undoubtedly be understood as referring to such *relative righting* as is realized *in the judgements of men.* The allusion is to Paris, (κακοῦ δὲ χαλκοῦ τρόπον | τρίβῳ τε καὶ προςβολαῖς | μελαμπαγὴς πέλει | δικαιωθείς). He was not *wronged,* but only *righted in the judgements of men* (δικαιωθείς), when he was regarded as being *inveterately black (in character),* μελαμπαγής. His character, when subjected to a moral crucial process, was like bad brass, when subjected to friction or other appropriate tests;—it showed itself to be base. Potter says that "there are few passages in Aeschylus more obscure than this antistrophe." Solanus of old gave up the attempt to interpret it. (*Rogabis forte, quid de hoc loco sentiam. Nescio equidem.*–Diss. de stylo Nov. Test., § 41.) But manifestly the word δικαιωθείς cannot mean either (forensically) *justified,* as Deyling dreamed, or *made (intrinsically) right.* It must refer only to such a *relative righting* as is realized when men see a bad character in its true light, and thus *judge* it rightly. A bad character when thus judged or *tested,* is detected and *detested.*

Hence the word δικαιόω came to signify, in classical Greek, *to condemn,*—the opposite pole of its New Testament meaning, *to justify.* Thus we read in Thucydides, iii. 40, that Cleon said to the Athenians regarding the Mitylenaeans;—"if you follow my opinion, you will do both what is just to the Mitylenaeans and what is advantageous to yourselves; but if you determine otherwise, you will not gratify them, but will rather *condemn* yourselves, (ὑμᾶς δὲ αὐτοὺς μᾶλλον δικαιώσεσθε); for if it was right in them to revolt, it was wrong in you to hold them under your rule." We need not marvel that the term should have this import. For he, who is justly *condemned*, is really *righted* (extrinsically). He is put right,—so far as people's judgements are concerned,—in relation to facts, and to law, and to his fellow-men in general. But we may well marvel that Pfochen, in his *Diatribe de Ling. Græc. Nov. Test. Puritate*, § 65, should appeal to the very passage of Thucydides, which we have just quoted, to prove that δικαιόω means *to justify* in classical Greek. He not only "nodded," like "good Homer," when he wrote that portion of his *Diatribe;* he was *sound asleep and dreaming.* He was contented to quote the passage at second hand. He quoted it from Camerarius on Matt. xi. 19; and he misunderstood both Camerarius and Thucydides. The word obviously means *to condemn.* It is supposed by many good critics that the term has the same meaning in the Heraclides of Euripides, 190.—Iolaus is pleading, before Demophoon at Marathon, the cause of the children of Hercules, who had been compelled to become refugees from Argos. He says,—

πῶς ἂν δικαίως ὡς Μυκηναίους ἄγοι
ὧδ' ὄντας ἡμᾶς, οὓς ἀπήλασε χθονός;
ξένοι γὰρ ἐσμέν· ἢ τὸν Ἑλλήνων ὅρον
φεύγειν δικαιοῦτ', ὅστις ἂν τ' Ἄργος φύγῃ;
οὔκουν Ἀθήνας γ'.

How can he drag us back again with justice
As subjects of Mycené, to that realm
Which hath already banished us? We there
Are only foreigners. But why should he
Whom Argos dooms to exile, by all Greece
Be also exiled? Not by Athens, sure.—Wodhull.

"Or do you *condemn* whosoever may be a refugee from Argos to be a refugee from all Greece? Surely not from Athens at least."

This import of the word is, in some respects, in striking contrast to the import of the term in the New Testament. But it had, nevertheless, so impressed itself upon the mind of Elsner, that he felt disposed to interpret Matt. xi. 19, in accordance with it,—reading the verse thus,—"The son of man came eating and drinking; and they say, Behold a man gluttonous and a winebibber,—a friend of publicans and sinners,—*and his doctrine is condemned by its disciples.*" But such an interpretation is an intolerable squeeze. It is supposed, however, by the same critic, and apparently on more plausible grounds, that Luther must have used the German word for *justify* (rechtfertigen) in this contrastive or contrary signification in Acts xii. 19,—"and when Herod had sought for him, and found him not, *liess er die Hüter rechtfertigen, he got the keepers condemned*, and commanded that they should be put to death."

Besides meaning *to condemn*, in classical usage, δικαιόω bore the kindred meaning *to punish*. This extension of import is entirely natural; for when a guilty being is justly punished, he is really *righted*,—so far as people's judgements are concerned,—in his relations to the political or moral system, into which his criminal conduct had introduced confusion. The term is frequently employed in this acceptation. A representative example or two will suffice. Herodotus, (i. 100), in describing the government of Deioces, the Mede, says, that "when he learned that any one had committed a misdemeanour, he sent for him, and *punished* him according to the desert of each offence," (κατ' ἀξίην ἑκάστου ἀδικήματος ἐδικαίευ). In speaking, again, of Cambyses, who fancied that the Egyptians were holding rejoicings over his ill success, he says, (iii. 29);—"When the priests led forth Apis, Cambyses, after the manner of a man demented, seizing his dagger, and aiming to thrust it into the belly of Apis, struck the thigh, and then, laughing, said to the priests, Ye knaves, these gods of yours are flesh and blood, and are sensible to steel! Truly worthy of Egyptians is this god! But it shall be to your cost that you have tried to mock me. Having thus spoken, he commanded those, whose office it was to do such things, to seize the priests, and to put to death whomsoever of the rest of the Egyptians they might catch celebrating the festival. So an end was put to the sacred festivities, and the priests were **punished**, (οἱ δὲ ἱρέες ἐδικαιεῦντο), and the wounded Apis pined away and died." (Compare also the oracle in V. 92. 2.) It is this meaning of the word which Hesychius signalizes,—to the entire neglect of the other significations which the term bears, at once in the classics and in the Scriptures. (He says, δικαιοῦν, μαστιγοῦν, νουθετεῖν, and again δικαιούμενον, κολαζόμενον, and again δικαιῶσαι, κολάσαι.) It is probable that in specifying δικαιούμενον, as meaning *punished*, he had reference to Plato's use of the word in the 11th Book of his *Laws*, ch. 12. 934. (Compare Timaeus's *Lexicon Platonic.* — δικαιούμενος, κολαζόμενος. It is worthy of note, also, that in his *Phaedrus*, § 61, Plato uses the word δικαιωτήρια to denote *places of punishment.*) The Cretans, going in a parallel line of thought, used θεμίζω in the same sense, *to punish*. (See Hesychius.) Suidas is more comprehensive than Hesychius. He says that δικαιοῦν has two significations, *to punish* and *to judge to be right*, (δικαιοῦν δύο δηλοῖ, τό τε κολάζειν, καὶ τὸ δίκαιον νομίζειν). He then, after having cited examples, adds, what amounts to a statement, that the word also means *to condemn*, (δικαιοῦσαν, καταδικάζουσαν). In another place,—reproduced entire in Phavorinus's Lexicon,—he mentions that the word means *to pronounce to be right*, or, *to judge to be right*, (ἐδικαίου, δίκαιον εἶναι ἔλεγεν,—ἐδικαίου τοίνυν αντὶ τοῦ ἔκρινε, δίκαιον εἶναι ἐνόμιζεν) : and he then specifies its two contrary poles of import—*to justify* and *to condemn*, (ἐδικαιώθησαν, δίκαιοι ἐκρίθησαν· σημαίνει δὲ καὶ τὸ ἐναντίον κατεδικάσθησαν δικαίως). In giving examples of this latter import of the word—*to condemn*—he quotes a passage from Dio Cassius, and then says that "Dio in many other places uses the word in this signification," (πολλαχοῦ δὲ οὗτος κέχρηται τῇ λέξει ταύτῃ ἐπὶ τοῦ εἰρημένου σημαινομένου). He specifies a passage in confirmation. But the passage which he quotes really exhibits the use of the word in its other meaning—*to punish*, and indeed *to punish* (*capitally*) :—"Ye are all worthy of death. Nevertheless

I shall not put you all to death: but I shall *punish* a few, whom I have already seized, and the rest I dismiss," (ἀλλ' ὀλίγους μὲν οὓς καὶ συνείληφα ἤδη, δικαιώσω, τοὺς δὲ ἄλλους ἀφίημι). We learn from Cicero that the word was conventionally used by the Sicilians in the sense of *punishing capitally.* (ἐδικώθησαν–[i. e., εδικαιώθησαν]– —inquit, hoc est, ut Siculi loquuntur, *supplicio affecti ac necati sunt.* Lib. v. in Verrem., c. 57.) Aelian uses the full expression, ἐδικαίωσαν τῷ θανάτῳ, *they executed.* (*Varia. Hist.*, lib. v. 18.) It is an interesting coincidence, that, in the terminology of Scots law, a criminal, who is executed, is said to be *justified.* The same expression occurs, too, among the Germans. (*Germani nostri, de facinoroso, e vivis ex judicis sententia sublato, dicunt,— er ist justificirt.–Wolf.* Rom. vi. 7.)

It has been disputed whether or not δικαιόω is ever used in classical Greek with its New Testament import—*to justify* (*a person*). Pareus assumes and asserts that this is its customary import. (*Graecis quoque* δικαιοῦσθαι, *semper idem valere quod* ἀπολύεσθαι *vel* δίκαιον νομίζεσθαι; *raro idem quod* νομίζεσθαι *censeri simpliciter, vel* ἀξιοῦσθαι *dignum censeri, vel* κολάζεσθαι *poenam luere, vel* τὰ δίκαια πάσχειν *aequum pati seu consequi.* Com. in Rom. Dub. vii. in cap. iii.) He spoke, however, at perfect random, and in absolute ignorance. We have seen that Pfochen contended that the word does mean *to justify* (*a person*), in classical as well as in biblical Greek. His theory regarding the "purity" of the New Testament diction was at stake. He was animated with literary pique in reference to Cocceius's Hebrew; and he aspired to put Hebraisms under ban. But he had to borrow and to bungle a quotation from Thucydides, which he found in Camerarius, ere he could produce even the appearance of evidence. In the passage referred to, the word means, as we have seen, *to condemn*, not *to justify.* Georgi is more prudent than Pfochen, for, though he is equally determined to find no Hebraism in the New Testament use of the term, he does not cite any passage from the classics in support of his opinion. He merely rides off under a cloud of references to *Taco Haio van den*

Honert, Clausingius, Schwartzius, Kirchmaierus, and says that no other passage occurs to him besides those which are specified by these distinguished authors, (*In quorum sententiis et nos, cum praeter eos locos, quos summi viri observarunt, nullus alius succurrat, acquiescimus.*–Vindiciæ, N. T. ab. Hebraismis, lib. ii. cap. ii. § 10.) This cloud of references, however, is nothing at all but a cloud of dust. Deyling too asserts that the word is used in classical Greek in its New Testament acceptation. (*Dissert. de voce* **δικαιοῦν,** § 4.) But he adduces no instances, and misinterprets Suidas. There really seems to be no evidence attainable, or, at least, there is none that has as yet been attained, that suffices to establish an exact identity of import in the use of the word in any one passage of the classics, and its use in the New Testament. (*Nihil itaque hactenus,* says Gataker, *a quoquam allatum comparet, unde vocis istius usus Apostolicus a veteri lingua Graeca descendisse comprobetur.*–De Novi Instrumenti Stylo, cap. viii.) The use of the word in the classics branches out, as we have seen, in different directions. There are the two main references, (1), the reference to *things* or *acts,* and (2), the reference to *persons.* In both of these references the word takes up into itself, to an emphatically dominant degree, a judicial element. In its fundamental notion it meant indeed *to make right,* or *to right.* But thence it came conventionally to signify (1) *to right (a thing) in one's judgement,—to judge it right,—to judge;* and (2) *to right a person, to treat a person rightly* or *justly, to condemn, to punish, to put to death.* The predominantly judicial and forensic or quasi-forensic import of the word is manifest. And, assuredly, no instance occurs,—so far as the researches of critics have hitherto extended,—in which the word signifies, when *a person* is the object of its action, *to make (inherently, or intrinsically, or psychologically, or metaphysically, or physically, or therapeutically) right or righteous.*

The reason why the word, when employed in biblical Greek, in reference to persons, took that particular pole of judicial, forensic, or quasi-forensic righting, viz., *justifying* or *making out to be right*, or *declaring to be possessed of righteousness*, which is the opposite of the classical pole of *condemning, punishing, and putting to death*, is to be found in the mother-tongue of the Hebrews,—the language in which it was natural for their thoughts to take shape. In that language the adjective (צַדִּיק),—which is the analogue, and indeed, as is evidenced by the main syllable, the etymological relative, though far removed, of the Greek δικαίος, (*right* or *righteous*), has an all but exclusive reference to persons, and means *morally right*, that is, *righteous* or *just*. It is invariably translated in our English Authorized Version either *righteous* or *just*. With the single exception, apparently, of its use in Deut. iv. 8, it is, in the scores upon scores of instances in which it occurs, applied to describe the character of *persons*. In Deut. iv. 8, the word is used to characterise the divine *statutes* and *judgements*. Such being the signification of the adjective, it is not to be wondered at that in those conjugations of the verb,—the *pihel* and *hiphil*,—in which we have the duplicate analogues of the Greek δικαιόω,—there should be a phase of reference altogether different from *judging a thing to be right*, or *condemning a man*, or *punishing him*. The Hebrew conjugations took, most decisively, a judicial, forensic, or quasi-forensic direction; but it was altogether in reference to persons, and exclusively *in bonam partem*. Hence the peculiarity, or *idiotismus*, of the import of δικαιόω in biblical Greek; and hence, too, apparently, the difficulty which the Greek Fathers experienced in forming an accurate conception of the New Testament import of the word. They were ignorant of *the fixed shape of the Hebrew vessel, into which the variable import of the Greek word had been poured.*

The forensic import of δικαιόω throughout the New Testament in general, and in the evangelical passages in particular,—will be confirmed,—if confirmation is needed,—by an appeal to the usage of the analogous Hebrew verb, (in its two conjugatives, *pihel*, צִדֵּק; and *hiphil*, הִצְדִּיק.) The confirmation will be intensified if we take along with us the Septuagintal translation of the passages. The Hebrew word occurs in Pihel five times in all. (1.) Job xxxii. 2, "against Job was his wrath kindled, because *he justified himself* (צַדְּקוֹ נַפְשׁוֹ) rather than God," (ἀπέφηνεν ἑαυτον δίκαιον ἐναντίον κυρίου). The meaning cannot be that Job *made himself inherently righteous.* It manifestly is,—*he made himself out to be righteous, he vindicated himself.* The idea was correctly rendered by the Septuagint translator. (2.) Job xxxiii. 32,—"If thou hast anything to say, answer me: speak, for I desire *to justify thee,*" (צַדְּקֶךָּ, θέλω γὰρ δικαιωθῆναι σε). Elihu calls upon Job to speak in his own defence, in self-vindication, if he was conscientiously able; so that he might *show himself to be righteous.* (Subjekt ist niet Elihu, sondern Hiob.–*Hahn.*) (3.) Jer. iii. 11,—"The backsliding Israel hath *justified herself* more than treacherous Judah," (צִדְּקָה נַפְשָׁהּ מִ־—ἐδικαίωσε τὴν ψυχὴν αὐτοῦ—ἀπό), that is, *hath shown herself to be more righteous, hath comparatively* (in relation to Judah) *righted herself in the judgement of all who are fit to judge in the case.* (4 and 5.) Ezek. xvi. 51, 52,—"thou hast multiplied thine abominations more than they, and *hast justified* thy sisters (וַתְּצַדְּקִי אֶת־אֲחוֹתֵךְ—καὶ ἐδικαίωσας τὰς ἀδελφάς σου) in all thine abominations which thou hast done,"—"they are more righteous than thou, (תִּצְדַּקְנָה מִמֵּךְ); yea, be thou confounded also, and bear thy shame, in that thou *hast justified thy sisters.*" This twofold passage throws light upon the preceding. The meaning is not that Jerusalem had *made* her sisters, Sodom and Gomorrah, *subjectively righteous.* But, by the enormity of her wickedness, she had *shown them to be (comparatively) righteous.* She had, as it were, judicially vindicated them, and declared them to be righteous.

The Hiphil (of צָדַק) still more emphatically corresponds to the Greek verb, (δικαιόω): and there are twelve instances,—(not *six hundred* or so, as Deyling most hyperbolically asserts—*Dissertatio de voce* δικαιοῦν, § 5),—in which the word occurs in this conjugation. (1.) Exod. xxiii. 7,—"Keep thee from a false matter; and the innocent and righteous slay thou not: for *I will not justify the wicked,*"

(לֹא־אַצְדִּיק רָשָׁע). On the contrary, God would condemn the wicked. The forensic import is obvious. (2.) Deut. xxv. 1,—"if there be a controversy between men, and they come unto judgement, that the judges may judge them; then *they shall justify the righteous*, and condemn the wicked," (וְהִצְדִּיקוּ אֶת־הַצַּדִּיק—καὶ δικαιώσωσι τὸν δίκαιον). The forensic import is evident. It is no more the part of judges, in justifying the righteous, to make them inherently righteous, than it is their part in condemning the wicked, to make them inherently wicked. The word for condemn, however, (הִרְשִׁיעַ), originally means *to make wicked.* When used forensically, as here, it must mean *to make out to be wicked, to judge to be wicked, to treat in judgement as wicked, to condemn.* (3.) 2 Sam. xv. 4,—"Absalom said moreover, Oh that I were made judge in the land, that every man which hath any suit or cause might come unto me, *and I would do him justice*," (וְהִצְדַּקְתִּיו—καὶ δικαιώσω αὐτόν), that is, *and I would right him*, in the sense of *pronouncing in his favour*, or *declaring him righteous.* It is assumed by Absalom that the pursuer, who would come to his bar, would have good ground of complaint. The forensic import of the word is indubitable. (4.) 1 Ki. viii. 32,—"Then hear thou in heaven, and do, and judge thy servants, condemning the wicked, to bring his way upon his head; and *justifying the righteous*, to give him according to his righteousness," (וּלְהַצְדִּיק צַדִּיק—καὶ τοῦ δικαιῶσαι δίκαιον). The judicial reference is explicit,—"judge thy servants." (5.) 2 Chron. vi. 23. This passage is the duplicate of the preceding. (6.) Job xxvii. 5,—"God forbid that I should justify you," (חָלִילָה לִּי אִם־אַצְדִּיק אֶתְכֶם—μή μοι εἴη δικαίους ὑμᾶς ἀποφῆναι). It cannot be supposed that Job had any reference to the production, in his comforters, of inherent righteousness. It was in his judgement—the court of his conscience—that he could not right them. (7.) Ps. lxxxii. 3,—"Defend the poor and fatherless: *do justice to* the afflicted and needy," (עָנִי וָרָשׁ הַצְדִּיקוּ—ταπεινὸν καὶ πένητα δικαιώσατε). The meaning is, *right the afflicted and needy, vindicate them, make them out to be righteous (in their suit), pronounce in their favour.* Hence it is added in the next verse,—"Deliver the poor and needy; rid them out of the hand of the wicked." The forensic import of the word is unquestionable; and, if further evidence were requisite, it would be found in the preceding verse,—"How long will ye *judge unjustly*, and *accept the persons* of the wicked?" (8.) Prov. xvii. 15,—"He that *justifieth the wicked*, and he that condemneth the just, even they both are abomination to the Lord," (מַצְדִּיק רָשָׁע—ὃς δίκαιον κρίνει τὸν ἄδικον). The Sept. translation, as in Job xxvii. 5, affords an admirable commentary on the forensic import of the word. The expression must be forensically interpreted. If it referred to the therapeutic production of inherent righteousness, the man who thus justified the wicked would be far from being an abomination to the Lord. (9.) Isai. v. 23,—"Woe unto them who *justify the wicked for reward*, and take away the righteousness of the righteous from him," (מַצְדִּיקֵי רָשָׁע—οἱ δικαιοῦντες τὸν ἀσεβῆ). The expression manifestly describes the corrupt practices of venal and unrighteous judges, (*bestechliche und ungerechte Richter.*-Gesenius). It is altogether forensic in its reference and import. (10.) Isai. l. 8,—"He is near that *justifieth me;* who will contend with me? let us stand together: who is mine adversary? let him come near to me," (קָרוֹב מַצְדִּיקִי—ἐγγίζει ὁ δικαιώσας με). The whole scenery is forensic. (11.) Isai. liii. 11,—"By his knowledge shall my righteous servant justify many," (בְּדַעְתּוֹ יַצְדִּיק צַדִּיק עַבְדִּי לָרַבִּים—δικαιῶσαι δίκαιον εὖ δουλεύοντα πολλοῖς). There are considerable difficulties in connection with the interpretation of the various clauses of the verse; and much diversity of opinion has prevailed among critics regarding the connection of several of the words, and the interrelation of the clausules. But, notwithstanding all that Bellarmin has said, there is no good reason whatsoever, on the hypothesis that the oracle is really Messianic, for supposing that the word, *he shall justify*, has any other than a forensic signification. If, with the majority of modern critics, we accept the construction of the word which underlies the Auth. English Version, as also Luther's, then the pronoun, in the expression "*his* knowledge," or "the knowledge *of him*," (בְּדַעְתּוֹ), will be, not subjective, but objective, "the knowledge *which has him for its object*," (*cognitione sui*, not, as in the Vulg., *cognitione sua*): and the meaning of the phrase, "he will justify many," or "he will justify *to* many," (יַצְדִּיק לָרַבִּים), will be,—not quite, perhaps, as Cocceius puts it,—*he will be the cause and donor of righteousness to many*, (**Justificat** *hic construitur cum dativo*, q. d. *justitiae causa et donator fiet multis*.—Com. *in loc.* and Lex. *sub. voc.*);—but, *he will be the occasion of justification to many.* The idea will be, that, as it is God, the divine Father, with whom it lies to justify or to condemn, so the Messiah, acting in court as the believer's Advocate or Intercessor, successfully pleads his cause by putting in, as a plea, or *justificamentum*, as Vitringa expresses it, his own righteousness. He thus becomes the occasion, or meritorious cause, of the believer's justification. The representation is strictly forensic; but it directs the eye rather to the bar, than to the bench. If, however, it should be deemed more natural to understand the pronoun subjectively, in the expression, "by *his* knowledge;" and if, with Lowth, we should regard it as unnatural to have in Hebrew the adjective *righteous*, (צַדִּיק), before the substantive *my servant*, (עַבְדִּי), then we may construe the expression, as Jonathan, Jarchi, the Septuagint, and the Syriac do,—thus,—*by his knowledge shall he justify the righteous*, and leave the remainder of the verse as forming two annexed clausules, *my servant unto many*, (or, *as my servant unto many*), *and he shall bear their iniquities*. In this case the reference of the words, *by his knowledge shall he justify the righteous*, would be to the forensic procedure of our Lord, as it shall be realized in its consummation, on the great day of judgement. Comp. Rom. ii. 13, 16. The interpretation of the verb given by Gesenius, and substantially accepted by Knobel, &c., *he shall guide to the true religion*, taken in connection with his translation of the preceding phrase, (בְּדַעְתּוֹ), *by his wisdom*, is certainly quite aside from the scope of the context, and indeed of the whole oracle. For the Messiah, throughout, and particularly in the conclusion of the 11th verse, is represented not as a teacher, but as a priest. (*Nostro loco non de sola* *admonitione et institutione, sed justificatione sermonem esse, totum quoque vaticinium docet, quum Messia, in eo, sacerdos, qui se ipsum sacrificium ad homines expiandos obtulerit, non vero doctor describitur.*–Reinke, *in loc.*) There can be no good reason, then, for doubting that the term is to be understood, here too, as having a forensic acceptation. (12.) The last passage, in which the Hiphilic word occurs, is Dan. xii. 3,—" They that be wise shall shine as the brightness of the firmament; and they that *turn many to righteousness*, (וּמַצְדִּיקֵי הָרַבִּים), as the stars for ever and ever." This, the last passage in which the Hiphilic word occurs, is the only one in which it seems, *prima facie*, to be used otherwise than forensically. Bellarmin makes capital of it, (*De Justificatione*, ii. 3). And yet, if it be the case that it would be necessary,—even on the hypothesis that the term must be rendered in an efficaciously therapeutical manner, *they that make many righteous*,—to understand the human agency as being only instrumental, *they that are instrumental in securing the inherent righteousness of many;*—may we not, by introducing the same idea of instrumentality, retain the otherwise invariable usage of the term,—*they who are instrumental in securing the justification of many?* If there be a legitimate sense in which one man may be said to *save* another, (James v. 20), viz., instrumentally, by leading to the saving Saviour; and if there be a legitimate sense in which one man may *sanctify* another, viz., in a way equally instrumental; may it not be likewise legitimate to speak of one man *justifying* another, viz., instrumentally, by leading to that "righteousness of God," which is " unto all, and upon all them that believe," and which is the ground of justification. It is on this principle that Cocceius explains the expression, (**justificantes multos**, *h. e. qui operam dederint, ut multi justificarentur, sive, quorum ministerio multi justificati erunt.*–Lexicon *s. voc.*) So do many others. Venema translates the expression,—"they who are justificators of many," (*justificatores multorum*), and refers it to rulers—the Maccabees—who *vindicated* and delivered the people who were their subjects. But if such interpretations should seem strained, it may be worthy of consideration whether we should not revert to that method of reading the text, which, before the era of the Masoretic punctuation, was adopted by Theodotion, whose Greek version of Daniel has superseded the original Septuagintal translation. He read the verse thus:—"They that be wise shall shine as the brightness of the firmament, and *apart from* (that is, *above* and *beyond*) *the multitude of the righteous,* as the stars for ever and ever." (καὶ οἱ συνιέντες λάμψουσιν ὡς ἡ λαμπρότης τοῦ στερεώματος, καὶ ἀπὸ τῶν δικαίων τῶν πολλῶν ὡς οἱ ἀστέρες εἰς τοὺς αἰῶνας καὶ ἔτι.) If this reading be correct, a diversity in the degrees of celestial glory would be intimated. They who *are wise* and *make others wise,* (*doctores,* Grotius;—מַשְׂכִּילִים—see chap. xi. 33, 35; and comp. Ps. xxxii. 8; Gen. iii. 6), shall be raised to pre-eminence above the rest,—above the commonalty, as it were,—of the righteous. (Jerome, in his *Commentary* on Daniel, says of the verse:—"Quem locum Theodotio et vulgata editio ita expressit,—*et intelligentes fulgebunt quasi splendor firmamenti, et* **de justis plurimi** *quasi stellae in aeternum et ultra.*" He had found, apparently, in his copy of Theodotion the reading ἀπὸ τῶν δικαίων οἱ πολλοί. He adds,—but not with great exegetical verisimilitude, as we apprehend,—"juxta Theodotionem dicitur, quod docti similitudinem coeli habeant, et absque doctrina justi stellarum fulgori comparentur: tantumque sit inter eruditam sanctitatem et sanctam rusticitatem, quantum coelum distat et stellae." It would appear,—the Masoretic punctuation apart,—that, instead of מַצְדִּיקֵי, Theodotion had read either מִצַּדִּיקִים or מִצַּדִּיקֵי. Compare, for the latter form, הַשָּׁלִשִׁי in 2 Sam. xxiii. 8, collating הַשָּׁלִישִׁים in 1 Chron. xii. 18.)—There are obvious difficulties connected with this reading of Theodotion. But it was reproduced, as Jerome remarks, in the Italic version. It is commented on by Theodoret, though, apparently, under the same form as Jerome had it, if we may judge of his text from his comment. And we should certainly be disposed to revert to this ancient reading, if there were no other alternative than to attribute to the Hiphilic Hebrew verb a meaning which is out of unison with its usage *in every other place in which it occurs.*

Such is the evidence derivable from the two Hebrew conjugations. It is confirmatory, to a remarkable degree, of the presumptive forensic or quasi-forensic import of the word δικαιόω in its New Testament application to the great doctrine of evangelical justification. And the confirmation is all the more considerable, when we take into account the truth of what John Campensis says of Paul,—"He uses, indeed, Greek words in writing, but in such a way, that he never forgets the Hebrew phraseology." (*Graecis namque, uti scis, sic in scribendo usus est vocabulis, ut tamen Hebraicae phrasis numquam oblitus esse videatur.*—Commentariolus in Ep. ad Rom., fol. 2.)

But although the passages quoted exhaust all the instances in which the Hebrew Pihelic and Hiphilic words occur; still, the Greek term itself is found in a considerable number of additional passages, both in the canonical books of the Old Testament and in the Apocrypha. In all these, however, with the one exception of Ps. lxxiii. 13, to which we have already referred, it is obviously used in a forensic or quasi-forensic manner. It denotes the *righting* which takes place *in judgement.* It is used, with a strictly forensic acceptation, in Isai. i. 17; xliii. 9; xliii. 26; xlv. 24; Ecclesiasticus xxxi. 5; xlii. 4; Mic. vi. 11; vii. 9. It is used, with a quasi-forensic acceptation, in Gen. xxxviii. 26; xliv. 16; Ps. xix. 10; li. 5; Isai. xlii. 21; Ezek. xvi. 52; xxi. 13; Tob. xii. 13; Ecclesiasticus i. 19; vii. 5; ix. 12; x. 29; xiii. 22; xviii. 2, 22; xxiii. 11; xxvi. 29.

The only other passage in which the Greek word occurs is Ps. cxliii. 2,—the passage which is partially quoted by the Apostle in Rom. iii. 20. In this passage the forensic reference is not merely determined by the sum of the evidence that bears upon the forensic import of the verb in Rom. iii. 20. It is still farther and conclusively established by the terminology of the first clause of the verse:—"*enter not into judgement* with thy servant; for in thy sight shall no man living be justified." The scenery is that of the tribunal. And since this is indisputably the case, we seem to be absolutely shut up to the forensic interpretation of the word in the verse before us, and thus to its forensic interpretation in the entire paragraph of which the verse before us is an integrant part.

And yet the cumulative evidence for the forensic interpretation is not exhausted. One item more we specify. The Apostle says,—"no flesh shall be justified *before him*," (ἐνώπιον αὐτοῦ). This expression is a continuation of the forensic scenery. God is *on his judicial throne. Men are standing at the bar.* The justification referred to is the justification that is realizable in a court of justice.

Thus every branch of evidence bears its appropriate burden of proof, that it is right to approach the passages, which treat of evangelical justification, under the influence of a tolerably settled persuasion that the word δικαιόω refers not to the therapeutical production of inherent righteousness, but to a judicial declaration of the reality of the substitutionary righteousness judicially found in the possession of believers,—and judicially found in their possession because it has been really apprehended and appropriated by faith in "Jesus Christ the righteous." It is righteousness that is, strictly speaking, *inherent in Christ.* It is mediatorial righteousness. It is divine righteousness. It is "God's righteousness." It is communicated,—but of course only imputatively,—to believers in Christ. It is imputed. Nevertheless, it is the real possession of believers. It is their *title to everlasting glory.*

The therapeutical production of inherent righteousness in the persons of these same believers is also and amply provided for. Justification is really in order to sanctification. It is a stepping-stone to something beyond itself. It is not the end. It is a means. Nevertheless, it is really and absolutely indispensable in its own subordinate place. And it is no disparagement to the greater blessing, which is realized in the production of inherent righteousness or holiness, that it is ruled under a different rubric than the term *justification.*

The future tense, which the Apostle uses when he says

"nobody *shall be justified* by works of law," is not to be accounted for, with Reiche, on the supposition that the reference is to the judgement of the last day. The Apostle is now entering on the consideration of justification, in its initial stage, as it takes place during the period of probation. See verses 21, 24. It is justification, as conditioned simply on faith. See verses 27, 28, 30. It is thus justification, *as it occurs on the occurrence of faith.* See ch. v. 1. Neither are we to suppose that the future tense, as such, is intended to express, definitely and sharply, the idea of what is called *moral possibility;* as if the Apostle's asseveration were absolutely equivalent to this,—"nobody *can be justified* by works of law." So Newcome, and the Unitarian *Improved version,* &c. This idea is doubtless implied; for the ideas of futurity and possibility run into one another. Still, it is eventuation in time which was present to the Apostle's mind when he said *shall be justified;* and non-eventuation in time is denied when he affirms, *shall not be justified.* The future, as distinguished from the past and the present, is used representatively. And the substance of the thought, though of course not its form, is equivalent to this,—*as nobody has been, or is, so nobody will be, justified by works of law.* The future used is, as some grammarians express it, though not very happily, *abstract future;* it is future, from which *futurity,* as an absolutely differentiating element, has been abstracted. It is future in which futurity is representatively expressed. It may, however, have been representatively fixed upon, in order to cut off, as Rambach says, future expectations, (*omnes spes futuras abzuschneiden*).

The Apostle, after saying *by works of law shall nobody be justified,* adds, as we have already noted, *before him,* (ἐνώπιον αὐτοῦ = לְפָנָיו = *coram ipso*). The expression is similarly, but not with equal felicity, rendered by Tyndale, and in the Geneva, *in his sight.* It is, as we have remarked, unquestionably forensic, (*in foro divino,* as opposed to *in foro humano*), and the scene, which it suggests, points to view the judge seated on his great white throne of judgement, with the parties to be judged standing *before him.* The words, as Origen observes, are not to be heedlessly passed by, "for it is one thing to be justified before God, and another thing to be justified before man." (*Hoc, quod addidit,* **coram ipso,** *non otiose prætereat, quia aliud est coram Deo justificari, aliud coram hominibus.*) "Many," says Paciuchelli, "whose character seems to the eye of men to glister in purity, are seen by the eye of God to be loathsomely polluted." (*Permulti emicant coram hominibus apparenti virtutum fulgore, qui tamen coram Deo sordescunt.*)

§ 5. *for through law is knowledge of sin,* (διὰ γὰρ νόμου ἐπίγνωσις ἁμαρτίας). The *law* referred to, is, of course, the same that is spoken of in the preceding clause,—*the revelation of God, viewed as authoritatively exhibiting the duty which devolves upon men, as men.* Thus viewed, it exhibits to the eye of the mind, and it is, what is now technically called, *the moral law.* (See on the former clause.) Through this law, says the Apostle, there is realized in everybody, (when duly self-conscious and self-cognizant), *knowledge of sin;* (not precisely "*the* knowledge," but certainly not "*a* knowledge," as Thomson gives it).

The Apostle does not mean,—*through the law is realized* **experience of sin, and that only,** inasmuch as through the law sin is roused up within us;—as Ernesti and others suppose. (*Das Gesetz macht nur das böse in uns rege und wirksam, und die Macht des Bösen fühlbar.*-Ernesti.) The word rendered *knowledge,* (ἐπίγνωσις), though occurring frequently in the New Testament, is not used in that shade of meaning. (See Rom. i. 28; x. 2; Eph. i. 17; iv. 13; Phil. i. 9; Col. i. 9, 10; ii. 2; iii. 10; 1 Tim. ii. 4; 2 Tim. ii. 25; iii. 7; Tit. i. 1; Philem. 6; Heb. x. 26; 2 Pet. i. 2, 3, 8; ii. 20.) Neither is it the case that the experience of sin is the "only" effect of the law.

Other commentators have supposed that the Apostle means,—*through the law is the nature of sin made known.* This is the interpretation of Thomas Aquinas, Sadolet, &c. (*Lex enim datur ut homo cognoscat quid debeat agere, quid vitare.*-Aquinas. *Lex nihil seipsa majus demonstrat neque altius, sed solam tibi notionem peccati insinuat.*–Sadolet.) But that the Apostle had some other idea in his mind is obvious from the fact, that the clause in which his conception is embodied, exhibits the ground on which the great doctrinal declaration, which is enunciated in the preceding clause, rests. Hence the ratiocinative particle *for*—"*for* by law there is knowledge of sin." But to say that law makes us acquainted with the nature of sin, is no reason why no one shall be justified by deeds of law. It rather, so far as it goes, affords a presumption that man might be justified by deeds of law. There are beings, somewhere, who are thus justified. To intrude the word "only," is, with Sadolet as well as Ernesti, an arbitrary addition to the inspired phraseology. And, moreover, it is not true that the law gives "only" the notion of sin. It gives us as really the notion of righteousness. And it imparts various wholesome influences, besides.

Theodoret takes a view of the expression, somewhat accordant with that of Thomas Aquinas; only, he obviously supposes that the word *law* has reference to the Mosaic or Old Testament revelation as such. "The law has given to men," he says, "a more accurate knowledge of sin," (ἀκριβεστέραν ὁ νόμος τοῖς ἀνθρώποις ἐπίγνωσιν τῆς ἁμαρτίας ἐντέθεικε). He adds, that nevertheless it did not impart power to work out virtue, (εἰς δὲ τῆς ἀρετῆς τὴν κατόρθωσιν ἐπαρκέσαι τοῖς ἀνθρώποις οὐκ ἴσχυσεν). He thus virtually intrudes the "only," which Sadolet and Ernesti arbitrarily supply, and which is furtively interjected, indeed, by many other critics, such as Seb. Schmidt, Heumann, Kistemaker, Glöckler, Köllner, Rückert, de Wette, Baumgarten-Crusius, &c. It was introduced by Luther into the first edition of his version, (1522)—"for through the law cometh **only** the knowledge of sin," (*kompt nur erkenntnis der sünd*). It was retained in all the editions that followed till that of 1530, when it was thrown out,—Emser having, meanwhile, found legitimate fault with the interpolation. Coverdale, however, even in 1535, retained the interpolation,—"For by the lawe commeth *but* the knowlege of synne." Theophylact's interpretation is similar to that of

Theodoret,—at least so far as the first part of Theodoret's explication is concerned. The interpretation of Wordsworth and Mac-Evilly corresponds. And so does that of Grotius, who regards the clause, absurdly enough, as introduced to show that the law, though unable to justify, is nevertheless of some use. (*Ne quis putaret legem plane fuisse inutilem, ostendit ejus usum egregium, nempe quod notitiæ illae actionum turpium, quas mali mores in Aegyptiaco maxime incolatu oblitaverant, manifesta voluntatis Divinæ revelatione factae sunt rursus conspicuae.*) Melancthon's interpretation is similar. The clause, he says, anticipates an objection, (*occupatio est*); it shows the use of the law. The use of the law is "to accuse and terrify the conscience," (*accusare et perterrefacere conscientiam.*-Com. 1540; Enar. 1556). Both Melancthon and Grotius, as also Oecolampad, Bugenhagen, and Ferus, seem to have altogether overlooked the power of the ratiocinative particle *for*, (γάρ), which shows that a reason is rendered for the preceding statement, not an apology for the existence of the law.

Koppe, in a still more exceptionable manner, limits the reference of the word *law* to the Old Testament revelation as a book: so Bolten. Koppe interprets the clause thus;—"for in the Old Testament scriptures it is testified that all men are sinners," (*ipsi illi libri divini testantur omnes homines esse scelestos*). He thus understands the *knowledge* spoken of as subjective in the readers of the epistle, rather than as subjective in all men who have become developed into moral consciousness:—*for by the Old Testament scriptures is the knowledge communicated to us of all men's sinfulness.* It is, however, an insuperable objection to this interpretation that the word *law*, in the preceding clause, has already sublimated itself into a notion very different from that of *the Old Testament Scriptures in general.*

Bahrdt imposes upon the word *knowledge* an idea still more remote from the reality than Koppe's. He makes it mean *demonstration* or *proof;* and interprets the whole clause thus:—"your Mosaic law, (being but a clumsy system of carnal ordinances), is the greatest *proof* of your corruption," (*euer Mosaisches Gesetz ist gerade der grösste Beweiss von eurer verdorbenheit*). Oertel, borrowing from Bahrdt's *Exposition*, still further exaggerates this outré interpretation, and translates the clause thus:—"for a positive religion is always the characteristic of a rude and savage nation"! (*denn nach der Erfahrung ist vielmehr positive Religion selbst allemal der Character einer rohen und verwilderten Nazion.*) Bahrdt and he thus actually make ἐπίγνωσις equivalent to *Merkmal*, and they understand by νόμος the positive element of religion, as distinguished from morality, (*im gegensatze der moralischen Tugend-religion*)! Such interpretations are a burlesque on exegesis.

Olshausen goes much too far in another, though upward, direction, when he interprets *the knowledge of sin* referred to as being equivalent to that *repentance* into which John the Baptist baptized. (*Die* ἐπίγνωσις ἁμαρτίας *ist also gleichbedeutend mit der* μετάνοια, *auf die Johannes der Täufer, als Frucht der alttestamentlichen Oekonomie, taufte.*) It is a knowledge, he says, that has within it the germ of faith. He thus confounds the offices of *the law* and *the gospel*, for it is assuredly a view of the contents of the gospel, as distinguished from the law, that generates in the soul that *repentance* which is animated by faith, and is "unto life."

We need not specify other untenable interpretations of the Apostle's expression. It evidently means, "for by law there is knowledge of sin," or, as Wycliffe renders it,—"forsothe by lawe is knowinge of synne," that is, *for by means of law,—law in its moral element, and howsoever revealed,—by means, in short, of the moral law, which prescribes to man his duty as man, and which is thus the rule of moral life, and the test of moral character, men, everywhere, who are in the normal state of moral self-consciousness and self-cognizance, know that they are sinners.* When men compare their actual conduct with the law, they know that they have violated its sacred precepts. They feel convicted of guilt. And thus it is impossible that they can be justified by deeds of law. The law enjoins absolute obedience from the first moment of moral probation, onward. And he who has failed, at any time, to yield this perfect obedience, can never thenceforward present at the bar of the Judge of all the earth a perfect righteousness of his own. A perfect righteousness, on the part of a moral creature in probation, is a righteousness, which extends, unbroken, *from the commencement to the conclusion of the probationary career.*

The word translated *knowledge,* (ἐπίγνωσις, as distinguished from γνῶσις), has an intensification of import, which cannot be reproduced in English. And, indeed, the word *knowledge,* though etymologically identical with the uncompounded Greek term, is, conventionally, by no means an absolute synonym. We must call in the aid of another derivate of the same wide-spread root, in order to get a nearer approximation to the import of the simple Greek vocable. The verb *to* **know,**—(an older word than the Greek γιγνώσκω, and from which, under the form γνο–, parts of the Greek verb are directly derived),—properly means in Greek *to take* **note** *of.* And the compound verb, from which the noun before us is derived, (ἐπιγιγνώσκω), properly means *to take note of (by fixing the attention) upon* an object, and thus, in reference to certain objects, *to become conscious of, to recognize.* The idea of the Apostle, in the expression before us, is this ;—*for by means of law men fix their attention* **upon** *certain acts of their life,* and **take note** *of their sinfulness.* When they view their actions in the light of the law, they *recognize* them as sins; and become *conscious of themselves as sinners.* Hence some have translated the expression thus ;—"for by law is the *acknowledgement* of sin." It is thus that Melancthon, Calvin, Beza, Limborch; and Bengel, Baumgarten-Crusius, van Hengel, &c., render the words. And not incorrectly; for *knowledge,* as we have said, is not a precise synonym of the original term. It is, however, nearer than *acknowledgement,* and better adapted to the majority of the passages in which the term occurs.

VER. 21. Νυνὶ δὲ χωρὶς νόμου δικαιοσύνη Θεοῦ πεφανέρωται, μαρτυρουμένη ὑπὸ τοῦ νόμου καὶ τῶν προφητῶν,

Eng. Auth. Vers. *But now the righteousness of God without the law is manifested, being witnessed by the law and the prophets;*

Revised Version. *But now without law God's righteousness has been manifested, being attested by the law and the prophets;*

§ 1. Cameron supposes that this verse is to be closely connected with the 18th of the first chapter! He thinks that it exhibits that which is the antithesis to the "wrath of God," which has been revealed from heaven. And he regards all of the disquisition that intervenes as parenthetical. (*Haec sunt conjungenda cum vers* 18 *cap. primi; et quae interjecta sunt parenthesi sunt includenda.*) This is rather an outré conception of the connection. But there is certainly a return, in the contents of the verse, to the subject matter of the theme of the epistle, as announced in the 17th verse of the first chapter. In what is contained in the intervening discourse,—chap. i. 18—iii. 20,—the Apostle makes a circuit, having it as his aim to show that men in general,—indeed all men,—whether Gentiles or Jews, need that *righteousness of God*, which is "revealed in the Gospel." They need it, because they are personally unrighteous, and if they are personally unrighteous they never can be pronounced righteous, or be justified, on the ground of a complete righteousness of their own. There is, however, as the Apostle declares, another righteousness,—*God's righteousness*,—which is available to them, which may be appropriated by them, and on the footing of which they may be justified and made heirs of everlasting life and glory. Of this righteousness, the Apostle resumptively speaks in the verse before us.

§ 2. Such being the relation of the contents of this verse to the preceding context, it is proper that in a text, which aims at exhibiting, by means of paragraphs, the natural groupings of the Apostle's discourse, there should be some obvious indication that the inspired writer is now crossing the boundary line of one of his concentric circles of thought. Such editors, hence, as Bengel, Griesbach, Scholz, Tischendorf, and Knapp, Tittmann, Hahn, Goeschen, Vater, Schott, Naebe, Muralto, Ornsby, &c., have done well in making here an interruption in the flow of the text, and indicating by a break in the continuity of lines, that we have arrived at a group of ideas, which deserves to be considered in some measure apart. De Brais contends that *a new chapter* should have commenced at this point. D. G. Herzog actually makes what amounts to a capitular division, and entitles it, —*Commentary on the* 17*th verse of the first chapter.* The Commentary, he thinks, extends to the close of chapter iv.

§ 3. *But now,* (Νυνὶ δέ). Some critics have supposed that this expression has a logical, rather than a temporal, import. Instead of understanding it as having reference to that "fulness of the time," which, in the ongoing of the ages, had just been reached, they suppose that it points, logically, to the condition of things that is indicated in the immediately preceding statements:—*but now,* that is, *but in this condition of things.* The expression is so understood, substantially, by Bullinger (*non est nota temporis*), Day (*but yet*), Koppe (*atqui vero*), Fritzsche (*atqui*), de Wette, Meyer, Alford, Matthias, &c. But it is certainly better to regard the adverb as having its usual temporal import:—*but now,* that is, *but in this new era in the divine dispensation of things,—"in these last days."* The Apostle intensely realized that, as a preacher of the Gospel, he was connected with the inauguration of a new epoch. And hence, at the very commencement of the epistle, he says that he was "separated unto the Gospel of God, *which he had promised afore* by his prophets in the holy Scriptures;" and in the 25th and 26th verses of this 3d chapter, he speaks of the "propitiation" as emanating from a design "to declare God's righteousness for the remission of sins *that are past,* through the forbearance of God,—to declare, I say, *at this time,* (ἐν τῷ νῦν καιρῷ), his righteousness."

Comp. Gal. iv. 4 ff. (Grotius says,—"**Nunc vero,** *id est, nostris temporibus hac in parte felicissimis.*" Mussus exclaims,—**Nunc.** *O seculum aureum! Seculum gratiae! Seculum evangelii, hoc est, faustae felicisque annunciationis!*) The great majority of expositors take the same view of the expression.

(It is perhaps not unworthy of being noticed that νυνί, the lengthened and strengthened form of νῦν, is always, in New Testament usage, followed by δέ. The compound expression occurs some twenty times or so. The instance in the verse before us is omitted in Schmid's Concordance. He there reads νῦν δέ, as also in the text of his posthumous *New Testament.* And he is followed by the *Englishman's Greek Concordance,* (ed. 1844): although it is νυνὶ δε that is read by Erasmus, Stephens, Beza, the Elzevirs, Leusden, Mill, Bengel, Wetstein, Griesbach, Tischendorf, Lachmann, &c.)

§ 4. *apart from law God's righteousness has been manifested,* (χωρὶς νόμου δικαιοσύνη θεοῦ πεφανέρωται). By *God's righteousness,* (δικαιοσύνη θεοῦ), we are to understand, as in chap. i. 17, *the righteousness* (*for unrighteous men*) *of which God is the author, the righteousness provided by God* (*for unrighteous men*),—*the divinely-originated righteousness* (*which is to unrighteous men who avail themselves of it, in place of their own righteousness, so far as a title to everlasting life is concerned*). It is not Christ himself, as Zuingli, though somewhat hesitatingly, says, but the righteousness wrought out and brought in by Christ. It is, indeed, the work of Christ viewed in a specific aspect, —viz., as exactly fitted to supply for us,—*so far as regards a title to everlasting life,*—the place that should have been occupied, during our probationary term of existence, by perfect, and perfectly uninterrupted, righteousness of our own. This *righteousness of God,* says the Apostle, *has now been manifested,* (νυνὶ δὲ . . . πεφανέρωται). Manifested, how? It has been made manifest in its actuality or reality. It has been shown as a thing that really is,—shown, namely, to such as were in a position to discern it, and as were at the same time willing to take note of it. Shown, where? In the innocent lives of believers, says Grotius, (*apparet rebus magnis, ex vita scilicet innocentissima Christianorum*). Fritzsche had a similar idea. God's righteousness, says he, has been manifested, that is, it has become actual and historical through faith in Christ, (*die Unsträflichkeit vor Gott ist durch den Glauben an Christus, in so fern dieser seine rechtfertigende Kraft bewährt hat und fortdauernd bewährt, factisch und historisch geworden*). But such an idea is very far apart from the Apostle's, and proceeds from a total misapprehension of the nature of God's evangelical righteousness. We read in chap. i. 17, that God's righteousness *is revealed in the Gospel.* Many critics suppose, along with Beza, Melville, Seb. Schmidt, Limborch, and Bengel, that the Apostle had the same idea present to his mind in writing chap. iii. 21; and that he, consequently, means that the righteousness "has been manifested" *in the Gospel.* So undoubtedly it has, secondarily. But primarily it was manifested in the facts which are announced in the Gospel. It was manifested in the career of Christ Jesus;—in the events, inner and outer, of his life and death;—in what he voluntarily did and voluntarily endured. These events constitute the subject-matter of the Gospel; and in them there was exhibited to view what subserves, so far as a title to glory is concerned, the place of a perfect righteousness of man's own. God's righteousness for unrighteous men was, in these events, *manifested* in actual fact. It had, indeed, been "promised afore." (See chap. i. 2.) But, though promised, it was "a mystery" in some respects, "kept secret since the world began." It could be only dimly seen. It was obscure. It was veiled. But "now it is made manifest." (See chap. xvi. 25, 26. Comp. 2 Tim. i. 10; Tit. i. 3.) It "has been manifested" in Him who was none else than God Himself "manifest in flesh."—In our authorized English version the verb is rendered "*is* manifested." A similar rendering is given by Wycliffe, Tyndale, and the Geneva. But the perfect tense represents the manifestation as *a completed historical fact:* and such an idea is peculiarly appropriate, when we regard the manifestation as accomplished in the life and death of the Saviour. In the expression, again, "*is* revealed," (ἀποκαλύπτεται), as occurring in chap. i. 17, the present tense as appropriately represents the continuous disclosure which is afforded in the enduring and, indeed, "everlasting" Gospel.

God's righteousness has been manifested, says the Apostle, *apart from law*, (χωρὶς νόμου). The expression is rendered in our authorized English version, as in Wycliffe and the Geneva, "without *the* law." And there is, perhaps, no good reason why we should greatly reprobate such a translation. Yet, as Origen pointedly remarked even in his day, and Beza after him, and Pareus after Beza, and Oltramare after Pareus, the expression in the original is anarthrous, while in the following clause the same noun is articulated. And as we can reproduce to a nicety, in our English idiom, both forms of expression, there is no valid reason for the introduction of the article in translating the phrase before us.

The *law* referred to is not merely *the law of nature*, as Origen supposed. Nor is it merely *the Jewish law*, as Chrysostom and Ambrosiaster; Grotius too, and Wetstein; and Rückert, and Fritzsche, and the great body of the modern German expositors contend. It is that same law which is spoken of in the preceding verse,—through which is knowledge of sin, and by obedience to the works of which no flesh shall be justified. It is that *Authoritative Instruction* of God which exhibits the duty of man, considered simply and generically as man. It is that *Authoritative Instruction*, consequently, whether as explicitly revealed in words to the Jews, or as implicitly revealed without words to the Gentiles all the world over. Such appears to be the reference of the Apostle. And such is substantially the view taken of his reference by Beza and Pareus; though Oltramare says that "all the commentators" have been agreed that the reference is exclusively to the Mosaic law. (*Tous les commentateurs s'accordent à y voir la loi mosaïque.*) Oltramare would translate the phrase, with unnecessary emphasis, and with the unnecessary assumption of a plurality of laws,—*independently of all law, (indépendamment de toute loi,—en dehors de toute loi)*; and Vaughan, in like manner, would render it, "apart from *any* law."

The construction of the phrase has been matter of considerable dispute. Augustin connected it with the words, *God's righteousness*, supposing that it was the Apostle's design to indicate that the righteousness specified was obtained by men, not from the law, but from God;—not by means of the assistance of the law, but by the Spirit of God. (*Non itaque sine lege manifestata, sed sine lege justitia, quia justitia Dei est, id est, quia nobis non ex lege sit, sed ex Deo.*-De Gratia Christi, I. 9. *Justitia Dei sine lege est, quam Deus per Spiritum gratiae credenti confert sine adjutorio legis, hoc est, non adjuto a lege.*"-De Spiritu et Litt. 9.) Klee approves of Augustin's construction; Flatt too; and so does Reiche, (*χωρὶς νόμου gehört nach der Stellung und Tendenz der Rede zu δικαιοσύνη*). So, too, Winzer. Theophylact, before them, adopted the same construction, (*τὴν δικαιοσύνην τοῦ Θεοῦ, τὴν χωρὶς νόμου*). So did the authors of our Authorized English Version. So, too, Macknight, Owen, &c., &c. But Erasmus, Beza, Fritzsche, and others, legitimately object to it on the ground of the peculiar adjustment of the phraseology. (We should have expected, if Augustin's idea had been correct, some such structure as Νυνὶ δὲ ἡ χωρὶς νόμου δικαιοσύνη κ. τ. λ.)

The majority of critics connect the phrase (*χωρὶς νόμου*) with the verb (*πεφανέρωται*):—"God's righteousness *has been manifested without law.*" And this undoubtedly is the correct construction, so far as the nexal point of grammatical coherence is concerned. But it must be borne in mind (1) that, so far as logical relation is concerned, the verb, with which the phrase is connected, must be viewed not as abstracted or reft from the whole concrete affirmation of which it forms a part, but as completing and bounding it. And then (2) the position of the phrase, as prefixed, not affixed, to the affirmation, fits it for overshadowing the whole, and for thus shedding its logical influence over the affirmation in its entirety.

This position of the phrase, in the foreground of the affirmation, shows, moreover, that it is intended to bear the burden of a special emphasis. In enunciation it should be betoned. For there is an antithetic reference to the statements of the preceding verse in relation to the moral law :—"*by works of law* there shall nobody be justified before God; for *through law* is recognition of sin." But though it is thus in vain for unrighteous men to have recourse to *law* (*the moral law*) in order to obtain justification; still their case is not hopeless. Justification may be attained in another way. "But now, *apart from law,* God's righteousness has been manifested." The nature of the case thus led the Apostle to give prominence, in the collocation of his phraseology, to the idea expressed in the phrase, "apart from law."

The phrase is exegetically translated by Luther, "without the aid of the law," (*ohne Zuthun des Gesetzes*). Campensis and Calvin explain it in the same manner, (*absque ullo adminiculo legis,* – Campensis. *Sine legis adminiculo.*– Calvin. *Sine adminiculo legis.*–Mussus). Augustin had attached to it the same idea. (*Vide supra.*) So do many others, as, for example, de Wette and Rückert, (*ohne Mitwirkung*). But this explication, though correct so far as it goes, is too narrow. The justifying righteousness has been manifested in a sphere of things *apart from law,*—so far as methods of justification, available to men, are concerned.

It is true, indeed, that in working out the justifying righteousness, Christ had respect to the law. He fulfilled it. He suffered its penalty. He magnified it, and made it honourable. But, so far as the righteousness is available to men for justification, it is, in the manifestation that has been made of it, a thing *apart from law.* It lies, to men, in a sphere that is altogether different from the sphere within which the law is dominant and says—"Do this and Live." (*Sine lege,* says Aquinas, *scilicet, causante justitiam.*)

It is also true that so far as mere duty is concerned, the law is for ever a perfect rule of life to man; and, as such, it goes hand in hand with the evangelical righteousness of God. In this relation of things it is not separated from *God's righteousness for unrighteous men.* And, correspondingly, *God's righteousness for unrighteous men* has not, in this relation of things, been manifested apart from law. But this is not the aspect of the case which the Apostle is at present contemplating. He is considering what it is which can furnish unrighteous men with a title to everlasting life. And he finds it, not in the righteousness which men themselves can work out by obedience to law, but in the righteousness of God, which has been manifested in a sphere of things altogether apart from this their obedience, and altogether apart, consequently, from the law as requiring their obedience.

The phrase was exegetically rendered by Tyndale, *without the fulfillinge of the lawe.* It is explained by Pareus as being equivalent to "without works of law," (*absque operibus legis*). Day gives the same explanation,—"without the law, that is, without the strict observation of the law." So does Carpzov, (*in phrasi* χωρὶς νόμου *subintelligitur, ex versu* 20, ἔργων). So Olshausen. And Calvin's interpretation is coincident:—he says that the word "*law* may be understood as meaning *works,*" (*ut lex pro operibus accepta intelligatur*). Theophylact took the same view; for, after quoting the expression, *without law,* he adds, exegetically, "for God justifies us, although we have not works," (δικαιοῖ γὰρ ἡμᾶς ὁ θεὸς, κἂν μὴ ἔργα ἔχωμεν). The idea running through all these parallel explanations lies, manifestly, on the right line; and the Apostle really means that, independently of those works which the moral law—(whether viewed apart, or as underlying, and regulating ceremonial observances)--independently of all the works which the law enjoins, and which, if fully performed by man, would constitute such a righteousness as would entitle to everlasting life,—God's righteousness,—the righteousness which God gives as a gift to unrighteous men,—has been manifested. Haldane admirably expresses the Apostle's idea by explaining the expression thus,—"without any regard whatever to the obedience of man to the law."

§ 5. *being attested by the law and the prophets,* (μαρτυρουμένη ὑπὸ τοῦ νόμου καὶ τῶν προφητῶν). By the expression *the law and the prophets,*—which Carpzov strangely regards as a Hendiadys for *prophetic law,* (*sine dubio autem verba* τοῦ νόμου καὶ τῶν προφητῶν *sunt hendiadyoῖν pro* νόμου προφητικοῦ *posita*) — we are evidently to understand *the Old Testament Scriptures.* These Scriptures originally consisted of the Pentateuch; the other parts being accretively superadded. The Pentateuch, consequently, was the original *Divine Instruction,* authoritatively exhibiting the duty of the Jews. (It was the original תּוֹרָה or νόμος.) Being such, it was very generally singled out and signalized, even after the growth of the volume of the book to its ultimate proportions, as *the law.* At other times the expression *the law* was extended to the entire body of the written revelations, inasmuch as the sum total of the ultimate volume was indeed the culminated or completed *Instruction* or *Teaching* of God, (הַתּוֹרָה), and was of uniform authority throughout, (ὁ νόμος). See Rom. ii. 12; John x. 34; xii. 34; xv. 25; 1 Cor. xiv. 21. Here the Apostle disintegrates, to his view, the volume of the book into the original *law,* the Pentateuch, and *the prophets*—the additional writings,—all of which were composed by inspired men (נְבִיאִים) who spake in the name of God, and for God, (προφῆται). The same dualism of representation is found in Matt. v. 17; vii. 12; xxii. 40; Luke xvi. 16; &c. Compare also Luke xvi. 29, 31, in which the parallel expression, *Moses and the prophets,* is found. In Luke xxiv. 44, instead of a dualism, there is a triplicity of groups, corresponding to the triple sections of the Hebrew Bible, as we at present have it, —*the law of Moses, the prophets, and the Psalms,* (the Psalms being specified as the first of the *Chethubim*). The general division, however, when the Unity of the volume was kept in the background of thought, was that which is reproduced here by the Apostle in the expression,—*the law and the prophets.*

Matthias supposes that the Apostle's dual expression is not intended to be a comprehensive designation of the Old

Testament "volume of the book," but is meant to point out, specifically, two constituent elements of the book, (1), "the word of God so far as it is *law*," strictly so called; and (2), "the word of God so far as it is *promise*," (*Wort Gottes sofern es Gesetz ist; und Wort Gottes, sofern es Verheissung ist*). But such an interpretation proceeds upon an erroneous view of the meaning of the word *law* in ver. 19th, to which Matthias refers for a parallel use of the term, and also upon an arbitrary and erroneous view of the meaning of the word *prophets* or *prophecy*. The expression employed by the Apostle manifestly designates the complex Scriptures of the Old Testament; and we may rest assured that, when he selected the dual representation, his mind spread itself delightedly over the varied testimonies to the evangelical righteousness of God which are, under appropriate representations, found in both the specified portions of the volume of the book.

It is, of course, impossible for us to know what were the particular testimonies which elicited his special attention, as his mind flashingly traversed the contents of *the law and the prophets*. We need not doubt that he thought of Abraham when he glanced at *the law*, for he dwells upon his case, in relation to the evangelical righteousness, in the fourth chapter of this epistle. We may rest assured too that in turning to *the prophets*, he thought of what David says in the 32nd Psalm, for he quotes from that psalm in the same 4th chapter. He would also think of the testimony from Habakkuk, which is quoted in chap. i. 17, and which is, indeed, *the Old Testament fountain-head of the Apostle's phase of the New Testament theology*. And we may reasonably suppose that his mind took a bird's eye view of all the prominent passages, both in *the law* and in *the prophets*, in which the propitiation of the Messiah is referred to, or the salvation that is bound up in that propitiation: for, in all these passages, the one great and glorious idea is either explicitly exhibited or implicitly suggested, that justification,—unattainable, as it is, through the personal righteousness of unrighteous men,—is attainable through that work of the Saviour which is, in one of the most gracious of its phases, *God's righteousness for the unrighteous.* We know that the Apostle was familiar with such passages, for we read that, on another occasion, "he expounded" to the Roman Jews "and testified the kingdom of God, persuading them concerning Jesus, both out of the law of Moses, and out of the prophets, from morning till evening." (Acts xxviii. 23.) In this matter he looked as through the eyes of Christ himself, who, "beginning at Moses and all the prophets, expounded unto his disciples in all the Scriptures the things concerning himself." (Luke xxiv. 27.) "These are the things," said he, "which I spake unto you, while I was yet with you, that all things must be fulfilled, which are written in the law of Moses, and in the prophets, and in the psalms, concerning me." (Luke xxiv. 44.) And Peter saw as Paul saw. "To Christ," says he, "give all the prophets witness, that through his name whosoever believeth in him shall receive remission of sins." (Acts x. 43.)

When the apostle represents *God's righteousness* as *attested* (μαρτυρουμένη) by *the law and the prophets*, the word is to be understood in its ordinary acceptation. "The law and the prophets" *bear testimony* to the righteousness. They speak of it; and they speak of it in such a way as to corroborate the announcement or proclamation of the New Testament evangelists. The expression indicates that evidence of the actual and divine reality of the righteousness either was or might be desiderated. Van Hengel would translate the word *celebrated*, (*quae* **laudatur** *a lege et prophetis*), instead of *attested:* Bretschneider renders it *recognized*, (*cognitus*): Schleusner, *predicted and promised*, (*quam praedixerunt et promiserunt Moses ceterique prophetae*): Calvin, Beza, Er. Schmid, &c., *verified by the testimony of*, (*testimonio comprobata*). But the majority of translators have done well in adhering to the ordinary import of the original term. The tense of the participle (μαρτυρουμένη) indicates that the attestation of the righteousness by the law and the prophets was viewed by the Apostle as a present thing. It had been, indeed; and it would be. But the idea to which he gives expression, is, *that it is.* If the tense had been past, the idea of attestation might have been obscured or complicated, and must have merged in pure prediction or promise. But even "now" the Old Testament continues to bear witness to the New. It bears present witness.

Why did the Apostle specify this fact,—that the Old Testament Scriptures bear testimony to *the Evangelical righteousness* which is the theme of the great New Testament annunciation? Why did he, as Oltramare strongly expresses it, "interrupt his proposition," that he might introduce the idea? Whatever was the reason, or whatever were the reasons, we may be sure that it was not to gratify, merely or at all, a taste for rhetorical antanaclasis or oxymoron, in setting off the expression *by law* against the expression *apart from law.* His aim might be various. (1.) He might love the grand idea,—so felicitously expressed by Augustin,—"the New Testament lies concealed in the Old; the Old Testament lies revealed in the New," (*Novum Testamentum in vetere latet, vetus in novo patet,*–Quaest. in Heptateuch., lib. ii. 73:—*Novum Testamentum in veteri velabatur: vetus Testamentum in novo revelatur,*–Sermo clx. 6.) The Apostle, from the mere largeness of his mind, and its love of magnificent harmonies, might thus interject the statement,—*attested by the law and the prophets.* (2.) He might, too, as Theodoret suggests, and as Fritzsche maintains, desire to hold up to view the dignity, worth, and glory of that which was the grand theme of his preaching. It was no crotchet. It was no minute and unimportant detail. It was the solar centre of divine revelation, out of which innumerable rays of light and heat were emanating, and back into which they might all be traced. The Gospel which he preached, and which exhibited the evangelical righteousness, had been "promised afore by God's prophets in the Holy Scriptures," (chap. i. 2). It was the mark to which prophetic fingers had pointed in all preceding times. (3.) And thus, too, as Chrysostom, Theophylact, and Œcumenius remark, it was no novelty, though "news." It was no new-fangled and upstart theory of things. It was a light that had dawned in the remotest antiquity, though it had only now reached the zenith of its effulgent glory. It had advanced with the ages, and grown with the growth of successive epochs, until "the fulness of the time." (4.) There can be little doubt that the Apostle had in view the reconciliation of the minds of his Jewish brethren to his evangelical teaching. He wished to show them that he was not overturning the Jewish faith, but only recalling it to its original purity, simplicity, and divine intent. This was one of the means that he wisely put into operation when he tried and plied all means, if, by any means, he might gain some of their souls. God Himself had set him the example, for, as Œcolampad reminds us, Moses and Elias were both of them sent to the mount of transfiguration to bear testimony to the Christ, (*Christo glorificato in monte testimonium perhibebant Moses et Elias*).

VER. 22. δικαιοσύνη δὲ Θεοῦ διὰ πίστεως Ἰησοῦ Χριστοῦ, εἰς πάντας, καὶ ἐπὶ πάντας τοὺς πιστεύοντας· οὐ γάρ διαστολή·

Eng. Auth. Vers. *Even the righteousness of God* which is *by faith of Jesus Christ unto all and upon all them that believe: for there is no difference:*

Revised Version. *even God's righteousness through faith in Jesus Christ, unto all, and upon all the believing; for there is no difference.*

§ 1. *even God's righteousness through faith in Jesus Christ,* (δικαιοσύνη δὲ Θεοῦ διὰ πίστεως Ἰησοῦ Χριστοῦ,). This clause is annexed to the preceding proposition, in order to explain, epexegetically, the particular *righteousness of God* referred to, which "has been manifested," and which is "attested by the law and the prophets." The Peshito detaches it, and erects it into a self-contained proposition, by supplying the substantive verb:—"But God's righteousness by means of faith *is* of Jesus Christ, &c." Wycliffe's version is similar,—"Sothli the rightwysnesse of God *is* bi the feith of ihesu crist, &c." Tyndale's version corresponds with Wycliffe's. So does Worsley's. Turnbull's is similar, —"and the righteousness of God, through faith in Jesus Christ, is for all and upon all who believe." Zinzendorf's translation is substantially the same, (*Diese gerechtigkeit Gottes durch den glauben an Jesum Christum ist vor einen jeden, &c.*) So de Saci, &c. It is, however, quite unnecessary to intrude into the Apostle's phraseology such an important supplement. The words form a natural additament to the proposition that goes before. The particle (δέ), which is rendered *even* in our Authorized English Version, is used in the case of such epexegetical annexes. See, for example, Rom. ix. 30,—"The Gentiles have attained to righteousness, *even the righteousness which is of faith*," (ἔθνη κατέλαβεν δικαιοσύνην, δικαιοσύνην δὲ τὴν ἐκ πίστεως). See also 1 Cor. ii. 6. (*Winer*, iii. 53. 7. *b.*) Though the translation *even* is perhaps as good a version as can, in the case before us, and in similar cases, be given in English to the Greek particle, yet it is certainly an imperfect reproduction of the idea of the original. The particle bears an epexegetically connective and quasi-adversative import; for it introduces a clause which is intended, as has been remarked by de Dieu, Day, Bengel, and others, to differentiate that particular *righteousness of God* which has been referred to. It is only, of course, a certain *righteousness of God* which is meant;—that, namely, which is "through faith in Jesus Christ." (*Exponitur quaenam sit ea justitia quam Dei esse dixerat.*-De Dieu.) Hence the idea of the Apostle, in his annexation, might be paraphrastically exhibited thus:—"God's righteousness, I have said, "has been manifested. It is true; and an all-important "truth. *But* let it be borne in mind that the righteousness "of which I speak is not that in the possession of which "God himself is righteous; but it is that which he has "provided for unrighteous men,—that which is to them "through faith in Jesus Christ." Hence Thomson renders the particle "however,"—"the righteousness of God *however* through faith of Jesus Christ." Mehring renders it "but," (*sondern*, as if the Apostle's word had been ἀλλά). The

Vulgate translation corresponds, (*autem*). Beza, on the other hand, brings out freely the idea of resumption and epexegesis, by translating it "I say," (*inquam*):—"God's righteousness, I say, &c." Castellio's version is the same. Bullinger, before them both, had given the same version, (δὲ *enim hoc loco* **inquam** *valet*). So Ostervald and Martin, (*dis-je*). Good old Thomas Wilson's corresponds,—"*I mean* the righteousness of God, &c." Tyndale aims at expressing the same idea, but not very felicitously:—"The righteousness *no dout* which, &c." Luther is paraphrastic:—"But *I speak of* such righteousness as, &c." (*Ich sage aber von solcher Gerechtigkeit vor Gott, die da kommt, &c.*) The Geneva version corresponds with our own:—"*to wit*, the righteousness of God, &c." And, on the whole, it would be difficult to find a more appropriate rendering than what has been given in our Authorized Version. (Winzer renders the particle by *nempe*. The German critics often give *aber*, as does Meyer; or *und zwar*, as do Rückert and Philippi.)

"Even God's righteousness, *through faith in Jesus Christ.*" Fritzsche supposes that we must mentally carry down from the preceding verse the verb *has been manifested*, and interpose it before the expression, *through faith in Jesus Christ*:—"God's righteousness, I say, *has been manifested* through faith in Jesus Christ." Noesselt had the same idea (*Vindiciae*, Rom. iii. 21—28). But this interpretation proceeds on a misunderstanding of what it is which constitutes *God's righteousness;* and it is objectionable, moreover, on the additional ground that it assumes the suppression, in the clause before us, of that which, according to Fritzsche's theory of interpretation, must have been the principal idea. (We should have expected πεφανέρωται δὲ κ. τ. ἑξῆς, instead of δικαιοσύνη δὲ κ. τ. λ.) Benecke would supply the same verb, and in the same manner; but then he takes a peculiar view of the expression, *through faith in Jesus Christ*, (διὰ πίστεως Ἰησοῦ Χριστοῦ). He adheres, like Paulus, to the literal translation, "through faith *of* Jesus Christ," and understands by faith, the "faithfulness" (*treue*) of Christ,—the unfailing faithful activity, which is characteristic of Jesus Christ, (*die göttliche*

Gerechtigkeit offenbart sich durch die Treue Christi, durch die unablässig treue Wirksamkeit desselben). But Benecke, too, had a wrong conception of what is meant by the expression, *God's righteousness;* and, over and above the other objection, which is as applicable to his interpretation as to Fritzsche's, it seems abundantly evident that the *faith* here spoken of must be the same that is referred to in chap. i. 17, and in chap. ix. 30; in which passages there is no mention of *Jesus Christ,* and consequently no scope for the supposition that the faith referred to may be *subjective in Jesus Christ.* Lange's notion corresponds almost throughout with Benecke's, (he interprets πίστις as denoting Christ's *glaubenstreue*). Bosveld is at one with Lange,—as with Fritzsche and Benecke,—in supposing that the verb, *has been manifested,* must be mentally carried forward into this verse. He believes that the Apostle means that it is *through the faith of Jesus Christ* that *God's righteousness has been manifested.* But he supposes that the word *faith* is here to be understood objectively, as denoting *the Gospel* and *the gracious Gospel-economy* of Jesus Christ, (*Kan ik, naar mijn oordeel, door het geloof van J. C. te dezer plaatse, onmogelijk iets anders verstaan, dan het* **Euangelij** *of de* **Geloofsleer van J. C.** *en de daar uit voortvloeijende, of daar mede gepaard gaande* **Bediening** *en* **Bedeeling der Genade**, *welke hij, door de verkondiging van zijn Euangelij, onder de menschen heeft ingevoerd.*) It is an inadmissible view of the *faith* specified.

There is no need for supplying any verb before the attributive clause, *through faith in Jesus Christ.* The Apostle's style is curt, abrupt, emphatic, and pregnant. And although, no doubt, he might have filled out his phraseology in some such way as might have been rendered into English thus:—"even God's righteousness, *which is attainable by unrighteous men* through faith in Jesus Christ," or, "*which may be appropriated* through faith in Jesus Christ;" yet, there was no necessity for such explicit unfolding of his idea. His condensed expression readily unfolds itself within the thought of the appreciative reader. And its amplitude of import is none the less realized that its form is so characteristically compressed. We have many instances, in the Apostle's writings, of a similarly abrupt and pregnant way of using prepositions. (See chap. i. 17; Gal. i. 1; &c.)

The expression, "*through* faith," (διὰ πίστεως), suggests the mere intermediacy and instrumentality of faith in relation to the blessing enjoyed in justification. The Efficient Cause is beyond.

The word *faith* falls to be discussed in connection with chap. i. 16, 17. Its import is nothing recondite; otherwise it would be a term altogether unsuitable for being used in an exhibition of the duty of universal man, uncultured as well as cultured. *Faith* is such a persuasion or conviction of the mind in reference to things unseen, and, so far as direct intuition is concerned, unknown, as supplies the place of vision or invisaging. Its *moral* power, in its relation to the Gospel of Jesus Christ, is resolvable into the peculiarity of its object, and not into any peculiarity in the act. What is needed, consequently, in order to continuous, and continuously increasing, peace, joy, hope, gratefulness, holiness, and devotedness, is that faith be continuously, and with continuously increasing breadth and depth of range, directed to its glorious personal object. He who "lives by faith" in Jesus, is continuously present with Jesus in the most exalted way in which presence can be realized; he is present dianoetically,—in mind, in thought. And the power of the presence of Jesus, as dianoetically and reciprocally realized, is, when the presence becomes to the inner eye intensely self-evidencing and luminous, imperial. It is apparently in virtue of this mighty *moral* power of *faith in Jesus* that it has been divinely invested with what is called its *justifying* function.

When the Apostle says, "through faith *of* Jesus Christ," (Ἰησοῦ Χριστοῦ), he evidently means, "through faith *in* Jesus Christ." The genitive of the Saviour's complex name is objective, (*genitivus objecti*). See Gal. ii. 16; ii. 20; iii. 22; Eph. iii. 12; Acts. iii. 16; Jas. ii. 1: and compare such expressions as Mark xi. 22, "faith *in* God" (πίστιν θεοῦ); "the faith *of* the Gospel" (Phil. i. 27); "faith" or "belief *of* the truth," (2 Thess. ii. 13). The Apostle might, indeed, have used a different expression, as, for example, "through faith which is *in* Christ Jesus, (διὰ πίστεως τῆς ἐν Χριστῷ Ἰησοῦ, the reading of A, but an evident gloss). See 2 Tim. iii. 15; and compare 1 Tim. iii. 13. But that which he employs is sufficiently explicit; and when Crell, Oertel, Macknight, Ritchie, &c., imagine that the peculiarity of the expression is intended to indicate, not that Christ is the object of faith, but that he is its inculcator, (*the faith which Jesus Christ hath enjoined*); and when Rauwenhoff, (*De δικαιώσει*, p. 88. ff.), van Hengel, &c., think that it is intended to represent Christ as the author or Efficient Cause of faith, (*faith in God, of which Jesus Christ is the author, fides cujus auctor est Christus*); they seem to forget altogether that the Apostle is but unfolding, more systematically and elaborately, that which is the grand burden of the whole of New Testament theology, and indeed of the whole Bible,—"Believe *on the Lord Jesus Christ*, and thou shalt be saved." He is explaining the way of salvation; and thus pointing the sinner's faith to Him who is emphatically the Saviour. It is true, indeed, that Christ, as the great Teacher, inculcates faith. It is also true that in an important sense he is its Author. It is likewise true that faith, in its ultimate issue, ascends to God, as God, and fixes on Him; while Jesus is "the Way" of ascent. All this is indisputable. But it is likewise true,—and emphatically so "now"—"at this time"—"in these last days,"—that "this is God's commandment, That we should *believe on the name of his Son Jesus Christ*" (1 John iii. 23.) "Neither is there salvation in any other: for there is none other name under heaven, given among men, whereby we must be saved." (Acts iv. 12.) It is "Christ" who is "the end of the law for righteousness to every one that believeth." (Rom. x. 4.) "For God so loved the world, that he gave his only begotten Son, that whosoever believeth *on him* (*on God's only begotten Son*) should not perish, but have everlasting life." (John iii. 16.)

"Jesus Christ" being the object of the faith through

which *God's righteousness for unrighteous men* is attainable, —it must be implied that it is *in* "Jesus Christ" that the *righteousness* is found. *Justifying faith* must undoubtedly embrace, at least implicitly, the justifying *righteousness*. It does embrace it; so that the *righteousness* becomes *the righteousness which is (to the soul) by faith.* (Rom. ix. 30; x. 6.) Faith is the hand that receives the gift and uses it. It is the hand that accepts "the robe of righteousness" and puts it on as "the garment of salvation." (Compare the Peshito version, ܒܐܝܕ ܗܝܡܢܘܬܐ *by the hand of faith: idiotismus linguae non sine emphasi hic accipiendus.*-Reusch.)

As *righteousness*, however, is only one of several aspects of the work of Jesus Christ, in its relation to the necessities of unrighteous men, it is possible that it may be often only *implicitly* believed in. And, for all popular and practical purposes, it is better to follow the example of the Apostle, and to present "Jesus Christ" himself, in the totality of his living personality, as the *explicit* object of the sinner's faith.

Lachmann, in his earlier text, omitted the word *Jesus*, on the authority of B. But in his later text he re-admitted it,—a fact overlooked by Tischendorf (1859),—and he thus acquiesced in the reading of almost all other editors. The complex designation *Jesus Christ* or *Christ Jesus* is a favourite combination with Paul. He uses it with great frequency. And no wonder. It is delightfully significant —bearing, as it does, the most interesting relations, both man-ward and God-ward.—When the Apostle has occasion, as in the passage before us, to use the double appellation *in the genitive*, he almost invariably collocates the words as we find them here, *Jesus* first, and *Christ* second. We say "almost," for there are several exceptional passages, such as Eph. iii. 1; Phil. ii. 21; iii. 8; 1 Tim. i. 1, 2; Philem. 1; though in most of these the reading is more or less disputed. But when he has occasion to use the appellation in the dative, he almost invariably collocates the words in the reverse order, and speaks of *Christ Jesus*. See Rom. iii. 24; vi. 11, 23; viii. 1, 2, 39; xv. 17; xvi. 3;

1 Cor. i. 2, 4, 30; iv. 15; xv. 31; xvi. 24; Gal. ii. 4; iii. 14, 26, 28; v. 6; vi. 15; &c. We say again, "almost invariably," for exceptional passages are found in Rom. xvi. 18; 1 Thess. i. 1; 2 Thess. i. 1.

§ 2. *unto all, and upon all the believing,* (εἰς πάντας, καὶ ἐπὶ πάντας τοὺς πιστεύοντας). Some expositors suppose that it is requisite to carry down mentally, from the preceding verse, the verb *has been manifested,* (πεφανέρωται), in order to effect a transition, in thought, to these words. This is the opinion of Seb. Schmidt, Belsham, de Wette, Stuart, Dr. Jo. Brown, Krehl, Alford, &c. By this expedient an independent, though elliptical, proposition is formed. Bos, indeed, would throw the preceding part of the verse into a parenthesis, in order to get the benefit of the verb. But there is not the slightest occasion for such devices; or for supplying any such participle, even, as *being* or *coming,* (οὖσα, γενομένη, ἐρχομένη). The clause is just a farther *annex* to the expression *God's righteousness.* And the prepositions, *unto* and *upon,* are sufficient links of attachment: although it is perfectly legitimate to unfold and expand, as best we may, the idea which is underlying the exceedingly condensed phraseology of the Apostle. In attempting this evolving expansion we should certainly refrain from having recourse to the verb *has been manifested,* for the manifestation referred to was a completed act long before the *righteousness* could come within the sphere of the cognizance of many of those who ultimately enjoy it. We should content ourselves with the substantive verb:—"even God's righteousness, *which is attainable* through faith in Jesus Christ, *and which is* unto all, and upon all who believe."

There is some difficulty in determining the correct reading of the clause. Griesbach suspected that the words *and upon all* (καὶ ἐπὶ πάντας) are spurious. Years before him Semler was positive that the Apostle had only written *unto all,* (*Paulus scripserat tantum unam phrasin,* εἰς πάντας.—Apparatus, &c., p. 34. See also p. 56). Wakefield says that either the one or the other of the two clauses "is an interpolation." Noesselt is of Semler's opinion. (*Vindiciae loci Rom.* iii. 21—28.) Greve condemns the second clause. Lachmann has omitted it from his text. He reads simply *unto all who believe.* Belsham, before him, omitted the same clause from his translation, saying that it "obscures the sense." The omitted clause is not found in א A B C. It is wanted in the Coptic, Æthiopic, Armenian, and the Erpen-Arabic versions. And it is occasionally omitted by some of the Fathers in quotation. This last circumstance is of little or no moment. The clause is found in D E F G K L, and in most cursive mss.; in the two Syriac versions, the Vulgate, the Polyglott-Arabic, and the Slavonic; and it is found in the texts of Rufinus's Origen, Chrysostom and Theophylact, and commented on by Theodoret and in Œcumenius. Ambrosiaster, too, has the two clauses, though, as his text at present stands, he strangely connects them thus,—"unto all or (*vel*) upon all who believe!" There are certainly some very great MS. authorities for the omission of the second clause; and yet we cannot but feel disposed, along with Bengel, Tischendorf, Fritzsche, Scholz, Meyer, Oltramare, &c., to retain it. It seems to be more difficult to account for its admission into the text, if spurious, than for its omission, if genuine. It could scarcely have been added as a marginal gloss to explain the phrase "unto all." That very simple phrase did not need explanation: and though it had needed elucidation, it is not likely that the more difficult phrase "upon all" would have been appended for the purpose. If therefore the phrase were apocryphal, it would be difficult to account for its origination and admission. But, on the hypothesis of its original canonicity, it is not difficult to account for its accidental or intentional omission. The principle of ὁμοιοτέλευτον might account for the accidental omission of the clause:—

ΧΥΕΙΣΠΑΝΤΑΣ
ΚΑΙΕΠΙΠΑΝΤΑΣ

Even though the clauses should not have occupied entire lines in any of the early codices, nevertheless their identical termination might mislead the eye. And the eye, if once misled, would not have the benefit of the interpretative understanding for a check on its misreading, inasmuch as the sense of the passage remains unembarrassed though the second clause be omitted. It is possible, besides, that some transcriber, finding the two clauses in the codex he was copying, yet not perceiving (with very many modern critics) any peculiarity in the second, to distinguish it in import from the first, might come to the conclusion that it had been unwarrantably intruded by some predecessor, and might thus omit it. The omission of the clause, says Bengel justly, might very easily occur. (*Facillima omissio.*) We cannot hesitate, therefore, to concur with the great body of critics in retaining the entire expression, as it stands in *the received text.*

But what then is the distinction between the two clauses? There is none at all, say many expositors. The one is a mere repetition of the other, it is maintained; and the repetition only intensifies the idea that the righteousness is indeed available to all who believe. "We are not nicely to distinguish between *unto* and *upon*," says Koppe, (*neque in* εἰς *et* ἐπί *est argutandum*). "No difference," says Alford, "in the two prepositions must be sought." "There is no difference," says Köllner, (*es ist kein Unterschied*). "I see no difference," says Sclater, "more than betwixt Aaron's beard, and the beard of Aaron." It is a *pleonasm*, says Bullinger. It is an "elegant and emphatic pleonasm," says Stein. (*Dissert. de Dicto classico Rom.* iii. 22—26, p. 10.) It is only, says Bugenhagen, a redundance of words, (*copia tantum est verborum*). "The repetition expresses intensity," says Hodge in his *abridged ed.* In his last edition, however, he drops the remark. But Calvin was of the same opinion, (*ad auxesin diversis loquendi formis idem repetiit*). So is Fritzsche, Reiche, Ritchie, Terrot, Maier, Hinton, &c. And yet this idea wears the aspect of extreme unverisimilitude. The Apostle was fond of using his prepositions distinguishingly. (See Gal. i. 1, and Rom. xi. 36.) And it should certainly be our very last resort to suppose that his discriminative use of the two which are employed in the case before us is unmeaning. There does seem to be an ascent in the thought. And unless it is utterly impossible to work out this climactic idea,—in consistency with sobriety, and with the scope of revelation, and with the facts of human experience,—we should not fall back upon the idea of mere indiscriminative accumulation.

Theodoret had the notion that by the clause *unto all*, the Apostle refers to the Jews; and that by the clause *upon all*, he refers to the Gentiles, (τὸ γὰρ εἰς πάντας, τοὺς Ἰουδαίους λέγει· ἐπὶ πάντας δὲ, τοὺς ἐκ τῶν ἄλλων ἐθνῶν). His notion has been taken up and echoed by a considerable number of succeeding expositors; as by Bengel, for instance, who, with a touch of the whimsical, explains the *unto* as meaning *into*, and represents the Jews as being the natural vessel for receiving the righteousness; whereas the Gentiles, *upon* whom it is, are, says he, like the soil that receives the superabundance of the rain of grace, (**in omnes,** *Judaeos, qui sunt tanquam vas proprium.* **Super omnes,** *Gentiles, qui sunt ut solum, recipiens pluviam superabundentem gratiae*). Wesley echoes Bengel. Boehme makes the same distinction; and Ch. Schmid. Long before, Gennadius (in Œcumenius) set it in a less artificial light than Bengel. In modern times Jatho has revived this ancient interpretation. Matthias, too, adopts it; but he modifies it so far as to refer the first clause, *unto all*, to the Gentiles, and the second, *upon all*, to the Jews. He contends at great length, and with great earnestness, for the interpretation; and finds, indeed, a reference to the same twofold distinction in the expression, *by faith to faith*, in chap. i. 17; only there he reverses his own order of reference, and supposes that the Jews are referred to in the first expression, *by faith*, while it is the Gentiles that are aimed at in the second expression, *to faith*. We cannot but feel that there is a thoroughly artificial strain in this method of accounting for the two clauses, and their respective prepositions, and we are sorry that Ernesti had really too much ground for his too severe remark, when, with special reference to the exposition of Bengel, he says,—"These explanations are so utterly absurd that one can scarcely read them without laughing," (*Das sind nun* *freilich alberne Erklärungen, dass man sie kaum ohne Lachen lesen kann*).

Grotius tries another vein. He thinks that only one class of persons is referred to in both clauses, but that the preposition *unto* or *into* denotes the fact that the righteousness referred to really *is* in believers, while the preposition *upon* indicates the fact that it is so in them as to be *apparent* to others, (εἰς *significat justitiam illam esse in credentibus*, ἐπί *etiam apparere*). Rauwenhoff echoes the opinion of Grotius, (*De* δικαίωσει, *p.* 34). Jowett has a somewhat similar idea. He says, "of the two prepositions, εἰς represents the more internal and spiritual relation of the Gospel to the individual soul, as ἐπί its outward connection with mankind collectively." Aquinas, before them, worked in the same vein:—he explained the first preposition as meaning *in the heart*, and the second as denoting what is *above* human power and in excess of human merit, (**in omnes,** *scilicet in corde, non carnalibus observantiis*,—**et super omnes,** *quia videlicet facultatem humanam ac merita excedit*). Abelard conjures similarly with the second of the two expressions. He interprets it as meaning,—"in the higher element of their being, that is, in their soul," (*supra omnes fideles, id est in superiori eorum parte, id est in anima*). Mussus is more judicious, and improves upon Aquinas:—*Justification and grace,* he says, *like Christ himself, come from heaven. Hence the expression* **upon all.** *God sends a plentiful rain of grace upon us,* (*Super nos gratias Deus largissimas pluit*). Seb. Schmidt, more naturally, interprets the *unto* as having reference to the *manifestation* of the righteousness, and the *upon* as having reference to its *application;* though he does not doubt that in both the clauses the *all* are one and the same class,—believers. Meyer is of the same opinion, so far as regards the assumption that it is one and the same class of persons who are referred to in the two clauses. But he would explain the *unto* as denoting the *destination* of the righteousness, and the *upon* as denoting its actual *collation.* So de Dieu, and Winzer, and Ryke. The same seems to be the view of Ewald, (*bestimmt für alle und kommend über* *alle die glaubenden*). The same is substantially the view taken by Philippi and Hofmann, (*Schriftbeweis*, i. 331). Philippi seems to think that the idea of a stream underlies the Apostle's phraseology. The Evangelical Righteousness, like a stream, reaches *to* all believers, and pours itself *upon* all, (*Sie kommt an Alle heran, und ergiesst sich über Alle, wie ein Strom*). Olshausen, before him, had the same idea, and Rambach before Olshausen. From Olshausen Hodge adopts the idea in his 1864 edition. Basil Cooper, again, sees in the preposition *upon*, or *over*, a reference to the protection of a shield; while Baumgarten-Crusius sees in *unto* an indication of the *commencement* of faith, and in *upon* an indication of its farther *development or increase*, (*im* εἰς πάντας *wird der Glaube ausgedrückt, mit welchem die Menschen herankommen, im* ἐπὶ πάντας *der, in welchem sie beharren*). But all of these are of opinion that it is one and the same class of persons who are referred to in both clauses.

There are obvious gleams of truth in several of these expositions,—so far as features of distinction are pointed out in the ideas suggested by the two prepositions. The notions of Grotius, indeed, and Jowett, and Aquinas, are obviously off the scent. But Seb. Schmidt, Meyer, Olshausen, Philippi, and Baumgarten-Crusius, are evidently snuffing the air in the right direction. So is Oltramare, who says that *unto* denotes that the righteousness is "for all," (*pour tous*), and *upon*, that "it rests on all," (*elle repose sur tous*). Others of the best critics are of substantially the same opinion. And, were we shut up to believe that it is only one class of persons that is referred to in the two clauses, we should certainly acquiesce, in substance, in the same view.

But, along with Wetstein, Heumann, Bosveld, Flatt, Moses Stuart, Haldane, Chalmers, Cox, Knight, Mehring, Wardlaw, &c., we feel persuaded that the Apostle had reference, in the two clauses, to two distinct classes of persons,—distinct, at least, when viewed as classes. And it is only, we apprehend, when this idea is taken, that we can account satisfactorily for the two clauses, and explain, at once with perfect precision and with fulness of significance the distinction subsisting between the two prepositions. Instead, then, of regarding the attributive expression *the believing* (τοὺς πιστεύοντας) as belonging equally to the two clauses, *unto all* and *upon all*, we would regard it as subjoined to, or rather as merging itself in, the second of the two, for the very purpose of limiting the reference of the second *all*, and thus differentiating its range of application from the unlimited sweep which is naturally characteristic of the first *all*. We would thus place a comma after the first clausule, *unto all*, but would interpose no comma between the expression *upon all* and the superadded expression *the believing*.

We cannot see or conceive the least objection, of a grammatical or hermeneutical nature, to this bifurcation of the clausules. And when we consider the expressions of absolute universality which the Apostle employs in verses 19, 20, while indicating the need that all men lie under, in consequence of their personal unrighteousness, of having recourse to the righteousness revealed in the Gospel;—the expressions, to wit, *the whole world—every mouth—all flesh*:—we see the utmost propriety in exhibiting,—when he begins to hold up to view the evangelical righteousness of God in its gracious counterpart-relation to men's necessities,—the counter universality, in all its amplitude, of the provision of grace. Hence the befittingness, we had almost said the hermeneutical necessity, of the unlimited expression *unto all*, as designating,—in the merciful correspondence and adaptation of the divine plan to the full range of human wants,—the unfettered freeness of God's evangelical righteousness to all unrighteous men, without distinction or exception. The righteousness is *for all*. It was provided *for all*. It was wrought out *in behalf of all*. It is tendered *unto all*. It is free *to all*. For Christ "gave himself a ransom *for all*." (1 Tim. ii. 6.) He "tasted death *for every man*." (Heb. ii. 9.) He is "a propitiation for the sins of *the whole world*." (1 John ii. 1, 2.) All these expressions are but other aspects of the idea that the Evangelical Righteousness of God is *unto all*. The Gospel of God's grace,—which equally announces the *ransom*, the *death-tasting*, the *propitiation*, and the *righteousness*,—is a message of mercy "to every creature." It has relations to man, as man, in whatever external circumstances, and in whatever intellectual, social, or moral state he may be found.

But while the divine Righteousness,—provided for the unrighteous,—is "*unto* all" without limitation, it is "*upon* all the believing." *Upon* is the radical and natural import of the preposition; and it is emphatically its predominant import in the New Testament. The Righteousness has not only been "brought *near*" to believers. (Isai. xlvi. 13.) A farther advance has been made. It has been brought over *upon them*. (Comp. Luke v. 36.) And it is thus *on them*. (Comp. Matt. xi. 29; xxvii. 29; Luke ii. 25; iv. 18; Rev. iv. 4.) It rests on them. (Comp. 2 Cor. xii. 9; 1 Pet. iv. 14.) It envelops them. (Comp. John xx. 7.) It remains on them. (Comp. John i. 33; iii. 36.) It, as it were, clothes them. (Comp. ἐπίβλημα in classical and Septuagintal Greek, and ἐπιβόλαίον in the Sept.-Coll. Luke xix. 35; 2 Cor. iii. 13, 15.) Melville approves of this idea, (*ea induti vestiuntur, ne eorum pudenda appareat nuditas*). It is to them as a "garment of salvation" thrown over them. When they have it, they are "covered with the robe of righteousness." (Isai. lxi. 10.) We do not doubt, indeed, that the Apostle had Isai. lxi. 10 in his eye when he penned the expression before us; although he does not reproduce the prophet's idea in an exactly parallelistic form. Both the prophet and the Apostle delighted to contemplate and to represent the saving grace of God in its aspect of Righteousness; and this Righteousness had evidently, to their eye, some closer relationship to those who believe on the Messiah than it has to those who believe not. For, undoubtedly, the ideas of Eyre, on the one hand, that all the elect are justified *before* they believe, (*Vindiciae justificationis gratuitae*), and of Maurice, on the other, that all men are justified *whether they believe or not*, (*Essays*, pp. 200—4), are, in the most emphatic manner possible, contradictions of the representations of Scripture.

The believing, (τοὺς πιστεύοντας). The expression,—so far as regards its tense,—has a reference to the "now" which is specified in ver. 21st; and it expresses, as Melville remarks, continuousness of faith, (*constantiam fidei, et in fide ad extremum usque perseverantiam innuens*). For continuousness of faith is necessary in order to the continuous enjoyment of the blessings which are wrapped up in the divine evangelical righteousness. The life must be "a life of faith." Momentary faith may, indeed, suffice for momentary blessings. More than momentary, and yet temporary, faith may suffice for more than momentary, yet temporary, blessings. But perpetual faith,—faith that is "held fast unto the end,"—is needed for perennial life, for everlasting glory.

§ 3. *for there is no difference*, (οὐ γάρ ἐστιν διαστολή). In both the preceding clausules the primary emphasis rests upon the word *all;* though a secondary intonation should be laid upon the contra-distinguished prepositions. The point of the emphasis lying on the word *all*, looks to the distinction in things religious that was commonly made by the Jews between themselves and the Gentiles. The Apostle, carrying along with him the idea of this emphasis, more especially as it was laid upon the last *all*, vindicates, in the expression before us, his use of the indiscriminative word. "There is no difference," viz., *in regard to the matter on hand, between believing Jews and Gentiles. They both equally need the evangelical righteousness of God. It is equally available for both. And both, as believers in Jesus Christ, have equally attained it, and equally enjoy the blessings which it involves.* This principle of indifferentiation in relation to the Righteousness of God is applicable to men, not only considered as Jews and Gentiles, but also considered in all possible diversities of physical, intellectual, moral, and social condition. There is no difference, in the matter referred to, between sovereigns, for instance, and their meanest subjects; between the cultured and the most uncultured; between the sage and savages; no difference between the most punctilious Pharisee who observes every ceremony of the church, and, gathering up his garments, steps fastidiously aside from every indecency of social life, and the most reckless offcasts who "rough it" on the highways of life, or riot and rot in the lowest of our city dens. As Cardinal Cajetan remarks, the *righteousness of God through faith in Jesus Christ is, was, and will be upon all who believe.*

VER. 23. Πάντες γὰρ ἥμαρτον, και ὑστεροῦνται τῆς δόξης τοῦ Θεοῦ,

Eng. Auth. Vers. *For all have sinned, and come short of the glory of God;*

Revised Version. *For all sinned, and are fallen short of the glory of God,*

§ 1. The last clause of the preceding verse forms, in the common editions of Luther's version,—such, at least, as we possess,—and in the Geneva, and in Bengel's German version, the first clause of this. And were the arrangement of the verses to be re-arranged, this grouping of the clauses,—a grouping approved of by Calvin,—would perhaps deserve to be preferred. To admit it now, however, would only be to embarrass references in dictionaries, concordances, &c. This embarassment is aggravated by Castellio, by the editors of the French Geneva, and by Ostervald and Martin, who, in their respective editions of the Bible, swallow up the Stephanic 23rd verse altogether in the 22nd, so that they have only 30, instead of 31, verses in the chapter. But such a departure from the conventional Stephanic adjustment and enumeration is greatly to be deprecated. In many cases the actual versicular division is obviously imperfect. In some it is very infelicitous. But it would be perplexing in the extreme to interfere with it now. And almost all the evils arising from the existing improprieties, either in the capitular or in the versicular divisions, may be obviated by printing the text continuously from paragraph to paragraph, as is done in the Testaments of Bengel, Griesbach, Lachmann, Tischendorf, &c.

§ 2. *for all sinned*, (πάντες γὰρ ἥμαρτον). Such is doubtless the proper translation of the apostle's expression. He might have used the perfect tense, and said "for all have sinned," (ἡμαρτήκασι), but then he would have shifted his standpoint of contemplation. He would have been in the attitude of one who was making some kind of mensuration of the rise, progress, and consummation of the sum-total, or of some part, of the sinning of those to whom he referred. He chooses, however, to say, "for all sinned,"—looking back simply to *the historical fact* of the occurrence of sin in the past life of "the believing." It was a fact that they had all sinned. It was a fact that they were sinners. They had failed in their duty. They had violated the law of their God,—the law that was continually echoed in their hearing by the voice of their own consciences, within their breasts.

Seb. Schmidt supposes that the reference of the verb is to the first sin of Adam. (*Malumus* ἥμαρτον *accipere de peccato omnium hominum in praeterito, quod est peccatum primum Adami ad omnes pertinens.*) Olshausen thinks that there is a principal, though not an exclusive, reference to that original sin. And Musculus, Aretius, Er. Schmid, Cocceius, Vitringa, Bengel, Benson, &c., are of opinion that there is a reference to both original and actual sin. So Trapp, who says, "the first man defiled the nature, and ever since the nature defileth the man." Stein maintains that the reference is, 1st, to *originating original sin*, 2nd, to *originated original sin*, and, 3rd, to *actual sin* so far as it is *involuntary*, but by no means so far as it is *elective and voluntary!* (*Dissert de Dicto classico Rom.* iii. 22—26.) Feurborn thinks that the passage is a decisive argument against the papistical doctrine of *the immaculate conception of the Virgin*,—her freedom, that is, from original sin! But any phase of such an idea, is entirely out of joint with the Apostle's argument. His reference is obviously to the fact which he has substantiated from chap. i. 18 to chap. iii. 20,—the fact that all are guilty of actual personal transgressions. It is on the ground of such actual unrighteousness that the Apostle builds his plea for the evangelical Righteousness of God.

When he says, "*for* all sinned," we are to understand the conjunction as bearing its usual reason-rendering signification. The clause which it introduces renders a reason for the affirmation with which the preceding verse concludes,—"there is no difference,"—no difference, namely, among the believing, so far as regards the relation which they sustain to the evangelical Righteousness of God. There is no difference,—*for* all of them were guilty of unrighteousness;—the best of them, the best of the Jews as truly as the worst of the Gentiles. Seb. Schmidt is disposed to take a different view of the conjunction. He has the notion that, as the Apostle has stated in verses 21st and 22nd that there is a way of justification for the unrighteous, so in verses 23rd—26th he explains, as in a sort of independent section, what this way is. Hence he would regard the conjunction as introducing, in some indefinitely explanatory way, a new paragraph:—"*Indeed* all sinned," (*particula non tam causalis est, quam explanativa,*—**Nimirum omnes peccaverunt**). But the Apostle's discourse is not a formal dissertation, partitioned off into sharply defined logical *heads* and *particulars.* It rolls freely and unconstrainedly along, wave succeeding wave. And as the current of thought runs, and indeed rushes on, the phraseology coincidently rushes onward and hither or thither,—sometimes regurgitating at a particular turn, sometimes dashing itself impetuously forward as on sunken reefs, or sweeping irresistibly around some majestic peak of everlasting rock. And, moreover, we must not attempt to lick such a conjunction as *for* into any shape that may suit our artificial divisions of things. It certainly just means *for.* There can be no doubt that the statement, "*for* all sinned," is intended to vindicate the affirmation at the conclusion of the preceding verse—"for there is no difference." All "the believing"—of whatever nationality, of whatever moral development,—needed to have the righteousness of God *upon them*, "for" it was a historical fact in their experience that they had *sinned*.

§ 3. *and are fallen short of the glory of God*, (καὶ ὑστεροῦνται τῆς δόξης τοῦ Θεοῦ). It is somewhat difficult to reproduce to a nicety, in our English idiom, the idea embodied in the verb which we translate *they are fallen short of*, (ὑστεροῦνται). Were we to say, with our Authorized Version, "they *come* short of," a somewhat erroneous idea would be suggested:—this, to wit, that the Apostle refers to what *happens* rather than to what *is*, (that is, in such a case, to what *has happened*). The same objection lies against the translation of Dr. Peile, and of the "Five Clergymen," *they fall short of*. If we should suppose, however, that the authors of our Authorized Version intended the auxiliary *have*, which they have used in translating the verb *sinned* ("for all *have sinned*"), to be carried forward to the verb *come short of*, then their version, though apparently less precise, would be really more correct. It would still, however, be somewhat objectionable; partly because, by the use of the perfect tense, it *seems* to be using too great freedom in reproducing the Greek present, and partly because it really *is* something else than an exact reproduction. For the Greek present does not indicate an accomplished fact. It only expresses an existing condition. Hence, too, Mace's version is objectionable;—*have forfeited*. Turnbull's is more objectionable still,—*have lost*;—though certainly both of these translations lie on the right line of things. On the whole, we cannot find a better translation, if we adhere to literality, than the one we have given, "and *are fallen short of* the glory of God," though it is far from being perfect. The Apostle's idea might be fairly and fully, though of course very freely, expressed thus,—"*and are unentitled to the glory of God* (though they might and should have been possessed of a title to it, in virtue of perfect righteousness of their own)."

The verb, by reason of its etymology, graphically represents the condition of those who are left behind in a race; (*ad verbum sonat* **posteriorantur.**–Erasmus). They fail to arrive at the goal in time to claim the proffered prize. They are thus unentitled to the prize. Such is the condition of sinful men. They have not run well in the race that was set before them. They have turned aside "like a deceitful bow." They have loitered. They have dallied. They have failed to improve their golden opportunity. And it is now therefore out of the question for them to entertain the idea of meriting "the glory of God." They are, by their own fault, unentitled, now and for ever,—so far at least as their own merit is concerned,—to "the glory of God."

The import of the verb helps, in a considerable measure, to determine the reference of the expression, "the glory of God." That reference has been greatly disputed. Theodoret explains the expression as meaning *the grace of God*, that is, we presume, *the glorious grace of God*, that grace of God which is his glory; and he regards, therefore, the verb as simply meaning, *they are in want of*,—"they are needful of the grace of God," (τῆς χάριτος ἐνδεεῖς). Dionysius à Ryckel echoes Theodoret's explication. In some codices of the Vulgate the word *grace* is substituted for the word *glory*:—"they are in need of the *grace* of God." Aquinas reads "glory," but he explains it in a way kindred to that of Theodoret:—"they need justification, which redounds to the glory of God," (*justificatione quae in gloriam Dei cedit*). So de Lyra, (*gloria Dei. i. gratia sui per quam apparet gloriosus*). Vatable had a similar idea. He says that *the glory of God* means "the gratuitous remission of sins through Christ," (*gloriam Dei vocat gratuitam peccatorum remissionem per Christum*). Œcolampad and Musculus are, in substance, of the same opinion. Emser too: he explains the expression as meaning *the grace of God, from which glory and honour are derived*, (*Das ist, seiner gnaden, aus welcher uns eere und glorien volget*). Pelagius had a somewhat similar notion, (**egent gloria Dei,** *quia non habent suam*). All this group of interpretations clusters around the assumption that the verb simply denotes *need*. It is so translated in the Vulgate, (*egent*). And hence the Rheims version of the verse is this,—"for all have sinned: and doe neede the glorie of God." So Wycliffe,—"For alle men synneden, and have nede to the glorie of God." So de Saci, (*et ont besoin de la gloire de Dieu*). Such a translation, however, does not express the precise idea of the original verb. The verb implies, indeed, the notion of *want*, but it is of want under the phase of *short-coming*,—want, that suggests the idea, not so much of *need* and *desirability*, as of *destitution*.

Melancthon regards the phrase—*the glory of God*—as meaning *the glory of which God approves*, the glory of personal righteousness, *that righteousness which God judges to be glory*. (*Carent illa gloria quam Deus approbat, carent illa justitia, quam Deus judicat esse gloriam*. Comment. 1540.) He would thus look upon the entire phrase, *and are fallen short of the glory of God*, as an echo of the import of the preceding expression, *they sinned*. Strigel's view coincides with Melancthon's. So does Stengel's, and Bisping's, and Lange's, (*die Gerechtigkeit des Lebens als Lebensruhm oder Glanz von dem Urtheilsspruch Gottes bezeichnet*). Bullinger's interpretation is something similar:—"the glory of God," says he, "is that glory of moral perfection which God should have in man, (*integritas quam deus in homine habere debebat,—die eere die Gott an uns haben solt*). Seb. Schmidt's interpretation is just a particular phase and development of the same fundamental idea:—he contends for the idea advocated by not a few of the old Lutheran interpreters, such as Feurborn, that *the glory of God* is *the image of God in man*. Calov maintains the same view. Alting, too, in substance, (*gloria Dei designat eam partem imaginis Dei, in qua ejus gloria potissimum elucet*). Glassius also, (*Phil. Sac.* iii. 1, 30—1). The same view is taken by Rambach and Carpzov; Ernesti and Olshausen; and also, substantially, by Rückert, Brandes, &c. Conybeare's translation of the clause is, "and none have attained *the glorious likeness of God*." In support of this interpretation, appeal is sometimes made to 1 Cor. xi. 7, in which man,—as distinguished from woman, who is "the glory of the man,"—is said to be "the image and glory of God." But even there the "image" is distinguished from the "glory:" and, moreover, it is not something in the man, but it is the man himself who is said to be, and who is, the "glory of God;" and it is the male, too, as distinguished from the female. It is not the case, besides, that that "glory" has been lost. It remains in the nature, as distinguished from the moral character. It is an objection to the interpretation, in all its phases, that it attaches to the expression, *the glory of God*, an import which, without the aid of contextual side lights, must appear to be arbitrary;—an import, moreover, which is aside from the ideas that are commonly attached to the phrase in the terminology of Paul. It is connected, besides, with an exposition of the whole clause, which, in relation to the preceding clause, seems to form a redundancy. And, to crown all, it fails to do justice to the peculiarity of the verb which is employed,—*they are fallen short of* (ὑστεροῦνται): for the verb naturally indicates, not the loss of a previous possession, or the destitution which is consequent on that loss, but a state of apparently hopeless distance from an unattained prize.

Luther translates the clause thus,—"and want the glory which they ought to have in God," (*und mangeln des Ruhms, den sie an Gott haben sollten*). He seems to mean, —if we may gather his idea from his marginal remark,— that sinful men cannot glory in God as their God. (*Können in der Wahrheit nicht sagen, Du bist mein Gott, ob sie wohl mit dem Munde viel von ihm rühmen,—they cannot in truth say, Thou art my God, although they boast much of him with the mouth.*) Somewhat analogous to this idea of Luther is the interpretation of Erasmus (in his *Paraphrase*), —"they cannot glory of their righteousness before God." Hunnius takes the same view,—"They are in want of all ground and occasion of glorying before God," (*carere omni materia et occasione gloriandi coram Deo*). Günther takes the same view, and, indeed, quietly substitutes, in his Comment on Luther's translation, "before God" for "in God," (*Im Papstthum wollen sich wohl viel Mönche desselben rühmen, aber es ist eine lügenhaffte Prahlerey.* **Denn**

wir mangeln alle des Ruhms, den wir vor Gott haben sollen). Este gives a preference to the same interpretation, (*non habent unde coram Deo gloriantur*). De Paris accepts the same interpretation; so Winzer; and, long before, Calvin seems to have accepted it, (*non habent unde apud deum glorientur.*—**Gloriam Dei** *accipit pro ea, quae coram Deo locum habit,*—which last clause is strangely mistranslated thus by Owen,—"*the glory of God* I take to mean the approbation of God"). The same view is taken by Heumann, Wolf, Zachariä, Koppe, Brentano, &c. It is, when hermeneutically viewed, a most unlikely interpretation,—attaching, as it does, a difficult, arbitrary, and unnatural idea to the relation that is expressed by the genitive in the phrase *of God*.

The interpretation, which Owen, and Oltramare too, falsely ascribe to Calvin,—"they came short of *the approbation of God*,"—is, nevertheless, espoused, in substance, by quite a considerable group of expositors. Tyndale translates the expression thus,—"and lacke the prayse that is of valoure before God." His position in this group of expositors is ambiguous. But that of Grotius is unequivocal, (*approbatio hominis quae fit a deo*); and the same interpretation is adopted by Crell, and Day, and Turretin; by Macknight too, and Flatt, and Bosveld, and Bolten; by Rosenmüller (ultimately, though he does not carry it out consistently); by Fritzsche also, and Stuart, Alford, Dr. Jo. Brown, Dr. Da. Brown, &c. Dr. Da. Brown claims for it,—but on utterly insufficient data,—the patronage of "the best interpreters." It cannot, we apprehend, represent correctly the idea of the Apostle. He never, so far as we can see, uses the noun in question (δόξα) in the sense of *approbation;* and indeed the term, as we apprehend, never bears such a signification in any of the New Testament writings. There are passages, certainly, which can be interpreted on the hypothesis that the word has the meaning contended for. But the meaning is not essential to their luminous explication, and they are more lucid when the term receives its common and Hebraizing import of *glory*.

A few critics have imagined that the Apostle's idea is this:—"They fail to glorify God." Œcumenius proposes this interpretation, (οὐκ ἔφθασαν τοῦ δοξάζειν τὸν θεόν); and Origen, long before him, seems to have held it, (*Quomodo enim peccator auderet dare gloriam Deo?*). Chalmers and Knight espouse it. Doddridge, Haldane, and Webster and Wilkinson, put it in the foreground of their complex and therefore compromising explanation. It is evidently a leap in the dark, and has been suggested, apparently, by the lexical affinity of the noun *glory* to the verb *to glorify*. But to *glorify* God is to *promote* his glory. And since there is no word equivalent to *promote* in the Apostle's phrase, the essential element needed for the authentication of the proposed explication is wanting.

When Abelard interpreted the expression as meaning, "they have need to glorify God," (*opus habent quasi ex debito Dominum glorificare*), he lost hold of the Apostle's expression at both its ends. He misunderstood both what is meant by "the glory of God," and also what is meant by the verb which expresses man's relation to the "glory."

When Meyer and Krehl suppose that the phrase, *the glory of God*, must, so far as the substance of thought is concerned, be tantamount to *the righteousness of God*, they seem, like so many others, to be groping in the dark, and catching at mere possibilities, however arbitrary or indistinct. We need not attempt to refute such conjectures. Neither need we take special note of various other sporadic interpretations, which have been devised by individual critics, but have rarely been approved of by any but their inventors;—such, for instance, as the theory of Matthias, who explains the expression as meaning—*glory such as God's*, (*Ruhm, wie er Gottes ist*); and the notion of Palairet, who imagines the expression to be used by hypallage for *the glorious God;* and the notion of Hofmann, who supposes that the relation of the genitive brings out this idea, "glory such as is befitting God," (*wie sie Gotte selbst eignet*,–Schriftbeweis, i. 551). Neither need we enumerate the various indiscriminative explications which have been proposed, such as that of Ch. Schmid, "the benefits of divine adoption," (*beneficia divinae adoptionis*), or that of van Hengel, "the communion of God, and all the blessings thence arising," (*Dei communione omnibusque bonis hinc oriundis carere*). There is no need for chasing, in their flights, all the vagaries of men who are ingenious, or who are determined to be ingenious, or who, feeling that they are baffled, hide their perplexity under the broad shield of a commonplace platitude.

The simplest, readiest, and by far the most likely and befitting of all the interpretations which have been proposed, is that which regards *the glory of God* as *that everlasting state of grandeur and bliss which belongs to God, within which he dwells, and admission into which he grants to all such as, during their state of probation, become meet to enjoy it.* It is, in so far as it is available to men, the glory, which is coupled with *honour and immortality.* (Rom. ii. 7.) It is the glory which goes hand in hand with *honour and peace.* (Rom. ii. 10.) It is *eternal life.* (Rom. ii. 7.) It is, in its man-ward relation, the "inheritance, which is incorruptible, and undefiled, and that fadeth not away, reserved in heaven." (1 Pet. i. 4.) It comprehends "the things which God hath prepared for them that love him," and which mortal "eye hath not seen, nor ear heard, neither have entered into the heart of man." (1 Cor. ii. 9.) We need not attempt, therefore, to describe it, or to conceive it. We would, in the attempt, only embody our own childish conceits. It is called "the glory *of God,*" because it belongs to God. It is his in possession. And it is of his bounty that he confers it on any of his creatures. Jesus enjoyed it *with Him before the world was.* (John xvii. 5.) And of all who believe in Jesus it may be said, "God hath called them unto *his eternal glory* by Christ Jesus." (1 Pet. v. 10.) They are heirs of it just now; joint heirs with Christ Jesus. (Rom. viii. 17, 18.) By and by they shall rise up higher, and entering on its actual possession, they shall be *glorified.* (Rom. viii. 30.) But this *glorification* of believers will be "to the glory of God's *grace,* wherein he hath made them accepted in the Beloved." (Eph. i. 6.) In themselves they have forfeited all title to such *glory.* "They sinned, *and are unentitled to the retributive glory of God.*" This view of the expression is that which is taken, apparently, by Chrysostom and Theophylact, (who contrast the *glory* which men have forfeited with the *shame* which is their due). It is given by Œcumenius (as an alternative interpretation). It is the interpretation which is given in the anonymous Venetian Commentary issued from the Aldine press in 1542, (*carent gloria Dei, id est, felicitate perpetua*). It is the interpretation of Beza, Hemming, Melville; Piscator, Pareus, Willet, Sclater; Vorstius also, and Dickson, and Vitringa, Zwinger; Locke too, and Varenius, Bengel, Whitby, Boysen; and also in more modern times, of Morus, Böhme, Glöckler, Baumgarten-Crusius, Oltramare, Mehring, &c. All men are, as in themselves, unentitled to celestial glory. Even all believers, as in themselves, are unentitled to it; and it is to them exclusively—though Alford does not see this—that the Apostle here refers. The fact that all believers—whether Jews or Gentiles—"are unentitled to the glory of God," is evidence that there can be no difference or distinction among them, so far as regards their relation to the evangelical *righteousness of God*, and their entire dependence on it for justification, and for the consequent attainment and enjoyment of everlasting life. "There is no distinction *here*," as Luther, interpretatively, has it, (*Denn es ist* **hier** *kein Unterschied*).

VER. 24. δικαιούμενοι δωρεὰν τῇ αὐτοῦ χάριτι διὰ τῆς ἀπολυτρώσεως τῆς ἐν Χριστῷ Ἰησοῦ,

Eng. Auth. Vers. *Being justified freely by his grace, through the redemption that is in Christ Jesus:*

§ 1. *being justified*, (δικαιούμενοι). The grammatical relation of this participle to what goes before has not been determined with unanimity by critics. Ostervald and Ewald, for instance, connect it with ver. 22nd, by throwing ver. 23rd, along with the last clause of ver. 22nd, *for there is no difference*, into a parenthesis. But this method of connection not only renders the composition unnecessarily rugged and abrupt, it renders the nominative case of the participle unaccountable in relation to the accusative case of *all the believing* in ver. 22nd. It is not easy to avoid the conclusion that the participle is in the nominative case, because the Apostle was conscious of continuity of thought in passing from ver. 23rd to ver. 24th.

But if there be this continuity of thought, is not the idea, participially expressed in ver. 24th, rendered subordinate and ministrant to the idea which is embodied in the affirmation of ver. 23rd? One would naturally come to this conclusion when following, unsophisticatedly, the unconstrained leadings of the phraseology. And yet such a relation of the verses has seemed to many critics, who looked at the subject exegetically and doctrinally, to be almost if not altogether unaccountable. They are at a loss to comprehend how the Apostle should adduce the fact that all believers are *justified freely by God's grace* as evidence that they all *sinned and are unentitled to the glory of God.* Such a relation of ideas seems to them to be a species of inexplicable *topsy-turvy* or *bouleversement.* Hence, apparently, the Peshito translator has supplied, before the participle, the conjunction *and*, (ܘܡܙܕܕܩܝܢ). Luther makes the same supplement, and changes the participial form of the expression into the indicative mood,—"*and* become righteous," (*und werden gerecht*). The same change is made by Wycliffe, (*and ben justified*), and the Geneva. Erasmus,—noting that the participle is in the present tense, *being justified*, whereas in the Vulgate it is, according to the exigencies of the Latin language, in the past, "having been justified," (*justificati*),—makes a similar change. He renders the expression *but are justified*, (**justificantur autem**, *addita de meo conjunctiuncula, quo sensum redderem dilucidiorem*). Tyndale gives the same translation. So does Melancthon; and Limborch and Koppe approve. Bengel adopts Luther's conjunction, "and are made righteous," (*und werden gerecht gemacht*). And so do Seb. Schmidt, Zinzendorf, Maier, &c. Van Ess intensifies the conjunctive idea by rendering the expression thus,

—"so they become righteous," (*so werden sie gerecht*). Fritzsche does not object to the introduction of the conjunction *and*, and the transmutation of the participle into the indicative mood. And Calvin, though not intruding the conjunction, says that the participle is put for the verb, (*participium loco verbi positum more Graecis usitato*). In accordance with this view, Peter Martyr, omitting the conjunction, translates the participle, "(they) are justified," (*justificantur*).

But such a transformation of the Apostle's expression is a liberty which, certainly, should not be taken, unless one is reduced to hermeneutical straits. And there are no such straits in the case before us; for the Apostle's idea is sufficiently self-luminous, if we retain the natural subordination of the participial clause to the affirmation that goes before. At *this particular point of his discourse* the Apostle is intent on showing that all believers are equally unentitled,—considered in themselves,—to the glory of God. And he adduces the fact of their free justification by God's grace as affording decisive evidence of the immeritoriousness of their character, and of the consequent moral imperfection that has attached to their probationary career. In other conjunctures of argumentation the Apostle would no doubt have, inversely, adduced the fact of men's sinfulness—as attested by consciousness and conscience—and their consequent failure to achieve, by personal worthiness, a title to everlasting glory, as evidence of the necessity of *free justification by God's grace through the redemption that is in Christ Jesus*. But there is a reciprocity in the relations of the two facts specified; and in this particular angle of his reasoning the Apostle views the subject retrogressively. Taking his stand on the fact of gratuitous justification, he reasons backward to the establishment of his momentous allegation that all, of whom this gratuitous justification is predicable, have *sinned*, and are consequently *unentitled to the glory of God*. Beza's ultimate translation of the participial expression preserves the proper relation of the clauses,—"ut qui justificentur," &c.,—*as being such as are justified, &c., inasmuch as they are justified, &c.*

Eras. Schmid adopts Beza's version. Piscator defends it. Kolding contends for it. (*Disput. Theol. de Dicto classico, Rom.* iii. 24—26.) And the idea on which it is founded, the subordination of the participial clause to the preceding affirmation, is maintained by Winer, (*Gram.* iii. 45. 6, b.), and advocated by Philippi, Matthias, Mehring, &c. It is adopted too by de Wette and Reithmayr. It is certainly the only natural and unconstrained interpretation of the phraseology. Oltramare would retain for the participle its usual participial power; but, instead of linking it, in subordination, to the preceding affirmation, he supposes that it forms the commencement of a new sentence, which finds its irregular apodosis in verse 27th:—"Being justified freely by his grace, &c., &c., &c., where then is boasting?" It is an ingenious interpunction and construction,—which, unknown to Oltramare, had been suggested by de Paris; but it is forced, and it gratuitously introduces anacoluth into the Apostle's composition. It inverts, too, the natural relation of the interrogation, *where (then) is boasting?*—lifting it up into a primary position, instead of leaving it as a natural conclusion, lying at the base of what has been previously established. There is no need for having recourse to any violent expedient to reduce the Apostle's words and ideas to symmetry and order. When we understand them aright, and look at them as from his own standpoint, so far as that can be ascertained by the unconstrained interlinking of the details of his phraseology, there is already beautiful kosmos and no chaos.

In justice, however, to those translators and expositors who have sought to merge or transmute that participial relationship of subordination which is naturally suggested by the initial expression in ver. 24th, viewed in relation to the affirmation contained in ver. 23rd; and by way of apology for those other critics who have thrown ver. 23rd into a parenthesis; it should be conceded that in the farther progress of the Apostle's train of thoughts, from the middle of the 24th verse onward to the close of the 26th, he *lets go* the relation of subordination, and expands, before his own mind and the minds of his readers, the subject of justification, as really being, in its relation to the evangelical righteousness of God, the principal theme of the entire paragraph that extends from ver. 21st to ver. 31st. The Apostle, indeed, gives no notice, by any peculiarity in the grammatical inter-relations of his phraseology, that he *lets go* the idea of subordination which is expressed at the commencement of ver. 24th. And thus his language is far from being moulded on the principles of a finely finished, and still farther from being conformed to the principles of a fastidiously finical, rhetoric. It rolls on at large, spreading out irregularly, now on the right hand and now on the left, but always sweeping powerfully along. Yet it is unquestionable that from the middle of the 24th versè, the current of thought widens out into the great subject of justification in general, apart from its particular bearings, in the shape of demonstrative evidence, upon the sinfulness and consequent immeritoriousness of those who are the recipients of its blessings.

Basil Cooper,—noticing the intimate relation which subsists between the evangelical "*righteousness* of God," and what is called *justification*, and noting at the same time the affinity, in Greek, of the terms denoting *righteousness* (δικαιοσύνη) and *justified* (δικαιούμενοι),—proposes to coin, as an equivalent in English for the latter term, the word *enrighteoused*:—"being *enrighteoused* freely by his own grace." He would form the verb *enrighteous* (that is, *to render righteous*) after the analogy of the verb *enrich*, (*i. e.*, *to render rich*). It is a bold expedient,—almost a daring adventure of invention. But, taking the tyranny of usage into account, it cannot possibly succeed; the more especially as it veils from view the judicial element of justification, which, in the original Greek, is emphatically prominent. When believers are said, in the passage before us, to be *justified*, the meaning is not that they are *enrighteoused* in the sense of *being made righteous*. It is that they are judicially made out and declared to be possessed of righteousness, — righteousness that had just been attained through faith,—righteousness such as forms an unchallengeable title to everlasting glory. (*Justitia Dei hic nihil aliud est, quam jus ad vitam, quod Deus nobis procuravit in Christo, dum is obediens est factus usque ad mortem. Seu est obedientia Christi, qua is, ordinante ita Deo, meruit nobis jus ad vitam.* – Horchius, Apparatus ad Epist. ad Rom. § 62.) God, while acting as the Supreme Magistrate of the Universe, can, even in that capacity, regard it as a right and befitting thing that,—in consideration of the relation of believers to the work of Christ, of which they avail themselves as if it were their own righteousness,—they should be constituted heirs of everlasting life.

§ 2. *freely, by his grace,* (δωρεὰν τῇ αὐτοῦ χάριτι). The word *freely* (δωρεάν) is translated *gratis* in the Vulgate. The translation is retained in the Rheims. Bosveld gives what corresponds to it in Dutch, *te geefs*, (which he prefers to the kerkelijke uitdrukking *om niet*). It is a correct translation. The term means *gratuitously*, or *after the manner of a gift*, (*Geschenkweise*, Passow, de Wette, Meyer, &c.) It is translated *for nought* in 2 Thess. iii. 8. (Comp. חִנָּם.) And it is *for nought* to believers themselves, so far as the ground or meritorious cause of God's action is concerned, that they are justified. The term is translated *without a cause* in John xv. 25. (Comp. חִנָּם.) And so far as believers themselves are concerned, so far as regards merit on their part, their justification is *without a cause.* It is apparently because of this usage of the word that van Hengel regards it as being here "a word of negation," (*vocabulum negans*), in opposition to the phrase *by his grace,* which he regards as "a formula of affirmation," (*formula aiens*). Dr. John Brown draws a similar distinction between the two expressions, saying that in "the former of the two the Apostle looks to the recipient of justification, and says, It is *free,*—there is no cause of it in man: in the second he looks to the author and bestower of justification, and he says, It is *by God's grace,*—there is no cause of it in God but sovereign kindness." But this distinction, if carried out so very sharply as Dr. Brown proposes, becomes arbitrary and inexact. For the word rendered *freely* (δωρεάν) is eminently fitted to lead us to look away from man to the giver of the gift, (the giver of the δωρεά or δῶρον); and in the latter phrase there is a special emphasis, as we shall see, not upon the word *grace*,—though a word of momentous significance in relation to the matter in hand,—but upon the pronoun *his*, as specifying the august Personality whence the "good and perfect gift" descends.

Freely, (δωρεάν);—the word "excludes merit," says Hemming, "not Christ's indeed, but ours," (*meritum excludit, non Christi, sed nostrum*). It excludes, says Aquinas, "the merit of preceding works," (*absque merito praecedentium operum*). It excludes more, says Beza; it excludes the works that come after faith, as well as the works that go before it, (δωρεάν, *i. ex gratuito dono ac mera liberalitate; ita ut non modo antecedentia, sed etiam consequentia fidem opera excludantur*). If the justification be gratuitous on the part of God, it must be to man "without money and without price." It would no longer be a gift to believers, if they purchased or deserved it by their merit. Luther translates the word, "without merit," (*ohne Verdienst*). So does Sharpe. Bellarmin explains it admirably, so far as its theology is concerned, "out of his mere liberality," (*ex mera ejus liberalitate*). Limborch explains it happily, so far as its philology is concerned, as meaning *donatitie*.

By his grace, (τῇ αὐτοῦ χάριτι). The position of the pronoun before the word *grace*, shows, as Meyer has remarked, that it is to be betoned. It is from God that the gift comes down. It is by *His* favour that believers are justified. This betonement of the pronoun is acknowledged by Philippi and van Hengel, and was noted long ago by Cardinal Cajetan. The Syriac translator, apparently overlooking the emphatic reference to the author of the gift, omits the pronoun altogether, and then transposes the two elements of the Apostle's complex expression, *by favour gratuitously*, (ܒܛܝܒܘܬܐ ܡܓܢ). But, as the Apostle gives it, the entire expression points us at once to the efficient, and also to the impulsive cause of the justification of believers. God is the *Causa efficiens*, the Efficient Cause:

the grace that is in Him is the *causa impulsiva*, the impulsive cause.

The *grace* referred to is, of course, subjective in God. And when Dionysius à Ryckel, Bellarmin, and others, represent it as grace subjective in man, infused grace,—"the formal cause" of justification, as distinguished from the *causes* that are *efficient, final*, and *material*,—they bring from the recesses of polemical theology an intolerable thumbscrew to apply to the inspired phraseology. It is, certainly, not grace "infused" into men, and thence "inherent" in them in the shape of *faith, hope, and charity*, that is referred to by the Apostle. Such an idea is an utter inversion of the Pauline doctrine. God "justifieth the ungodly." (Rom. iv. 5.) He justifieth; and then, and thence especially, he sanctifieth. In the passage before us the word *grace* has manifestly its common signification, its signification of *favour*. It denotes a mode of the divine *love*. It is the divine love in its relation to the undeserving:—the divine love, consequently, in so far as it is free in its outgoings. It is the same divine love which is still more strongly represented as *mercy* (ἔλεος) when its objects are viewed in the *tout ensemble* of their guilt and misery.—The believing, says the Apostle, are *justified freely by God's favour—God's mercy;* and, this being the case, it follows that it must be true that they have all *sinned*, and are, as viewed in themselves, *unentitled to the glory of God.* "Juniors," says Melancthon, "are to be warned that the monks are guilty of corrupting the word *grace* when they interpret it here of infused qualities, while, without doubt, it signifies *gratuitous compassion.*" (*Hic juniores monendi sunt de corruptela vocabuli* **gratiae,** *quod interpretati sunt Monachi de qualitatibus infusis, ut ipsi loquuntur, cum hic sine ulla dubitatione significet* **gratuitam misericordiam.**–Enarratio, 1556.) As to the *formal cause* of justification, see Davenant's *Disputatio de justitia habituali et actuali.*

"Freely, by his grace:"—The latter expression, says Baumgarten-Crusius, explains the former. (*Den Begriff des δωρεάν erklärt das daneben stehende τῇ αὐτοῦ χάριτι.*) The

Apostle thus twice declares, says Calvin, that the whole is of God, (*itaque bis expressit totum esse Dei, nihil nostrum*). He "doubles, as it were," says Day, "the same word, that he might the more exclude *debt* and *merit*." For, to use a favourite idea of Augustin, if grace be grace in any way, it must be grace or gratuitous in every way. Beza translates the twofold expression thus, "gratis, that is, by his grace," (*gratis, id est, ejus gratia*). And the best view, apparently, that can be taken of it, is to regard the latter portion of it—*by his grace*—as reduplicating on the former,—at once echoing the idea that is expressed by the word δωρεάν, and thus intensifying it, and also pointing out emphatically the Being from whom the gift descends.

§ 3. *through the redemption which is in Christ Jesus*, (διὰ τῆς ἀπολυτρώσεως τῆς ἐν Χριστῷ Ἰησοῦ,). The Peshito translator introduces this clause with the conjunction *and*, —"and through, &c." But the insertion of such a particle is an intrusion,—an interruption to the continuous flow of the Apostle's exhibition. Cramer, Rosenmüller, and Koppe translate the preposition (διά) "on account of," (*propter*), as if it had been followed by an accusative, instead of a genitive. It must, however, be rendered *through*, or *by means of*, and denotes the real objective medium through which justification is reached:—the objective medium in distinction from the subjective medium, which is faith in Christ, (see ver. 30th);—the *real* objective medium in distinction from the verbal objective medium, which is the testimony of the Holy Spirit, the Gospel.

The English, or rather the Latin, word *redemption* is not a perfect synonym of the term employed by the Apostle, (ἀπολύτρωσις). But it is the nearest approximation to a homologue that can be found. The Greek term etymologically means *a ransoming off*. The Latin and English term etymologically means *a buying again, a buying back*. Wycliffe's translation here is "the redemcioun *or the agenbiyng*." In the application of the two terms to the spiritual condition of men, in their relation to the economy of mercy, the distinguishing idea of each is emphatically realized. Men are *bought again* or *bought back;* and they are *ransomed off.* They are "bought *again*" or "bought *back;*" for they were not always captives and slaves: their primitive condition was one of freedom. And they are "ransomed *off:*" they are liberated in virtue of the ransom which has been paid. It is this last idea, of course, which was in the Apostle's mind; as his thought would be running in the groove, not of the Latin term "*re*demption," but of the Greek term which he uses, (ἀπολύτρωσις), and which, in virtue of the preposition prefixed to it, is stronger and more complex in its import than either of the Hebrew terms which might also be present within the field of his consideration, (גְּאֻלָּה and פְּדוּת).

Wakefield translates the word *deliverance:* and says, "This is the meaning of the word in abundance of places throughout the version of the LXX., without any notion of an *equivalent price* or *purchase;* so that to bring proof to this purpose were useless to the unlearned reader, and an insult to the learned." Bruce and Whitwell give the same translation. And Locke, though using the word *redemption,* maintains that it does not import that "there was any compensation made to God, by paying what was of equal value, in consideration whereof they were delivered; for that," he adds, "is inconsistent with what St. Paul expressly says here, viz., that sinners are justified by God gratis, and of his free bounty." But if any one, he continues, will persist in it that the word "implies an equivalent price paid, I desire him to consider to whom: and that, if we will strictly adhere to the metaphor, it must be to those whom the redeemed are in bondage to, and from whom we are redeemed, viz., sin and Satan." "Nor could the price," he says, "be paid to God in strictness of justice; unless the same person ought, by that strict justice, to have both the thing redeemed and the price paid for its redemption. For it is to God we are redeemed, by the death of Christ, (Rev. v. 9)." Oltramare, also, strenuously contends that the word means *deliverance* only, without any reference to purchase, (*sans aucune idée de rachat*).

Now, it must be admitted that the uncompounded term

for *Redeemer* (λυτρωτής) is applied in Acts vii. 35 to Moses. God sent him to be "a ruler and *a redeemer.*" The word is translated *deliverer* in our *Authorized Version.* And Moses delivered Israel *without paying a ransom.* It must also be admitted that in the Sept. the uncompounded verb (λυτρόομαι) is frequently employed to express acts of deliverance *unaccompanied with the payment of a price or ransom.* See Exod. vi. 6, "I will redeem you (λυτρώσομαι ὑμᾶς) *with a stretched-out arm, and with great judgements:*" xv. 13; Deut. vii. 8; ix. 26, (ἣν ἐλυτρώσω ἐν τῇ ἰσχύϊ); xiii. 5; xv. 15; xxi. 8; xxiv. 18; 2 Sam. iv. 9; vii. 23; 1 Kings i. 29; 1 Chron. xvii. 21; Neh. i. 10, (οὓς ἐλυτρώσω ἐν τῇ δυνάμει σου τῇ μεγάλῃ); &c. It must likewise be conceded that the two Hebrew words (גָּאַל and פָּדָה) corresponding to the uncompounded Greek verb (λυτρόομαι) do not embody in their constitutional structure or make a distinct reference to the idea of a ransom. In this respect they differ from the Greek term; and hence, no doubt, we are to account for the free Septuagintal application of the word to deliverances which were unaccompanied with the payment of a ransom.

(The origin of the Hebrew, גָּאַל, is hidden in obscurity. See Fürst. But it is radically connected, we doubt not, with גָּעַל, and apparently too, though more remotely, with חָלַל. Its primary import was probably some phase of action, consisting in, or corresponding to, *cutting, piercing,* and thus *opening, loosening, letting free, setting free, &c.* Hence the conciliation of the two divergent stems of import which are attached to the word, *to release,* and *to defile.* Compare חָלַל in Hiphil and Pihel. The radical import of פָּדָה seems to have been similar,—*to divide, to separate,* and hence *to let go, to let go free, to set free.* The radical import of the corresponding word in Chaldee, פְּרַק, and the Syriac, ܦܪܩ, is remarkably consentaneous,—*to break, to break off.* The Chaldee word, the Syriac, and the English term *break,* are etymological relatives.—In none of the Semitic terms is there any inherent reference to *a ransom.*)

Nevertheless the Greek word does embody, in its make

or structure, a reference to *a ransom*, (*a* λύτρον, *something given in order to the release, the* λύσις, *of an object;* or, more commonly, λύτρα, in the plural, *things given for release*). In the active voice,—in which, however, it does not occur in the New Testament, nor, so far as we have noticed, in the Septuagint, for Bretschneider is certainly wrong in adducing Numb. xviii. 15, 17, Dan. iv. 24 (27), as instances,—in the active voice, we say, the verb properly means *to release on receipt of a ransom.* In the middle voice it bears the same signification; see Numb. xviii. 15, 17: but it more frequently means *to release by giving a ransom.* See Lev. xxv. 25, 33, 48, 49, &c., &c. And even in those passages in which the distinctive idea of *ransom* is merged, and the Hebraistic idea of *deliverance* is thoroughly predominant, it is not *mere deliverance* that is meant. John Locke had a glimpse of this fact when he says,—"Redemption signifies deliverance, *but not deliverance from everything, but deliverance from that to which a man is in subjection or bondage.*" This is so far correct, and on the right line of things. But the *deliverance* from subjection or bondage that is legitimately designated *redemption* is something more still. It is deliverance which is effected *in a legitimate way,* and *in consistency with the rights and claims of all parties concerned.* Illegitimate deliverance, even from subjection or bondage,—deliverance effected over the belly, or at the expense of real and recognized rights,—is *deliverance* indeed, but it is no *redemption.* There is nothing in it that lies on the line of things that is indicated in the staple part of the Greek or Latin term, nothing that lies on the same line of things as *ransom;* and hence it cannot be described as *ransoming* or *redeeming.* This idea of a regard to rights is emphatically imbedded in the New Testament usage of the term in all its branches. It is also imbedded in the usage of the term in the Septuagint. And we believe that it will not be found to be wanting in the usage of the term by any author who was competent to observe the proprieties of the language which he employed. It is because of this idea, inherent in the term, that it is so peculiarly applicable, and so frequently applied, to the deliverance of Israel from their Egyptian bondage. See Exod. vi. 6; xv. 13; Deut. vii. 8; &c., &c.

As to the compound term which is used by the Apostle in the passage before us, (ἀπολύτρωσις), it is not the case, as one might be led from Wakefield's remark to suppose, that it occurs "in abundance of places throughout the version of the LXX." As it does not occur in the classics at all, so it does not occur in the Septuagint at all. And the compound verb from which it is derived occurs only twice, viz., in Exod. xxi. 8 and Zeph. iii. 3 (1). In the latter of these passages it is applied by the Septuagint translator to Jerusalem, *the redeemed city,* (ἀπολελυτρωμένη πόλις). In the former it is used in the active voice, and means *to release on receipt of a ransom,* (ἐὰν μὴ εὐαρεσθῇ, ἀπολυτρώσει αὐτήν. Compare Philip, *in Demosthenes,* 159, —ἀπελύτρωσε ταλάντων ἐννέα). The noun employed by the Apostle occurs, however, in other nine passages of the New Testament: and while in each of them the idea of *deliverance* is prominent, there are none of them which oblige us to merge the reference, explicit or implicit, to *ransom* as the ground, or reason, or meritorious cause, of the deliverance specified. We shall glance at the passages :—

(1.) The first is Luke xxi. 28,—"And when these things begin to come to pass, then look up, and lift up your heads; for your *redemption* draweth nigh." When that "redemption draweth nigh," then "the kingdom of God is nigh at hand," (ver. 31). It is consequently a *deliverance* intimately connected with the work of the Redeemer, and indeed secured by it;—It is thus a deliverance based on something beneath itself, something that meets and settles all legitimate claims. It is, in an important sense, *purchased.*

(2.) The next passage is Rom. viii. 23,—"even we ourselves groan within ourselves, waiting for the adoption, to wit, the *redemption* of our body." It is certainly a deliverance that is here, also, referred to; but as it is "in Christ" that "all shall be made alive," (1 Cor. xv. 22), the deliverance is undoubtedly conditioned on his work as its meritorious cause. It is *purchased.*

(3.) 1 Cor. i. 30,—"of him are ye in Christ Jesus, who of God is made unto us wisdom, and righteousness, and sanctification, and *redemption.*" The term doubtless denotes, again, deliverance,—deliverance full and final: but it is deliverance on the ground of something beneath itself, and "in Christ Jesus." It is *purchased,* like the other deliverances referred to.

(4.) Eph. i. 7,—"In whom we have *redemption* through his blood, *the forgiveness of sins,* according to the riches of his grace." Here the term is explained for us. It is used to denote *the forgiveness of sins,* and is therefore emphatically a deliverance: but it is deliverance "through Christ's blood." It is deliverance conditioned on something beneath itself. It is purchased deliverance.

(5.) Eph. i. 14,—"which is the earnest of our inheritance, until the *redemption* of the purchased possession, unto the praise of his glory." If "the purchased possession" (ἡ περιποίησις) be the acquired and peculiar people who are the reward of "the travail of Christ's soul," or whatever it be, it is manifest that its *redemption*—still future—is a deliverance: but it is doubtless a deliverance which is procured and secured by what the Redeemer has done. It is a *purchased* deliverance.

(6.) Eph. iv. 30,—"And grieve not the Holy Spirit of God, whereby ye are sealed unto the day of *redemption.*" The term manifestly denotes deliverance,—still future,—and coincident no doubt with the "redemption of the body." But it is deliverance secured by something underneath itself,—something which is its reason, ground, or meritorious cause. It is *purchased* deliverance.

(7.) Col. i. 14,—"in whom we have redemption [through his blood], *even* the forgiveness of sins." It is a parallel passage to Eph. i. 7, and is to be similarly explained. It is manifestly a *purchased* deliverance.

(8.) Heb. ix. 15,—"for this cause he is the mediator of the New Testament, that by means of death, for the *redemption* of the transgressions that were under the first Testament, they which are called might receive the promise of eternal inheritance." The term is here used in a manner that is grammatically peculiar. (Compare Dan. iv. 24.) But there can be no doubt that it involves the idea of *deliverance*, deliverance *from* transgressions; and as little, that the deliverance referred to is in consideration of something beneath itself. It was deliverance "by means of death." Christ's death, or the surrender of his life, was the ransom. (Matt. xx. 28.) The deliverance was thus *purchased* deliverance.

(9.) Heb. xi. 35,—"Others were tortured, not accepting *deliverance*." It would have been better to have retained Wycliffe's version, "redempcioun." For though it is assuredly deliverance that is spoken of, it is most probably deliverance in consideration of a ransom; and it was undoubtedly deliverance in consideration of something offered as its condition or price.

So far, then, as we can learn anything from the New Testament usage of the compound term employed by the Apostle, we have reason to come to the conclusion that, in the passage before us, it will not denote, barely and abstractly, simple *deliverance*. It will, indeed, denote *deliverance:* but the deliverance referred to will be deliverance *on the ground of something that meets all rightful claims*. It will be, in some legitimate sense, a *purchased deliverance*. It will be, in short, deliverance *on the ground of a ransom*.

That this is the case seems to be put beyond the range of reasonable doubt when we consider that our Lord himself expressly states that he "came, not to be ministered unto, but to minister, *and to give his life a ransom for many*," (καὶ δοῦναι τὴν ψυχὴν αὐτοῦ λύτρον ἀντὶ πολλῶν). See Matt. xx. 28; Mark x. 45. Paul iterates the Saviour's idea,—"There is one God, and one Mediator between God and men, the man Christ Jesus, *who gave himself a ransom for all*," (ὁ δοὺς ἑαυτὸν ἀντίλυτρον ὑπὲρ πάντων),—1 Tim. i. 5, 6. If Paul, then, understood the Gospel, and if Christ understood his own mission, there *was* a ransom given,—intentionally given. And as the giving of a ransom is the way for *ransoming*, and *ransoming off;* as it is the payment of "the price of redemption," (*redemptionis pretium*); we may be sure that the redemption, for which the payment was made, and of which there is mention in the passage before us, will involve a reference to the price that was paid. The redemption which is "in Christ Jesus," will be *purchased deliverance*. It will be *a ransoming off*. It will be a deliverance that is based upon that *ransom* which it was the end of our Saviour's mission to present.

This conclusion is fortified when we look to those passages in the New Testament in which the uncompounded term is used in relation to the work of Christ; and used after that work was completed and understood. It is said, for instance, in Tit. ii. 14, that "our Saviour Jesus Christ gave himself for us, *that he might redeem us from all iniquity*, and purify unto himself a peculiar people, &c." The redemption specified rests upon the fact that Christ "gave himself for us." It is said in 1 Pet. i. 18,—"Ye know that ye were not *redeemed* with corruptible things, as silver and gold, from your vain conversation received by tradition from your fathers, *but with the precious blood of Christ, as of a lamb without blemish and without spot*." The price of the redemption is expressly specified. And in Heb. ix. 12, we read,—"Neither by the blood of goats and calves, *but by his own blood*, he entered in once into the holy place, *having obtained eternal redemption for us*." The price of the redemption is, again, very obviously indicated. The other passages in which the uncompounded term is employed are not of such significance and importance, doctrinally considered. They are these,—Luke i. 68, "Blessed be the Lord God of Israel; for he hath visited and *redeemed* his people;"—Luke ii. 38, "and spake of him to all them that looked for *redemption* in Jerusalem;"—Luke xxiv. 21, "We trusted that it had been he which should have *redeemed* Israel." But even in these passages, as in the corresponding Old Testament passages concerning the redemption of Israel, it is not bare deliverance that is referred to, but deliverance that meets all legitimate claims. It is deliverance that has some relation to what constitutes a ransom, or to what is equivalent to a ransom.

That it is a *purchased deliverance*, or a *ransoming off*, that is referred to in the passage before us, is farther confirmed by all those more or less analogous passages in which *buying*, or *buying off*, is ascribed to Christ:—1 Cor. vi. 20, "ye are *bought* with a price," (ἠγοράσθητε γὰρ τιμῆς); —1 Cor. vii. 23, "ye are *bought* with a price," (τιμῆς ἠγοράσθητε);—Gal. iii. 13, "Christ hath *redeemed* us (*bought us off*, ἐξηγόρασεν) from the curse of the law;"—Gal. iv. 5, He was "made under the law, to *redeem* them (to *buy them off*, ἵνα ἐξαγοράσῃ) that were under the law;"—2 Pet. ii. 1, "denying the Lord that *bought* them," (τὸν ἀγοράσαντα αὐτοὺς δεσπότην);—Rev. v. 9, "thou wast slain, and hast *redeemed* us to God," (and *didst buy us* to God, καὶ ἠγόρασας τῷ θεῷ);—Rev. xiv. 3, "which were *redeemed*," or, "*bought*, from the earth," (οἱ ἠγορασμένοι ἀπὸ τῆς γῆς); Rev. xiv. 4, "these were *redeemed*," or, "*bought* from among men," (οὗτοι ἠγοράσθησαν ἀπὸ τῶν ἀνθρώπων).

We regard it, then, as established, that the "redemption" mentioned by the Apostle in the passage before us is not mere and bare deliverance; but *deliverance procured by a price paid,—deliverance by a ransom.*

It is no valid objection to this conclusion, that the Apostle has said, in the preceding part of the verse, that believers are "justified *freely by God's grace.*" It is to no purpose that Locke urges this objection; for the whole provision of the *redemption* is, just as truly as the act of *justification*, a *gift* of God,—an outflow from his *grace.*

Neither need it be objected that the ransom must have been paid to "sin and Satan." For to whomsoever, or to whatsoever, it must have been paid, it is a matter of fact that it has been paid. Men *are* "bought with a *price*." (1 Cor. vi. 20; 2 Pet. ii. 1.) Christ "*gave* himself a *ransom*" for "many,"—for "all." (Matt. xx. 28; 1 Tim. ii. 6.) But there is no difficulty in ascertaining the recipient of the ransom. Sin is not an Entity separate from the sinner. To pay, therefore, a price to sin, would be to pay a price to the sinner himself. That were absurd. And as for Satan, he has no right of property in men, and no right to use men, or to abuse them. God cannot acknowledge that he has any such rights, and hence it could not be to him that the ransom was paid. Some of the ancients, inclusive of Origen, stretched metaphors into absurdities when they excogitated such an idea. And it is unworthy of Lützelberger to have reproduced the idea, (*Grundzüge des Paul. Glaubenslehre*, p. 81). The *price* or *ransom* which Christ paid was the *offering* which he made, the *sacrifice* which he presented. It was *himself*. (Gal. i. 4; Tit. ii. 14.) And we know that he "gave himself for us; an offering and a sacrifice *to God* for a sweet-smelling savour." (Eph. v. 2.) All the sacrifices that typified him were presented *unto God*. It is God who is *propitiated* in Christ Jesus. (1 John ii. 1, 2.) It was *His* claims which required to be satisfied. This is an idea to which, in interesting contrast to the frivolous speculations of some of the other fathers, Athanasius delighted to give prominence. (ἑαυτὸν ὑπὲρ ἡμῶν διὰ τοῦ θανάτου προσενέγκῃ τῷ πατρί. *Cont. Arian.* ii., p. 347; &c., &c., ed. 1686.)

Does any one reiterate the idea of Locke, that it would be incongruous that the price of redemption should be paid to the Being who, at the same time, receives the persons redeemed? Is it thought to be inconsistent that God should thus receive both the price and the persons for whom the price was paid? Is it contended that men are "redeemed *to* God," and that therefore it cannot be supposed that the price of their redemption was exacted *by* God? Such suggestions owe their birth to the attempt to run out, to their extremity, certain isolated analogies by which the work of our Lord is represented to us. They ignore the fact that that work is unique; and that it finds, therefore, no perfect parallel among human transactions. Finding no perfect parallel, the language which is borrowed from human transactions, to represent it, must be inadequate; and it should not, therefore, be stretched to its utmost possible extent. There was, of course, no literal or financial *price;* no literal bargaining and *ransom;* no literal or commercial *redemption*, or, *buying back*. There was something far more sublime and divine. But, in one of its multiform aspects, the unparalleled and glorious and most gracious reality may be faintly, and yet significantly and efficiently, represented and bodied forth under the notion of a *price of redemption* or a *ransom.* It must, however, ever be borne in mind that it is such *a price of redemption* or *ransom* as is at the same time a manifestation of unparalleled divine philanthropy, unpurchased and unpurchasable benevolence; and yet too, and at the same time, an *offering* and a *sacrifice;* and also *a righteousness for the unrighteous.* When the expressions *price of redemption* and *ransom* are thus limited by the unique peculiarities and glory of the great reality to which they are applied, there is no difficulty in meeting Locke's objections. There is no difficulty in supposing that God may, in one of the manifold susceptibilities of his nature, experience *anger,* while in another he experiences and cherishes *benevolence* and *grace.* Such a dualism of feeling is possible even to ourselves. It is a polarity that is, in truth, inevitable, on the supposition of contrary moral relationships. There is hence also no difficulty in supposing, that in one line of the multiform relationship in which God stands to his universe, he may require to manifest displeasure; while in another line of the same multiform relationship, he will delight to manifest compassion and mercy. There is no difficulty in supposing that these two lines of relationship may exist concurrently, and may also objectively meet in the same individuals; provided the individuals be viewed under different aspects, and as bearing different *rapports.* And thus there is no difficulty in supposing that God, in one respect of his many-sidedness, may require satisfaction; while, in another, he graciously makes provision for the satisfaction which he requires. It may thus be the case that he requires a price of redemption for men; and that at the same time he provides for its payment; and that he thus provides for its payment, that men may be "redeemed *to* Himself." The principle of the matter is just this,—*God may require one thing in order to another.* If this principle be disputed, all the elements of moral character and of personal activity are eliminated from our notion of the Divine Being. Impersonality is maintained, and Pantheism, emptied to boot of infinite self-consciousness, is assumed. But if the principle be admitted, then the whole of the doctrine of redemption, as exhibited in Scripture, with all its alleged antilogies, but real harmonies, is transparently self-consistent. Men may require to be redeemed *from* exposedness to God's *wrath*, his *wrath to come*, his *wrath to the uttermost*, that they may be redeemed *to* the enjoyment of his everlasting favour and glory.

The word which the Apostle employs in the passage before us, (ἀπολύτρωσις), and which we translate by the Latin and English term *redemption*, is, of course, to be distinguished from the word λύτρον, or *ransom*, which is imbedded in it. The distinction, however, has been often overlooked. And the oversight has occasioned not a little confusion in theology. In the Vulgate version the one word *redemptio*, or *redemption*, has, unhappily, been employed as the translation of both the Greek terms: and hence the work of Christ, as actually accomplished on Calvary, has often been confounded with its results, as contingently realized in men. And thus, as well as for reasons that go deeper, theological battles have been fought regarding *the extent of redemption;* some contending for *universal redemption*, the redemption of the whole race of mankind, others for *limited redemption*, the redemption of the believing or the ultimately saved. Origen,—as represented by Rufinus,—failed to distinguish between the two terms. (**Redemptio** *dicitur id, quod datur hostibus pro his, quos in captivitate detinent, ut eos restituant pristinae libertati.*) So, in modern times, did Richard Baxter; and hence the title of his posthumous work,—*Universal Redemption of Mankind by the Lord Jesus Christ.* So, too, John Goodwin; and hence the title of his incomplete work,—*Redemption Redeemed; wherein the most glorious Work of the Redemption of the World by Jesus Christ is, by expressness of Scripture, clearness of argument, countenance of the best authority, as well ancient as modern, vindicated and asserted, in the just latitude and extent of it, according to the counsel and most gracious intentions of God, &c., &c.* So, too,

Jonathan Edwards. In his *History of the Work of Redemption*, he says that the term *redemption* "strictly signifies *a purchase of deliverance*." He must have been thinking, of course, of the Latin term, not of the Greek word employed in the New Testament. But, though thus defining, inexactly enough, the "strict signification" of the Biblical terminology, he unhappily, throughout his book, gives reins to greater inexactness still, and takes the word "more largely," as denoting "all God's works that were properly preparatory to the purchase, and accomplishing the success of it." Multitudes of others have had their minds warped by the same confusion. Dr. Adam Clarke, for example, says, "ἀπολύτρωσις properly means the price laid down for the redemption of a captive."

It was, hence, good service to theology, as well as to exegesis, when Erasmus drew attention, long ago, to the inaccuracy of the Vulgate in using the word *redemption* for *ransom*. Beza, too, did well in following up the remark of Erasmus, (Matt. xx. 28.) And all accurate modern critics are careful to distinguish between the two terms. It is, hence, altogether inexcusable in Dr. Da. Brown to explain the word *redemption* in the passage before us, as meaning "the payment of a ransom (in Christ's death)." He adds:—"that this is the sense of the word 'redemption,' when applied to Christ's death, will appear clear to any impartial student of the passages where it occurs." It might, we reply, *if there were any passages at all in which Christ's death is designated an ἀπολύτρωσις*. We have seen, however, in our enumeration and consideration of the passages in which the term occurs, that *there are none such*. Christ's death, as the culmination of his dedicated and devoted life, is indeed the price of ἀπολύτρωσις. It is a *ransom*. The things wherewith the atonement was made, and in which it consists, were λύτρα. Their sum-total was λύτρον.

(The definitions of the term given by Hesychius and Suidas are admirably adapted to express its genuine and distinctive import. Hesychius says, λύτρα,—πάντα τὰ διδόμενα εἰς ἀνάκτησιν ἀνθρώπων, *all things whatever that are given for the recovery of men*, their recovery, to wit, ἐξ αἰχμαλωσίας, *from captivity.* Suidas says, λύτρα,—μισθός, ἢ τὰ παρεχόμενα ὑπὲρ ἐλευθερίας, *a price, or, things given for freedom.* Such was the work of Christ. But the ἀπολύτρωσις itself was, as the word is explained by Hesychius and Phavorinus, ἀποφυγή, ἀπόλυσις.)

In all ordinary cases, indeed, deliverance instantly eventuates when a ransom is paid,—(so that the distinguishing idea of ἀπολύτρωσις may be loosely attached to the paying of the λύτρον, even as the distinguishing idea of the λύτρον clings tenaciously and inherently to ἀπολύτρωσις). Nevertheless, cases are easily conceivable, in which the ransom might be paid, while yet the deliverance would not eventuate. The spiritual case of men is one of them. Their actual deliverance is wisely conditioned on a subjective contingency,—the forth-putting of faith. And thus it is of the greatest moment to distinguish carefully between the λύτρον paid for them, and their ἀπολύτρωσις. Olshausen, hence, misses the mark, so far as precision is concerned, both in the first and second of his particulars, when he specifies, as the three distinguishing representations of the work of Christ, 1. *Redemption,* ἀπολύτρωσις, 2. *Reconciliation,* καταλλαγή, 3. *Propitiation,* ἱλασμός.

When Christ paid the price of redemption for men, he *bought* them, it is true, with the price. (1 Cor. vi. 20; vii. 23; 2 Pet. ii. 1.) They are hence his by a new right. He is entitled anew to all that they are. They are bound to be his servants, and to do his work, and to make his will the rule of their activity, and to regard his glory as the end and pole-star of their being. But as men are free-agents, and not chattels, the new right that has been acquired over them by Christ, can issue in their actual consecration to his person and service and will, only by the intervenience of the free determination of their own will. Hence, also, *the buying of them* (τὸ ἀγοράζειν) does not, as a matter of fact, issue in *the buying of them off*—(τὸ ἐξαγοράζειν)—from the curse of the law, which they had broken, (Gal. iii. 13), unless scope is made for what is implied in the word "off" by the intervenience of faith. Without that intervenience, it is not fit that the *buying* should be a *buying off.* Without that same intervenience, moreover, it is impossible that they can be "bought (and brought) *out of* every kindred, and tongue, and people, and nation," (Rev. v. 9), and "from the earth," (Rev. xiv. 3), and "from among men," (Rev. xiv. 4). And, in like manner, without that intervenience, they cannot be *ransomed off* from the evils that are involved in sin. They are *ransomed*, indeed, in the sense of being *bought*. They might be said to be *redeemed*, so far as the mere etymological make of the Latin word suggests the meaning of the term. They have been *bought again*. But they are not *ransomed off*. They are not *redeemed*, when we take the Latin word *redemption* as a conventional synonym of the Greek word that is used by the Apostle in the passage before us.

The *redemption* which is "in Christ Jesus" is thus more than *the payment of a price*. It is *deliverance in consideration of a price paid*. That we must regard as settled. But what deliverance is it? Is it the entire, full-orbed, deliverance which is in Christ Jesus for men? Or is it some special aspect of this entirety? If it were the entire and full-orbed deliverance, it would include not only the pardon of sin, (Eph. i. 7; Col. i. 14), and justification too, and the sanctification of the soul, (1 Pet. i. 18; Tit. ii. 14), but also the redemption of the body, (Rom. viii. 23), and indeed the emancipation of the entire being from all the internal and external evils of sin. We scarcely think that the term should be here understood in this, its greatest possible amplitude of import. It is probable that it was rather one particular aspect of the great sum-total that was present to the Apostle's thoughts, when he said of believers, that they are "justified *through* the redemption which is in Christ Jesus." He seems to have been contemplating a certain specific element of redemption, which requires to be specially realized *in order to justification*. And hence we conclude that he was looking at that prominent side of the great whole which he specifies and explains in Eph. i. 7, and Col. i. 14;—in which passages he says, "in whom (*i. e.*, in Christ) we have redemption, (through his blood),—*the forgiveness of sins*." It is, apparently, *deliverance from the penal consequences of sins that is referred to.* And Oltramare consequently is not very far wrong when he translates the word *pardon:* and Philippi is right when he says that Gal. iii. 13 presents to view a consentaneous idea: for *deliverance from the penal consequences of sins* is *deliverance from the curse of the law.* Believers are "justified *through* this deliverance," not, as Calvin supposed, because the redemption constitutes the matter of the justifying righteousness, (*materia nostrae justitiae*); nor, as Day similarly supposed, because redemption is justification,—"justified by the justification which is by Christ Jesus;" but because, in the very nature of things, as divinely concatenated, a title to eternal glory cannot possibly be conferred until men are released from exposedness to eternal woe. Sinners, as sinners, stand in a certain positive relation, —downward or hell-ward; and in a negative relation,— upward or heaven-ward. It is clear that a positive upward or heaven-ward relation, of the nature of a title to "glory, honour, and immortality," could not be conferred until the actual relation downward and woe-ward be cancelled or neutralized. *Men must be pardoned, that they may be justified.* The one blessing, indeed, includes the other. Pardon involves justification: and justification involves pardon. Each is the obverse of the other. Each is the other's complement. And the two are, in fact, an indissoluble unity. But, nevertheless, it is a two-sided unity. And though there is, in general, only a specification of one of the sides, there is at other times a distinctive and distinguishing reference to each. There seems to be such a reference here. Believers are "justified *through* the redemption which is in Christ Jesus." It is in consequence of the purchased deliverance which they enjoy from the penalty of their sins, a deliverance which they have "in Christ Jesus," that they are still further blessed,—"justified," and thus constituted heirs of everlasting life and glory.

The expression, "*which is in Christ Jesus,*" (τῆς ἐν Χριστῷ Ἰησοῦ), is finely significant. It represents Christ Jesus as containing within himself the fulness of the blessing of redemption. Redemption is "in" him, just as salvation and eternal life are "in" him. They are "in" him for men. There is store of them; enough and to spare. And men have only to go "to" him,—though go "to" him they must,—go to him in spirit,—go to him by faith, —that they may get "*out of* his fulness," as out of an inexhaustible treasury, these, and all the other blessings that, as sinners, they require. The representation is, of course, metaphorical; but yet simply and sublimely significant: for it is because of something "in Christ," it is because of something which was effected by Christ, that believers are redeemed from the curse of the law, from the penalty of their sins, and thus and thence "justified freely by God's grace." Our English translation, "the redemption *which is in Christ Jesus*," is identical with the Vulgate version. It is approved of by Bengel; and is obviously the most natural interpretation of the phraseology. (We may fill out the phraseology thus,—διὰ τῆς ἀπολυτρώσεως τῆς οὔσης ἐν Χριστῷ Ἰησοῦ. It perplexes the idea to supply γενομένης, with Fritzsche and Philippi. And thus) Beza's translation was far from being an improvement,—"the redemption made in Christ Jesus," (*redemptionem factam in Jesu Christo*). And yet Luther's is similar, (*die Erlösung so durch Christum Jesum geschehen ist*). Rückert concurs with Luther in substituting the preposition "through" for "in." So J. J. Herzog, (*Diss. Exeget. de loco Paulino, Rom.* iii. 21—31). Day renders it "by." So Bullinger, (*per*). So Crell. But such a substitution or transmutation is altogether uncalled for, and mars the simplicity and significance of the representation. Krehl retains the "in;" but he awkwardly explains it as denoting "union with Christ," (*indem sie mit Christus in Verbindung und enge Gemeinschaft treten durch den Glauben*). It evidently points out to us, and is simply intended thus to point out, where it is that redemption is in store, and may be found. "This redemption," says Seb. Schmidt, "is with the Lord Jesus, because it was he who acquired it, and acquired it for the very purpose of having it in his power to possess it, and give it, and apply it to whomsoever he pleases." (*Haec Redemptio apud dominum Jesum est, quod ille eam sic acquisiverit, ut eam possideat, et det, atque applicet, cui vult.*)

VERS. 25, 26. ὃν προέθετο ὁ θεὸς ἱλαστήριον, διὰ πίστεως ἐν τῷ αὐτοῦ αἵματι, εἰς ἔνδειξιν τῆς δικαιοσύνης αὐτοῦ διὰ τὴν πάρεσιν τῶν προγεγονότων ἁμαρτημάτων | ἐν τῇ ἀνοχῇ τοῦ θεοῦ, πρὸς τὴν ἔνδειξιν τῆς δικαιοσύνης αὐτοῦ ἐν τῷ νῦν καιρῷ, εἰς τὸ εἶναι αὐτὸν δίκαιον καὶ δικαιοῦντα τὸν ἐκ πίστεως Ἰησοῦ.

Eng. Auth. Vers. *Whom God hath set forth* to be *a propitiation through faith in his blood, to declare his righteousness for the remission of sins that are past, through the forbearance of God; to declare,* I say, *at this time his righteousness: that he might be just, and the justifier of him which believeth in Jesus.*

Revised Version. *whom God set* (*publicly*) *forth* (*as*) *propitiatory,*—(*available*) *through faith in his blood,—for demonstration of his righteousness because of the pretermission of the sins of former times in the forbearance of God, —in order to the demonstration of his righteousness in the present time, that he may be righteous even in justifying him who is of faith in Jesus.*

§ 1. We connect these two verses together, partly because they are a unit, whether considered grammatically or doctrinally, and partly because Robert Stephens has fixed upon an awkward point in the unit for his versicular disjunction. Had he postponed the disjunction to the close of the clause, *in the forbearance of God,* (ἐν τῇ ἀνοχῇ τοῦ θεοῦ), the verses might have been considered apart. This postponement is adopted in our English Authorized Version; in the Dutch versions, old and new; in the Lutheran; in Diodati; in Bengel's German version; in Beza's ultimate text (1588—9, and 1598); also in Calvin's ultimate French translation, and hence in the French Geneva, and in the English Geneva, and in Ostervald's and Martin's Bibles, and in Beausobre and Lenfant's New Testament; &c., &c. In such a case as this,—as distinguished, for instance, from that of the last clause of the 22nd verse of this chapter,—there is good reason to justify a departure from the Stephanic arrangement, provided the verses are to be printed, not in continuous paragraphs, but, as has been too customary, in detached morsels, like proverbs.

§ 2. The two verses, in conjunction with the four which precede, are among the most important in the Bible. The entire paragraph, which consists of these six verses, is, as we have already indicated, an expansion and explanation of the theme of the epistle, as propounded in chap. i. 16, 17, and, as such, it is the very "marrow of divinity." It is eminently and preeminently rich in the distinctively essential elements of that evangelism which constitutes the true glory of the Bible, as a revelation of mercy from the Infinite God. And hence every clause in it, every clausule, every expression, every word, deserves to be carefully scrutinized, analyzed, weighed, and considered in its varied relations to the surrounding words, and to the sum-total of the doctrine of the Apostle, and of the inspired writers in general. Almost all expositors seem to have realized, with more or less depth of conviction, and with feelings varying according to their illumination and the ratio of their evangelical sympathy with the Apostle, that they had here to deal with words of peculiar significance,—and with ideas which, in the Apostle's own judgement, were of transcendent moment. Luther draws attention, in the margin of his Bible, to the importance of the section. He says, over against ver. 23rd ff.,—"This is the chief point, and the very central place of the epistle, and of the whole Bible," (*Merke diss, da er saget*:—**Sie sind allzumal Sünder, &c.** *Ist das Hauptstück und der Mittel-Platz dieser Epistel, und der ganzen Schrift, &c.*) Calvin, on ver. 24th, and referring to the contents at once of that verse, and of the two which follow, says,—"There is probably no passage in the whole Bible that more exhaustively exhibits the justifying righteousness of God: for it shows its efficient cause, the mercy of God; its material cause, Christ with his blood; its formal or instrumental cause, faith springing from the Word; and its final cause, the glory of the divine justice and goodness." (*Nullus est forte in tota Scriptura insignior locus ad vim istius justitiae illustrandam. Ostendit enim Dei misericordiam causam esse efficientem: Christum cum suo sanguine esse materiam: formalem seu instrumentalem esse fidem e verbo conceptam: finalem porro divinae et justitiae et bonitatis gloriam.*) "There is no passage," says Matthias, "in Paul's epistles which exhibits the doctrine of justification in a manner so condensed, so profound, and so clear." (*Keine Stelle der paulinischen Briefe enthält die Lehre von der Rechtfertigung so kurz und doch die tiefste Wahrheit so klar enthüllend wie v. 24—26 dieses Capitels.*) Melancthon says,—"This whole period (viz., ver. 24th ff.) contains the very head and front of Paul's discussion." (*Haec tota periodus, quae sequitur, est principalis propositio et status in hac disputatione Pauli.*-Enarratio, 1556.) "Lo! here, here," says the classic Mussus, "is the great and ineffable mystery of all Christian philosophy." (*Ecce, Ecce magnum et ineffabile omnis Christianae Philosophiae mysterium.*) "In these verses," (viz., ver. 21—26), says John Jacob Stolz, "is the quintessence of the Pauline doctrine concerning Christ. Whosoever understands them, understands the Apostle; whosoever misunderstands them, runs the risk of misunderstanding the entire epistle." (*In diesen Versen ist die Quintessenz der Paulinischen Christus-lehre. Wer hier den Apostel verstehet, der weiss was derselbe will; Missverstand dieser verse wirkt auf das Verständniss der ganzen Epistel*). "This passage," says E. J. Greve, "contains the principal theme of the Epistle; and this theme is the foundation of the whole evangelical system." (*Deze plaats bevat de voornaame hoofdstelling van den brief, welke tevens de grondslag van 't gantsche Euangelisch leerstelsel is.*) "There is perhaps," says Dr.

Chalmers, "no single passage in the Book of inspiration which reveals, in a way so formal and authoritative as the one before us, the path of transition by which a sinner passes from a state of wrath to a state of acceptance. There is no passage — to which, if we would only bring the docility and the compliance of childhood—that is more fitted to guide and to turn an inquiring sinner into the way of peace." "These six verses," says C. P. Shepherd, "which contain the first enunciation of the doctrine of justification in this epistle,—the first overflow, so to speak, of that matter of which the Apostle's heart and mind were full,—contain also in a short compass the completest expression of the Christian doctrine." They are emphatically, to use the language of Nösselt, (in his *Interpretatio et Vindiciae loci classici de justificatione Rom.* iii. 21—28), *nobilissimus locus.* They are preeminently, on the subject of justification, *locus classicus*, or, as Kolding, Stein, and others, in their *Dissertations,* express it, *Dictum classicum de justificatione.* The passage is, as Philippi designates it, "the proper seat" (*sedes propria*) of the Pauline doctrine of justification. "This," says Seb. Schmidt, "is a full exposition of the whole business: wherefore the verses should be most diligently studied by us." (*Sane haec plena est totius negotii expositio: quare hi versus diligentissime nobis observandi sunt.*) Verses 25th and 26th, in particular, are of the greatest significance in reference to the nature of the work of Christ. The "nerve," as Tischendorf expresses it, of the whole argument in favour of the accredited evangelical view is found in them, (*in quo loco profecto nervus inest totius causae nostrae comprobandae.*-De vi mortis Christi satisfactoria, p. 20). And as, therefore,—to borrow the remark of the great Vitringa,—"this passage is a brief compend of the divine wisdom, and is, moreover, rich in meaning and power, it must be doubly deserving of the most careful consideration possible," (*Naardien nu dese plaats des Apostels een kort begrijp van de Goddelijke wijsheit, en daar te boven rijk in sin en kragt is, soo salse de alder-naukeurigste overweginge dubbelt waardig zijn*). Well might Vinke exclaim in reference to it,—"Glorious Gospel!"

(*Heerlijk Evangelie*). It was in the 25th verse that the poet Cowper found peace to his spirit, after it had well-nigh drifted into utter despair. "*I flung myself,*" he says, "*into a chair near the window, and seeing a Bible there, ventured once more to apply to it for comfort and instruction. The first verse I saw was the 25th of the 3rd of Romans* :—'whom God hath set forth to be a propitiation, through faith in his blood, to declare his righteousness for the remission of sins that are past, through the forbearance of God.' *Immediately I received strength to believe, and the full beams of the Sun of Righteousness shone upon me. I saw the sufficiency of the atonement he had made for my pardon and complete justification. In a moment I believed, and received the peace of the Gospel.*"—"*Unless,*" he adds, "*the Almighty arm had been under me, I think I should have been overwhelmed with gratitude and joy. My eyes filled with tears, and my voice choked with transport. I could only look up to heaven in silent fear, overwhelmed with love and wonder. But the work of the Holy Spirit is best described in his own words;—it is 'joy unspeakable and full of glory.'*"–Taylor's Life of Cowper, pp. 37, 38, ed. 1835. It is not, however, astonishing that Jones, with his entire lack of evangelical insight, should say of the entire paragraph, ver. 21—27, "This passage must appear to every reader very obscure and involved." It must, indeed, to every reader whose eye will not look on Christ Jesus,—Christ Jesus "the crucified," Christ Jesus as *thus* the Saviour. But to those who see light in His light, it must appear to be the very focus of Biblical illumination on the subject of which it treats. And the multiplicity of rays which converge in it, and emanate from it, irradiates, indeed, but neither dazzles nor bewilders. With not one of them would we dispense. Every word is precious. And the fulness of the Apostle's phraseology is so emphatic, so exquisitely intensifying, so genial withal, and fresh, and warm, that we cannot but pity Gilbert Wakefield,—in many respects a noble man, though unhappily blinded on one side of his spiritual being,—when he remarks that "the author is exceedingly *verbose* upon this subject." Would he have liked that the Apostle had nimbly skipped through his theme, as with *hop, step, and leap?*

§ 3. *whom God set (publicly) forth,* (ὃν προέθετο ὁ θεός). It is Jesus Christ who is referred to,—Jesus Christ, "*in whom* is redemption." The Apostle is about to explain how it is that there is "redemption" in Him. It is because *God set him forth, &c.* The verb which we translate *set (publicly) forth,* (προέθετο), has been viewed by expositors from various standpoints, and has received different explanations. It might mean, as a medial verb, *to place before oneself, to propose to oneself,* that is, *to purpose, to determine.* This is the meaning which the word bears in the other two passages in which it occurs in the New Testament, Rom. i. 13, Eph. i. 9. And, in accordance with this meaning, the cognate noun (πρόθεσις) generally bears, in the New Testament, the signification of *purpose* or *determination.* (See Acts xi. 23; xxvii. 13; Rom. viii. 28; ix. 11; Eph. i. 11; iii. 11; 2 Tim. i. 9; iii. 10.) This is the meaning which is attached to the verb in the passage before us by Aquinas, Wycliffe (*purposid*), Purvey's revision (*ordeynde*), Mussus (*definivit, decrevit*), Beausobre et Lenfant (*avoit ordonné*), Böhme (προέθετο *scilicet* ἐν ἑαυτῷ), Wahl (*destinavit vel voluit*); so Fritzsche, and Oltramare; Mace too (*ordained*), and Vaughan, &c. All these would understand the expression thus:—"*whom God purposed (to be)* ἱλαστήριον κ. τ. λ. (The interpretation of Aquinas is,—"*eum Deus ad hoc ordinaverat secundum suum propositum, quod designat, cum dicit,* **quem proposuit Deus propitiatorem.**) Many other expositors have held what is substantially the same view of the verb: only, with more or less distinctness or indefiniteness, they seem to have considered that the word itself indicates the antiquity, or eternity, of the purpose. They seem, in short, to have, either decidedly or dimly, regarded the preposition in composition (the πρό) as having a relation to time. Hence the Peshito version, (ܗܢܐ ܕܩܕܡ ܣܡܗ, which is translated *proposuit* by Tremellius, but which really means *foreordained*). Chrysostom took the same view, (δηλῶν δὲ πάλιν οὐ νεώτερον τοῦτο ὄν, οὐδὲ καινόν, φησί προέθετο,—*but as a proof that it was no novel or new thing, he says* **foreordained**). Œcumenius echoes it, (προέθετο, δηλοῖ παλαιὰν τὴν περὶ τούτου βουλήν). Theophylact re-echoes it, (προέθετο δὲ εἶπεν, ἵνα δείξῃ ὅτι πάλαι προώριστο ἡ διὰ τοῦ αἵματος τοῦ Χριστοῦ ἀπολύτρωσις). Vatable, Musculus, Pareus, and Elsner (*praefinivit*), Heumann (*zuvor verordnet*), Ostervald (*a établi de tout temps*), Martin, Koppe, Schleusner, and others, take substantially the same view. They all suppose that the Apostle refers to God's *purpose of old*, though it is not certain that all of them regarded the preposition in composition as definitely indicating the relation of antecedence in time. In either of its phases, whether as simply expressing *purpose*, or as expressing *purpose of old*, the interpretation is an unlikely explication of the Apostle's idea. In the phase that is given by the Syriac translator the power of the incorporated preposition is undoubtedly misunderstood, as is evident from the import of the cognate noun (πρόθεσις) in such passages as Acts xi. 23; 2 Tim. iii. 10. And if, in accordance with the other phase, the relation of antecedence in time is obliterated, and the mere idea of *purpose* or *design* expressed, there is nothing in the context, or in the nature of the case, to bespeak special favour for the interpretation. It is not the mere purpose of God in reference to the propitiation, but the fulfilment of his purpose in actual fact, that is available "for the display of his righteousness in the remission of sins." The position, moreover, of the verb—(its position, to wit, in relation to the word ἱλαστήριον)—shows that it is to be betoned while we read and interpret; and hence the subsequently mentioned "demonstration of God's righteousness in the remission of sins" is to be regarded as finding its starting-point in the action indicated by the betoned verb. And consequently we seem shut up to suppose that the action indicated, instead of being subjective and immanent, must be objective and transient. The verb, in other words, cannot bear the signification, *purposed*, or *designed*, or *ordained*, or *foreordained*.

De Dieu, though not speaking very decisively regarding the word, is inclined to attribute to the preposition in composition a temporal import. And, on the whole, he would interpret the term as referring to the types and predictions of the Old Testament:—*whom God formerly*, —that is, *under the Old Testament dispensation*,—*placed or revealed as a propitiation*, (**quem ante**—*nempe in veteri Test. per umbras legis, prophetarumque vaticinia*—**posuit placamentum**:— προέθετο *non accipiatur de exhibitione Christi, sed* **de praecedanea ejus revelatione in V. Test.**) It is a most unlikely explication. *Placed*, as meaning *revealed*, is surely a violent strain of exegetical contrivance.

While some of the expositors referred to above made a wrong use of the incorporated preposition, Melancthon, in his latest and best exposition of the Epistle, his *Enarratio* of 1556, erred in merging it out of view altogether. He translates the expression thus:—"whom God **constituted**," (*constituit*), or "**placed**," (*posuit*), "a propitiator." Tyndale, before him, had given the same interpretation. He translates the word "hath made:"—"whom God *hath made* a seate of mercy." Rilliet's translation is the same, (*dont Dieu* **a fait** *une victime expiatoire*). But there is certainly no good reason for annulling the force of the preposition.

Kypke duly recognized the importance of the preposition: and he fancied, indeed, that he saw in it a very special significance of evangelical meaning. He thought that it expressed a substitutionary idea; so that the verb would mean "put in place of" (*loco alterius substituere*):—"whom God *substituted*," or "*gave in our room* as ἱλαστήριον κ. τ. λ," (*quem Deus nostri loco dedit ut sacrificium expiatorium*). His translation was adopted by Rosenmüller, and Jo. D. Michaelis. But it was founded on a misunderstood expression of Euripides in his Iphig. A. 1592,—in which Calchas, referring to Diana's miraculous substitution of a hind for Iphigenia, says, ὁρᾶτε τὴν δὲ θυσίαν ἣν ἡ θεὸς προὔθηκε βωμίαν ἔλαφον ὀρείδρομον, *but see the sacrifice which the goddess hath set forth—hath placed before our eyes —at her altar,—a hind from the hills.* The verb does not bear the signification attributed to it by Kypke. It often means *to prefer*, but not *to substitute.*

It does bear, however, the signification which is attributed to it by Matthias, who renders it *published, promulgated,* or *proclaimed,* (*προέθετο nehme man im Sinne von* **öffentlich kundthun** *d. i.* **predigen liess**):—"whom God *caused to be announced* as having the power of propitiating." But this signification of the verb is appropriated to the calling or appointment of assemblies, or the promulgation of laws, and seems to be inapplicable to the case which the Apostle has in hand. More particularly does this appear when we consider that it is the actual historical occurrence of the propitiatory work of Christ Jesus, rather than its mere promulgation, that is "for the manifestation of the divine righteousness in the forgiveness of sins."

There is an oddity of interpretation given to the word by Jatho. He supposes that the Apostle means,—"whom God *exposed* (as) *for sale* a *ἱλαστήριον*;" and he imagines that "the price," at which we may, as it were, purchase the commodity, is specified in the following expression, *through faith in his blood,* (*προτίθεσθαι, von dem Seinigen zum Verkaufe öffentlich und Jedermann feil bieten.—Da aber von einem προτίθεσθαι die Rede ist, so wird hinzugesetzt, um welchen Preis Christus ein Sühndeckel für uns wird. Die Erlösungsthat ist freilich objectiv am Kreuze vollendet; aber für uns ist er ein ἱλαστήριον erst διὰ τῆς πίστεως ἐν τῷ αὐτοῦ αἵματι*). This extremely mercantile interpretation is founded, indeed, on an actual usage of the verb. (See Lucian, *Adv. Indoct.* 19.) For one need not marvel that a word which naturally signifies *to place before,* or *to set forth,* should be employed to denote the *forth-putting* of a thing for sale. But the explication, nevertheless, is a remarkable instance of that perverse species of ingenuity that ransacks possibilities for improbabilities, and leaves out of sight, however precious and appropriate it may be, what is lying on the surface, and thus obvious to the view of all.

There really seems to be no good reason why we should seek far and wide for a fitting explication of the term. Its primary import, as simply applied to the case in hand, suffices. Its primary import is *to place before;* and in the middle it will, as used in such a connection as the one before us, naturally mean, either *to place before oneself, to propose to oneself, to purpose,* or *to place before others on the part of oneself,* or *in behalf of oneself.* We have seen that it is not congruous to interpret the term here as meaning *to purpose.* And we therefore at once betake ourselves to the other natural offshoot of its radical import, and come to the conclusion that the Apostle means, that *God, in his own interest as the Moral Governor of the Universe, put Christ Jesus (publicly) forth as* ἱλαστήριον. The action of God in the case was intentionally public. It was designed for the benefit of the public, and for the vindication and glory of Himself, as standing at the head of the public,—the Monarch of the moral universe. God *exhibited* Christ. He *brought him forth* upon this human stage of things. He *put him forth,* he *put him before the public,* that the public might have the opportunity of taking due notice of his appearance, and of observing what was involved in the marvellous phenomenon. The word is frequently used with this special reference to the public—the public viewed more or less expansively. See, for instance, Herodot. v. 8,—"But the funerals of the wealthy are conducted in this way,—They *expose to (public) view* the corpse for three days, &c.," (τρεῖς μὲν ἡμέρας προτιθέασι τὸν νεκρόν). Herodot. vi. 21,—"For when Sybaris was taken by the Crotonians, all the Milesians, from the youth upward, shaved their heads, and *publicly exhibited* great grief," or "made public demonstration of great grief," (καὶ πένθος μέγα προεθήκοντο). See also iii. 148. See also Thuc. ii. 34,—"During this winter the Athenians *made a public funeral* (δημοσίᾳ ταφὰς ἐποίησαντο) of those who had died first in this war, in the following manner,—They *expose to view* for three days the bones of the departed, &c.," (τὰ μὲν ὀστᾶ προτίθενται τῶν ἀπογενομένων πρότριτα). Hence, too, the use of the word with reference to articles *set forth* or *exposed* for sale; and hence too its use to denote *proclamations,* and other acts of *making publicly known.*

It is worthy of note that the cognate noun, (πρόθεσις),

of which we have already spoken, and which, in the greater number of the instances in which it occurs in the New Testament, means *purpose*, has another meaning in a minority of passages; and this a meaning which connects itself with that signification of the verb which we have just been exhibiting. The word is used in reference to what is called the "*shew*bread," (=לֶחֶם הַפָּנִים or לֶחֶם הַמַּעֲרֶכֶת,—Sept., οἱ ἄρτοι τῆς προθέσεως,—Vulg., *panes propositionis*). See Matt. xii. 4; Mark ii. 26; Luke vi. 4. Comp. Heb. ix. 2. The expression is rendered in the margin of our English Bibles, "the bread *of setting before*." It was bread which was *set forth*. It was *set forth* by men before the Lord. And in some corresponding manner was Christ Jesus *set forth* by God before men. He was *shown* to them. The expression for "*shew*bread" is, of course, Septuagintal. And the cognate verb—the verb which occurs in our passage—is used in connection with it in Exod. xl. 4,—"Thou shalt bring in the table, and *set in order the things that are to be set in order upon it*," (καὶ προθήσεις τὴν πρόθεσιν αὐτῆς, *and thou shalt set forth its forth-setting*, viz., of loaves). It occurs with the same application in 2 Mac. i. 8, (προεθήκαμεν τοὺς ἄρτους). And in Ps. liii. 3; lxxxv. 13; c. 4, it bears the same signification of *setting forth*. In these passages of the Psalms, moreover, it occurs in the middle voice, and means *to set forth in one's own behalf*. The word does not bear the meaning of *purpose* in the Septuagint.

We think, then, that those critics have seized the Apostle's idea in the passage before us, who have, along with the authors of our *Authorized English Version*, interpreted the term which the Apostle employs as meaning *set forth*. It was thus that Pelagius interpreted it, (*in promptu ante oculos omnium posuit, ut qui redimi vult, accedat*). It was thus that Luther understood it, (*hat vorgestellt*). It is thus that it is rendered in the Geneva, and in the Bishop's Bible; and in the Dutch translations, old and new. Thus, too, was it understood by Cognatus, and Rollock; Bengel too (*ante omnium oculos posuit*), and Wetstein (*Christus proponitur publice*);

Deyling also (*proposuit in lucem—omnium oculis videndum exposuit*), Bos, Wolf, &c., &c. Thus, too, by Winzer, among the more modern critics, and Reiche, Rückert, de Wette; Stuart too, and Hodge, Meyer, Baumgarten-Crusius, Philippi, Bisping, Krehl, Umbreit; and Mehring, van Hengel, Lange, &c. Christ Jesus was *set forth* by God as ἱλαστήριον. In so far as he was ἱλαστήριος, or ἱλαστήριον, he was among men by the arrangement and agency of God. God placed him in our world;—*set him forth* before us and before the whole universe. He was *exhibited*, though of course not for the mere sake of exhibition, before men and angels.

§ 4. *propitiatory*, that is, *as propitiatory*, (ἱλαστήριον). A most important word, in a doctrinal point of view; and a word encompassed with no insignificant difficulties when hermeneutically considered,—though these are happily of such a nature as not to perplex materially the doctrinal exegesis.

The radical meaning of that class of Latin words which embraces such terms as *propitiatory*, *propitiation*, *propitiator*, *propitiate*, *propitious*, seems to be as yet uncertain.

Vossius supposes that the basis-idea is that of *nearness*, (**a prope esse propitius,** *quia, qui propinqui sunt auxilium ferre possunt; et presentes pro propitiis dicimus*). He adopted this notion from Alfenus in Gellius vi. 5; and Richardson accepts from him the etymology. But we doubt its validity. In its "letter" it seems to be all that could be desired; but in its "spirit" it has little to recommend it. Some other philologers, retaining the idea of *nearness*, add, as a distinct element in the etymology of the word, the idea of *movement, approach*, (*prope ito,—I go near*). The addition is ingenious, but undoubtedly fanciful; for the primitive word was evidently an adjective, (*propitius*), not a verb. We should suppose that we must go off, altogether, from this scent of the idea of *nearness*, (prope), if we would get to the primitive notion of the word;—for mere nearness is no guarantee for propitiousness. The hating and the hateful—the revengeful—may be near, as well as the forgiving, the compassionate, and the loving.

It has been supposed by some that the idea of *petition* is involved in the word, (*pro* and *peto;* see Leverett, *sub. voc.*). It is surely an absurd etymology. A *propitious* being is not one *who petitions for another.* He is one who may require to be petitioned, but not one who requires to petition.

Nonius Marcellus supposes that the word etymologically means *exceedingly pious,* (*prorsus pius, proprie pius,* or *porro pius*). It is, we presume, a fanciful and inadmissible explanation of the primary import of the term. And yet we are not unwilling to think that, so far as the introduction of the word *pious* into the sphere of our concept is concerned, there may be a movement in the right direction. We can suppose that there is between the two words, "*pi*ous" and "pro*pi*tious," not indeed an immediate or very near connection, but a real, though perhaps far removed, relationship. On the supposition that *kindness*—the peculiar feeling of *kind*red or *kin*ship—is fundamentally involved in the idea of *pious,* (*pius,* conf. ἤπιος),—then, assuredly, there is a *kind of piety* in *propitiousness.* There is at least the *piety* of *pity,*—a piety which may be characteristic of a parent in relation to his erring children, and of God in relation to the erring subjects of his sovereign rule. In Latin it was legitimate to speak of parents being *pious* toward their children, as of children being *pious* toward their parents; and of God being *pious* toward men, as well as of men being *pious* toward God. In English the word *piety* has got narrowed in its reference. It denotes almost exclusively a feeling of the moral creature toward the Creator,—that feeling that pervades the character and the conduct of those who realize that God is their God and their Father. But *pity*—another phase of *piety*—has not been equally turned aside from applicability to God. The Lord is "very *pitiful.*" And we may with propriety ask him *to pity us* in some specific way, or *to be propitious to us.* In Latin the worshipper could be represented as *piating* the Being worshipped. (*Tellurem porco,*

Silvanum lacte piabant,–Hor. *Ep.* ii. 1. 143.) The human *piety*, that is to say, of the worshipper, could be viewed as rising up and taking effect upon the Being worshipped, so that divine *pity* was the result. This same *piety* could also be viewed as taking effect upon the sin that had given offence, (*culpam piabunt*,–Virg. *Aen.* ii. 140). The offering or sacrifice which was presented by *piety* took effect in *piating* the offended God, and in *expiating* the offence that had been committed against him. Pro*pi*tiation was realized. We are thus not indisposed to think that there may be some interlacing, however complicated, between the word "*pi*ous" and the word "pro*pi*tiation." But still we wait for light.

The etymological import of the corresponding class of Greek words is, if possible, still obscurer. Indeed, it is enveloped in a darkness which is, as yet, utterly unpenetrated. If the word that signifies *propitiated* or *propitious* (ἵλαος) be connected, as Eustathius says it is, and as is admitted by many philologers, with the word that signifies *cheerful* or *joyful*, (ἱλαρός), then one might suppose that there might be some reference to the joyful light or radiance that beams from the countenance of the glad and kind. One naturally remembers that the moon is called ἱλάειρα, and one is almost tempted to connect, though remotely, the fundamental element of the word with the fundamental element of the word ἥλιος, *the sun*, and of the affiliated words ἕλη, εἵλη, *the light or heat of the sun*. It is a widely diffused element. We find it in German, *hell* (*clear*). We find it in Hebrew, הָלַל, *to be clear*. And it seems to turn up, with its aspiration made sibilant, in σέλας, *light, brightness*, and σελήνη, *the moon;* and compare, too, the Gothic *sauil, the sun*. If there be a filament of affinity running through this group of terms, and threading them into etymological unity, then we may suppose that, by a not unnatural lateral movement of the needle of thought, there may be some reason, in the affinity of things, for the connection which is suggested by the *Etymologicum Magnum* between the word for *propitious* (ἵλεως = ἵλαος) and the word for *mercy*, (ἔλεος). If the connection be real, then we should have a relationship of things corresponding to the relationship between "*pi*ty" and "pro*pi*tiousness." Eustathius has a fancifully operose and utterly impracticable derivation for ἵλαος. He resolves the word thus,—ἵεμαι λάειν, *I desire to see.* But his assertion that ἵλαος and ἱλαρός are connected is borne out by the fact that ἵλεως is sometimes used in the signification of ἱλαρός. (Hence Hesychius, ἵλεως, εὐμενής, ἱλαρός, and hence, *vice versa*, Suidas, ἱλαρώτερος, εὐπροσιτώτερος, *easier of access.*)

But, however obscure the etymological import of the words we have been considering, their conventional acceptation is by no means obscure. The verb *to propitiate* (ἱλάσκομαι) is always, in Homer, used with a reference to divine beings, and means *to appease, to placate, to win the favour of, to render propitious.* In subsequent writers its application was, not unnaturally, extended; and men were said *to propitiate men.* The Parians, for instance, are said by Herodotus to *have propitiated Themistocles by money,* (Πάριοι δὲ Θεμιστοκλῆα χρήμασι ἱλασάμενοι.—viii. 112). In the New Testament the words are invariably employed in reference to God. But in the Septuagint an instance or two occurs in which propitiation is spoken of as terminating on offended men,—men whose indignation might be regarded as formidable or dangerous. In Gen. xxxii. 20 (21) we read that Jacob said of Esau, "I will appease him (*I will propitiate him,* ἐξιλάσομαι τὸ πρόσωπον αὐτοῦ, = אֲכַפְּרָה פָנָיו) with the present, and afterward I will see his face; peradventure he will accept of me." In Prov. xvi. 14 we read, "The wrath of a king is as messengers of death; but a wise man will pacify it, (*will propitiate him,* ἐξιλάσεται αὐτόν)." It is added, "In *the light of the king's countenance* is life; and *his favour* is as a cloud of the latter rain."

The corresponding terms in Hebrew (כַּפֹּרֶת, כִּפֻּרִים, כֹּפֶר, כִּפֵּר) do not run in exactly parallel lines of import with the Latin and Greek terms. But their primary import is manifest. The verb (כָּפַר) means to *cover.* And, indeed, were it not the case that the English term *cover* verifies itself as a simple modification of the French *couvrir,*—which, like the Spanish *cubrir* and the Italian *coprire,* comes from the Latin *cooperire,*—one might have been almost tempted to have imagined that there might be some phraseological filament of kinship between it and the Hebrew term;—they are so like one another. Such a connection, however, —should it really be imagined,—would nevertheless be entirely imaginary.

There seems to be little reason to doubt that the primary meaning of כָּפַר is *to cover.* Hence the use of the term in the one passage in which it is found in Kal, Gen. vi. 14,—"and *cover it* (viz., the ark) within and without with pitch," (translated in our version "and *pitch it* within and without with pitch"). And thence, in the Pihel conjugation,—the conjugation in which the term generally occurs,—it bifurcates in its import, and signifies, either *to pardon,* on the one hand, (Ps. lxv. 3; lxxviii. 38; Jer. xviii. 23), or *to make propitiation* or *atonement,* on the other, (Exod. xxix. 36, 37; xxx. 10, 15, 16; xxxii. 30; Lev. i. 4; iv. 20, 26, 31, 35; v. 6, 10, 13, 18, &c., &c.) In both branches of signification the fundamental idea of *covering* is manifest. Sins are *covered,* and as it were *hidden out of sight,* both when they are pardoned and when they are atoned for or expiated,—when propitiation is made for them. In consequence of this twofold application of the Hebrew term, the corresponding Greek verb (ἱλάσκομαι) is sometimes anomalously used in the Septuagint, even in the middle voice, as meaning *to pardon.* (See 2 Kings v. 18; Ps. lxiv. 3.) And, indeed, Symmachus uses the active voice of the compound verb in the same acceptation, (ἐξιλάσκων ἁμαρτίας, Ps. lxxviii. 38). In the New Testament the compound verb (ἐξιλάσκομαι) does not occur at all, though it is it that is generally used in the Septuagint. And the simple verb (ἱλάσκομαι) occurs only twice, signifying, in one of the passages, (Heb. ii. 17), *to make atonement* or *propitiation for* (= the Septuagintal ἐξιλάσκομαι), and, in the other, (Luke xviii. 13), in which it is used in the passive, it means *to be propitiated so as to forgive,*—"God be merciful (be propitiated, be forgiving) to me a sinner."

The publican, doubtless, had regard to the typical sacrifice presented in the temple, where he was when he offered up his prayer. It was pardon, on the footing of a propitiation, which he desired.

As to the word which the Apostle employs in the passage before us, (*ἱλαστήριον*), it is evidently intended to exhibit the ground of the "redemption" which is "in Christ Jesus," and of the "justification" which is conditioned on that "redemption." "Christ Jesus" is characterized by what is "propitiatory," and has been "set forth publicly" by God as such: and hence there is redemption for men, and the possibility of justification. But there is some considerable difficulty with the specific hermeneutics of the term.

(1.) Some translators have rendered the word, as if it were a masculine noun,—*propitiator*. The Codex Fuldensis of the Vulgate reads *propitiatorem:* and so other ancient codices of the Vulgate. The same reading, too, had doubtless been found in some of the ante-Hieronymian codices. Pelagius gives it. And so does Ambrosiaster. Rufinus, in his translation of Origen, says that *Propitiator* was the most frequent translation in the Latin codices. Wycliffe's translation corresponds: he renders it "an helpere." Purvey, in his revision, renders it "forghyver" (*forgiver*). In Cranmer's Bible it is rendered "the obtainer of mercy." Erasmus's version is similar: he renders it "reconciler" (*reconciliatorem*); but in his Paraphrase and Notes he adheres, along with le Fèvre of Estaples, to the more literal translation, "*propitiatory,*" (*propitiatorium*). Vatable, while noticing that the Latin codices differ in their way of translating the term, seems to assume *propitiator* as his reading. Cajetan decides for the masculine noun, rendering the word *placator,* (*procul dubio, redimendo*). Este, too, prefers *propitiator.* So did Melancthon, both in his *Commentary* of 1540, and in his *Enarratio* of 1556. In his *Annotations* of 1522 he assumed the interpretation which is stereotyped in Luther's version, and to which we shall by and by refer. Strigelius and Hunnius follow Melancthon's ultimate opinion. Wahl gives the same translation. So does Bolten. And so does Schrader, (*Versöhner*). So, too, Reithmayr. Jaspis and Goeschen render it "*expiator*," (*expiatorem*). Semler, before them, had explained it in the same manner. Benecke renders it *a Freer-from-sin*, (Entsündiger). The Peshito version has been regarded by Tremellius and Schaaf as lending its authority to the same kind of rendering: but on merely conjectural and indeed mistaken grounds, for the term which it employs (ܚܘܣܝܐ) is used, both in 1 John ii. 2; iv. 10; and in Heb. ix. 9, in which last place, at least, it cannot mean *propitiator*.

This translation, as a free and easy rendering, might be accepted: but only as a free and easy rendering. Doctrinally regarded, it doubtless harmonizes with the Apostle's idea. But the word which he employs is evidently an adjective, not a substantive. It means *propitiatory*, not *propitiator*. (If *propitiator* had been the precise idea which was in the mind of the Apostle, we should have expected him to use ἱλαστής instead of ἱλαστήριον.)

(2.) In the common editions of the Vulgate the term is translated "propitiation," (*propitiationem*):—and this rendering has been followed in our Authorized English Version; as also in the Dutch, (*tot eene verzoening*). It is approved of by Er. Schmid, and Boysen, and Jowett, &c. Beza's translation is in substance the same, *placamen* in his first edition, and *placamentum* in all the subsequent editions,—a version of the word that has been adopted by Melville, Piscator, and others. It had, in its ultimate form, been adopted, we presume, from Castellio, who gives it. (Rollock improves it by rendering the expression *in placamentum*.) The Geneva version of 1557 corresponds with Beza's translation,—"a pacification." The subsequent Geneva has it, "a reconciliation." Diodati's version is similar, "per purgamento,"—"*for a cleansing* or *expiation*." The interpretation of Glöckler and Usteri corresponds,—"a means of propitiation," (*Versöhnungsmittel*,-Glöckler; *Sühnungsmit-*

tel,–Usteri). Sharpe translates the word too demonstratively, "the means of propitiation."

The remark that we made in reference to the other translation specified is equally applicable to this. As a free and easy rendering, it is admissible, and useful, and, in many respects, admirable. But it must be borne in mind that it *is* free and easy. For the Apostle's word is not a substantive, but an adjective. And its adjectival import would, doubtless, be fully-orbed before his mind when, passing over a variety of substantives, from among which he could have made a selection, (*ἱλασμός, ἐξιλασμός, ἐξίλασμα*, &c.), he chose the term which he actually employs.

(3.) A large number of interpreters suppose that the Apostle, in using the word, has direct reference to *the golden covering of the ark of the covenant*, which was within the Holy of holies; and they think that he intended to represent Christ as the antitype of that particular and very special part of the innermost contents of the temple. This has been a favourite view of the import of the word,—being founded on the fact that the term, as it occurs in the Septuagint, is almost always used as the designation of that golden cover. (See Exod. xxv. 17, 18, 19, 20, 22; xxx. 6; xxxi. 7; xxxv. 11; xxxvii. 6, 7, 8, 9; xxxix, 35; xl. 18. Lev. xvi. 2, 13, 14, 15; Numb. vii. 89.) In the only other passage, moreover, in which the term occurs in the New Testament, viz. Heb. ix. 5, it has its customary Septuagintal reference:—"and over it (viz., the ark of the covenant) the cherubims of glory shadowing *the mercy-seat*," (for such is the translation of the term in our English Authorized Version). Philo, too, refers to the lid of the ark as a symbol of propitiatory power, and as being called ἱλαστήριον. (He says,—*τῆς δ' ἵλεω δυνάμεως, τὸ ἐπίθεμα τῆς κιβωτοῦ. καλεῖ δ' αὐτὸ ἱλαστήριον. De Profugis*, p. 465, ed. 1691: and again, p. 668, *De vita Mosis*, he says, speaking of the ark, *ἧς ἐπίθεμα ὡσανεὶ πῶμα τὸ λεγόμενον ἐν ἱεραῖς βίβλοις ἱλαστήριον,—ὅπερ ἔοικεν εἶναι σύμβολον, φυσικώτερον μὲν, τῆς ἵλεω τοῦ θεοῦ δυνάμεως*·—he then proceeds to give his "ethical" or mystical interpretation of its import.) It is supposed by the expositors referred to that it was Christ, viewed in his propitiatory relation, and as the Protector of the honour of the law, who was typified by the *ark's lid*, or, the "mercy-seat." Hence, it is supposed, the cherubim, who were on either side of it, overshadowing it with their outspread wings, had their faces toward it, (Exod. xxv. 20), "desiring to look into" the wonders which were involved in his person and work (1 Pet. i. 12). And hence, too, the Lord said to Moses,—"there will I meet with thee, and I will commune with thee from above the mercy-seat, from between the two cherubims which are upon the ark of the testimony, of all things which I will give thee in commandment unto the children of Israel." (Exod. xxv. 22.) Afterwards,—when the affairs of the Judaic theocracy were fully set in order,—it was only once a year, and on the great day of atonement, that the Holy of holies was entered, and the mercy-seat approached. Peculiar solemnities were observed on the occasion. They are particularly described in Lev. xvi. The high priest, who alone was allowed to enter, had first to sacrifice a bullock, as a sin-offering for himself and his house; and then, taking incense within the vail, "that the cloud of incense might cover *the mercy-seat* (τὸ ἱλαστήριον) that was upon the testimony, that he die not," he was to "take of the blood of the bullock, and sprinkle it with his finger *upon the mercy-seat*, (ἐπὶ τὸ ἱλαστήριον), eastward," and "seven times *before the mercy-seat*," (κατὰ πρόσωπον τοῦ ἱλαστηρίου). It is added,—"Then shall he kill the goat of the sin-offering, that is for the people, and bring his blood within the vail, and do with that blood as he did with the blood of the bullock, and sprinkle it *upon the mercy-seat*, (ἐπὶ τὸ ἱλαστήριον), and *before the mercy-seat*, (κατὰ πρόσωπον τοῦ ἱλαστηρίου). And he shall make an atonement for the holy place, because of the uncleanness of the children of Israel, and because of their transgressions in all their sins; and so shall he do for the tabernacle of the congregation that remaineth among them in the midst of their uncleanness." (Lev. xvi. 11—16.)

Christ, it is supposed, is the true "mercy-seat," (the true

ἱλαστήριον), and as such, it is contended, is he referred to by the Apostle in the passage before us. This was the opinion of Origen, who certainly throws the reins on the neck of his imagination, and strikes, besides, his sharpest spurs into its sides, when he sets himself to describe the analogy that subsisted between the type and the antitype. He thinks, for example, that it is said that the cherubim were "in the two ends," and not said that they were upon *the right and left sides*, of the golden cover, because there is nothing *but what is right*—nothing sinister (*sinistrum nihil*)—in the soul of Christ. Chrysostom took apparently the same view of the word. Erasmus thinks that he did. It is certain that Theodoret took it, and Œcumenius and Theophylact. Luther too: He translates the word "throne of grace," (*welchen Gott hat vorgestellt zu einem Gnadenstuhl, whom God has set forth as a throne of grace.* See Heb. iv. 16). Tyndale gives the same translation,—*a seat of mercy.* Calvin leans, upon the whole, to the same interpretation. Peter Martyr approves of it, and Musculus. Mussus thinks it not improbable. Grotius adopts it. Cocceius decides for it. Vitringa contends earnestly for it, and is indeed very positive about it. (See his Tractate *De mysterio aurei arcae operculi*, and his *Commentary*, in which last he says, *Doch daar kan niet aan getwijfelt worden, omdat de Apostel dit woord gebruikt heeft, 't welke alleen aan de Grieksche Joden bekent was, of hy neemt het in de self de sin, in welke het by haar aangenomen was.*) Wolf is of the same opinion. Wetstein, too, assumes the interpretation, and gives some quotations to show that the Rabbis recognized some great mystery in the furniture of the Holy of holies. Bugenhagen, Ferus, and Crell, before Wetstein, took the same view; and Schlichting, and Felbinger, and John Locke;—and these were followed by the moderns of their school,—Taylor, Newcome, Wakefield, Belsham, Jones, &c. Hammond, too, maintains the same interpretation, (though he errs in saying that the Hebrew כַּפֹּרֶת is "indifferently rendered in the Old Testament ἱλαστήριον and καταπέτασμα;" being misled no doubt by Exod. xxvi. 34 and xxx. 6, in which two passages the

Septuagint translator had read כַּפֹּרֶת instead of פָּרֹכֶת). Deyling contends earnestly and elaborately for it. (See his *De Christo ἱλαστηρίῳ*, in which, however, he strangely maintains that the blood of atonement was not sprinkled *on* the *ἱλαστήριον*, but merely before it.) Venema pleads at length for the same view; but, in defending it, he says that on the great day of atonement the typical *ἱλαστήριον* "was exposed before the eyes of all," when the high priest passed through the vail, (*hoc operculum die solennis expiationis, Pontifice velum quasi removente, sanguine conspersum* **ante omnium oculos** *exponebatur*), forgetting that it is expressly said in Lev. xvi. 17, that "there shall be *no man* in the tabernacle of the congregation" when the high priest "goeth in to make an atonement in the holy place." Lavater supports and ingeniously unfolds the same view in two Dissertations, (*de Christo Jesu ἱλαστηρίῳ*). Andreae supplements Lavater's labours in another Dissertation, (*De Christo tanquam fidelium propitiatorio*). Leichfeldt contends for the same view. (*Disput. Theol. de Christo Propitiatorio.*) Seb. Schmidt takes the same view, and also Wolf, Baumgarten, Böhme, Wells, Krebsius, Carpzov, Nösselt, &c. Among more modern interpreters it has been accepted by Bosveld, Olshausen, Philippi, Umbreit, Wardlaw, Brandes, Lange, &c. Tholuck, too, in his 5th edition, settles down into it. In his 4th edition he wavered. In his three preceding editions he gave the preference to another interpretation, to which we shall by and by refer.

In support of this explication of the Apostle's idea it is sometimes alleged, as, for example, by Taylor, Owen, Knight, that "in all other places" in which the word occurs in the Greek Scriptures, whether of the Old Testament or of the New, its reference is to the "mercy-seat," or golden cover of the ark. This, however, is not true. For, not to refer to Amos ix. 1, (where the Septuagint translator had evidently read, by mistake, כַּפֹּרֶת for כַּפְתֹּר), the term is used five times in Ezekiel (viz., xliii. 14, 17, 20) as the translation of the word which is rendered "settle" in our English Version, (viz., עֲזָרָה—a term for a ledge round a large altar). It is not the case, then, that the word has, in Biblical Greek, an absolute or exclusive or monopolizing reference to the cover of the ark of the covenant.

And, on the whole, we are disposed to think that the interpretation, though venerable for its antiquity, and estimable for its evangelical relationships and aspirations, is too narrow, too artificial, and too bizarre to be legitimate. We doubt not, indeed, that the Apostle had in mind the Septuagintal translation of the word that designates the golden cover. We believe, too, that he would regard that cover as constituting an important item in the typical institutions that had relation to Christ Jesus as a propitiator. There is no good reason for supposing with Koppe, de Wette, Rückert, Fritzsche, Bleek, and others, that the Septuagintal translation for the golden cover arose from a misapprehension of the Hebrew noun on the part of the translator. It is evidently from the Pihel verb (כִּפֶּר) that the Hebrew noun (כַּפֹּרֶת) is derived: and that verb, in every instance in which it is used, has reference to *covering* that is connected with *propitiation.* The *covering* which it imports is either *propitiatory* or *propitious.* And doubtless the *covering* of the tables of the law in the ark of the covenant was, and was intended to be, in some way *propitiatory;* for there are insuperable objections to that theory of the "Holy of holies" that makes it merely and absolutely a symbol of Heaven. It is a symbol of heaven as specially and propitiatorily prepared for sinners. The sum-total of the representations in the tabernacle and temple was assuredly either interpenetrated with, or enveloped in, a propitiatory element. Doubtless, then, the cover of the ark was not intended to be *simply a cover.* It was intended to be a *cover* that *covered propitiatorily.* And hence its pihelic name in Hebrew. And hence the translation of that name in Greek;—though the translation,—in consequence of the total absence of the fundamental idea of *covering* in the Greek class of expiatory words,—is an extremely imperfect reproduction and reflection of the Hebrew original. The Greek translator, if using only a single term to render the single term of the original, was constrained, in consequence of the peculiarity of his language, either to suppress the idea of *covering* (ἐπίθεμα or πῶμα) while retaining the idea of *propitiatory*, (ἱλαστήριον), or, *vice versa*, to suppress, as Josephus does (*Ant.* iii. 6. 5), the idea of *propitiatory* (ἱλαστήριον) while retaining the idea of *covering*, (ἐπίθεμα or πῶμα). The Septuagintal translator chose, and chose wisely, the former alternative, inasmuch as it is the *propitiatory* idea that is emphatic in the original word. In Exod. xxv. 17 (16), and in xxxvii. 6, (*ed Comp.*), the two terms are combined,—"propitiatory cover," (ἱλαστήριον ἐπίθεμα). In all other passages the fragmentary expression, "the propitiatory,—" (τὸ ἱλαστήριον), is employed.

But while we would thus vindicate the Septuagintal translation; and while, therefore, we would not lose sight of the idea that the antitype of the *propitiatory cover* is found in the work of Christ, which has, for the sake of sinful men, propitiatorily covered, and thus honoured and magnified, that law on which the throne of the universe is established; we would still regard that cover as being only a part of the typical entirety that represented the full propitiatory element of the work of our Saviour. The sin-offerings, too, were propitiatory. The shedding of their blood was emphatically propitiatory. The sprinkling of the shed blood was propitiatory. The incense, too, was propitiatory. The whole action of the High Priest in connection with the sin-offerings was propitiatory. In order to the fulness of propitiation the life of Christ and the death of Christ required to be combined. His righteousness was indispensable; and so were his sufferings. We do not regard it, therefore, as natural, to understand the word *propitiatory*, in the passage before us, as simply designating the *propitiatory cover* of the ark; and more especially as there is nothing in the surroundings of the word to recal the reference to the "ark," or to indicate the relation of the symbolic cover to the ark's contents. The interpretation is too narrow.

It is to be borne in mind, moreover, that in Heb. ix. 5, and in all the passages of the Septuagint, except that first one (Exod. xxv. 17) in which the making of the propitiatory covering is ordered, the expression is articulated, "*the* propitiatory—," (τὸ ἱλαστήριον). If the reference, in the passage before us, had been to the *propitiatory covering*, we should have expected the definitive article.

And not only so; for as Christ Jesus was not a real and literal *covering*, a real and literal "propitiatory *lid*," we should have expected, if the Apostle were referring to that *lid*, that he would have used some such expression as Theodoret employs when he says that the Apostle teaches us that our Lord is "the *true* propitiatory,—" (διδάσκει τοίνυν ὁ θεῖος ἀπόστολος, ὡς τὸ ἀληθινὸν ἱλαστήριον ὁ Δεσπότης ἐστὶ Χριστός).

And then, besides, it is not natural to represent Christ himself, in the entirety of his personality, as the *propitiatory lid* or *cover* of the ark of the covenant. For that *propitiatory lid* or *cover* was the throne of the Shekinah. And it is no more natural to regard Christ, in the entirety of his personality, as the throne of the Godhead, or of the Father, than it would be, with Grotius, to regard the Godhead or the Father as constituting the throne of the Son. (See on Heb. i. 8.) It is *the propitiatory work* of Christ, in one of its elements,—his *active obedience to the law*, as we presume, (his *gehoorsaamheit*,–Vitringa),—which is the natural antitype of the propitiatory cover of the ark; and as it is on the ground of that *work*,—the actual active righteousness of Christ, as connected with his shed blood,—that God acts propitiously toward men, the *work* might be represented,—but certainly not *Christ himself* in his entire personality,—as *the mercy-seat*. It is no more necessary, and no more natural, to regard *the propitiatory lid* as representing Christ in his entire personality, than it would be to regard *the propitiatory blood* as also the type of the entire personality of our Saviour. The Apostle, however, in the passage before us, is speaking, not of the work of Christ as such, but of Christ himself:—"*whom* God set forth as propitiatory."

But, whatever may be thought of this reasoning, it is certain that Luther's translation of our word, "Gnadenstuhl," and Tyndale's kindred translation, "a seate of mercy," are altogether inappropriate. For neither in the Greek expression,—whether viewed in its fragmentary or in its complete form, (τὸ ἱλαστήριον or τὸ ἱλαστήριον ἐπίθεμα),—nor in the original Hebrew word, (כַּפֹּרֶת), is there the shadow of a shade of reference to "stool," or "throne," or "seat." This is utterly fatal to the accuracy of the translation. And besides, it is more than either "grace" or "mercy" that is referred to. It is *propitiatoriness.* God was gracious and merciful in sending Christ Jesus: but now that Christ Jesus has come, and lived, and suffered, and died, he is *propitiated* and therefore *propitious,* willing and ready to forgive, and to justify, and to glorify.

In conclusion, as regards this interpretation, we would say, not indeed with Rückert, that the time is now almost come when it should be passed by in silent contempt, or only referred to as an exegetical curiosity, (*diese Ansicht ist schon längst mit so vielen und so haltbaren Gründen bestritten worden, dass es bald an der Zeit zu seyn scheint, sie mit Stillschweigen zu bedecken, oder höchstens als Ballast ihrer Sonderbarkeit wegen mit fortzuführen*); but that it is certainly too narrow, too artificial, and too one-sided to satisfy the requirements of the Apostle's exposition of his great evangelical theme.

(4.) A large proportion of expositors suppose that the Apostle's word means *a propitiatory sacrifice.* They would regard it,—at all events the majority of them,—as having been originally an elliptical expression,—an adjective, (having for its understood complement some such word as θῦμα, ἱερόν, ἱερεῖον); but they think that it ultimately settled itself, in conventional usage, into the independent status of a noun. (They compare it with such expressions as καθάρσιον, or, in the plural, καθάρσια, χαριστήριον or χαριστήρια, σωτήρια, ἐπινίκια, διαβατήρια, τελεστήρια, γενέθλια, εὐαγγέλια, &c. &c.) Meyer alleges that Chrysostom took this view of the expression. The "golden-mouthed" father, at all events, according to him, regarded the Apostle's word as exhibiting our Saviour in the light of the antitype of the Mosaic sacrifices, (*den Antitypus der Thieropfer*). But it is more probable, as we have already indicated, that Chrysostom referred to the typical cover of the ark. His expression is quite indefinite, (καὶ ἱλαστήριον δι' αὐτὸ τοῦτο καλεῖ, δεικνὺς ὅτι εἰ ὁ τύπος τοσαύτην εἶχεν ἰσχὺν, πολλῷ μᾶλλον ἡ ἀλήθεια τὸ αὐτὸ ἐπιδείξεται,—*and he calls him for this same reason* ἱλαστήριον, *showing that if the type had such power, much more would the reality exhibit the same*). Le Clerc advocates the interpretation. Bos assumes it, (**Ellips.** *sub* θῦμα). Turretin prefers it. Rollock long before assumed it. Elsner takes the same view. So does Heumann. So Kypke. Michaelis introduces it into his Translation, (*zum Versöhnopfer*). It is defended by Koppe, Flatt, Storr, (**Opusc.** i. 190—1), Klee, de Wette, Reiche, Stuart. Terrot renders the expression "an expiatory sacrifice." Stolz gives a similar rendering, (*zum söhnopfer*). Köllner decides for the same interpretation. So does Meyer. So does Fritzsche, who, in reference to the *golden-cover* interpretation, exclaims, "Valeat absurda explicatio!" Greve, in his Free Translation, coincides with Stolz and Köllner, (*zoenoffer*). Chalmers says that the word "rather signifies the offering itself, than the place in which the blood of the offering was sprinkled." Van Ess introduces the interpretation into his translation, (*zum Sühnopfer*). Krehl, Baumgarten-Crusius, Oltramare, Bisping, Maier, Turner, decide for the same view. So does Tischendorf, (*De vi mortis Christi Satisfactoria*, p. 17). Ewald introduces it into his translation, (*zum Sühnopfer*). So does Schott, (*tanquam sacrificium quod vim haberet expiandi*). So does Conybeare, (*to be a propitiatory sacrifice*). Schleusner defends it in his Lexicon, though he draws somewhat on his imagination for authorities. Alford, as so frequently on Romans, echoes de Wette. Rilliet translates it "an expiatory victim," (*une victime expiatoire*). Many other critics accord.

It is undoubtedly, *in substance at least*, and *so far as doctrinal exegesis* is concerned, the correct interpretation of the Apostle's expression. If Christ Jesus was "propitiatory" at all, he was propitiatory as a sacrifice. His blood had propitiatory value. All the propitiatory acts of his theanthropic personality pointed to, and terminated in, the shedding of his blood upon "the wooden altar,"—the surrender of his human life as the consummation of his atonement for our sins. That such an idea was present to the Apostle's mind when he dictated the word before us, is put beyond all reasonable question by the very next words, "through faith *in his blood*." And yet there is no decisive evidence that the term in question was ever used substantively to signify *a propitiatory victim* or *sacrifice.* It *may* have been thus used. But there is no decisive evidence that it was.

Many critics, indeed, and some of great name, speak in such a way as to convey the idea that there is abundance of evidence for this substantive use of the word. Tholuck, for instance, speaks confidently; and that not only in his first, second, and third editions, saying that the word is found with this signification "in Josephus and Dio Chrysostom," but in his fourth also, in which he began to sift as well as to gather. He there affirms, on the authority of Winzer and Fritzsche, that the word occurs "in the classics" with the signification of *propitiatory offering.* In his fifth edition he gives no authorities, either primary or secondary, but he speaks confidently of the word as *currently* and *commonly* used by the classics in the signification contended for. (*ἱλαστήριον für Sühnopfer ist im Classischen ein gangbarer Ausdruk.—Das bei Griechen so gewöhnliche ἱλαστήριον.*) Meyer, again, in his first edition, also refers to Dio Chrysostom,—quoting as his authorities for the reference, Bos and Kypke. In his succeeding editions he drops all reference to secondary authorities, and gives the words of Dio himself, though not with perfect accuracy. He added, too, as other primary authorities for the acceptation of the word as a substantive, Nonnus, *Dionys.* 13, p. 382; Josephus, *de Macc.* 17, 20; Hesychius; and the Scholiast on *Apoll. Rhod.* 2, 487. Fritzsche had, in the meantime, appealed to most of the same primary authorities,—quoting the passage from Dio Chrysost. almost as Meyer gives it, and exactly as it is given by Bos, and reproduced by Kypke. De Wette took the same view, as we have seen. He asserts that the word is a substantive, meaning *propitiatory offering;* and he adds that this is demonstrable "from Dio Chrysostom, *Orat.* xi., p. 184, (see Kypke), and Hesychius." Alford so far follows de Wette as to assert that the word is itself a substantive, needing no supplemental substantive, such as *sacrifice* (ϑῦμα), to be tacitly supplied. And he then adds:—"we have this very word in Dio Chrysost. *Orat.* ii., p. 184, (cited by Stuart), where he says that the Greeks offered an ἱλαστήριον τῇ Αθήνᾳ, *a propitiatory sacrifice.*" Turning to Alford's authority, Moses Stuart, we find him asserting, like the other critics we have specified, that ἱλαστήριον, in "the common Greek idiom," stood for ἱλαστήριον ϑῦμα, *propitiatory sacrifice* or *offering:* and he then adds:—"So Dio Chrysostom, *Orat.* ii. 184, ἱλαστήριον 'Αχαιοὶ τῇ 'Αϑηνᾳ̃, *the Greeks* (made) *a propitiatory offering to Minerva.*" He still further adds:—"So Josephus, ἱλαστήριον μνῆμα, *a propitiatory monument,* Antiq. xvi. 7. 1. So in 4 Macc. xvii. 22, ἱλαστηρίου ϑανάτου αὐτοῦ *his propitiatory death.* Symmachus in Gen. vi. 14, ἱλάσεις ἱλαστήριον."

It is in this way that many of the modern critics,—and we might easily have added a troop of other names, such as Oltramare, Krehl, Maier, &c.—dispose of the word ἱλαστήριον, and establish, to the satisfaction of their own minds, that it is a substantive, signifying *a propitiatory sacrifice* or *offering.* All of them, it will be noticed, make capital, either at first or at second hand, of Dio Chrysostom. Let us therefore begin with him.

Bos referred to him,—leading the way. Kypke followed, and then Rosenmüller, Koppe, Tholuck, Winzer, Reiche, Fritzsche, de Wette, Meyer, Stuart, Tischendorf, Alford, &c. Alford seems to trust to him as his mainstay, citing Stuart. He has correctly cited Stuart. But Stuart was unworthy of his confidence. For, in truth, he had never seen Dio Chrysostom; and, merely guessing concerning the passage, he blundered in his notation of it; he blundered, too, in his translation; and he blundered, in addition, in his interpretation of ἱλαστήριον as occurring in the passage. He borrowed the quotation, though without acknowledgement;—apparently either from Kypke or from Koppe. In borrowing it, he unhappily borrowed a mistake as to the notation of the *Oration.* Kypke acknowledges,—like Reiche, and like de Wette in his various editions, and like Meyer in his first edition,—that he borrowed the quotation. He borrowed it from Bos. But, by a mistake of his pen or of his printer, he numbered the *Oration* referred to as ii. instead of 11, or xi. Koppe somehow or other committed the same mistake. Hence, apparently, Stuart's first blunder. Then, in the second place, he translates the quotation as if it were a historical remark of Dio in reference to some fact that had transpired—"the Greeks (made) a propitiatory offering to Minerva." But Dio is not referring, in the passage, to any historical event that had occurred, or that was supposed to have occurred. He does not say that *the Greeks made a propitiatory sacrifice to Minerva.* He is merely recording a *scheme* or *proposal* of Ulysses. And, in the third place, there is not the shadow of a shade of reference to anything of the nature of a *sacrifice* or *sacrificial victim.* Dio represents a proposal supposed to be made by the wily Ulysses to the Trojans, when the Greeks were suing for peace. The Trojans were for insisting that the Greeks should make some atonement (δίκην τινὰ ὑποσχεῖν) for having causelessly waged war. Ulysses denied that the war was causelessly waged. The Greeks were really insulted and provoked. But, added he, if some atonement should, in the circumstances, be really befitting, he himself would devise one. The Greeks, he was ready to pledge himself, *would leave behind them a large and beautiful monumental offering to Minerva,* (καταλείψειν γὰρ αὐτοὺς ἀνάθημα κάλλιστον καὶ μέγιστον τῇ Ἀθηνᾷ), *bearing the inscription,* ἱλαστήριον Ἀχαιοὶ τῇ Ἀθηνᾷ τῇ Ἰλιάδι, or thus,—

ΙΛΑΣΤΗΡΙΟΝ	PROPITIATORY.
ΑΧΑΙΟΙ	THE GREEKS
ΤΗ ΑΘΗΝΑ	TO THE ILIAN
ΤΗ ΙΛΙΑΔΙ	MINERVA.

The terminology of the inscription is, as was common in such cases, abrupt and elliptical. But the meaning is evident:—**This monumental structure is propitiatory. The Greeks have erected it, and dedicate it, to the Guardian Goddess of Ilium.** There is not, as will be at once perceived, any filament of reference to any *victim* or *sacrificial offering.* It would be nearer the truth to say that there is a reference to the famous *wooden horse.* And thus the mainstay of Stuart, Alford, Tholuck, de Wette, &c., &c., for interpreting ἱλαστήριον as in itself meaning *propitiatory sacrifice,* falls to the ground. There is nothing, moreover, in the inscription to establish the idea that ἱλαστήριον is "itself a substantive." The intended erection, or ἀνάθημα, which was to bear the inscription, was the concrete substantive,—the concrete substance,—which was to be adjectively qualified, or defined, or explained, by the word *propitiatory.*

Besides this passage in Dio Chrysostom, appeal is made, in support of the interpretation of the word which we are considering, to a passage in the reputed Josephus *de Maccabeis,* c. xvii.,—the Tractate that is sometimes called the *Fourth Book of Maccabees.* Tholuck, as we have seen, couples, in his first, second, and third editions, a reference to Josephus with his reference to Dio Chrysostom. This is the passage intended. Rosenmüller, Koppe, and Meyer quote it at length. Stuart adduces so much of it as he considered to be of service. The passage runs thus:—"By the blood of these pious ones, καὶ τοῦ ἱλαστηρίου [τοῦ] θανάτου αὐτῶν, divine Providence saved the previously afflicted Israelites." The clause which we have quoted in Greek is supposed to mean, *and by the propitiatory sacrifice of their death.* Krebs, in his *Observations on the New Testament from Flavius Josephus,* thus explains the passage. And it is, as thus explained, and thus only, that it can be regarded as lending some countenance to the notice that ἱλαστήριον is a substantive, meaning *propitiatory sacrifice.* Krebs's explanation of the clause, however, assumes the genuineness of the second article, which we have enclosed in brackets;—an unlikely assumption. The article, indeed, is found in Hudson's edition, and Havercamp's, and Dindorf's; but it is omitted in Weidmann's, 1691; and it is condemned as spurious even by Reiche and Oltramare, although by such a sentence of condemnation they deprive themselves of one of their few authorities for their interpretation of ἱλαστήριον. The genuineness of the article would certainly require to be thoroughly established before we could accept the interpretation of the expression given by Krebs. It seems to be an outré stretch of imagination to represent *the death* of the worthies referred to as being a *propitiatory victim* or *sacrifice.* Even Mehring's interpretation is intolerably violent, philologically, as the other is logically, —*by the propitiatoriness of their death,* (τὸ ἱλαστήριον *für* ἡ ἱλαστηριότης). It is certainly far more likely that the word was used as a simple adjective,—*and by their propitiatory death.* Moses Stuart, as we have seen, quotes the passage in support of his interpretation of ἱλαστήριον. But, in quoting it, he seems to assume the spuriousness of the second article, for he omits it. And yet the wonder is, that, when the passage was thus shorn of its only possible applicability to the end in view,—the support of his opinion that ἱλαστήριον is used substantively, and means *a propitiatory sacrifice,*—he should yet adduce it as evidence. But not only does he adduce it, (though inaccurately;—ἱλαστηρίου θανάτου αὐτοῦ, instead of αὐτῶν), he translates it "his propitiatory death;"—not observing that in this, his own translation, he actually excluded altogether the substantival idea for which he contends, and for the establishment of which he had quoted the passage.—This second mainstay, then, of the interpretation we are considering, breaks down.

A third mainstay is a note of the ancient scholiast on an expression in the 2nd Book of the *Argonautics* of Apollonius Rhodius, l. 487, (λωφήϊα ῥέξαι ἐπ' αὐτῳ | ἱερά). Moses Stuart does not refer to this scholium. But Reiche does, and Fritzsche, and Meyer, and Tischendorf; and Winzer before them. Oltramare, too, quotes it from Fritzsche. The scholiast uses the compound ἐξιλαστήρια to explain Appollonius's λωφήϊα, and it is supposed that this is evidence that ἐξιλαστήριον, and, by consequence, ἱλαστήριον, are substantives meaning *a propitiatory victim* or *sacrifice.* We feel surprised that the evidence should be deemed satisfactory, or as indeed of any weight whatever. A simple inspection of Apollonius makes it evident that λωφήϊα is an adjective. The old man counselled Paraebius to make atonement for the injury his father had done to the nymph. He exhorted him to rear an altar to her, *and to offer on it propitiatory sacrifices*, (λωφήϊα ῥέξαι ἐπ' αὐτῳ ἱερά). Λωφήϊα is thus a mere adjective qualifying ἱερά, *sacrifices*, and hence when the scholiast explains the phrase as a whole, and the word λωφήϊα in particular, (λωφήϊα ῥέξαι.—ἐφ' οἷς λωφήσει καὶ παύσεται ἡ τῆς Νύμφης ὀργή· τουτέστι καταπαυστικὰ τῆς ὀργῆς. λωφήϊα, ἐξιλαστήρια, ἐφ' οἷς λωφήσει καὶ παύσεται κακούμενος), there is no reason to suppose that he ignored the word ἱερά, as qualified by the adjective λωφήϊα, though he does not expressly quote it. We have nothing here to do with the twofold explanation given of the adjective. The first—καταπαυστικὰ τῆς ὀργῆς—is manifestly the only legitimate interpretation of the import of the word.—This third mainstay, then, of the notion that ἱλαστήριον is a noun signifying *a propitiatory sacrifice* has also broken down.

Our authorities are like to vanish from our hands the moment that we touch them. But Fritzsche has one more. And Meyer reproduces it; and Tischendorf. Oltramare, too, cites it, but not, like Meyer, as if at first hand. It is one of the cluster of authorities on which Tholuck rests in his fourth and fifth editions, reposing in the trustworthiness of Fritzsche. Wordsworth, too, has had regard to it. He accepts the interpretation of ἱλαστήριον "which renders it a *sin-offering* or *propitiatory victim;*" and he says in support of his choice,—"See the authorities in Fritz. p. 193, and in Meyer, de Wette, and Alf." Such is his array. But Alford's one authority, as we have seen, was Dio Chrysostom as quoted by Stuart. *It* has vanished. De Wette's main authority was the same Dio. But he has, in addition, a little subsidiary authority, which we shall consider forthwith. Meyer rests on five authorities,—Dio; Josephus de Macc.; Apollonius; the passage we are about to cite; and de Wette's small subsidiary addendum. Fritzsche overlooks this small subsidiary addendum; and thus his only remaining support is the passage we are about to consider. It is from the *Dionysiaca* of Nonnus, Lib. xiii. p. 382, v. 9,—ἱλαστήρια Γοργοῦς. But it was too bad in Fritzsche to stick down, at perfect random, such a quotation, as having a bearing on the subject in hand, thus leading, they knew not well whither, Meyer, Tholuck, Oltramare, Wordsworth, &c. The expression as given by Fritzsche is a *mere conjectural reading*, proposed by Falkenburg, and approved of by Moser, in lieu of an unintelligible expression in the text. Cunaeus gives another conjectural reading,—ἱερὰ ῥεύματα Γοργοῦς, and he had as good a right to his conjecture as Falkenburg had to his. The expression in Nonnus (xiii. 517) is, ἱκαστήρια Γοργοῦς. "I know not what it means," says Graefe, (*quae sint* ἱκαστήρια Γοργοῦς *plane ignoro*). But to suppose that Nonnus's expression could be *the propitiatory victims* or *sacrifices of the Gorgon* is utterly incongruous. The author is describing certain localities occupied by the Phrygians; and after specifying Budias, Temenias, Dresia, Obrimus, and the land of Doias, he adds the auriferous Celaenae, καὶ ἱκαστήρια Γοργοῦς. Whatever be his meaning, it may certainly be taken for granted that the Phrygians did not inhabit the *propitiatory sacrifices of the Gorgon*. Thus this authority, too, breaks down.

De Wette, as we have observed, has a small subsidiary reference in support of his interpretation of ἱλαστήριον. He says that the substantival import of the word, as meaning *a propitiatory sacrifice*, is demonstrable "from Dio Chrysostom *and Hesychius*." Meyer, too, appeals to Hesychius. So did Koppe before them both. But the appeal is entirely futile. Hesychius's explanation of ἱλαστήριον is καθάρσιον, θυσιαστήριον. With the latter word we have at present nothing to do. It is puzzling enough. But as to the former, it assuredly cannot determine anything in the present controversy; for καθάρσιον is not only an adjective in its essential nature, it is used in good Greek *adjectively* as well as *substantively*, and more frequently adjectively. Alberti supposes that Hesychius is explaining the meaning of ἱλαστήριον in its common Septuagintal application, as a designation of *the golden covering of the ark*. Be this as it may, it is obvious, at all events, that the lexicographer's explanation is no proof at all of the substantival import of ἱλαστήριον. And yet, in consequence of this word καθάρσιον, Hesychius is actually set down by Heumann as holding, along with "Grotius, Hammond, Clericus, Elsner, Beausobre, Bos, Turretin," &c., that the Apostle meant by ἱλαστήριον, *propitiatory sacrifice.* And in Tholuck's first three editions a corresponding but somewhat more accurate string of authorities is thus given,—"Hesych., Grotius, Clericus, Kypke, Elsner, Heumann, &c."

Strangely enough, Moses Stuart has adduced, in support of his view, another passage still,—a passage from the genuine Josephus, *Antiq.* xvi. 7, 1, ἱλαστήριον μνῆμα, *a propitiatory monument.* The expression is a real one. Stuart's translation is a correct one. The reference of the historian is to Herod, who had got a fright when sacrilegiously attempting to pillage the tomb of David. In consequence of the check which he had thus received, he erected, says Josephus, in white marble, at the mouth of the sepulchre, *a propitiatory monument of his fright,* (τοῦ δέους ἱλαστήριον μνῆμα), that is, *a monument of his fright, which was intended to be of atoning value.* The passage is an interesting and important one. But how it could ever have occurred to Stuart to adduce it to prove that ἱλαστήριον is used substantively, as signifying *a propitiatory sacrifice,* is beyond our power of imagination to conceive.

In his later editions Stuart adds to his list of testimonies an expression from Symmachus's version of Gen. vi. 14. Winzer had adduced the expression in 1829. It is also referred to by Reiche. That phrase in the Hebrew which is rendered in our version *thou shalt pitch with pitch,* is, it seems, rendered by Symmachus ἱλάσεις ἱλαστηρίῳ. It is, however, a rendering so outré that nothing can be made of it, at least for the determination of the import of ἱλαστήριον in Rom. iii. 25.

Le Clerc, it would appear, was running in the right tract when he said that he had not met, in his readings, with any instance of the substantival use of ἱλαστήριον, in the sense which he attached to it in the passage before us. The only authority that he could think of, that had any relevancy, was the interpretation which is given to the word in the Old Onomasticon, namely *propitiabile.* He refers to the ancient Glossary published by Labbeus; and he supposed that *propitiabile* is to be understood actively,—*able to propitiate.* But this is nothing to the point. It affords no evidence whatsoever that ἱλαστήριον means a *propitiatory sacrifice.*

The result of our investigation is, that there is no passage yet adduced in which our word, ἱλαστήριον, is used as a substantive signifying *a propitiatory sacrifice.* This is all the more remarkable, as there is no lack of similar adjectives which are used substantively in the manner referred to;—no lack, at all events, of such words in the plural number. (See καθάρσια, ἐπινίκια, εὐαγγέλια, &c.) The phraseological relations, moreover, of ἱλαστήριον are so very intimately connected with what has reference to atonement or expiation, that one would have expected abundant instances in the classics of its specific substantival employment, if it had really been made use of to designate a *propitiatory sacrifice.*

In these circumstances it would, we apprehend, be unwise to insist that the term should be translated, substantively, *a propitiatory sacrifice.* The idea, indeed, that underlies this translation, and that constitutes the whole pith and marrow of the doctrine that is infolded in it, was, as we have already indicated, undoubtedly present to the Apostle's mind. But it would appear that he inwrapped the idea in the folds of a term that is ampler in its reference than the proposed translation. He inwrapped it in the ample folds of an adjective, retaining its primary adjectival import and force:—"whom he set forth *propitiatory,*" that is, "whom he set forth *as propitiatory;*"—as propitiatory, namely, in the special and distinctive relations of his glorious theanthropic personality. That the word might thus be used adjectivally is beyond a doubt. The passage quoted from the reputed Josephus is evidence. The passage quoted from the real Josephus, *Antiq.* xvi. 7. 1, is incontestable evidence. The Septuagintal passage, Exod.

xxv. 17, in which the expression *propitiatory cover* (ἱλαστήριον ἐπίθεμα) occurs, is also incontestable evidence. So is the passage which Hase quotes in Stephens's *Thesaurus* from Nicephorus, (χεῖρας ἱκετηρίους, εἰ βούλει δὲ ἱλαστηρίους, ἐκτείνας θεῷ.—*Vita Symeon. Stylit.* in Actt. SS. Maii t. 5, p. 335, 17). There can thus be no doubt of the actual conventional usage of the word as employed adjectively. And its simple adjectival force in the passage before us is really all that can be desired. It is, in substance, approved of by Winzer, Matthias, and Mehring. It comprehends, and harmonizes, indeed, all that is aimed at in all the other interpretations; but it embraces them in the ampler folds of that indefinite applicability that is characteristic of its own peculiar adjectival import. If Christ Jesus be set forth as *propitiatory,* then it must be true that he was set forth as *a propitiator*, and set forth as *a propitiation*, and set forth as *a propitiatory sacrifice*, and set forth, too, as *the antitypical fulfilment of all the symbols of propitiation that were divinely instituted under preceding dispensations.* It was Christ himself, in his theanthropic personality, that was thus *propitiatory.* He was, in his intermingled *satisfactio* and *satispassio*, the meritorious cause of God's relation of propitiousness to the human family. It is in consideration of his propitiation that God, as the Moral Governor of the universe, is willing and is ready to forgive and to justify all such of the "ungodly" as will be induced to take up, by means of faith in the propitiator, that one mental position that will insure their voluntary reception of such divine influences as are needed to renew the heart and assimilate the character to the archetypal character of God.

The work of Christ Jesus, as propitiator, was that "ransom," (that λύτρον or ἀντίλυτρον), which he paid "for many," "for all,"—for *the multitudinous all,*—and on the ground of which there is that "redemption" which is spoken of at the conclusion of the preceding verse. It is a "ransom,"—a "price,"—*something precious* and *to be prized.* It *is prized* by God. It is *of unspeakable value* in the estimation of God. And in consideration of its incalculable value in moral government, as a thing that is so precious as to be more than an equivalent for the demands of strict justice in relation to transgressors of law, God,—even while realizing all the claims that lie upon him as the Great Moral Governor of the universe,—is willing to forgive the guiltiest of the guilty, and to render them heirs of everlasting life. But the word *propitiation*,—as comprehended in the word *propitiatory*,—is more expansive in its import than the words *ransom* and *price*; and it is better fitted, therefore, to bring into view some of the wide governmental principles that are involved in the unique phenomenon of the terrestrial life and violent death of Him who was both God and man,—"God manifest in flesh." Propitiation assumes, indeed, that the Great Moral Governor,—considered personally, and as distinct from his abstract Moral Government,—has been displeased. It assumes that he has been greatly offended. And greatly offended God has really been;—offended at rebellion and with rebels. His infinite heart has been stirred. His infinite conscience has been aroused. His holy indignation has sprung up and gone forth. But other feelings and other principles were at work all the time, and thence arose the idea and the scheme of propitiation. In the accepted propitiation the divine anger has been so turned away that God is now willing, and ready, and eager to forgive the guiltiest of the guilty, treating them for eternity as if they had never sinned. He is willing, ready, and eager, in consideration of the propitiation, to render them who had madly made themselves liable to everlasting death the heirs of everlasting life. The propitiatory work of Christ is thus that great unique fact in the divine moral government, in consideration of which God, as the Great Moral Governor, is willing and ready to forgive. Such is its essential nature. But let it ever be borne in mind that it was in virtue of a self-originated desire in the divine heart, —a desire to be willing to forgive,—that God Himself devised the scheme of propitiation.

§ 5. *through faith in his blood*, (διὰ πίστεως ἐν τῷ αὐτοῦ αἵματι). The clausule, "through faith," (διὰ πίστεως), is omitted in the Alexandrian Manuscript (A). And it is not made use of by Chrysostom in his exposition. It is omitted also from his text in Matthaei's codices. Mill says that he does not doubt that it has stealthily crept in from the 22nd verse, or from other passages of the epistle, (*illud* διὰ πίστεως *irrepsisse haud dubito ex* v. 22, *aliisve locis hujus epistolae.* –Prol. § 691). Locke thinks that the omission is "conformable to the sense of the Apostle." Matthaei, too, could suppose that the clausule had been imported for the sake of explication: but he would not modify the text in the face of such overwhelming manuscriptural authority, (*Sunt haec ita comparata, ut facile quis credat, explicandi caussa illata esse. Sed contra tot Codd. nihil tentandum videtur*). He is right in the conclusion to which he comes. For assuredly there is no legitimate ground, either internal or external, for suspecting the genuineness of the clause. Whitby had good reason for objecting to the soundness of Mill's judgement in this instance, (*judicium hic parvi facio.* –Examen. p. 57). Nevertheless Belsham considered himself justified in striking out the clause, and saying nothing about it. The copy of the epistle which Ambrosiaster must have had before him would seem to have been here imperfect. The preposition is omitted, though the word "faith" is retained, (*quem proposuit Deus propitiatorem fidei*). This corruption of the integrity of the clausule on the one hand, and its omission on the other, may be sufficiently accounted for on the ground either of accident, or of intentional attempt to relieve the text from a supposed confusion of ideas or perplexity of structure. In reality, however, there is neither confusion nor perplexity.

Another remark about the text. In the Stephano-Elzevirian text the article is inserted between the preposition *through* and the word *faith*, (διὰ τῆς πίστεως). And this reading is supported by B E K L, and the great majority of cursive mss. It is also found in the texts of Theodoret and Œcumenius. But the article is wanting in ℵ C D F G, 31, 80, &c., and is omitted by Eusebius, Basil, Cyril, Damascene, and Theophylact, and, what is of special moment, it is omitted by Origen in the three passages of his extant

Greek writings in which the passage is quoted. (See *Com.* on Matt., Tom. xii. 21; on John, Tom. i. 23, 38.) Griesbach suspected that it was spurious; and it has been omitted from the text by both Lachmann and Tischendorf. Alford, too, omits it. On the whole, the evidence is in favour of its omission: although this is one of the cases in which there is almost an equipoise of authorities. And, happily, it is one of the cases in which it is not of the slightest exegetical or doctrinal moment whether of the two readings be assumed. If the article be omitted, faith is spoken of indefinitely, and its specific reference as Christian faith is to be determined from what follows, or from the nature of the case. If, again, the article be inserted, the finger of the Apostle is, as it were, directly pointed to the Christian faith, of which he had already spoken, (ver. 22; chap. i. 16, 17), and with which, as was well known, he had specially to do as an Apostle of Christ Jesus. It was evidently a matter that lay almost indifferently at the option of the inspired writer,—to employ either the more or the less definitive mode of reference. And in other cases he sometimes,—and without any ascertainable doctrinal significance, —adopts the one mode of reference, and sometimes the other. See ver. 30. In English, our idiom will not permit us to make any difference in our translation, whether the article be present or absent in the original.

We accept, then, the clausule—"through faith;" and we accept it in its more indefinite reference. But how is it to be connected with what goes before? Baumgarten, D. G. Herzog, and Reiche suppose that the preceding part of the verse is parenthetical, and that the clausule is therefore to be added, as in a row, to the clausules of the 24th verse, being, equally with them, dependent on the participle "justified:"—"being justified freely by his grace through the redemption which is in Christ Jesus,—through faith." But this method of construction is inadmissible, inasmuch as the second half of the 25th verse, "for the manifestation of his righteousness, &c.," is obviously dependent on the expression, "whom he set forth as propitiatory;" which expression, therefore, cannot be parenthetical. Philippi connects the clausule with the verb *set forth*:—"whom he set publicly forth—through faith:"—an unlikely interlinking, though he explains himself as meaning that the forth-setting is "realized subjectively through faith," (*realisirt subjectiver Seits durch den Glauben*). The explanation is good; but the forth-setting itself was certainly altogether independent of human faith. It was a divine act which historically transpired more than eighteen hundred years ago. It was nothing but an act,—an act, in a double sense, transient. And in no legitimate sense or reference was it conditioned on the intermediacy of the sinner's faith.

There can be no doubt that the great body of expositors are right in attaching the clausule in question to the word *propitiatory*, (ἱλαστήριον). In *attaching* it, we say. For there is rather an adherence of notions than an intimate inter-knitting of ideas. The Apostle means that the propitiatoriness of Christ is, so far as its blissful results are concerned, realized by the sinner *through faith*. The Propitiation enters as a power within the precincts of the sinner's personality, so as to result in redemption or pardon, and justification, and eternal life, only when it is apprehended by faith. It is thus the case that Christ Jesus, as propitiatory, is available to sinners—through faith, and only through faith. The Apostle's idea might be exhibited thus:—"whom God set publicly forth as propitiatory,—*available as such,—realizable,—through faith*," or, as Day represents it, "*to be enjoyed and made ours through faith*." The attachment of clauses is, both phraseologically and doctrinally, akin to the expression in ver. 22—"God's righteousness through faith of Jesus Christ." God's evangelical righteousness is evangelical righteousness whether believed in or not. It is also evangelical righteousness for sinners, and free to them all, whether they have faith in it or not. But it is not "on them," unless they apprehend it by faith. They are not justified on the ground of it, until they believe. So the propitiation of Christ is a propitiation, whether believed in or not. But it issues not in that actual pardon of the sinner which, so far as its relation to man is concerned, is its normal aim and end, until it be apprehended by faith, (—faith as the *causa apprehendens* of the propitiation,—the ὄργανον ἀντιληπτικόν). The propitiation may be regarded as characterized by polarity of aim. At one of its poles,—the pole which points in the direction of the divine readiness to forgive,—it is unconditionally fixed. At its other pole,—the pole which points in the direction of the actual eventuation of forgiveness,—it is unfixed, until the sinner's receptivity for ulterior and purificatory influences is secured by the act of faith.

The Apostle adds to the expression *through faith*, the words *in his blood*, (ἐν τῷ αὐτοῦ αἵματι). The words are regarded by not a few critics as forming a distinct co-ordinate clausule, which is to be directly attached either to the word *propitiatory* or to the verb *set forth*. Baumgarten, indeed, and Reiche, think that it is to be connected with the participle *justified* in the preceding verse. Apart from this extreme view, however, Wetstein says, "these words are to be separated by a comma, both from those which succeed and from those which precede," (*Haec verba commate distinguenda sunt a sequentibus et praecedentibus*). Crell and Schlichting take the same view. Limborch prefers it. Jowett decides for it. Long before them Erasmus seems to have taken the same view. He translates the expression absolutely,—"his blood intervening," (*interveniente ipsius sanguine*). Vorstius adopts the rendering. In Cranmer's Bible there is a comma after "thorow faith," and then the clausule before us is translated "by the meanes of hys bloude." In Nösselt's edition of Theodoret, and in the Oxford edition of 1852, a comma is inserted, in the text, after the word *faith*. Conybeare, in his translation, makes a considerable transposition, connecting the words in question with the verb *set forth*:—"Him hath God set forth, in his blood, to be a propitiatory sacrifice by means of faith." Mehring makes a similar transposition; only he connects the words with the adjective *propitiatory*, (*welchen Gott dargegeben hat als die Kraft, durch den Glauben zu versöhnen, in seinem Blute habend*). With Mehring agree Schrader, Glöckler, Köllner, Matthias,

Vaughan, &c. With Conybeare agrees Meyer. And of substantially the same opinion are Vitringa, de Wette, Alford, and the Five Clergymen, who connect the words *in his blood* with the whole expression *whom God set forth as propitiatory.* In the existing Latin translation of Origen's *Homilies* on Leviticus the two clausules are transposed,—"whom God hath set a propitiator in his blood through faith," (*quem posuit Deus propitiatorem in sanguine ipsius per fidem.* Hom. ix., p. 351, *Tom.* ix. *ed. Lom.*) Beza is said by de Wette to approve of the separation of the two expressions. He is, on the other hand, adduced by Meyer as approving of the interblending of the two. The truth is that he wavered somewhat between the two interpretations; but certainly he never decided for the interblending of the expressions. In his first edition he spoke decisively in favour of keeping them apart,—connecting the second of the expressions with *propitiatory,* not with *faith.* (*Haec refero ad* ἱλαστήριον, *potius quam ad* προέθετο *vel ad* πίστεως.) In his second edition he began to hesitate. In his third his hesitation continued. Nevertheless, in both of these editions, he interposes a comma after *faith.* In his fourth edition he continued in his state of hesitation, but he removed the comma. In his fifth and last edition he still omitted the comma, but continued undecided, though on the whole he tended somewhat strongly in the direction of his early determination, (for he says, for the first time, in this edition, that if we should connect *in his blood* with *faith,* we should render the former expression in Latin, *in sanguinem;* whereas he gives it in all his editions, *in sanguine,* with the exception of the first, in which he paraphrastically renders it *fuso sanguine suo*). Some critics, such as Day, Wolf, &c., attempt to hook the expression *in his blood* by two distinct links, both to the proximate expression *through faith,* and to the more remote *propitiatory.* It is a clumsy coalition of ideas, and compromise of interpretations. Benecke and van Hengel separate the two expressions, but they regard them both as terminating in their reference on him who was *propitiatory.* He was propitiatory *by means of his faithfulness:* He was propitiatory *by means of his blood.* It is an interpretation that squeezes the Apostle's phraseology as in an iron vice.

There is really no necessity for having recourse to any hyperbaton or strain. There is no good reason why we should hesitate, even for a moment, to regard the words *in his blood* as pointing out the object on which the faith specified in the preceding expression terminates, and in which it reposes:—*through faith in his blood.* It is true, indeed, that the same expression does not elsewhere occur. But if we are never to accept an expression unless it be a repetition, we shall never get at all to a beginning of expressions. It is also true that Heumann, Koppe, Flatt, and others are guilty of critical licentiousness when they say that the Apostle, in exhibiting the object of faith, uses the preposition *in* (ἐν) for *unto* (εἰς). They have no right to allege such a commutation of prepositions;—although it is the case that, when the act of believing in relation to Christ is mentioned in the New Testament, it is connected with its object, generally, by means of the preposition *unto* (εἰς):—for the act of believing is represented as something going out *toward* Christ, and reaching *to* him. But when it reaches *to* him, it does not flit *from* him. It rests. It reposes *on* and *in* him. And hence the use, in the expression before us, of the preposition *in.* It occurs again in Eph. i. 15,—"faith *in* the Lord Jesus Christ;" Col. i. 4; 1 Tim. iii. 13; 2 Tim. iii. 15. Comp. Mark i. 15, (πιστεύετε ἐν τῷ εὐαγγελίῳ). It is likewise true that if the article before the word *faith* in the Stephano-Elzevirian text be genuine, we might have had a repetition of it before the expression *in his blood,* (διὰ τῆς πίστεως τῆς ἐν τῷ αὐτοῦ αἵματι). Comp. ver. 24, (διὰ τῆς ἀπολυτρώσεως τῆς ἐν τῷ Χριστῷ Ἰησοῦ). We *might* have had this repetition:—*the faith which is in his blood.* But we *might not;* for the whole expression, instead of being regarded by the Apostle as two-plied, might have been viewed as a unit:—*the faith in his blood,* i. e., *the thing, which is faith-in-his-blood.* Comp. Col. i. 4, (ἀκούσαντες τὴν πίστιν ὑμῶν ἐν Χριστῷ Ἰησοῦ); Eph. i. 15; &c. (And conf. Winer *Gram.* iii. 20. 2: and Fritzsche, in loc.)

De Wette and Alford say that it is necessary to disconnect the expression *in his blood* from the expression *through faith*, and to connect it with the preceding expression, *whom he set forth as propitiatory*, inasmuch as the succeeding expression, *for demonstration of his righteousness* (εἰς ἔνδειξιν τῆς δικαιοσύνης αὐτοῦ) "directly refers to it," and hinges on it. De Wette refers to Meyer in confirmation of this idea. But the reference, in this case, is of no moment. For Meyer's notion on the subject is not the result of his hermeneutics or philology, but the outworking of his theological theory. It is in short a mere opinion, unsubstantiated by any real evidence, philological, hermeneutical, philosophical, theological, or Scriptural.

Pelagius, Luther, and Calvin are obviously right in regarding the words in question, viz., *in his blood*, as designating the object of the faith which issues in justification. Every other construction is violent. Seb. Schmidt and Cocceius look at the words in the same light: and so, among more modern critics, do Winzer, Rückert, Olshausen, Tholuck, Tischendorf, Oltramare, Maier, &c. "Faith," as John Brown of Wamphray says, "looks for acceptance to nothing in itself, but goes quite out of a man's self, and rests upon the merits and death of Christ as only satisfactory to justice, and through which it expects to be accepted of God:—therefore it is *faith in his blood*." It is not, indeed, to be supposed that justifying faith fixes upon the blood of the Propitiator, simply because of the vital peculiarity or the peculiar vitality of blood, when viewed physiologically, as an element of the organization of the human body. There is a substrate of this implied in justifying faith. But it is not to the blood of Jesus, as merely running in his human veins, that faith has respect. It is to his blood as sacrificially shed. It is, in other words, to the surrender of his human life as the culmination of his terrestrial obedience, that faith refers. It is thus to his "obedience until death,"—his obedience subliming itself in death, or, reversely, to his "death" as instinct with the sublime moral element of "obedience,"—that justifying faith has respect. Faith looks to our Lord's glorious "passive righteousness," as animated with his perfect "active righteousness," which perfect active righteousness alone could sublime the passive righteousness into an atonement unspeakably meritorious. The sum-total of the ingredients of Christ's "passive righteousness," as animated and sublimed by his "active righteousness," was supererogatory. Christ was a supererogatory or superinduced member of the human race. His active and passive righteousness, in our human nature, was not for himself. It was for us. It was substitutionary. "He was wounded for *our* transgressions; he was bruised for *our* iniquities; the chastisement of *our* peace was upon him; that with his stripes *we* might be healed." (Isai. liii. 5.) He was made "a curse *for us*." (Gal. iii. 13.) The surrender of his life was the consummation of his propitiatory sacrifice. And hence it is that he is available in so far as he was propitiatory,—available to us for redemption, for pardon, for justification,—"through faith *in his blood*."

Though the same expression does not elsewhere occur, yet the New Testament is strewn with expressions which indicate that justifying faith must have either explicit or implicit reference to Christ's sacrificial oblation of his life. The glorified sing, "Thou hast redeemed us to God *by thy blood*." (Rev. v. 9.) The believing on earth say, "Unto him that loved us, and washed us from our sins *in his own blood*, &c., be glory and dominion for ever and ever. Amen." (Rev. i. 5.) They believe that "*the blood of Jesus Christ*, God's Son, cleanseth them from all sin." (1 John i. 7.) They are "elect unto the sprinkling of *the blood of Jesus Christ*." (1 Pet. i. 2.) Christ, as "an high priest," has "entered in once into the holy place, *by his own blood*, having obtained eternal redemption for us." (Heb. ix. 11, 12.) "We have redemption *through his blood*, the forgiveness of sins." (Eph. i. 7.) Of the cup that was given to the disciples after supper, our Lord himself said, "This cup is the new testament *in my blood*, which is shed for you." (Luke xxii. 20.)

It is only farther to be noticed that in the expression *faith in his blood*, the position of the pronoun *his*, (αὐτοῦ), as having precedence, in the Greek, of the word *blood*, intimates that it is to be betoned :—"through faith in *his* blood." The expression thus doubles back upon the word *propitiatory* that goes before, and represents faith as scenting out the distinctive element in Christ's relation to us, so far as *he* was propitiatory. It is the sacrificial element. He says "*his* blood," says Musculus, "to exclude the blood of beasts," (*addit* **ipsius**, *ut oblatorum pecudum sanguinem rejiciat*).

§ 6. *for demonstration of his righteousness*, (εἰς ἔνδειξιν τῆς δικαιοσύνης αὐτοῦ). This clause is omitted in the Peshito. And Gilbert Wakefield has dropped it out. Vitringa, too, in his exposition of the verse, ignores it; as does also Calvin :—though neither of them disputed or doubted the canonicity of the remark. There can be no doubt that it was part and parcel of the original text. The symmetry of the sentence conspires with the overwhelming mass of external authorities to establish its authenticity.

The word *demonstration* (ἔνδειξιν) shows that the Apostle was contemplating God in the relationship which he sustains to the great moral public. In that relationship God is Himself a public Personage. He stands at the head of a vast community of Intelligences. He is a Magistrate: a Moral Governor: King of men and angels. He is a Law-giver; and a Sovereign Administrator of the laws which he has enacted. As such, his conduct is not only an object of cognizance: it is also possible for it to become an object of deliberative scrutiny. And, as the moral state of the subjects of his realm cannot but be affected by the estimate which they form of his public procedure, it is natural to suppose that, as becometh an infinitely wise and benevolent Ruler, he should be desirous *to point out*, for public observation and consideration, the righteous principles by which he is regulated. Hence the ἔνδειξις, or *demonstration*, or *forth-showing*, here specified. It is, as Andrew Melville remarks, *a pointing out, as with the finger*, (*non secus ac si quis digitum intendat, hoc enim est* εἰς ἔνδειξιν).

When the Apostle says "*for* demonstration," the preposition (εἰς) evidently indicates the divine intention or aim. The entire expression is therefore but another phase of the expression that is employed in Eph. ii. 7,—"that he might show," (ἵνα ἐνδείξηται).

As it is intention or aim that is indicated, it is manifest that it must be some action that is referred to: for aims are relative only to acts. They are the ends contemplated in acts. And hence there can be no doubt that the clause *for demonstration of his righteousness* links on to the verb *publicly set forth* (προέθετο) at the beginning of the verse. It is not to that verb, however, nakedly and abstractly considered; for the verb does not stand naked or abstract in the Apostle's phraseology. The act of God was not a naked and abstract act. It could not be. It had an object; and an object that was complex or multiform in its relations. "God *publicly set forth* Christ as propitiatory," and, as such, "available through faith in his blood." It was this public forth-setting of Christ,—the forth-setting of him as propitiatory,—available, as such, through faith in his blood, —which was intended to be *for demonstration of his righteousness.*

There has been much diversity of opinion among interpreters regarding the *righteousness* which was intentionally pointed out by the public forth-setting of Christ as propitiatory. Some have supposed that the word means the divine *goodness* or *benignity* or *mercy.* This was the opinion of Abelard, (*ad ostensionem suae justitiae, id est, charitatis*); of Grotius too, (*malim hic de* **bonitate** *interpretari*); of Cameron too, who holds, indeed, that the word, when applied to God, has always this meaning, (**justitiae** *vocabulum in Script. semper notat Dei comitatem, misericordiam, salutem, et redemptionem, nunquam vero adhibetur ad id significandum quod vulgo* **justitiam** *dicimus*). Of the same opinion were Brentius, Limborch, Hammond, Wetstein (in the upshot), Semler, Koppe, Mace; Rosenmüller too, and Wakefield, Morus, Jaspis, and Reiche; Heberden also, and Geissler, Whitwell, &c. But it is not the case that the word *righteousness* (δικαιοσύνη) means *goodness* or *benignity;*

although it is doubtless the case that it is oftentimes a *right* and *righteous* thing to be *kind, good,* or *benignant,* and hence it sometimes happens that the same act is capable of being represented either under the aspect of *righteousness* or under the aspect of *kindness.* It is because this is the case that the Greek word for *righteousness* (δικαιοσύνη) is sometimes employed in the Septuagint to translate a Hebrew word (חֶסֶד) which means *kindness, lovingkindness,* or *mercy,* (see Gen. xix. 19; xx. 13; xxi. 23; xxiv. 27; xxxii. 10; Exod. xv. 13; xxxiv. 7; Prov. xx. 28; Isai. lxiii. 7); and, correspondingly, the Hebrew word for *righteousness* (צְדָקָה) is sometimes translated by a Greek term (ἐλεημοσύνη) which signifies *mercifulness,* or *goodness,* or *alms,* (see Deut. vi. 25; xxiv. 13; Ps. xxiii. 5; xxxii. 5; cii. 6; Isai. i. 27; xxviii. 17; lix. 16; Dan. ix. 16). In Matt. vi. 1 the word *alms* (ἐλεημοσύνην) occurs in the received text, and in many of the Uncial manuscripts, inclusive of א; but, instead of *alms,* it is *righteousness* δικαιοσύνην) that is the reading of B D, supported by the Vulgate, approved of by Griesbach, and accepted into the text by Lachmann and Tischendorf. The diversity of reading arises from the fact that it was possible to view the thing spoken of under two aspects. It might be viewed as *mercifulness;* and it might be viewed as *righteousness.* But still the word *righteousness* no more means *mercifulness* than the word *mercifulness* means *righteousness.* We cannot, then, accept the translation and interpretation of Grotius and his confrères in the passage before us.

Other critics have supposed that the word, as here used, means *truthfulness.* This is the view taken of the word by Ambrosiaster; and that is accepted by Zuingli, Bullinger, Hyperius (waveringly), Crell, Ferus, Gomarus, Turretin, Locke, Böhme, &c. It is supposed that the word denotes, as Turretin expresses it, God's fidelity in keeping his promises, (*fidelitas in implendis promissis*). But though such fidelity is certainly a phase of righteousness, it is nevertheless the case that the word *righteousness* does not denote *fidelity* or *truthfulness.* And the relation of the word to the cognate adjective and participle in the last clause of the 26th verse,—"that he might be *righteous*, (δίκαιον), and the *justifier*—the *adjudger as righteous*—(δικαιοῦντα) of him who believeth,"—proves that it was not that particular phase of righteousness which consists of *fidelity* or *truthfulness* that was present to the mind of the Apostle.

A large number of expositors suppose that the word refers to God's *justifying righteousness*, howsoever they may view that righteousness. This is the opinion of Chrysostom and Theophylact; also of Aquinas; and of Egidius Delphus; also of Luther, who translates the expression thus,—"the righteousness which is of avail before him," (*die Gerechtigkeit, die vor ihm gilt*). It is also the opinion of Tyndale, who translates the expression,—"the rightewesnes which before hym is of valoure." It is the opinion, too, of Melancthon (*Com.* 1540); and of Calvin, in substance, and of P. Martyr, Aretius, Rollock, Willet; Zuinger too, and Ferme, Elsner, Varenius, Heumann, Nösselt; and of Este too, and de Paris, and Reithmayr; and of Winzer, Oltramare, van Hengel, Edwards, Vaughan, Dr. John Brown, Bisping, Colenso, &c. The same is in substance the view of Baumgarten-Crusius, who explains the term as meaning *sin-forgiving righteousness*, (*Gerechtigkeit welche die Sünden vergiebt*). So, too, Krehl, apparently; for he says that *righteousness* means here *the forgiveness of sins*, (δικ. *ist hier* = ἄφεσις ἁμ.). So, too, Moses Stuart, who explains the phrase as meaning "the justification which God proffers, or of which he is author." So Whitby. So Belsham, (*for a declaration of his method of justification*). And so too Terrot, who translates the clause, ecbatically, thus,—"and thus God exhibits his method of acquitting sinners." But this interpretation, under all its phases, is liable to insuperable objections. Under the phase which it assumes in the hands of Belsham, Terrot, Moses Stuart, Krehl, Baumgarten-Crusius, &c., the distinctive import of the word *righteousness* is merged and lost sight of. The idea of righteousness, in fact, disappears. The term loses its identity; and is transubstantiated. The phase which the interpretation assumes in the hands of

Chrysostom and Theophylact is connected with a defective view of the nature of justification. (See on ver. 20 of this chap.) The phase which it assumes under the hand of Calvin is in the main remarkably kindred to the view of Chrysostom and Theophylact;—although, in his case, it is not associated with such a defective conception of the nature of justification. He supposes that the righteousness referred to is both immanent and transient. It is the righteousness in virtue of which God is Himself righteous, and by means of which, as communicated through Christ, he makes believers righteous. The combination, however, of these two ideas breeds hermeneutical confusion, by introducing perplexity into the relation of the clause to the immediately succeeding clause. And it proceeds on the erroneous supposition that the participle *justifying*, at the conclusion of verse 26th, means *making righteous*, rather than *pronouncing righteous*. We need not specify all the other phases of the interpretation under consideration. Only we may remark that the phase under which it appears in the hands of Luther, Melancthon, Elsner, Wolf, &c., is out of harmony with the upwinding of the sentence at the close of ver. 26,—"that *he might be righteous* (viz., in the estimation of his moral subjects,—the public of the universe) even in justifying him who believeth." The righteousness referred to is evidently immanent righteousness. It is, relatively to Him to whom it is ascribed, subjective. It is, in short, a divine attribute, and it is thus to be distinguished from that righteousness which is conferred in the economy of mercy, and which is God's great evangelical gift,—that righteousness which is revealed in the Gospel, and which was wrought out and brought in by Christ Jesus. That righteousness,—God's evangelical or justifying righteousness,—is but a special phase of the propitiatory work of our Saviour; and hence we could not expect the Apostle tautologically to say that "Christ was publicly set forth by God, as *propitiatory,* in order that *his evangelical righteousness* might be shown." We might have as legitimately expected him to say that Christ was set forth publicly as *the Lord our Righteousness*, for demonstration of God's *propitiousness.*

Flatt, Fritzsche, and others render the word "holiness," (*sanctitas*). It is a rendering that certainly lies on the right line of thought. Nevertheless there is a distinction between *righteousness* and *holiness.* And it is uncritical to ignore it. Schott's translation of the word,—the translation into which he ultimately settled,—is kindred to that of Flatt and Fritzsche, but far inferior. It is "probity," (*probitas*). And in explaining the phrase he shows his perplexity,—a perplexity that had distracted him for many years,—by combining, after the manner of Calvin, the two ideas of immanency and transiency,—"the probity which he has and which he confers," (*probitatem quam habet et quam tribuit*).

Schott is not the only one who, in perplexity, has sought to gather into a knot two or more divergent explanations. Vorstius long before him explained the phrase as meaning *partly* (partim) *God's truthfulness, or his goodness; and partly* (partim) *our justification,* (illa nostri justificatio, de qua jam saepius actum est). Day says,—"The word *righteousness* signifieth here both the *fidelity* or *truth* and the *goodness* or *mercy* of God." Beza, though contenting himself in his earlier editions with the notion of *faithfulness,* says, in his last edition, that by *righteousness* we are to understand at once *God's severity in avenging sins, and his fidelity in fulfilling his promises, and his mercy in imputing Christ's righteousness to believers.* Thus he twists for himself, very accommodatingly, a threefold cord. Pareus makes a quadruplicate of it, (see on ver. 26), supposing that there is a reference, 1st, *to God's universal rectitude and holiness;* 2nd, *to his truthfulness or fidelity in fulfilling his promises;* 3rd, *to his goodness and mercy;* and 4th, *and* chiefly, *to his judicial rectitude or justice, in virtue of which he renders to every one his due.* Œcumenius long before had flitted, in like manner, from idea to idea, in reference to the import of the word,—finding no rest for the sole of his foot. Many others are also hesitant, as Rückert, for instance, and before him Baumgarten, who gives, however, the preference to Luther's idea of *righteousness for imputation.*

But, undoubtedly, as already indicated, the word denotes *God's own subjective righteousness,*—or that principle in his infinitely perfect moral character which manifests its existence and energy in an undeviating regulation of all his voluntary acts, immanent and transient, by the idea of right. It is obvious that there is such a principle or element in the divine moral character; and it complexions with its own peculiarity and radiance all the relations in which God stands to his moral creatures. It complexions, for instance, his legislative relation, so that all his laws are right,—right as regards what is preceptive in them, right as regards whatever of a promissory nature is involved in them, and right as regards all that is comminatory in their sanctions. The same righteousness complexions his relation as the Sovereign Administrator of his moral laws. His administration is right throughout. Such of his laws as were enacted for perpetuity, he maintains to perpetuity. Such as were intended to be subservient to the interests of temporary dispensations, he maintains while the dispensations last,—cancelling them, or subliming them into laws higher and more comprehensive, when the dispensations close. He upholds the authority of all his enactments. He honours and magnifies them all.

It was, undoubtedly, this administrative phase of the essential righteousness of God which was present to the mind of the Apostle when he said,—*for demonstration of his righteousness.* There was, apparently, no other phase of the divine righteousness that was in danger of being beclouded by the phenomena of *forbearance* and the *pretermission* or *forgiveness of sins.* But there was some danger of men, when not imbruted into moral torpidity, and especially of the other members of the universal moral public, starting back, as in puzzled amazement, on finding that the breach of laws unchallengeably wise and good did not draw after it the penalty which had been threatened. How could such an anomaly in moral government, and that too an infinitely perfect moral government, be accounted for? The question is natural, and momentous. And *Christ Jesus, as propitiatory,* is the only answer that really solves the difficulty. Hence it is that he was set forth by God *for demonstration of the righteousness of his governmental procedure.*

It is this view of the righteousness here referred to that is, with more or less of accuracy in definition or description, attached to the term by a very large, if not a preponderant, body of expositors. Origen aims at it,—though confusedly, and giving undue prominence to the merely *judicial* element: for, certainly, God's judicial righteousness, or his righteousness as a Judge, is but one ingredient in his righteousness as Administrator of his vast moral government. This judicial element is, however, that which is specified, not by Origen only, but also by Sclater, de Wette, Alford, and Tholuck,—all of whom look in the right direction for the explication of the term. Others specify, but also with too great one-sidedness, God's *retributive* righteousness,—that phase of the divine administrative righteousness in virtue of which he renders blessing to the good and woe to the wicked. This is the view of Calov. And Philippi, identifying it with the view that singles out the *judicial* element, accepts it as his interpretation, (*seine Gerechtigkeit, nämlich seine richterliche, vergeltende Gerechtigkeit*). Others, again, suppose that it is God's *punitive* righteousness that is meant. This is the opinion of S. Schmidt, Cocceius, Schrader, Meyer, Maier. It is the opinion, too, of Brown of Wamphray, who calls it "vindicative justice." Others call it "*vindictive* justice." Haldane has the same opinion, and calls it "avenging justice." The explication lies in the right domain. For undoubtedly it is God's righteousness in its relation to the penal element of his administration that is specially in danger of being beclouded by *forbearance* and *forgiveness.* But yet it is unnecessary to detach or abstract, in thought, this one relativity from the sum-total of God's rectoral righteousness, when considering the God-ward end of things that was contemplated in the setting-forth of Christ as propitiatory. A cloud over the punitive element would cast its dark shadow athwart the whole of the divine administrative righteousness. Wardlaw holds that it is God's *public justice* that is referred to,—his *righteousness toward the great moral public.* This idea, too, is in the right domain; only it may be regarded as of unnecessary amplitude. For legislative righteousness, as well as that which is strictly administrative, is part and parcel of *public justice.* The interpretation may thus be regarded as erring somewhat by way of excess, while the other interpretation of "punitive righteousness" (*Straf-Gerechtigkeit*) errs by way of defect. If, however, the expression *public justice* be regarded as limited to the divine administrative righteousness, then the interpretation is perfect, with this one exception, that the word *justice* is not exactly equivalent to the original term, (δικαιοσύνη). It is *righteousness,*—as distinguished at once from *truthfulness* and *goodness* on the one hand, and from mere *justice* on the other,—that is the precise English homologue for the Apostle's vocable. Matthias's explanation of the reference of the word is not nearly so good as that of Wardlaw. He says that it means "the perfect agreement of the divine action with the divine law," (*die völlige Uebereinstimmung des göttlichen Handelns mit dem göttlichen Gesetz*). This would be (*mutato mutando*) an excellent definition of the righteousness of the subject: but it is not a correct representation of the righteousness of the supreme Governor. The law is not a rule for regulating the divine procedure: and if the divine procedure were to be rigidly bounded by its provisions, atonement and forgiveness would be absolute impossibilities.

We need not, however, consider, in detail, the varied aspects given to the interpretation under consideration by its various patrons. It is also approved of, in the substance of its import, by Melville, Hunnius, Sclater; Hombergk too, and Venema; and Macknight, Michaelis, Wetstein, Klee; Köllner also, and Stengel, Chalmers, Olshausen, Hodge, Tischendorf, Wordsworth, D. Brown, &c., &c. And the remark of John Brown of Wamphray is truly admirable:—"Though we be ready to overlook God's justice [his δικαιοσύνη] in the matter of our redemption, yet it is useful to consider seriously how justice as well as mercy kyths [shows itself] in it, and how they kiss and embrace each other, that the wisdom of God may be the more admired in the salvation of sinners, who can make justice and mercy, as it were, lay their shoulders together to help in our redemption, and mercy gain the day, yet so as justice should suffer no detriment; therefore doth he say that one end of Christ's being a propitiation for sin was *to declare his righteousness.*" (Expos. *in loc.*)

§ 7. *because of the pretermission of the former sins,* (διὰ τὴν πάρεσιν τῶν προγεγονότων ἁμαρτημάτων); a clause that has been found by expositors to be in several respects perplexing. The word which we have translated *pretermission* (πάρεσις) is peculiar. It occurs nowhere else in the New Testament; and nowhere in the Septuagint. It had struck the fancy of Chrysostom at a very particular angle of incidence; for he regards it as having its pathological signification of *paralysis.* The Apostle, he remarks, "does not say, *because of our sins,* but *because of our paralysis,* that is, *our deadness;* for there was no longer hope of health; but as the paralytic body needs the hand from above, so also the dead soul," (οὐδὲ γὰρ εἶπε, διὰ τὰ ἁμαρτήματα, ἀλλὰ διὰ τὴν πάρεσιν, τουτέστι, τὴν νέκρωσιν· οὐκέτι γὰρ ὑγείας ἐλπὶς ἦν, ἀλλ' ὥσπερ σῶμα παραλυθὲν τῆς ἄνωθεν ἐδεῖτο χειρός· οὕτω καὶ ἡ ψυχὴ νεκρωθεῖσα). He must, apparently, have construed the expression thus:—*because of the deadness of our souls, resulting from our former sins.* Œcumenius and Theophylact give the same interpretation. Theodoret adroitly skips over the word,—taking no notice of it; but he seems nevertheless to have assumed its pathological import, for he winds up his exposition by referring to God's preparation of *the medicine of salvation* for sinful men, (τοῦτο προκατασκευάζων αὐτοῖς τῆς σωτηρίας τὸ φάρμακον). Photius (in Œcum.) seems to take a different view of the import of the word; but yet he regards it as descriptive of what is subjective in men, instead of what is attributable to God. He seems to interpret it as denoting that *remissness* or *negligence* which is one of the characteristic phases of human sinfulness. He explains the Apostle's idea thus:—"Then when we should have been subjected to the punishment *of our remissness*, we experienced forbearance and philanthropy," (εἶτα δέον τῆς παρέσεως ἀπαιτηθῆναι δίκας, ἀνοχῆς καὶ φιλανθρωπίας ἐτύχομεν). He would apparently construe the expression thus,—*because of our remissness in committing our former sins.* But neither this interpretation nor that of Chrysostom, Œcumenius, and Theophylact, has approved itself to modern expositors: and no wonder. They are both exceedingly unnatural.

It would appear that in some of the early codices the word was either accidentally or intentionally altered into πρόθεσις, *purpose.* For, although this reading is not now found in any of the extant Greek manuscripts which have been collated, the corresponding Latin word, *propositum*, is found in Ambrosiaster's text and comment, and in Augustin's quotation of the text in his *De Spiritu et Littera, cap.* 13, and in manuscripts d and e. It is also found in Pelagius's comment, though not in his text. Ambrosiaster seems to have interpreted the clause thus:—"because of God's purpose (of mercy) in reference to our former sins," (*sciens deus propositum benignitatis suae, quo censuit peccatoribus subvenire, &c.*). Pelagius seems to have interpreted it thus:—*because of God's purpose* (*of justice*) *in reference to our sins*,—that is, *because of God's purpose to punish our sins.* "God set forth Christ a propitiation, that his purpose to punish our sins might not be carried into fulfilment," (*Propterea passus est Christus, ut propositum Dei sedaret, quo tandem punire decreverat peccatores*). This reading of the text, however, is a thorough derangement of the natural construction of the clause. And the interpretations founded on it are at best but ingenuities.

In ms. 46 the word πώρωσιν, *hardening*, is substituted for the term in our text. And in Matthaei's ms. f, or 116, as well as in 69, παραίνεσιν, *advice*, is found instead. The latter of these two readings,—if it be not a mistake for παράλυσιν, *paralysis*,—is unaccountable except on the principle of an almost incredible remissness. The former seems to be a conjectural emendation, in the direction of the interpretation of Chrysostom, Œcumenius, and Theophylact;

though Griesbach is certainly mistaken when he supposes that it was the reading which was in the text that lay before these fathers. They are both of them readings entirely out of the question. Their existence, however, concurs with the existence of the reading of Ambrosiaster, &c., and with the interpretations of the Greek fathers, to show that the Apostle's expression was felt to be perplexing.

In the Peshito version the word is passed by altogether, as well as the immediately preceding clause, *for demonstration of his righteousness.* The clause is rendered;— "because of our sins which we formerly sinned," (ܡܛܠ ܚܛܗܝܢ ܕܡܢ ܩܕܝܡ ܚܛܝܢ). This preterition of the word seems to be additional evidence that its interpretation was felt to be perplexing.

And yet there is no reason why we should despair of reaching the authentic idea of the Apostle.

There can be no doubt that the word is genuine. This much seems to be indisputable.

There can be no doubt that it denotes some act on the part of God. This, too, seems certain: and it is almost universally admitted by modern interpreters.

It is doubtless, too, some merciful act that is represented, —some act that made it desirable that the divine righteousness should be demonstrated by means of the propitiatory work of Christ Jesus: for, unquestionably, the clause is hung upon the immediately preceding clause, *for demonstration of his righteousness,* and adduces a reason why that demonstration of the divine righteousness was required. It is as if the Apostle had said:—"whom God set forth as propitiatory, &c., for demonstration of his righteousness,— *which demonstration was needed, or was rendered desirable, because of the pretermission of the former sins.*" God's pretermission of former sins might, as an act of mercy, have been liable to be misunderstood, to the depreciation and damage of the moral system of the universe,— to the unsettling of the minds of moral creatures in general, as regards the rightness and righteousness of the moral administration of the great moral Governor,—if means had not been devised to demonstrate the perfection of his administrative righteousness. But these means were devised and put into execution.

We have translated the word *pretermission*,—the translation contended for, and established, by Cocceius, both in his *Commentary* and in his *Monograph* on the word, (*Moreh Nebochim.—Utilitas distinctionis duorum vocabulorum scripturae, παρέσεως et ἀφέσεως*). It is adopted and defended by Vitringa. It is adopted by Momma, whose life, poor fellow, was sacrificed in his prime on the altar of Cocceianism. It is accepted by Bengel, Böhme, Fritzsche, Bretschneider, Wahl, van Hengel, &c., and approved of, along with the distinction which it is intended to indicate, by Rückert, Meyer, de Wette, Tholuck; and by Philippi, Oltramare, Maier, Alford, Krehl, Mehring, Matthias, Lange; and indeed by the great body of modern expositors. It is certainly the most literal translation of which the word is susceptible. The verb, from which the noun is derived, (παρίημι), means—*to send aside* or *pretermit, to let pass*, &c. And when used in reference to *faults, transgressions*, or *sins*, it naturally means *to let pass* (*unpunished*). The word "unpunished," indeed, is complementively supplied by Xenophon, in his *Hipparchicus*, vii. 10, (τὰ οὖν τοιαῦτα ἁμαρτήματα οὐ χρὴ παριέναι ἀκόλαστα). Such being the meaning of the verb, the noun, (πάρεσις), when used in reference to the same objects, naturally denoted "a letting pass by," (*Vorbeilassung*), that is *a letting pass by unpunished*, that is, *praetermissio, pretermission.* (It occurs in Dionysius, Hal. Antiq. Rom., vii. 37.—πολλὰ λιπαρήσαντες τὴν μὲν ὁλοσχερῆ πάρεσιν οὐχ' εὕροντο, τὴν δ' εἰς χρόνον ὅσον ἠξίουν ἀναβολὴν ἔλαβον,)—*though they failed, even after much importunity, to obtain a complete pretermission* (or, *letting-alone*, viz., of the case of Coriolanus), *yet they got such a postponement of it as they asked.*

Instead of *pretermission*, the Vulgate renders the word, *remissio, remission*, that is, *forgiveness.* And this meaning is accepted by Erasmus, Luther, Tyndale, Calvin, Piscator, &c. It is keenly defended by Elsner, and by Gebhardi in his *Programma* on the verse. It is supported by Kolding,

Wolf, Heumann, Winzer, Stuart. It is adopted by Schrader. And it has got a place in our Authorized English Version, and in the Dutch (old and new); and also in Castellio, Diodati, Ostervald, Martin, Beausobre et Lenfant, &c:, &c. The French Geneva renders the word *pardon*, and the English Geneva, *forgiveness*. The rendering,—whether *forgiveness* or *remission*,—is, for all practical purposes, a sufficiently good translation. For the sins referred to by the Apostle were indeed really forgiven. And their real forgiveness is *implied* in the Apostle's statement. Nevertheless, if the precise idea of *forgiveness* had been that which was in the Apostle's mind when the expression was dictated, it is remarkable that the common and kindred word for *forgiveness* (ἄφεσις) should have been passed by, and a term introduced that is never employed again in the epistles, and that is never found in any of the other writings of the New Testament. It is not the case, moreover, that, according to Greek usage, the word is a perfect synonym of the common word for *remission*, (ἄφεσις); although, doubtless, when *pretermission* was *permanent*, it practically amounted to *remission*. Thus in some instances *pretermission* and *remission* must have been tantamount. In some cases *offences pretermitted* would be virtually *offences remitted*. This was the case, as we shall see, in the instance referred to by the Apostle. But Elsner is assuredly under a mistake when he says that the word, as it occurs in Dionys. Hal. vii. 37, means *forgiveness*. Forgiveness in that case,—*forgiveness* properly so called,—was not asked. When Hesychius explains the word as meaning *forgiveness*, (πάρεσιν, ἄφεσιν, συγχώρησιν), we may regard him as giving only its approximative import. And we may take the same view of Suidas's explanation of the verb, (παριέναι, συγχωρεῖν, ἀφιέναι). What Cocceius says of the former of the two lexicographers is applicable to them both;—"here, as frequently, he does not explain the exactitude (or nicety) of the phrase," (*ut saepe, hic non explicat phraseos ἀκρίβειαν*).

Instead of either *praetermissio* or *remissio*, Seb. Schmidt, in his *Bible*, though not in his *Commentary*, gives *trans-*

missio, as the rendering of the Apostle's term. Wittich, before him, had given the same translation. So Alting (alternatively). And one Teuber, adopting it, supposed that the Apostle refers to the *transmission* or *transference* of sins to Christ as the sinner's surety. (See Wolf.) Teuber's interpretation is a mere excrescence of ingenuity, causing the Apostle to return, circularly, in his thought, so as to account for the propitiation by the propitiation. The translation on which the interpretation is founded,—if it be intended to draw a line of distinction between *transmissio* and *praetermissio*,—is at variance with the characteristic nature of the term. But if it be intended merely to represent, under a variation of phase, the idea of *praetermissio*, it is unimpeachable: only the variation of phase is such that it cannot be reproduced in English. It was thus that Grotius used the word in his explication of the clause; and hence, indeed, Wittich's use of it, and Schmidt's. Cocceius, too, interchanges *transmissio* with *praetermissio.*

Beza, though in his earlier editions accepting the translation *remission*, saw reason, toward the close of his career, to alter his mind; and, in the last two editions of his *Annotations*, he contended that the word was altogether different, in its import, from the common term for *remission*, ἄφεσιν. (*Perperam, meo quidem judicio, Vulgata; et eam interpretationem ego quoque cum ceteris in superioribus editionibus secutus:* πάρεσιν **remissionem** *interpretati sumus, quasi scriptum sit* ἄφεσιν. *Nam haec duo plurimum inter se differunt.*–Ed. 1594.) In the 1594 edition of his *Annotations* he rendered the word "overlooking" (*dissimulatio*), and, ultimately, in his 1598 edition, he adopted "passing-by," (*pratereundo peccata*). He would have employed the noun *preterition* had it not been, in his estimation, ambiguous. His pupil Melville, however, accepted *preterition.* This ultimate translation of Beza,—with which Hammond's interpretation coincides,—though doctrinally admissible, is philologically inadmissible, as it proceeds on an erroneous derivation of the term, (from πάρειμι, *to pass by*, instead of παρίημι, *to let pass by, to send aside:* conf. ἄφεσις, from ἀφίημι, *to send off, to dismiss, to forgive*).

We need not specify other interpretations of the term, such as that of Pareus,—"*relaxation*, namely of the bonds of our sins." It is reproduced by Trapp. The word obviously means *pretermission*, or *the act of letting pass by unpunished*. The real distinction between this *pretermission* and *remission* will appear after we have ascertained the objects of the *pretermission*.

The Apostle specifies them thus:—"the pretermission *of the former sins*," (*τῶν προγεγονότων ἁμαρτημάτων*), or, as Wycliffe renders the phrase, "of bifore goynge synnes," or rather, to use another archaism, "of the fore-gone sins." Some have conceived that the expression means, *of our previous sins*, that is, *of the previous sins of us who are believers*. And they have either supposed that the reference is to *the sins of believers committed before conversion*, or thought that there is a pointing as of the finger to the general principle, that it is *past, as distinguished from future sins, which are pretermitted or remitted*, inasmuch as sins must *be*, before they can *be remitted* or *pretermitted*. It is the one or the other of these views,—merging as they do in the common notion that the Apostle is making mention of *the past sins of believers*,—that is entertained by le Fèvre, Erasmus, Bugenhagen, Aretius; and by Piscator, Hyperius, Calov, and Baxter; and by Wesley, Reiche, Barnes, Mehring, Purdue, &c. Wesley's note is, "*past sins*, all the sins antecedent to their believing." And the same phase of interpretation is given to the expression by Calov, Reiche, Mehring, Purdue.

It seems manifest, however, that the Apostle intends an antithesis between the expression "for demonstration of his righteousness, because of the pretermission of the *former* sins," and the expression in the succeeding moiety of the sentence, "for the demonstration of his righteousness in the *present* time, that he might be righteous even in justifying him who believeth," (*ἐν τῷ νῦν καιρῷ κ. τ. λ.*) And hence there seems to be an antithesis intended between two great cycles of time, as these cycles stand separated from each other by the meridian line of the fact of the propitiation. The one cycle comprehended the age or ages that preceded the accomplishment of the propitiation. It is past. The other comprehends the New Testament age that is running on. The expression, *the former sins*, will therefore naturally mean *the sins of the former age or ages*, (τῶν ἐν τῷ πρὶν καιρῷ γεγονότων ἁμαρτημάτων). And this is, in substance, the view that is generally taken of the expression. It is undoubtedly the right view.

There is, however, among the expositors, who are thus far agreed, a difference of opinion as to the particular extent of the reference. A very considerable number of them, inclusive of Grotius, Hammond, Winzer, Meyer, Rückert, de Wette, Tischendorf, Alford, Conybeare, Matthias, &c., suppose that the Apostle refers to the sins of men, indefinitely, whether Gentiles or Jews, and whether believing or unbelieving, who lived under the preceding dispensations. And of this class of interpreters several interpret the word *pretermission* as equivalent to the *overlooking* that is spoken of in Acts xvii. 30,—"the times of this ignorance God *winked at*." And some identify both the *overlooking* and the *pretermission* with the *sufferance* or *permission* that is mentioned in Acts xiv. 16,—"God in times past *suffered* all nations to walk in their own ways."

But it is not likely that the *pretermission* in the passage before us is identical with the *sufferance*, or even with the *winking-at* or *overlooking*, that are referred to in Paul's addresses in the *Acts of the Apostles*. For, (1), the *sufferance* and the *overlooking* or *winking-at* express the action of God in reference to Gentile nations as distinguished from the Jews. And, (2), they point not so much to God's sovereign clemency, or to the restraint of his rectoral wrath in relation to sins that were actually committed, as to the sovereign withholding of special agencies or instrumentalities, like those of the Mosaic theocracy, for the prevention of the actual commission of sins. God *suffered* Gentile men to walk in their own sinful ways; he *suffered* them, for he did not specially interpose to hinder them. He "*winked at* the times of ignorance;" he no more *specially* interfered than if he had not seen what was going on. It is, however, an entirely different relationship that is indicated in the *pretermission* of which the Apostle here speaks. It is a relationship of sovereign mercy that is akin to that which is indicated in the expression that is found at the conclusion of the second clause of the sentence,—"that he may be righteous, *even in justifying him who believeth.*" It is a relationship akin to that involved in justification.

Philippi supposes that *the former sins* referred to are the sins of *the Jews,*—under the currency of their peculiar economy,—*of the Jews* as distinguished from *the Gentiles.* (Comp. Heb. ix. 15.) But this interpretation seems to err both in the way of being too narrow in one respect, and too wide in another. It is too narrow, as excluding from view God's gracious acting in relation to many who lived and died before the rise of the Jewish theocracy, and in relation to some, if not many, who lived and died during the period of its currency, but yet outside of its pale. It is too wide, as bringing into view an immense multitude of people who, though Jews, and blessed with the high privileges of Judaism, were yet by no means the objects of the *pretermission* of which the Apostle speaks, the *pretermission* that is akin to *justification.*

We agree with Cocceius and Beza, as well as with the expositors who regard the Apostle as speaking of *remission,* or *forgiveness,* in supposing that *the former sins* referred to are those of believers. They are the sins of all those who, in former dispensations, lived and died in faith,—faith explicit in the Messiah that was to come, or faith implicit in the propitiousness of God,—faith, in either case, "working by love," and thus "purifying the heart," and beautifying the life. The expression, therefore, "*the* pretermission of *the* former sins," will, in its demonstrative element, fold back upon itself, so as to convey this idea,—"the pretermission *of those particular former sins which were actually pretermitted.*" The Apostle assumes, as an indisputable fact, that there were sins, in the former ages, which were pretermitted; and he accounts for their pretermission by pointing to the propitiatory work of Christ Jesus. By means of this propitiatory work, God's righteousness in relation to the pretermission is demonstrated and vindicated.

It is implied in the Apostle's remark that it would not have been a *right* and *righteous* thing to have pretermitted any of the sins of former ages, had not the propitiation been divinely precontemplated. Such pretermission or non-punishment would have been inconsistent with the divine *righteousness.*

It is also implied, in the use of the word *pretermission* in reference to these *former sins,* as distinguished from the word *remission,* that it is only on account of the propitiatory work of Christ Jesus that there is an absolute and final deliverance from the real penalty of sin. Mere *pretermission* is mere *non-punishment.* And it is, besides, mere *non-punishment for the time being.* It does not involve any immunity for the future. So far as mere *pretermission* is concerned, there is no security that the penalty of the sins shall not be by and by inflicted. It is different with *remission* or *forgiveness.* When sins are *remitted* or *forgiven,* there is, *de jure,* immunity for all time to come. The sinner is no longer liable to the penalty of his sins. His sins are pretermitted indeed. But they are remitted too. The latter invariably implies the former; though the former does not invariably imply the latter. The sins, however, of the believers who lived and died in former times were not *merely pretermitted,*—their souls, at death, being reserved, as de Lyra supposes, *in limbo.* They were also *really remitted.* And hence God is represented frequently in the Old Testament as *forgiving.* There was "forgiveness with him." He not only "passed by transgression." (Mic. vii. 18). He was "a God of pardons." Olshausen is wrong, we conceive, when he says that "under the Old Testament there was no real, but only a symbolical forgiveness of sins," (*Im A. T. war keine reale, sondern nur eine symbolische Sündervergebung*). But yet, as the remission of *the former sins* was grounded on a work that was future; and as it was therefore, *de facto,* without its meritorious cause, as an *ens* actually eventuated, —there was scope for the Apostle, when expressly treating of the propitiation as the ground of the blessings of salvation, to substitute the word *pretermission* for the word *remission,* as being, in a system of philosophic Theology, peculiarly suggestive of the indispensability of the work of our Saviour to render a condition of non-punishment secure and final. When distinguishing, on the one hand, *pretermission* from *remission*, and when regarding, on the other, the actions of God and the corresponding states of men in their strict relation to the category of time, we may say that the *pretermission* of *the former sins* was developed or transmuted into their *remission* on the occurrence of the propitiatory work of Christ Jesus. But we can take this view, and use this language, only when occupying the peculiar standpoint indicated. And, when occupying other and more familiar standpoints, from which we see that the future and the past are alike, as regards certainty, to God, and that hence the work of Christ, in its relation to the *passing by* of iniquities, was, before its accomplishment, as really available, and as sure, as if it had been actually completed from the foundation of the world,—it is both natural and right to speak of the *remission* of the former sins, and to speak of their *remission* as having actually happened in the ages that have gone by. For all popular and practical purposes, the translation of the term in question, as given in our Authorized English Version, and in the great majority of other versions, need not be disturbed.

It is different, however, with the preposition (*διά*) which is rendered *for* in our Authorized English Version. It received the same rendering from Wycliffe (*for* remiscioun) and in the Rheims. The idea intended was, apparently, the notation of the *end*, or *aim*, or *final cause* of the "demonstration of the divine righteousness." Calvin took the same view, (*Tantundem valet praepositio causalis, acsi dixisset, remissionis ergo, vel in hunc finem ut peccata deleret*). The preposition is thus regarded as meaning *in order to:*— a most unlikely import. It is translated *through* by Reiche, (*διά bezeichnet hier das, wodurch sich die δικαιοσύνη zeigt*). Koppe gives the same rendering. So also Heumann. And Luther seems to have regarded it in the same light:— he translates the whole expression freely,—"in this that he forgives sins," (*in dem, dass er Sünde vergiebt*), that is, *through the forgiveness of sins.* Tyndale follows Luther,—

"in that he forgeveth the synnes that are passed." So Cranmer's version, and the English Geneva of 1557, &c. The English Geneva of 1560 has, similarly, "*by* the forgiveness of the sins that are passed." The French Geneva ultimately settled in the same translation, (*par la remission*). In the 1562 edition it is "*pour* la remission." Macknight's translation is, in substance, accordant: he renders the preposition "in:"—"*in* passing by the sins which were before committed." Many others translate and interpret in a corresponding manner. But the translation and interpretation could be warranted only in a case of extreme hermeneutical perplexity. The idea involved ignores the peculiar force of the preposition, when governing the accusative case; and it proceeds on an erroneous view of the reference of the word righteousness. There can be no reasonable doubt that the preposition has its usual and distinctive import, "on account of," (*propter*), and that it brings into view one of the *occasions*,—or one of the *occasioning* or *impulsive causes* (but certainly not, as Grotius says, the *efficient cause*)—of that demonstration of God's righteousness which was purposely made in the propitiatory work of Christ Jesus. This occasion, or occasioning cause, was *the fact of the pretermission of sins under former dispensations.*

§ 8. *in the forbearance of God*, (ἐν τῇ ἀνοχῇ τοῦ θεοῦ). These words stand, according to the versicular division of Robert Stephens, at the commencement of the 26th verse,—an exceedingly awkward position. The awkwardness is increased when they are preceded, as in the Elzevir of 1624, and in Mill's edition, and Wetstein's, as well as in many others of lesser note, by a semicolon at the close of verse 25. In Henry Stephens's edition of 1587 there is even a full point. This is repeated in Ornsby's recent edition of 1865. The linking of the words is evidently retrospective, instead of prospective. They are a pendant to the immediately preceding clause,—*because of the pretermission of the previous sins*,—and should certainly not have been versicularly separated from it. Erasmus has a comma between the two clauses. Robert Stephens himself has no more in his versiculated edition of 1551, and in his grand folio edition of 1550. Vater, in modern times, contents himself with a comma. But Bengel, Schoettgen, Griesbach, Lachmann, Tischendorf, as well as Knapp, Tittmann, Hahn, Naebe, Alford, Scrivener, Buttmann, &c., have done well in obliterating every vestige of interpunction. J. C. Herzog wisely recommends this non-interpunction. (*Obs. Phil. de interpunctionum positu in Epist. ad Rom.*) And, what is somewhat remarkable, Robert Stephens, in his 1549 edition, has no point of any kind. Neither has Robert Stephens the Second in his 1569 edition. Beza, while retaining the comma, boldly departed in his fourth, as also in his last, edition, from the versicular division of Stephens, and remanded the clausule to its proper position at the conclusion of the 25th verse. He was followed by the French Geneva, and the English Geneva, and our Authorized English Version, and the modern Dutch, and the common editions of Luther's version; and also by Diodati, Ostervald, Martin, Beausobre et Lenfant, &c.; and by Bengel in his German version, &c. But, as perplexities in the matter of reference are the inevitable consequence of disturbing the Stephanic divisions, it is doubtless preferable, while adhering to the arrangement of Robert Stephens, to take means to avoid its inaccuracies and infelicities, by printing our Bibles on the system of continuous paragraphs, after the plan of Bengel, Lachmann, Tischendorf, &c. The system of artificially setting every verse apart, as if it were a distinct and detached proverb, and of consequently beginning each verse with a capital letter, and on a new line, is certainly as effective a contrivance as could well have been devised for throwing difficulties in the way of understanding the Word of God.

The expression, *in the forbearance of God*, (ἐν τῇ ἀνοχῇ τοῦ θεοῦ), has, in general, been regarded as intimately connected, either with the participle, (προγεγονότων), which we may freely translate *previous*, or with the noun, (πάρεσιν), which we have rendered *pretermission*. Œcumenius takes the former view, (ἐπιτείνει τῶν ἀνθρώπων τὸ ἔγκλημα, τῷ τὰς ἁμαρτίας γινέσθαι ἐν τῇ ἀνοχῇ τοῦ Θεοῦ). So do Luther, Erasmus Schmid, Seb. Schmidt, and Piscator; Heumann too, and Raphel, Elsner, Carpzov, &c., and Rückert, Baumgarten-Crusius, Tischendorf, Oltramare, and van Hengel, &c. In the hands of these expositors the expression assumes various modifications of shape,—some more strained, as that of Er. Schmid (*Deo* illa *tolerante*), and some more ingeniously adapted to the exigencies of the case, as that of Oltramare and van Hengel, *in the time of the forbearance of God*,—"the sins that previously occurred *during the forbearance of God*." This latter view seems to have been that of the Peshito translator. But it is more natural to connect the expression with the prominent idea of the preceding clause,—the idea that culminates in the word *pretermission*. The expression will thus denote the immanent sphere of that divine attribute *in* which the transient acts of the divine pretermission took place,—"because of the pretermission, *in the forbearance of God*, of the previous sins." God pretermitted the previous sins, in the exercise of his forbearance. He, as it were, *held himself up*, and thus *restrained himself*, when provoked to inflict the punishment that was deserved. (Comp. ἀνέχομαι.) He did not yield in his action to the impulse of indignation. He bore and forbore. This view of the connection of the expression is approved of by Koppe, Glöckler, de Wette, Fritzsche, Meyer, Olshausen, Philippi, Matthias, Tholuck, Mehring, &c. It is not, perhaps, necessitated, as Fritzsche thought it was, in virtue of the collocation of the words. (Fritzsche thinks that if the expression had been dependent on προγεγονότων, it would have run thus, τῶν ἐν τῇ ἀνοχῇ τοῦ Θεοῦ προγεγονότων ἁμαρτημάτων, or thus, τῶν ἁμαρτημάτων τῶν ἐν τῇ ἀνοχῇ τοῦ Θεοῦ προγεγονότων. But it might, with equal conclusiveness, be argued that if the expression be dependent on πάρεσιν, it would have run thus,—διὰ τὴν ἐν τῇ ἀνοχῇ τοῦ Θεοῦ πάρεσιν κ. τ. λ., or thus, διὰ τὴν πάρεσιν τῶν προγεγονότων ἁμαρτημάτων, τὴν ἐν τῇ ἀνοχῇ κ. τ. λ.) Yet it is certainly far more natural to regard the forbearance of God as the condition of his pretermission of sins, than as the condition of the commission of sins. And, assuredly, when we go up to the first sin, which must not be excluded from the scope of the divine pretermission, there is no legitimate sense in which it can be said of it, that it was committed *in the forbearance of God.* God's *forbearance,* or *endurance,* or *toleration,* or *longsuffering,* presupposes the existence of sin. Until sin existed there was no more scope for forbearance than there was for pretermission or forgiveness.

We need not specify in detail the various *outré* constructions and explanations of the clausule we have been considering, such as the construction of Wolle, who would connect the clausule with the conclusion of ver. 22nd, throwing all that intervenes into a parenthesis, (*De Parenth.*, p. 66); and such as the interpretation of Gebhardi, who considers that the clausule means "because the divine Saviour bore them," i. e., "bore the sins that are remitted," (ἐν τῇ ἀνοχῇ τοῦ Θεοῦ, i. e., διὰ τὸ ἀνέχεσθαι αὐτὰ τὸν Θεόν, *propterea quod ea non nudus homo, sed verus deus, exantlavit,*–Programma, p. 7.) The introduction of the word "God," instead of the pronoun, need not be regarded, with Gebhardi, as indicating an extremely great emphasis. Neither does it explain the case to say, with Rückert and Meyer, that the Apostle speaks objectively from his own standpoint, as distinguished from the divine standpoint; for the third personal pronoun would have been, to the Apostle, as thoroughly objective as the noun. The truth of the matter is, that in the interchange of the noun and pronoun there is scope for variation; and in individual instances the choice may be determined by stereotyped prepossessions of taste or by temporary impressions or impulses, which it might be in vain for us to attempt to hunt up or ascertain. Matthias sees in the use of the noun an intentional antithesis to what is human. (*Das nomen scheint jedoch, ähnlich wie* 2 Cor. i. 4; v. 21, *wohl absichtlich wiederholt, um einen Gegensatz gegen den Begriff Mensch hervortreten zu lassen.*) It may be so. We cannot tell. Or it may be that, in the living intercourse of the Apostle's soul with the Father of lights, his thoughts, instead of simply running out into mere logical sequences, soared into immediate communion with "God."

§ 9. *in order to the demonstration of his righteousness in the present time,* (πρὸς τὴν ἔνδειξιν τῆς δικαιοσύνης αὐτοῦ ἐν τῷ νῦν καιρῷ). It is very generally supposed that these words double back epanaleptically upon the words of the preceding clause,—"for demonstration of his righteousness because of the pretermission of the previous sins in the forbearance of God." They constitute, says de Wette, a corroborative repetition (*verstärkende Wiederaufnahme*) of the preceding clause. The Apostle, says Grotius, repeats what he had said, as he often does on other occasions when he is wishful to fix an idea deeply in our minds, (*Repetit quod dixerat, ut saepe solet, ubi quid altius vult infigere animis*). "He repeats what he had said," says Este, "that he may add *in the present time.*" Hence Conybeare translates the clause, interpolatingly, thus;—"[Him (I say) hath God set forth] in this present time to manifest his righteousness."

This epanaleptic view of the relation of the clause to the preceding one is, we cannot doubt, a misapprehension of the Apostle's idea. It is, at least, in the main, a misapprehension. We say "in the main," for it is evident that there is some element of epanalepsis. The expression *in order to the demonstration of his righteousness* (πρὸς τὴν ἔνδειξιν τῆς δικαιοσύνης αὐτοῦ) manifestly repeats, with extremely slight variation, the expression *for demonstration of his righteousness,* (εἰς ἔνδειξιν τῆς δικαιοσύνης αὐτοῦ). And if, as is probable, the reading which inserts the article—"in order to *the* demonstration," (πρὸς τὴν ἔνδειξιν)—be correct, there will be embodied in the second expression a consciously repetitious reference to the first. The article is found in ℵ A B C D, and is approved of by Fritzsche, and admitted into the text by both Lachmann and Tischendorf. The Textus Receptus omits it, under the sanction of the great majority of the cursive mss. and of E K L, and of the text as it stands in Chrysostom, Theodoret, Theophylact, and Œcumenius. But while there is, to the extent indicated, an epanaleptic element in the expression, we conceive that so far as the clauses, in their entirety, are concerned, they run out *abreast* from the great evangelical apophthegm of the Apostle—*whom God set forth as propitiatory*, (ὃν προέθετο ὁ θεὸς ἱλαστήριον). The lines of thought do not coalesce; they run parallel. There is, in short, a bifurcation of idea. In the first clause the relation of the propitiation to God's merciful dealings under the ancient dispensations is pointed out; and in the second there is reference to its relation to his merciful dealings under the current dispensation. The propitiation, as we learn from the first clause, was *for demonstration of God's righteousness in* **pretermitting** *sins under the former dispensations.* And the same propitiation, as we learn from the second clause, was *for the demonstration of his righteousness in* **remitting** *sins under the present dispensation.* The Apostle, indeed, does not attempt to exhibit the antithetic harmony of these two relationships of the propitiation by any studied and fastidiously balanced concinnity of phraseology. But the antithesis of the two ideas, and their harmony, were evidently lying in his thought.

In the diversity of prepositions which is employed, (εἰς and πρός),—and which we have attempted to reproduce, though in the second case paraphrastically, by rendering the one *for*, and the other *in order to*,—there is probably mere phraseological variation. And, for aught that is discernible, their positions might have been reversed, without affecting the substantive import of the sentence. If we would distinguish between the two, the first (εἰς) indicates *tendency toward*, the second (πρός) *direction toward.* But as both are intended to denote *purpose* or *aim*, they really coalesce in import; for the *tendency* of an aim, is just the *direction* of a purpose.

The expression *in this present time*, or, as Heinfetter has it, *in the now time*, (ἐν τῷ νῦν καιρῷ), is used, not in antithesis to the future, as Origen supposed, but in contradistinction to the past. It exhibits a pole of thought that is opposite to that which is indicated in the expression *the previous sins*, (τῶν προγεγονότων ἁμαρτημάτων). There is hence no reference to a mere point of time,—a mere epoch in the world's history, such as "the fulness of the time," when Christ was "set forth as propitiatory." The phrase does not limit itself, chronologically, to the period of the occurrence of the Saviour's propitiatory work. It represents an entire cycle of time,—a cycle within which there are enjoyed peculiar results of the great propitiatory work,—which peculiar results, as well as the proleptic blessings enjoyed in preceding ages,—find their vindication in the nature of the propitiation. If the Apostle had spread out his idea, it would have been somewhat to the following effect:—"in order to the demonstration of his righteousness *as regards that treatment of sin in the present time which corresponds to its pretermission in the past time.*" The treatment of sin referred to is *remission*, more especially as viewed on the other side of its totality, *justification.* See the remaining clause of the verse, (εἰς τὸ εἶναι αὐτὸν δίκαιον καὶ δικαιοῦντα τὸν ἐκ πίστεως).

Some expositors, who felt that the usual epanaleptic explanation of the clause lacked lustre and likelihood, and who yet did not apprehend the fine bifurcation of idea that is realized in the two clauses, have fallen on various unnatural expedients to work out into symmetry the Apostle's thought. Beza, for instance, supposes that the expression, *in order to the demonstration of his righteousness at the present time,* depends on the latter fraction of the preceding clause, *in the forbearance of God,*—"forbearance divinely exercised in order to the demonstration of his righteousness in the present time." Rückert, Baumgarten-Crusius, and Jowett take a similar view of the connection. Sebastian Schmidt, again, and Maier think that it is a different *righteousness* altogether that is referred to in the second clause. They suppose that in the first clause it is God's *sin-punishing righteousness* that is meant, while in the second the reference is to his *sinner-justifying righteousness.* Olshausen and others take a similar view. Mehring is exceedingly perplexed with the clauses, and thinks that they constitute one of the most difficult passages of the epistle, (*wir in den Worten* εἰς ἔνδειξιν *bis* ἐκ πίστεως

'Ιησοῦ *eine der schwierigsten Stellen des Briefes vor uns haben*). He, too, supposes that the word *righteousness* means, in the second clause, *God's justifying righteousness*, attributable to the believer, although it means in the first His own *essential and ever-immanent attribute of righteousness.* And he regards *the manifestation of God's justifying righteousness in the present time* as that *in consideration of which* the manifestation of his rectoral righteousness took place in the forth-setting of Christ as propitiatory. Hence he discriminates strongly between the import of the two prepositions, (regarding πρός as meaning *in Beziehung auf, in Betracht*, oder, wenn man es recht versteht, *gegenüber*). In all these efforts, however, at explication, there is "labour" and "vanity." They are violent and unnatural.

§ 10. *that he may be righteous even in justifying him who is of faith in Jesus*, (εἰς τὸ εἶναι αὐτὸν δίκαιον καὶ δικαιοῦντα τὸν ἐκ πίστεως 'Ιησοῦ). It is impossible to give in English a very felicitous translation of this clause. The paronomasiac relation between the adjective which we translate *righteous* (δίκαιον) and the participle which we translate *justifying* (δικαιοῦντα) cannot be reproduced. If we were to give the translation, *just*, to the adjective, the link of coincident relation to the participle would be exhibited. But *just* is too narrow a signification. And were it adopted, we should be constrained to substitute the noun *justice* for *righteousness*, not only in the immediately preceding clauses, but also in verses 21st and 22nd, and in chap. i. 17th. In this substitution, however, we should so pinch the great evangelical idea of the Apostle as to wring from it not a little of its life's blood. One has, in this emergency, some sympathy with Basil Cooper, who proposed to maintain the paronomasia by rendering the clause thus,—"so that he is *righteous*, and also the *enrighteouser* of him which believeth in Jesus." But such a coinage is, as we have seen, too startling in its violence. It is too great a leap. And it would not suit, besides, those cases in which the verb *to justify* is used to designate the action of human judges; and those others, also, in which it is employed to denote the action of the divine Judge at the summing up of human affairs. Neither, indeed, would it suit this or any other passage of the New Testament. We must be content, it would appear, to forego the beautiful paronomasia of the original.

But not only so. In foregoing the paronomasia, we find it to be impossible, unless we should darken the inspired idea by entirely unidiomatic phraseology, to give an extremely literal rendering to the paronomasiac expression. An extremely literal rendering would be the following:—"that he may be *righteous, and justifying* him who is of faith in Jesus." It is intolerable. And hence more or less freedom must be used in reproducing the idea. Tyndale translates thus:—"that he myght be counted *juste, and a justifiar* of him which belevith on Jesus." The Eng. Geneva corresponds:—"that he might be *just, and a justifier* of him which is of the fayth of Jesus." Our Authorized Version has followed in the wake of these precursors, though not slavishly:—"that he might be *just, and the justifier* of him which believeth in Jesus." Substituting, as we must do, the word *righteous* for the word *just*, the version is justifiable, or, as we should rather say, partially justifiable, only on one supposition, the supposition that the *righteousness* referred to in the preceding clauses is *God's justifying righteousness*, imputable to believers, in contradistinction to his *immanent rectoral righteousness*. This supposition, however, we have seen to be untenable. And even though it had been tenable, the idea embodied in the version would still be only *partially* justified. For it would be difficult to account for the expression "that he may be *righteous*,"—as, by the hypothesis assumed, there is no reference, in what goes before, to God's own personal righteousness. It would, too, be specially difficult, and indeed impossible, to account for the betoned emphasis and prominence that are assigned, in the collocation of the phraseology, to the word *righteous* as distinguished from the word *justifying*.—On the supposition, again, that the righteousness spoken of in the preceding clauses is God's rectoral righteousness, as vindicated by the atonement in relation to the pretermission and remission of sins,—on this supposition, the clausule, *that he may be righteous*, is naturally and easily accounted for. But when it is added, *and the justifier, &c.*, there seems to be the intrusion of an idea which,—*when taken abreast with the idea contained in the clausule* "that he may be righteous,"—appears to be here out of place; and peculiarly so when we remember that the expression *the justifier* is, in the original, participial, *justifying*.

The truth is that the Apostle's expression is a complexity that culminates, *not in duality, but in unity*. And it is only because of its intransferable paronomasia that there is apparent duality. The culmination takes place in the word *righteous*, as is manifest, not only from the purport of the two preceding clauses, and from the collocation of the adjective and the participle, but likewise from the fact that the substantive verb is used, like the kindred verb γίνομαι in verses 4th and 19th, logically,—to denote not what God is to be absolutely, in his own perfect subjectivity, but what he is to be relatively, in the minds of the moral creatures who constitute the vast moral public of the Universe. The Apostle could not mean that Christ was set forth as propitiatory, that God *may be regarded as justifying the believer in Jesus*. He means that Christ was set forth as propitiatory, that God *may be regarded as righteous even in justifying the believer in Jesus*. The logical import of the substantive verb makes it manifest that it is the word *righteous* which is to be betoned, and that the participial addition is subordinate and subsidiary. The inspired idea might be paraphrastically exhibited thus:—*that he may be, in the estimation of the moral public, righteous even in justifying the believer in Jesus*.

The expression which we have rendered *even in justifying* (καὶ δικαιοῦντα) is rendered by Turnbull, "while justifying;" by Scarlett, "even when justifying." Matthias and Mehring give the same translation, (*auch wenn*). So does Purdue. Whitby has, "and yet the justifier;" Conybeare, "and yet might justify." Hodge intensifies it, "although the justifier." Archbishop Magee, before him, had sanctioned the same rendering, (*Atonement and Sacrifice*, Diss. xlii., p. 465 of vol. i., ed. 1832). Macknight has it, "when justifying;" and Chalmers, without professing to give a translation, quietly adopts Macknight's idea. He says, "it is now made manifest that God might be just *while he justifies* those who believe in Jesus." So far as the theology of the passage is concerned, any of the free and easy translations specified might be accepted. But, as a matter of exegesis, the rendering, *righteous even in justifying*, undoubtedly hits, as precisely as possible, the nail on the head. It is far superior to the dualizing interpretation of de Wette, adopted by Bisping and partially by Alford, *righteous on the one hand and justifying on the other*. And it is certainly nearer the centre of the Apostle's thought than the idea that is embodied in the version of Luther,—"that he *alone* may be righteous, and make righteous him who believeth in Jesus," (*auf dass er allein gerecht sey, und gerecht mache den, der da ist des Glaubens an Jesu*). Coverdale's rendering is a faithful transcript of the great Reformer's *Douche* translation:—"that he onely mighte be righteous, and the righteous maker of him which is of the faith on Jesus." (*Biblia*, 1538.) Calvin seems to have had the very same idea as Luther. (*Definitio est illius justitiae, quam dato Christo ostensam fuisse dixit; sicuti primo capite docuerat patefieri in evangelio. Duobus autem membris eam constare affirmat. Prius est, Deum esse justum, non quidem ut unum ex multis: sed qui solus in se omnem justitiae plenitudinem contineat. Neque enim integra et solida laus, qualis debetur, ei aliter tribuitur, quam dum solus obtinet justi nomen et honorem, toto humano genere injustitiae damnato. Alterum deinde membrum statuit in justitiae communicatione, dum scilicet suas divitias Deus apud se minime tenet suppressas, sed in homines effundit.*) But the notion suggested by the word *alone* is, exegetically, an intrusion. The notion, too, suggested by the expression *make righteous* is a deviation from the proper forensic import of the term. And, moreover, the entire translation and interpretation rest,—however inconsistently,—upon the assumption that the *righteousness* specified in the preceding clauses as the righteousness whose demonstration was contemplated in the propitiation, is God's justifying righteousness, or, as Luther expresses it, *the righteousness which avails before God*, (*die Gerechtigkeit die vor ihm gilt*). Bengel did well to throw out, in his German translation, Luther's *alone*. And Piscator, too, did well to substitute, in his German translation, "pronounce righteous" (*gerecht spreche*) for Luther's and Bengel's "make righteous," (*gerecht mache*).

We have already indicated that the substantive verb, "that he *may be* righteous when justifying," is to be understood logically,—as denoting what it is desirable that God should be *in our apprehension*. The two preceding expressions, *for demonstration, in order to the demonstration*, prepare us for this relativity of the substantive phrase. And as the Apostle seems, in these two preceding expressions, to be referring to the righteousness of God's immanent nature, as distinguished from the righteousness of his transient acts, it is not likely that he could be supposing that, in that inner and ultimate respect, the atonement was the condition of the existence of God's righteousness. It was rather the case that the essential righteousness of God was the condition of the existence of the atonement. Christ was set forth as propitiatory, not that God might be righteous in his nature, even in justifying the unrighteous, but that the righteousness of his nature might appear;—that, in the apprehension of the moral public, he might be righteous when justifying the unrighteous who believe in Jesus. (*Afin-qu'il soit trouvé juste.*–Calvin.) This logical import of the substantive verb has been generally recognized by expositors.

It has not, however, been so generally noticed that the entire clausule, *that he may be righteous even in justifying him who believeth in Jesus*, is epexegetical, not of the two preceding clauses, (1), *for demonstration of his righteousness because of the pretermission of the previous sins in the forbearance of God*, (2), *in order to the demonstration of his righteousness in the present time*, but only of the latter of the two. Grotius, Reiche, and others regard the clausule as constituting a *thirdly* in the exhibition of the divine aim in the propitiatory work of Christ, and as being thus a re-repetition of the idea embodied in the first clause. Rückert regards it as exhibiting the final result of the whole, (*das Endergebniss des Ganzen*). Fritzsche, Meyer, Philippi, &c., regard it as epexegetical of the two preceding clauses; Maier similarly, as exhibiting the final aim of the two preceding *demonstrations.* But Matthias is evidently right in supposing that the Apostle's design is to exhibit, epexegetically, the peculiar idea of the second clause in its antithesis to the peculiar idea of the first. Christ was set forth as propitiatory, not only, (1), *for demonstration of God's righteousness because of the pretermission of sins, in the forbearance of God, during the former dispensations;* but, (2), *for demonstration of his righteousness at the present time, that he may be apprehended to be righteous when he justifies those who believe in Jesus.* The righteousness of justification in the present time, as distinguished from the righteousness of pretermission in the past time, is the great idea of the Apostle. The righteousness of both of these modes of dealing with sinners is demonstrated and vindicated by the propitiatory work of Jesus.

The clausule is rendered ecbatically by some few expositors, such as Rückert:—*so that he is righteous.*—Struensee, Stolz, and Colenso take a similar view. So did T. Edwards, and Michaelis, (*so dass Gott gerecht bleibt, &c.*) So Peile, (*to the effect that he is righteous*). But the obvious epexegetical relation of the words seems, independently of the use and wont of the preposition in connection with the articulated infinitive (see chap. i. 20), to make it certain that a telic import is intended.

The concluding expression, *him who is of faith in Jesus*, (τὸν ἐκ πίστεως Ἰησοῦ), is idiomatic. Felbinger, in attempting to translate it with extreme literality, (*den der aus dem Glauben Jesu ist*), yet failed by inserting, as Luther had done before him, the article before *faith,*—" out of the faith of Jesus." The expression suggests derivation, and is regarded by some as distinctly denoting filiation. Glöckler, for instance, takes this view, (**Aus dem Glauben seyn** *heisst aber so viel als:—aus dem Glauben abstammen, geboren seyn, also durch den Glauben wiedergeboren seyn zu einem* *neuen Leben*). Conybeare says that the expression means *the child of faith*, and in his version he renders it, plurally, *the children of faith*. So Wittich, (ὁ ἐκ πίστεως, *est, quasi genitus ex fide*). But this is to condense into too definite a shape the natural indefiniteness of the original. There is rather the suggestion than the assertion of filiation. And perhaps the idea, as it lay in the Apostle's mind, amounted to no more than this,—that the individuals referred to *derived their distinguishing peculiarity from faith in Jesus*. Their great spiritual characteristic had its origin in faith,—faith that terminated on Jesus, and found in Him the *righteousness* which God judicially recognizes in justifying the ungodly. Sclater explains the expression in a manner that gives it a grotesquely polemical tinge,—a tinge of the date of the extremely polemical seventeenth century. His explanation is this,—"as if he should say, *him that, renouncing the sect of merit-mongers, embraceth the supposed heresie of solifidians*." The genitive "*of* Jesus" is, of course, to be regarded objectively. The entire phrase denotes the "faith of which Jesus is the object;" not the "faith of which he was the subject," or "of which he is the author." (See on ver 21.)

Of Jesus (Ἰησοῦ) is omitted from the text by Tischendorf, so that the expression with which the verse concludes is, according to his reading, *him who is of faith*. The word was condemned, too, by Mill, and suspected by Griesbach. Fritzsche, Meyer, and Oltramare approve of its omission. It is wanting in F G 52. f. g. But it is found in ℵ A B C K, and in the great majority of cursive mss., as also in the Philoxenian Syriac and Ethiopic versions, and in Chrysostom, Theophylact, and Œcumenius. The Vulgate, Coptic, Theodoret, Pelagius, Ambrosiaster, read, complexly, *Jesus Christ*. The Peshito reads *our Lord Jesus Christ*. The Erpen-Arabic, *our Lord Jesus*. These three latter readings seem to have been supplemented; but they are certainly confirmatory of the genuineness of the word *Jesus*. (In D L and many cursives Ἰησοῦν is found instead of Ἰησοῦ,—a manifest error of negligence,—ῑν̄ for ῑῡ. The same error occurs in Œcumenius, in the quotation of the text, though the immediately succeeding explanation shows that he really read Ἰησοῦ. The authorities, then, that have Ἰησοῦν are also confirmatory of the genuineness of Ἰησοῦ.) There can be little doubt that the reading of the received text is correct. It is wisely approved of by Lachmann, Philippi, and van Hengel. And we certainly like to find the act of faith led up to its great and glorious Personal Object,—*Jesus*, our Saviour.

VER. 27, Ποῦ οὖν ἡ καύχησις; Ἐξεκλείσθη. Διὰ ποίου νόμου; Τῶν ἔργων; Οὐχί· ἀλλὰ διὰ νόμου πίστεως.

Eng. Auth. Vers. *Where is boasting then? It is excluded. By what law? of works? Nay; but by the law of faith.*

Revised Version. *Where then is the glorying? Shut out. Through what kind of a law? Of works? Nay, but through the law of faith.*

§ 1. The Apostle has finished that grand paragraph (verses 21—26) which explains, *in extenso*, what it is that renders the Gospel "the power of God unto salvation." His explanation had been given, *in brief*, in chap. i. 17. But it was befitting to resume it, and expand it in the full affluence of its details.

The Apostle had evidently felt, in his own spirit, the intensest interest as he proceeded with the evolution of the details. Each item, as it turned up, seems to have sent a thrill through his heart. His ardour grew and glowed. He could not but admire the divine method of justification. Its symmetry, its completeness, its exquisite adaptations, and the might of the moral influences with which it was charged, charmed his soul. He stood arrested and rapt as he gazed. At length words came. And he utters forth, in abrupt and exceedingly condensed bolts of jubilant thought, some of the corollary-ideas which, in the midst of the consciousness of his ecstasy, he felt rising up with irrepressible and almost tumultuating energy within his mind. (Verses 27—31.) Foremost among these are references to the unbecoming feelings and incorrect notions, as regards the way of justification, that were unhappily characteristic of the great mass of his countrymen. And thus he says:— "*Where then is the glorying? Shut out. By what kind of law? Of the works? Nay, but through the law of faith.*"

§ 2. *Where then is the glorying?* (Ποῦ οὖν ἡ καύχησις;) Such is the most literal, and doubtless the most correct rendering of this clause. In our *English Authorized Version* the article is ignored:—"Where is boasting then?"— a translation yielding, indeed, a sense that is far from being repugnant to the Apostle's idea, but that, nevertheless, sweeps out into a wider circumference of reference than he intended. Vaughan says that the article has its *generic* force. But it is not *glorying in general* to which the Apostle is referring. It is not *glorying in general* that is put under ban. It is some particular glorying,—the glorying of some particular class of persons. The Apostle does not specify the persons to whom he refers; but his mind was fixed on them, and hence the article:—*Where then is the glorying?* It is almost, but not altogether, tantamount to the expression,—*Where then is their glorying?*

The Vulgate reads, "where is then *thy* glorying?" or as Wycliffe gives it, "where is therfore thi gloriynge?"—(*ubi est ergo gloriatio tua?*) The same reading is found in the pre-Hieronymian codices d. e. f. g. It is hence the reading of the Latin Fathers. It is found, too, in the Greek Uncials F and G; but not in the Greek Fathers. It is a mistake to refer to Theophylact as supporting it, though it is the case that, in freely explaining the clause, he applies it directly, and in the second person, to *the Jew*, (εἰκότως οὖν ἐρωτᾷ τὸν Ἰουδαῖον, ποῦ ἐστιν ἡ καύχησίς σου, καὶ ἡ μεγαλοφροσύνη; οὐ λέγει δὲ, ποῦ ἐστιν ἡ ἀρετή; οὐδὲ γὰρ εἶχον ἀρετὴν, ἀλλὰ καύχησιν μόνην. The clause οὐ λέγει δὲ, ποῦ ἐστιν ἡ ἀρετή;

shows that Theophylact did not read *ποῦ ἐστιν ἡ καύχησίς σου*;) There can be no doubt that the introduction of the pronoun *thy* into the Latin versions, and of the kindred personal pronoun, *of thee,* in that single Greek text which is dually represented by F and G is to be accounted for on the assumption of an effort to exhibit the force and reference of the definitive expression—"*the* glorying." There is no evidence, however, that the Apostle was sisting, as it were face to face with himself, a single representative Jew, and addressing him. He is rather looking at the mass of his countrymen collectively, as in verses 2nd and 29th. And his attitude is that of one who is speaking *of* them, rather than *to* them.

The *Five Clergymen* and Shepherd supply a different pronoun. They render the clause, "Where is *our* boasting then?" It is not, as we conceive, a felicitous rendering. The Apostle was not in the mood to transfer to himself, even in a figure, that particular, and particularly odious, failing of his countrymen in general, which it was his wish to reprobate, and which seemed to him to be utterly inconsistent with that way of justification which he had just been exhibiting and expounding. He stands apart, as an inspired expositor of the Gospel, and, looking upon both Jews and Gentiles as respectively massed before his mental eye, he does not seek, for the moment, to realize or identify, or, at all events, to take into particular account, his own ethnological relationship.

If freely substituting a pronoun for the merely definite article of the original,—as it would be, perhaps, in some respects, not undesirable to do,—we would make our selection not from the sphere of *the first person,* nor from the sphere of *the second person,* but, as already indicated, from the sphere of *the third person,* in which we have an English pronoun akin both etymologically and conventionally, to the article. We would say,—"where then is *their* glorying?" But the fact that both the second and the first persons have been respectively proposed, is evidence that the definitiveness of the expression has been realized, and should not be ignored.

It has, indeed, been very generally realized. Luther inserts the article in his translation, (*Wo bleibet nun der Ruhm?*), and has been followed, among German translators, by Piscator, Felbinger, Reitz, Zinzendorf, Heumann, Bengel, Michaelis, Stolz, &c. The Dutch translators, old and new, have likewise inserted it. So did the French Geneva of 1562, (*Où est donc la vantance?* It is Calvin's ultimate translation. His translation of 1556 was, *Ou est donc la gloire?*) The English Geneva, too, inserted the article,—*where is then the rejoicing?* So did Diodati. Among critics, too, Fritzsche gives due prominence to the idea intended by the article, (*ubi est igitur hactenus saepe audita gloriatio?*) So does Meyer, (*der Artikel bezeichnete die bewusste, schon mehrerwähnte—*). So does Philippi, (*der Artikel ein bekanntes, oft getriebenes und gehörtes, oder öfter schon herborgehobenes und zurückgewiesenes Rühmen*). Oltramare, too, remarks that the article denotes the notoriety of the glorying, (**Où est donc cette gloriole?** *L'Article indique qu'il s'agit de quelque chose dont on a conscience, qui est notoire*). These are a fair specimen of the whole body of good translators and critics.

When duly recognizing the article, an interesting particularity is imparted to the psychological scene that is pictorially presented to the mind's eye. We see the Apostle standing, as it were, on some elevated platform, and looking round and round inquisitively. He seems to be in quest of some object with which he has been familiar, indeed too familiar. But he cannot see it in all that plane of things that is around him. He exclaims,—not in a disappointed, but in a glad and jubilant tone,—*where then is the glorying?—that glorying which is always so obtrusive of itself?—that glorying which is scarcely ever absent when a Jew is present? Where, I say, is this glorying?*

Fritzsche supposes that the Apostle has no particular reference to what was characteristic of the Jews, as distinguished from other religionists. Mussus supposed that he makes equal reference to Jews and Gentiles (*qui inaniter alter alteri se invicem preferebant*). Krehl echoes Fritzsche's opinion, (*Die Frage ist nicht an die Juden gerichtet, sondern ganz allgemein*). And many of the more polemico-theological expositors, such as Calvin, Sclater, Cocceius, Haldane, never start the question whether or not there is a particular reference to the Jews. Hodge thinks that there is no such particular reference. But it is really the case that the Apostle has had all along, down through the chapter, the spiritual condition of the Jews in view. He has been seeking so to lay his subject as to meet their peculiar wants, and more particularly their peculiar prejudices in favour of themselves, their religious haughtiness and conceit,—their glorying in relation to themselves. In the immediately preceding chapter, moreover, he makes express reference to their *glorying*. See verses 17 and 23. And the fact that in the 29th verse of the present chapter he goes on to ask,—"*Is he the God of the Jews only? is he not also of the Gentiles?*" —is evidence that it was the Jews, and the self-glorification of the Jews, that occupied in particular the attention of his mind.

We need not suppose, indeed, that in asking, *Where then is the glorying?* he allowed his mind to be utterly oblivious of corresponding tendencies in others. We may reasonably suppose, on the contrary, that he gives expression to his thoughts and feelings regarding the glorying of the Jews, because he realized that this element of the spirit of Judaism was too apt to be imported into Gentilism, and would be in danger of infecting and infesting the Christian church as a whole. Men everywhere are too prone to haughtiness and self-glorying,—too apt *sese jactare*. Pride is one of the disfigurements of humanity in general. And even from behind a profession of faith in Christ, and of justification by faith alone, and of the abnegation of glorying in the matter of justification, the forbidding lineaments of a supercilious spirit may lower forth. Paul knew this: and hence, we doubt not, he had an aim that went far beyond the Jews when he asked, *where then is the glorying?*

Nevertheless we cannot doubt that when he said *the*, he was thinking of *the Jews*. Chrysostom was of the same opinion. So was Origen before him. So were Theodoret, Œcumenius, and Theophylact, after him; Ambrosiaster too, and Pelagius;—and almost all who read the clause thus, *where then is thy glorying?* So also Erasmus, Grotius, Bengel: Heumann too, and Böhme, Rückert, Meyer, de Wette; Philippi also, and Oltramare, van Hengel, &c.,—and indeed the great majority of expositors.

Some have supposed that the word (καύχησις) means here *ground of glorying*, (*materia gloriandi*=καύχημα). Beausobre et Lenfant, for example, (*où est donc le sujet de se glorifier?*) Flatt too, and Brentano; Reiche also (καύχησις *ist hier Gegenstand und Grund des Rühmens*); and Rilliet (*Que devient donc la raison de s'enorgueillir?*). De Wette, too, took the same view in his first edition;—only gradually laying it aside. But the interpretation is a manifest mistake, arising from a natural tendency to confound the Apostle's rhetorical representation with the philosophy of things that was underlying it. In that philosophy the Apostle realized that all *legitimate occasion of glorying* was shut out. But in the hieroglyph which he was engaged in painting on the walls of the chamber of his mind's imagery he refers to *the glorying itself*, as distinguished from its historical occasion or logical ground.

Some have erred in another direction in their attempt at reproducing the Apostle's idea. They have rendered his word *glory*, instead of *glorying*. So, among the German translators, Luther, Emser, Ulenberg, Piscator, Felbinger, Reitz, Heumann, Bengel, Michaelis, Struensee (*der eigne Ruhm*), Kistemaker (*Selbstruhm*), van Ess; but not Zinzendorf, (who renders it properly *Rühmen*, instead of *Ruhm*). De Wette, Matthias, Mehring, are careful to give the same translation as Zinzendorf; and de Wette expressly calls attention to the error of the other rendering.

In our *English Authorized Version*, as in the Rheims, the word is rendered *boasting*—a far superior translation to *glory*. It is also far superior to *rejoicing*,—the translation which is found not only in *the Eng. Geneva*, but also in Tyndale. Nevertheless we question whether it be equal to *glorying*, the translation which is given by Wycliffe, and which not inaptly represents the Vulgate version, *gloriatio*.

The advantage of *glorying* over *boasting* arises from the fact that it has not got so fixed a twist *in malam partem.* It more readily adjusts itself to the expression of what is right and becoming, when such expression is required.

It is often required. There is a befitting, as well as an unbefitting, *glorying.* The word that is here employed by the Apostle is used by him again in chap. xv. 17, "I have therefore *glorying* through Jesus Christ in those things that pertain to God." So in 2 Cor. i. 12,—"For our *glorying* is this, the testimony of our conscience, that in simplicity and godly sincerity, not with fleshly wisdom, but by the grace of God, we have had our conversation in the world, and more abundantly to you-ward." In 2 Cor. vii. 4, too, he says—"Great is my boldness of speech toward you; great is my *glorying* of you." He says again in 1 Thess. ii. 19,—"For what is our hope, or joy, or crown of *glorying?* Are not even ye, in the presence of our Lord Jesus Christ at his coming?" Indeed, in almost all the passages in which the noun for *glorying* (καύχησις) is employed, it is used to denote *legitimate and befitting glorying.* The kindred noun (καύχημα),—rather denoting *the ground of glorying* than *the act of glorying,*—is also almost always used *in bonam partem.* And the affiliated verb is indeterminate in its moral reference. Sometimes it is employed to denote illegitimate *glorying.* And at other times we read of *glorying in the Lord* (1 Cor. i. 31); *in Christ Jesus* (Phil. iii. 3); *in the cross of our Lord Jesus Christ* (Gal. vi. 14); *in God* (Rom. v. 12); *in tribulations* (Rom. v. 3); *in hope of the glory of God* (Rom. v. 2). It is the same word that is employed by the Septuagint translator in that *glorious* passage about *glorying,*—Jer. ix. 23, 24,—"Thus saith the Lord, Let not the wise man *glory* in his wisdom; neither let the mighty man *glory* in his might; let not the rich man *glory* in his riches: but let him that *glorieth glory* in this, that he understandeth and knoweth me, that I am the Lord which exercise lovingkindness, judgement, and righteousness, in the earth: for in these things I delight, saith the Lord."

There is, then, a becoming *glorying,* as well as a *glorying* that is unbecoming. The English word *glorying* is excellently adapted to turn, as needed, either way, to the left hand or to the right. As a matter of fact, indeed, *glorying*, among men, is a state of mind that is generally found pointing toward the left rather than toward the right. It is *glorying* that is, too, *glorifying to self,—vain-glorying.* It makes men *braggarts* either in fact or in spirit. It lies on one line with *overweening self-applause.* This is the form of *glorying* that is naturally assumed by inordinately sensitive self-consciousness;—by selfishness. But there may also be the *glorying* of disinterested admiration. And although the admiration be not absolutely disinterested, although it have relation to what has filaments of connection with self, and is beneficial to self,—nevertheless, if self be kept in its own little place, at the feet of the Infinite One, and if it occupy its own appropriate attitude while there, not distending itself as if it were a lord among its fellows, but bending lowly as a servant of all,—then its *glorying* is becoming and good. The word, however, has, as a matter of fact, a preponderance of association, in human language, with what is unbeseeming and inordinate. And hence, when it is employed, in the Bible, to denote what is befitting and right, there is, as it were, an element of apology accompanying its application,—there is a consciousness of an effort to vindicate for the term a sublimer association. It is as if the Holy Spirit were saying to men,—"If your hearts be "set on *glorying*, let it be noble glorying,—glorying that "has true glory in it. See that ye glory only in really "glorious objects. Glory, if you please, in the Lord; glory "in the cross of Jesus Christ. Glory, too, in whatever gives "legitimate occasion for advancing the glory of God; glory "in your tribulations, glory in your infirmities. And when "you glory in what turns round to promote your own glory, "see that, nevertheless, the chief ground of your glorying be "the glory that accrues to God. Only thus anticipate your "crown of glorying (1 Thess. ii. 19). Only thus glory in the "testimony of your purified conscience (2 Cor. i. 12), or in "any of your acts of self denial (2 Cor. xi. 10)." Men, then, would require to take heed in *glorying*. If there be the smallest relaxation in the moral tension of the soul, when glorying is indulged in, one will be apt to become "a fool in glorying." (2 Cor. xii. 11.)

The peculiarity of the Apostle's word is now evident. It is a word that had, in general, a bad association connected with it. That association clings to it in the interrogative corollary before us, and in some other passages. In these passages it denotes such *glorying* as resolves itself into *boasting;* and hence the vindication of our *Authorized Eng. Version* in the case before us. The only objection to the translation is the difficulty of subliming, for other occasions, the word *boasting.* It is, indeed, sometimes sublimed, as, for instance, in Ps. xxxiv. 2; xliv. 8. But this exaltation of the term does not come to it so naturally as to the word *glorying.* There is something in the make of the word, as well as in its conventional associations, that persists in pointing *in malam partem*, suggesting not only *abundance of noise* (conf. the Latin *boo* and the Greek βοάω), but also *inflation* and *emptiness.* The term seems to have a filament of connection with the noun *boss*,—the inflated or protuberant part of a shield; and most probably it has a link of relation to the Scotch adjective *boss*, which means *empty.* A boaster is an *empty braggart.*

We hold, then, by the translation *glorying.* And when the Apostle asks, *where then is the glorying?* we assume that he is using the term with its current ill-omened association attached to it. Seb. Schmidt, indeed, supposes that it is used with its sublimer reference. He thinks that the query is an *occupatio*,—the anticipation of an objection, on the part of an opponent, to the Apostle's doctrine of justification by faith. Such an opponent would be ready, as S. Schmidt supposes, to step forward and say to the Apostle,—"If this doctrine of yours, O Paul, be accepted, where is there scope for glorying?" "There is none," replies the Apostle; "for what you count legitimate glorying, I count illegitimate." S. Schmidt thus comes round, in the upshot, to the generally received view. But his notion of a formal dialectical colloquy is too cumbrous and artificial. It has, however, been reproduced by Taylor. Day, though on other grounds, takes substantially the same view with Schmidt of the import of the word. He says, "Note that the Apostle speaks not here of an unlawful or unjust or causeless boasting, or of boasting only before men, (for so any man might boast, and so did the Jews boast): but he speaks of a lawful, just, and well-grounded boasting, and a boasting before God, such a boasting where nothing is to be imputed to the grace and favour of God, but all to a man's own self." In other words, Day supposes that when the Apostle asks, *where is the glorying then?* he is inquiring concerning that glorying that would have been legitimate if Adam had not sinned, and that is legitimate in heaven among angels who have never sinned. He did not note the article *the*, which ties down the reference to some sort of boasting that was common enough, too common, on earth. Neither did he take into account that there are no moral creatures anywhere who could attain to any moral excellence apart from "the grace and favour of God." Even in heaven, the angels, who have never fallen, will think but little of their own worthiness when it is placed side by side with the prevenient loving-kindness of God. Their glorying will be in God.

The Apostle evidently uses the term in its sinister reference:—*Where then is that self-glorifying glorying of the Jews that has been sounding abroad so loud and so long, proclaiming how good and godly they are, and how eminently entitled, considering the great merit of their circumcision and other ceremonial observances, to get to heaven and eternal glory? Where*, says the Apostle, *is this glorying?* It is as standing on the platform of the doctrine of justification that he puts the question. It would be wrong, however, to say, with Calvin, Hemming, Musculus, Melville, and Day, that he speaks "after a kind of *insulting* manner." The associations of the word *insulting* lie on the line of malignity. For the same reason, we would not say, with Aretius, that he speaks *derisively*. But we would not deny that there is a jubilant tone of logical, theological, and ethical triumph in the interrogation. (He is, says Bullinger, *veluti* ἐπινίκιον *canens*. The "where?" says Bengel, is *particula victoriosa*. Compare 1 Cor. i. 20; xv. 55.)

§ 3. *It was shut out*, (Ἐξεκλείσθη). This is one of the cases in which, for all popular purposes, the perfect tense in English might be advantageously employed to represent the aoristic Greek:—*It has been shut out.* The aorist, however, is more graphic when the scene that was present to the Apostle's mind is vividly reproduced. It might be conceived of as follows:—The Apostle looks about inquisitively on the platform of thought on which he was standing. But he does not discern the object of which he was in quest. Then a jubilant flash shoots from his eye; and he exclaims, *Where is the glorying?* He pauses for an answer. The answer at length comes,—"It was shut out," that is, "It *is* not here, because it *was* shut out." It is in some such manner that the aorist is to be accounted for. If, however, the scenic nature of the representation be ignored, the logical value of the idea will be sufficiently preserved by translating the verb either in the perfect tense, "It has been shut out," or in the present, "It is excluded," (or, as Tyndale gave it in 1526, "Hitt is excluded").

The expression implies that the *glorying* referred to had,—so far as scenically viewed,—tried to intrude. It had, as it were, struggled hard to get a footing. But it was unsuccessful. It was thrust out; and shut out. An interdict was laid upon it. It was put under ban.

The logical substrate of the representation is obvious:—*There is no legitimate scope for the glorying of the Jew,* (or *of any man*). *One has but to understand the real nature of that justification which lies at the basis of salvation, in order to see that the glorying of the Jew* (or *of any man*) *is an absurdity as well as a sin.* It is not the case that the Jew can find, either in his own worth, or in the favour of God, any good reason for pride of heart or superciliousness of spirit. He cannot even find a good reason for great self-complacency.

The majority of the Greek fathers suppose that the Apostle's expression assumes that there was once, to the Jews, an opportunity for glorying, but that now, since the appearance of Christ, that opportunity was gone. *The time for it is past*, says Chrysostom, (οὐκέτι γὰρ ἔχει καιρόν).

There is no longer room for it, says Theodoret, (οὐκ ἔτι χώραν ἔχει). Œcumenius repeats the same idea. The Apostle's expression, says he, *shows that there was once room for glorying*, (δεικνὺς ὅτι καὶ χώραν εἶχέ ποτε). Theophylact, too, as is his wont, echoes Chrysostom. But the idea has no warrant in the inspired text, or in the nature of the case. It arose from not distinguishing between the Apostle's rhetorical representation, and its logical substrate. According to the rhetorical representation, the *vain-glorying* was eager to intrude itself. But according to the logical substrate of the representation, there never was, and there never can be, any legitimate scope for the Jewish, or for any, self-applauding glorying, in the matter of justification and salvation. Michaelis's rendering of the expression is based on this logical substrate of thought. But, for this very reason, it obliterates the fine dramatic representation of the Apostle. It is this:—"all occasion for it has been cut off," (*alle Gelegenheit dazu ist abgeschnitten*). It is an excellent logical explanation; but certainly it is no translation at all of the Apostle's expression.

§ 4. *Through what kind of a law?* (Διὰ ποίου νόμου;) That is, *Through what kind of a law was the glorying shut out?* The Apostle keeps up the rhetorical colloquy.

It will be noticed that the question is not, *Through which law?* The Apostle does not so much inquire for *the particular law* by means of which the glorying had been shut out, as ask information regarding *the nature of the law*. To speak in the language of Aristotle's predicaments, the inquiry points, not in the direction of the οὐσία, but in the direction of the ποίοτης of the law. *What kind of a law is it?*

Chrysostom supposes that the Apostle uses the word *law* conciliatingly,—*to tone down the appearance of novelty that attached to his doctrine*, (ἐμφιλοχωρῶν τοῖς ὀνόμασιν, ὥστε παραμυθεῖσθαι τὴν δοκοῦσαν εἶναι καινοτομίαν). Day, again, supposes that he uses the word "by a Mimesis,"— "repeating the word *law*, that he might in a slighting manner imitate the Jews, who did *crack of the law*, and had it always in their mouths, though they kept it not." Tholuck, in his 5th edition, takes a somewhat similar view, (*Das Jüdische Pochen auf das Gesetz zu Schanden zu machen, spricht der Apostel auch von einem Gesetze des Glaubens*). But there was a deeper reason for the employment of the term. When it was said that *the glorying was shut out*, the language had reference not so much to the power of physical force, as to the interposition of authority. (*Quo jure est exclusa?*–Bugenhagen.) The glorying had no *right* to be within; and an interdict had been laid upon its entrance. What, then, was the tenor of that interdict? How did the order or *ordonnance* run? What was the purport of the legal instrument by which the ejectment was effected? *What manner of law* is it?—Such seems to be the Apostle's idea. In the light of it, the difficulties vanish which have so grievously perplexed some of the most inquisitive expositors. We shall refer to these difficulties after we have noticed the remaining clauses of the verse.

§ 5. *Of works?*—Wycliffe, *Of dedis doyinge?* (Τῶν ἔργων;) Literally, *Of the works?* There is real significance in the article, although our idiom will scarcely admit of its introduction into an easy-going translation. The expression does not refer to *works* indefinitely, nor even to *good works* indefinitely. The article is not, as Vaughan supposes, generic. The expression refers, very definitely, to certain peculiar works,—*the works*, namely, *which were specially prized and punctiliously performed by the great body of the religiously inclined among the Jews, and on the ground of which they thought themselves exceedingly good, and entitled to be exceedingly sure of the everlasting glory of God.* The Apostle, as it were, says:—*Through what sort of law has the boasting (of the Jews) been shut out? Is it through a law that enjoins, as the human condition of justification, such works as the Jews are scrupulously careful to perform, such as circumcision, a punctilious observance of holy days, a careful distinction of meats, a tithing of mint, anise, and cummin, &c., and, in addition, a fair outside compliance with the precepts of the decalogue?* The force of the articulated expression might be tolerably well exhibited by the introduction of the pronoun *their*:—*Is it through* **a law that enjoins their works** *that their boasting has been shut out?* The word *works* is, of course, objective in relation to the word *law.* It denotes the objects supposed to be authoritatively or legislatively enjoined.

§ 6. *Nay, but through the law of faith,* (Οὐχί, ἀλλὰ διὰ νόμου πίστεως). The Jewish glorying is excluded *through the law that enjoins faith* as the human condition of justification and salvation. That is *the kind of law* by means of which *the glorying was shut out* from the platform of divine things, in the midst of which the Apostle found himself standing, while he was surveying and exhibiting the wonders that are in and around the great propitiation. It is not faith itself that is called a *law;* although there is an important sense in which it is *a rule of life.* But the Apostle is speaking of *a law that enjoins faith,*—a law, or order, or *ordonnance,* or commandment, or divine statute, that, with the force of an evangelical Imperative, lays hearers of the Gospel under obligation to *believe and live.* The Greek expression is unarticulated,—"law of faith." We cannot, in our English idiom, reproduce it. We cannot say "through law of faith." Neither can we here say "through faith's law." We must say either, "through *a* law of faith," or, "through *the* law of faith." Either translation is legitimate, though neither is an exact reflection of the original expression. In such a case as the Apostle had in hand, "*the* law of faith" is "*a* law of faith." For that kind of law which consists in "*a* law of faith" is neither more, nor less, nor else, than *the* actually enacted, and therefore *the* actually existing, law of faith. "This is God's commandment—(*God's law*)—that we should believe on the name of his Son Jesus Christ," (1 John iii. 23).

§ 7. Such is the purport, we apprehend, of the jubilant

outburst of condensed utterances contained in this 27th verse. The key to the whole aggregation of expressions is the idea that there is a particular reference to the great body of the religiously disposed Jews,—to *their glorying* on the one hand, and to *their works* on the other. In the light of this idea most of the difficulties vanish which have caused perplexity to not a few of the most earnest investigators.

Many have wondered, for example, why the Apostle should speak both of *a law of works* and of *a law of faith*. The twofold use of the word *law* has excited their wonderment. Œcumenius wondered, and thought that he explained the matter when he remarked that the expression *law of works* is used periphrastically for *works*, and the correlative expression *law of faith*, for *faith*, (νόμου ἔργων, τῶν ἔργων περιφραστικῶς, καὶ νόμου πίστεως, τῆς πίστεως περιφραστικῶς). But, of course, his explanation explains nothing. It gives no reason whatever for the use of the word *law*. Theophylact says that *faith is called a law* by the Apostle out of respect for the Jews, who honoured the term, (Ἰδοὺ καὶ τὴν πίστιν νόμον καλεῖ διὰ τὸ τοῦ ὀνόματος παρὰ Ἰουδαίοις τίμιον). But, as we have seen, it is not the case that faith is called *a law*;—no more than *works* are. Theodore of Mopsuestia speculated on the subject, and evidently with ingenuity; but his remarks have unhappily not come down to us in an uncorrupted state; neither has the exposition of Pelagius. Theodoret, again, begins his explanation in a rather unpromising manner. He says that it is not inconsiderately that *faith is called a law*, (οὐχ' ἁπλῶς δὲ τὴν πίστιν προσηγόρευσε νόμον),—thus committing the mistake into which Theophylact afterwards fell. But ere he ends his exposition he comes round to a much more accurate view of the expression, and speaks of *faith in Christ* as having been *legislatively ordained (as a duty)*. (He says of the new covenant, prophesied of by Jeremiah, αὕτη δὲ πιστεύειν νομοθετεῖ τῷ χριστῷ.) Aquinas got fairly off the scent on the subject. He seems, like Theodoret, to have thought of the New Covenant spoken of by Jeremiah (xxxi. 31—34); and he concluded that by *the law of works* is meant *the law of God, viewed as inculcating outward works,* while by *the law of faith* is meant *the same law inwrought into the heart, and thus regulating the new heart's inner movements, the first of which,* says he, *is faith.* (*Legem autem fidei vocat legem interius descriptam, per quam non solum exteriora facta, sed etiam ipsi motus cordium disponuntur, inter quos primus est motus fidei.*) Abelard went still farther in the same direction, and actually explains the expression *law of faith* as meaning *love springing from faith,* (**per legem fidei,** *ut dictum est, Jesu Christi, id est, charitatem ex fide nostrae salvationis per Christum venientem*). Melancthon saw that such explanations of the Apostle's phraseology were far aside from the mark, and from evangelical truth. Yet he could not work his way into the Apostle's representation. In his *Annotations* (1522) he says that the expression *law of faith* just means *faith,*—the word *law* being used abusively, (*Lex fidei, abusu vocabuli, ipsam fidem signat*). He thus looked at the expression in the same light as Œcumenius. But in his *Commentary* (1540) and *Enarratio* (1556) he attributes more significancy to the word *law.* He says it means *doctrine. The law of faith,* he thus explains as meaning *the doctrine concerning faith* (*doctrina de fide; doctrina quae concionatur de fide*). In this, his ultimate explication, many succeeding expositors acquiesced, as Hunnius, Balduin, Beza; Sclater, Calov, Wittich, Vitringa, &c.; and in later times Kypke, Nösselt, Christian Schmid, Koppe, Morus, Weingart; Böckel too, and Flatt; Tholuck also, in his 1st and 2nd editions, and Turner, &c. "*Law,*" says Turner, "is equivalent to *a system of doctrine.*" There is in such an interpretation of the phrase a tittle of basis, inasmuch as the Hebrew word (תּוֹרָה), corresponding to the Greek word (νόμος), does bear ineradicably in its make the idea of *instruction* or *revelation.* Yet it never means *doctrine,* in the systematic-theology sense of the term,—doctrine in the sense of *dogma.* And in the passage before us the scenic nature of the case demands the retention of the distinctive conventional force of the Greek term,—*law.* Peter Martyr accepts the interpretation of Melancthon; but he improves it a little, saying, "by the word *law* the Apostle means *doctrine*, since it has the power of controlling and governing," (*Voce autem Legis, intelligit Apostolus doctrinam; quoniam ea vim habet moderendi ac regendi vires nostras et voluntates ad aliquid agendum*). Aretius gives a similar modification, but more happily than Martyr, to Melancthon's notion. Bullinger, however, who wrote before Melancthon's *Commentary* and *Enarratio* appeared, felt fairly puzzled, and proposes several shifts to account for the use of the word *law*. Perhaps, he says, it may mean *principle* or *mode*:—or perhaps it is a catachresis; or perhaps, he adds, it is a mimesis (as in John vi. 29). The secret of his perplexity is found in his erroneous view of the scenic representation. He supposes *glorying* to have been thrust out by mere *brute-force* as it were, (*gloriatio convulsa jacet, convulsa, inquam, fidei non operum robore*). Musculus, too, is puzzled, and could only come to the conclusion, that whatever the expression may mean (*ut ut accipiamus*), the Apostle evidently intended to discriminate between *the law of Moses* and *the grace of the New Testament*. Melville does not attempt to explain the expression. He simply wondered and adored. "Here," he says, "the name *law* is given to faith, wonderfully and qualifiedly, but divinely and significantly"—(*Hic legis nomen mirifice et modificate, sed divinitus et significanter, fidei tribuitur*). Zuingli took much the same view as Œcumenius. The expression, in his opinion, is just a peculiarity of Greek speech, (*schema Graecanici sermonis*). "By the law of faith?" just means, he thinks, "by faith?" and the preceding query, "by what sort of law?" just means *how?* (*quomodo?*). In more modern times the difficulty has continued to be felt. Tholuck, as we have seen, held, in his 1st and 2nd editions, by the notion that *law* means *doctrine*. In his subsequent editions he shifts his ground, and holds that the word denotes an *authoritative rule of action*, (*norma, verpflichtende Richtschnur*). Grotius had taken substantially the same view, (*vivendi regula*); and indeed Calvin too; and it has been approved of by Hodge, Maier, Philippi, Alford, Oltramare, &c. Seb. Schmidt, on the other hand, supposes that the word *law* means *scripture*, and is used partitively, as the word *scripture* sometimes is, as when we speak of *a scripture* and *another scripture.* He would interpret the verse, in formal colloquy, as follows:—"**Jews**:—*Where then is glorying?* **Paul**:—*It has been excluded.* **Jews**:—*Through what (part of) Scripture?—through that which enjoins works?* **Paul**:—*Nay, but through that which enjoins faith.*" This interpretation of the word *law*, however, is extremely, and indeed absolutely, arbitrary. So is that of Reiche, Moses Stuart, Rückert, &c., who understand by it *a religious system, dispensation, economy, or order of things,* (*Religionsverfassung, Religionsordnung,* οἰκονομία). Correspondingly, and correspondingly unsatisfactory, is the view of Webster and Wilkinson, *principle or system,* and of Da. Brown, *principle or scheme.* And correspondingly objectionable is the affiliated view of Dr. Chalmers,—shaped far too much in the mould of the nomenclature of modern science,—*method of succession.* "The law of faith," says he, "is that law by which the event of a man's justification follows upon the event of his faith,—just as the law of gravitation is that law upon which every body above the surface of the earth, when its support is taken away, will fall towards its centre."—We need not detail other efforts of perplexed and perplexing exegesis. All such efforts are superseded, and all apology for them, as soon as the scene is realized, which was psychologically present to the Apostle when he asked the question—*Through what kind of a law?* That which he calls *the glorying* had been thrust out from the scene of things in the midst of which he found himself as an expounder of the Gospel; and a ban was laid upon it to prevent its entrance. It was *legally* shut out. When fully realizing this, the Apostle asks,—*by what kind of a law? By a law that enjoins the works (of which the great body of the Jews make so much)? Nay, but by the law that enjoins faith.*

Other difficulties, besides those which circle around the expression *law of faith,* have been felt. They centre in the expression *law of works,* and have reference to the legitimacy of the Apostle's argumentation in that direction. Is it not the case, it has been asked, that *the law of works* does really shut out glorying from the hearts of men, and that most effectually? Understanding by *the law of works* the law *that prescribes the outworking of a perfect righteousness as the condition of everlasting glory,* is it not the case that such a law, when not kept, shuts out all ground of glorying? Is it not by it that *the knowledge of sin* is realized? And as *the knowledge of sin* is nothing less and nothing else than the knowledge of that which humiliates, and which consequently makes glorying an absurdity, how is it that the Apostle says that glorying is excluded, *not by the law of works,* but only by *the law of faith?* Such is the difficulty that has been felt. Kypke felt it much, and hence could not persuade himself that, when the Apostle asked *by what kind of law?* he meant *by what kind of law is glorying shut out?* He would understand the verse somewhat as follows:—*Where then is legitimate glorying,—glorying, for instance, in hope of the glory of God? and how may we attain to that glorying? It has been (alas!) shut out, but how may it be brought in?—By what kind of law? Of works? Nay, but by the law of faith.* (*Per qualem legem oritur gloriatio?*) But such an impenetration and interpretation of the clause *by what kind of law?* seems to be an inversion, rather than an explication, of what is natural. Erasmus, however, had felt the same difficulty, and hence he interprets the verse as follows:—*Where then is thy glorying, O Jew? It is taken away from thee by that Gospel which puts all the nations of the earth on a level. Salvation and righteousness are brought nigh to the Gentiles also. But by what law* (are salvation and righteousness thus brought nigh to the Gentiles)? *The Mosaic, which prescribes ceremonies? Nay, but by a new law, which exacts nothing but faith in the Son of God.* Here, too, there is the most arbitrary interjection of an idea not expressed by the Apostle, viz.,—*Salvation and righteousness are brought nigh to the Gentiles also,* (*Defertur et gentibus salus et justitia*). And when this intruded idea is linked into the query *by what sort of law?* there seems to be again a total inversion of what is natural.—Semler, likewise, was perplexed, and would supplement the clause thus:—*by what kind of law* (*can the favour of God be obtained*)? Utterly arbitrary. Bengel also was perplexed. John D. Michaelis gives the following translation of the clause:—*Through what law are we justified?* (*Durch welches Gesetz werden wir gerecht?*) And Mehring, although not aware of Michaelis's translation, proposes the very same supplement and interpretation. It is, of course, utterly arbitrary. Rückert, in his 1st edition, proposed a similar interpretation; but he felt constrained to abandon it in his 2nd, (*nur die gewöhnliche Annahme kann den philologischen Verstand befriedigen; sie muss also festgehalten werden*). De Wette, too, in his earlier editions, felt extremely perplexed, not knowing whither to turn himself. He did not see that it was possible to supplement and interpret the expression *by what sort of law?* in any other way than this:—*by what sort of law* (*is the glorying shut out*)? and yet, if thus interpreted, it seemed to him that the Apostle's interrogative introduction into his representation, and his consequent exclusion, of *the law of works*, was "a mere rhetorical and almost senseless figure, serving to give emphasis to the affirmation *by the law of faith*," (*Es ist besser—διὰ—οὐχί als eine blosse rhetorische, fast gedankenlose Figur, zur Hebung der Affirmative διὰ—πίστεως dienend anzusehen*). He ultimately, however, threw out the inconsiderate and gratuitously irreverent expression, "almost senseless," and attained a somewhat more satisfactory and sensible view of the passage, by realizing that the Apostle was picturing a scene, while building up an argument and establishing a corollary. But he did not, as we apprehend, get to the Apostle's real standpoint. When one gets to that:—

It is seen, (1), that it is the idea of the *right* of self-glorying,—the *right* as distinguished from the *fact*,—to which the Apostle is referring,—so far as regards the logical substrate of his representation. Men may *in fact* glory when they have *no right* to do so. The Jews thus gloried. But it is the *right* which the Apostle,—so far as regards the logical substrate of his representation,—disputes and denies.

It is seen, (2), that, in the psychologically pictorial scene which the Apostle pourtrays, he represents glorying as shut out, and kept out, not so much by a mere exertion of strength or force, as *by a law.* And he asks,—*By what manner of law?*

It is seen, (3), that, in his answer to this question, the Apostle does not suppose the actual existence of two divine laws, and then give the preference, for his present purpose, to one of the two. On the contrary, he assumes that there was only one divine law of ejectment, only one enactment or *ordonnance.* And assuming this, he explains, in his own vivid and vigorous way,—by negation and affirmation,—that the quality (the ποίοτης) of the law was such, that, instead of enjoining *the works* which were so highly prized by the great mass of the Jews, it enjoined *faith in the evangelical righteousness of God.*

Hence it is seen, (4), that there is a reason for the presence of the article in the excluded interrogation, (τῶν ἔργων;)

And hence it is seen, (5), that it is irrelevant to ask the questions, *does not the moral law exclude all undue glorying as well as the law of faith? Do not indeed all divine laws exclude all undue glorying?* They do. But the Apostle makes no reference to any really existent divine law but one,—*the law of faith.*

VER. 28. Λογιζόμεθα οὖν δικαιοῦσθαι πίστει ἄνθρωπον χωρὶς ἔργων νόμου.

Eng. Auth. Ver. *Therefore we conclude that a man is justified by faith without the deeds of the law.*

Revised Version. *We reckon then that a man is justified by faith without works of law.*

§ 1. The precise relation of this verse to the preceding context seems to have been the subject of earnest consideration from the most ancient times. Hence the diversity of reading as regards the connective particle;—some thinking that it is illative, *then* or *therefore*, (οὖν),—"we reckon *then*;" some thinking that it is rationative, *for*, (γάρ),—"*for* we reckon." If the former,—viz., *then*, (οὖν),—be the correct reading, the statement of the verse will be of the nature of an inference or corollary from what goes either immediately or more remotely before. If the latter,—viz., *for*, (γάρ),—be the correct reading, the statement of the verse will be confirmatory of what goes immediately before—*the* (*Jewish*) *glorying is excluded by a law of faith*, for *we reckon that a man is justified by faith without works of law.* We are persuaded that *then* (οὖν) is the correct reading, and that the statement of the verse is a corollary from what goes before, *viewed generally*, whilst there is doubtless a *more particular reference* to the peculiarly rich unfolding of the plan of justification into which the Apostle's discourse has effloresced in verses 21st—26th.

The diplomatic authorities in support of *for*, (γάρ), instead of *then*, (οὖν), are, indeed, very weighty. ℵ A D E F G, besides several cursive manuscripts, have *for* (γάρ) as their reading. It is, besides, the reading of the Vulgate, (*enim*); and also of the prae-Hieronymian codices d. e. f. g. It is most likely, therefore, that it was the reading of the Greek codices from which the original Latin version or versions were made. It is, of course, the reading of Ambrosiaster and Pelagius, and also of Augustin.

The inferential *then*, (οὖν), on the other hand, is the reading of B C K L, and of the great mass of the cursive manuscripts. It is supported, moreover, by the two Syriac versions, and also by the texts of Chrysostom, Theodoret, Œcumenius, and Theophylact. The purport, too, of the *comments* of Chrysostom, Œcumenius, and Theophylact assumes the same reading. (Œcumenius, indeed, explains the οὖν by τοιγαροῦν.)

In consequence of *then* (οὖν) being the reading of the great body of the cursive manuscripts, it was reproduced in the early printed editions. It is the reading of Erasmus's editions and of Stephens's. Of Beza's too; and of the Elzevir of 1624, and its successors. It is hence the reading of the *Received Text.*

In Robert Stephens's great edition of 1550, the reading *for* (γάρ) is mentioned in the margin, under the authority of two manuscripts, δ and ι; and Mill contended that this reading was the genuine one. He says that some reader, thinking that the Apostle's statement was an inference from what goes before, put *then* (οὖν) in the margin, and that afterwards this reading, as apparently more suitable, was admitted into the text. He remarks, however, in opposition to the reading, but certainly with no great cogency of argumentation, that there is not more reasoning, in support of justification by faith, in the preceding than in the subsequent part of the Epistle, (*verum non magis arguit Apostolus justificari nos per fidem ex superioribus, quam ex parte maxima reliquae hujus Epistolae*). Bengel, though not absolutely decided, was favourable to the reading preferred by Mill. Griesbach was quite decided. He received it into his text; and he has been followed by Knapp, Tittmann, Lachmann, Scholz, Alford, &c. Newcome says,—"The true reading is γάρ." Rückert approves of the reading; and so do Fritzsche, Meyer, Philippi, Reithmayr, Oltramare, van Hengel, Matthias, Mehring, the Five Clergymen, T. Schott, &c.

Vater is undecided, though he gives *then* (οὖν) in his text; (γάρ *certe aequiparandum fuerit*). But Matthaei decided for *then*, (οὖν). H. A. Schott, too, in his last edition, decided for it. And Tischendorf gives it both in his 1849 edition and in that of 1859. It is approved of by Reiche, by Stengel, by de Wette, by Krehl, by Hofmann, by Lange, and with emphasis by Maier.

We think that Maier is right. This is a case in which Bengel's maxim should rule—*proclivi scriptioni praestat ardua—the more difficult reading is to be preferred to the easier.* It is not easy to see how *then* (οὖν) could ever have supplanted *for* (γάρ); whereas, it is easy to see how a transcriber, who was not considering comprehensively both the warp and woof of Paul's discourse, might be tempted to substitute *for* in place of *then,* under the idea that *then* must have been a previous transcriber's mistake. If *for* be read, then the verse hooks itself on, closely and readily, to the immediately preceding verse, and gives a reason why it was by *a law of faith* that *self-glorying* was shut out. Thus this is an easy-going reading. But if the other reading (οὖν) be adopted, then there is immediately started the question, *whence is the inference drawn?* And this is a question more easily started than laid or answered. It does not seem natural to regard the corollary as deduced from the immediately preceding verse; for in that verse there is no argumentative basis for a corollary,—there is no attempt at argumentation. There is merely jubilant interrogation and asseveration. It would hence be awkward to regard the corollary as deduced from that verse. But if so, there seems to be difficulty in accounting for the introduction of the corollary at all, especially after, and immediately after, the preceding verse. It seems, therefore, to be almost incredible that any transcriber should have turned the easy-going *for* into the difficult *then.* But we can perfectly understand how the reverse alteration should have commended itself to some superficially thoughtful readers.

We would abide, then, in this case, by the reading of the *Received Text.* And we would regard the verse as forming *an independent corollary* to the Apostle's preceding discussion. It *stands abreast* with the corollary of verse 27th. And in a paragraphed text it would be well to join Muralto, and also Tyndale of old, in making use of a new line. We would go further than Muralto and Tyndale, and begin the next verse too with a new line,—letting this one stand by itself as a distinct utterance. Indeed, the entire knot of verses 27th—31st is not rightly understood unless it is regarded as a cluster of distinct and abrupt utterances, with which the preceding argumentation,—so triumphantly wrought out,—is jubilantly, as well as logically, crowned, as with appropriate *corollae.*

§ 2. There is another matter regarding the reading of the text which may be advantageously disposed of here;

though it is by no means of such significance as the connective conjunction. In the *Received Text* we read *πίστει δικαιοῦσθαι ἄνθρωπον*. This is the common order of the words in the cursive manuscripts; and it is found also in K L. But in ℵ A B C D E the order is the following,—*δικαιοῦσθαι πίστει ἄνθρωπον*, and this is the order that has been followed by Griesbach, Lachmann, Scholz, Tischendorf, &c. In F G the expression is *δικαιοῦσθαι ἄνθρωπον διὰ πίστεως*,—an evidently tinkered reading, yet certainly favouring that order of the words that gives precedence to *δικαιοῦσθαι*. We accept the reading of ℵ A B C D E; and we are all the more firmly persuaded of its genuineness, that it accords best with that view of the verse's relations that is suggested by the connective particle *then*, (οὖν). It is true, indeed, that several of the authorities that support this particle are in favour of the reverse order of the words; while several of the authorities that support *for* (γάρ) are in favour of that order of the words which we accept. But this confusion is of small significance, and need excite but little marvel, when we take into consideration that it is not likely that transcribers in general would be men of exquisitely sensitive exegetical tact. It is not probable that many of them would make much effort to transfer themselves, in a matter of minute nicety, to the precise standpoint of such a peculiar mind as that of Paul. Hence there was sufficient scope for the introduction of small incongruities, when the order of the text seemed confused.

If the arrangement of ℵ A B C D E be accepted, it is in fine harmony with the idea that the Apostle is referring to *his general discussion regarding justification*. The word *justified* is the proper term to be betoned; and hence its position in advance. But if the Apostle had been merely confirming the affirmation regarding the "law of faith," which stands at the conclusion of verse 27th, then we should have seen a special congruity in reversing the arrangement of ℵ A B C D E, and giving all the emphasis possible to the word *faith*.

But this whole subject of emphasis is slippery, and runs itself up, when considered broadly and profoundly, into complexities of vocal as well as logical harmonies, and into the idiosyncrasies of particular minds.

§ 3. *We reckon then,* (Λογιζόμεθα οὖν). Such is perhaps as good a translation of the verb as can in English be attained;—although *reckon* is a rather inadequate term to express the inner logical or quasi-logical process suggested by the original term. The word does not exactly mean, *we logically conclude, we conclude,* though this was the idea of Theophylact (συμπεραίνει τὸν λόγον, καὶ φησιν ὅτι ἐκ τῶν εἰρημένων πάντων συλλογιζόμεθα), as also of Beza, Melville, and many others. The word denotes, says Calov, *a logical inference,* (*logicam illationem*). It means, says Heumann, *to make a syllogism,* (*einen Schluss, einen Syllogismum machen*), that is, *to collect out of premisses a legitimate conclusion.* Hence in the English Geneva of 1557 it is rendered *we gather;* and in our Authorized English Version, *we conclude.* This is not, however, the Pauline import of the word. It nowhere, in all his writings,—although he very frequently employs it,—bears such a meaning. Calvin's translation, too, is rather overdrawn,—*we settle then,* (*constituimus ergo*). Not so the translation of the Vulgate and Erasmus,—*arbitramur.* It is, on the contrary, as Beza remarked, in danger of being viewed on that side of its usage which makes it merely mean, *we are of the opinion.* That, indeed, was Zinzendorf's translation, (*wir sind der Meynung*). It was, too, Fritzsche's interpretation,—who thought that there was a touch of irony or "acrimony" in the expression,—(*nempe puto*). But, undoubtedly, more is meant than mere opinion. Absolute certainty is implied; but it is *reasonable certainty*—certainty that is the result of that *inner discoursing,* or *discursive process* of the reason, that lays the foundation of rational conviction. It is certainty that is the result of that inner *reckoning,* or *counting of the logical votes,* which determines the acceptance of an idea, (λογίζομαι, τῇ χειρὶ ψηφίζω.–Hesychius. λογίσομαι, ἀναψηφίσομαι, ἀναριθμήσω.–Suidas). Melancthon merged too much this reference to an inner process, when he translated the word *we pro-*

nounce (*pronunciamus*) in his *Commentary* of 1540, and *we assert* (*adseveramus*) in his *Enarratio* of 1556. Luther's version is better,—*we hold,* (*halten wir*). Tyndale's is far too weak,—*we suppose.* Wycliffe's is better,—*we demen,* although it goes off upon another line of things,—*the inwardly judicial,* as distinguished from the *logical.* *We reckon* is, on the whole, as good a version as our language will admit of. The idea is not inaptly expressed in a colloquial Americanism—*we calculate;* for the notion of *counting* or *calculation,* as Melville noted, is inherent in the original word.

When the Apostle, then, says,—*I reckon,* he not only represents himself as *thinking,* he realizes that he was *thinking reasonably.* And when he says,—"I reckon *then,*" he looks back upon the sum of his previous *thinkings,* as expressed in his *discoursing,* more especially as that discoursing culminated in the paragraph that concludes with verse 26th. As he thus looks back, he rests in the result which he had reached. And he quietly assumes that his readers had gone with him, and will rest too:—"*we* reckon then." He and they were satisfied and sure. About what? Let us see:—

§ 4. *that a man is justified by faith,* (**δικαιοῦσθαι πίστει ἄνθρωπον**). This, with the appended clause, *without works of law,* is, says Calvin, the "principal proposition," (*principalis propositio*). It is "the proposition of the whole epistle," (*propositio hujus epistolae*), as an ancient owner of our copy of Stephens's 1549 New Testament has noted in the margin. It was imperfectly understood in the ages that preceded the Reformation; and, at the time of the Reformation, it became a battlefield of contending theologies and theologians. "This passage," says John Campensis, "has been hitherto misinterpreted, and has occasioned everywhere tragedies of quarrel, the end of which is not yet." (*Hic locus parum huc usque meo judicio feliciter intellectus, maximas in toto orbe excitavit tragoedias, quarum nondum finem videmus.*–Commentariolus.) It is the expressed essence of the Apostle's doctrine.

We need not, however, elaborately expound it, for, as it is obviously the recapitulation in miniature of the whole preceding discussion, each element that enters into its entirety has already been subjected to examination.

As to the word *justified* (δικαιοῦσθαι), see on ver. 20th. A man is evangelically *justified* when he is *made out to be in possession of that righteousness which is the title to eternal life.* That righteousness is God's. It belongs to God. It was manifested in Christ Jesus. It was wrought out and brought in by Christ Jesus. It is revealed in the Gospel. It is the gift of God. See chap. i. 17; iii. 21—24; Phil. iii. 9; Rom. x. 6—10; 2 Cor. v. 21; &c.

It is *by faith* (πίστει) that man is justified,—*faith that lays hold of the righteousness of God* either explicitly or implicitly. The righteousness of God is apprehended explicitly when the revelation regarding it is understood and believed. It is apprehended implicitly when the revelation of God's propitiousness in general, or of Christ in particular as the Propitiator, or of Christ as the Saviour, is understood and believed, even although the peculiarly Pauline aspect of the great reality is not realized. Faith in God as "the Lord-God,-merciful-and-gracious,-longsuffering,-and-abundant-in-goodness-and-truth,-keeping-mercy-for-thousands,-forgiving-iniquity-and-transgression-and-sin," involves implicitly faith in Christ as a Saviour. Faith in Christ as a Saviour involves implicitly faith in Christ as a Propitiator. Faith in Christ as a Propitiator involves implicitly faith in the propitiatory sacrifice of Christ. And faith in the propitiatory sacrifice of Christ involves implicitly, and as its obverse, faith in the meritorious righteousness of God, as wrought out by Christ, and as constituting for man, in place of his own perfect righteousness, his title to everlasting life.

The dative expression, *by faith*, (πίστει,—*the dynamic dative*), denotes instrumentality. To speak in the language of the schools:—Faith is not the efficient cause of justification. God is that. Faith is not the meritorious cause. God's righteousness, as wrought out by Christ, is that. Neither is faith the material cause. The soul of man, as a substance, is that. Neither is it the final cause. Man's good,—the universe's good,—Christ's glory,—God's glory,—all these, culminating in the last, constitute the final cause of justification. Neither is faith the formal cause. God's judicial action, his judicial finding, his judicial declaration, is that. But *faith* is still, nevertheless, in a certain respect, a cause. It is an instrumental cause. So is *the word of faith*. The two,—*the word of faith* and *the act of faith*,—constitute as it were one complex instrumentality,—the one pole of which touches the mind of God, whose word *the word of faith* is; while the other pole touches the mind of man, whose is *the act of faith*. But this stiff scholastic way of viewing the subject, though possessing advantages in the direction of distinction and precision, is far from doing perfect justice to the full realities of the case.

When the Apostle says "that *a man* is justified by faith," his expression means, "that *every man who is justified at all* is justified by faith." Some translators render the expression, not *a man*, but *man*. So Wakefield, Macknight, Newcome, Scarlett, Thomson, Cox, &c. The translation is of course legitimate, (corresponding to the *l'homme* of the French translators and the *der Mensch* of the German). But *a man* is better:—for in the use of our indefinite article we have an advantage even over the Greek language. The Apostle is not referring to *man as a species*, or to *man in general:* and hence the advantage of the translation, *a man*. The *species man* is not justified. Neither is *man in general*. It is some men only. But whensoever *a man*, be he who he may, is justified, it is *by faith that he is justified*. Beautiful, however, is the remark of Chrysostom,—"He does not say *a Jew*, or *one who is under the law*, but, expatiating wide, and throwing open the door of salvation to the world, he says *man*, using the name that is common to the race," (οὐκ εἶπεν Ἰουδαῖον, ἢ τὸν ὑπὸ τὸν νόμον ὄντα, ἀλλ' ἐξαγαγὼν τὸν λόγον εἰς εὐρυχωρίαν, καὶ τῇ οἰκουμένῃ τὰς θύρας ἀνοίξας τῆς σωτηρίας, φησὶν ἄνθρωπον, τὸ κοινὸν τῆς φύσεως ὄνομα θείς).

§ 5. *without works of law*, (χωρὶς ἔργων νόμου). Such

is manifestly the correct construction of the expression. Glöckler's hysteron-proteron translation—*without the law of works*—is extremely unnatural and violent. It proceeds, moreover, on the erroneous hypothesis that the Apostle is referring particularly to ver. 27th; and it is based, besides, on a misinterpretation of the expression *law of works*, as occurring in that verse. When the Apostle says that *a man is justified without works of law*, he means that he is justified *without any works whatsoever, performed in obedience to that law, which, in its wider sphere of relationship, exhibited the duty of men as men, and in its narrower sphere exhibited the duty of Jews as Jews.* Man is justified by faith *without any works of law, moral or ceremonial.* Man's *good works* of every kind, whether simply moral, or whether having in addition an interpenetrating element of what is ceremonial, form no part of the meritorious cause of justification. The meritorious cause, or ground, of justification is Christ's good work alone,—his righteousness, —the righteousness of God. It is not hence to be inferred, indeed, that good works are not good. Neither is it to be inferred that they are not absolutely indispensable as moral meetness for heavenly glory. They are absolutely indispensable. "Without holiness no man shall see the Lord." But they form no part of the sinner's title to glory. They do not enter at all as an element into the ground of his justification. Justification is thus distinct from sanctification. But it must ever be borne in mind that it is subordinate too. It is the means; sanctification is the end. We are justified that we may be sanctified. We are pardoned that we may be purified. Faith is enjoined, not that it may remain idle and alone, but that it may work, and work by love, and thus result in "the fulfilling of the law."

§ 6. Luther introduced into his translation of this verse the word *alone*,—"through faith alone," (*allein durch den Glauben*). The word does not modify in the least the doctrinal idea of the Apostle. It simply gives a little more edge or emphasis to it,—emphasis that was doubtless in thorough accordance with the thought and feeling of the inspired writer. Nevertheless, the additament was unnecessary and uncalled for, and should not have been made. It is not the business of a translator to make the idea of his author more emphatic than the author himself has made it. Its introduction gave, moreover, the enemies of the truth a handle for saying something about "adding to the words of the Book." It gave them an opportunity for throwing dust into the eyes of their dupes. They were not slow to take advantage of it:—and quite a little library of literature grew up around the intruded word. The apologies for Luther were in the main triumphant;—and thoroughly so when considered in relation to the peculiar shape which the impeachments assumed in the hands of his Roman Catholic opponents. In Schleenaker's **Disputatio Theologico-Apologetica pro genuina B. Lutheri versione, Rom. Cap. 3. versic. 28,** we have an excellent summary of the contents of these Apologies. It was shown:—

(1.) That the Vulgate—the Received Text of Roman Catholics—had frequently inserted the same word *only* for the sake of emphasis, although there was no corresponding word in the original; as for example in 1 Sam. x. 19.

(2.) That the Saviour himself, in quoting Deut. vi. 13,—as he did when he was tempted (Matt. iv. 10),—had used the word *only*, although it does not occur in the original Hebrew.

(3.) That the Septuagint translators had again and again introduced the same word without any corresponding Hebrew term; as for example in Gen. iii. 11.

(4.) That the Peshito translator had used the same liberty; as for example in Rom. iv. 5.

(5.) That even Roman Catholic translators who came after Luther,—such as Emser and Dietenberger,—had used the same liberty; as in Mark xiii. 32 for example, where both the translators specified introduced the word *only*. And yet Emser was one of the most zealous in raising a hue and cry against Luther for his *only* in the passage before us.

(6.) In the Nürnberg Bible of 1483, the corresponding

passage in Gal. ii. 16 is translated "*only* through faith,"—(*nur durch den Glauben*); and the same passage is translated in the Italian Roman Catholic version, published at Venice in 1546, *ma solo per la fide di Giesu Christo.*

(7.) Many of the Fathers were accustomed to use the expression, *by faith only*, when discoursing on justification. For example, Ambrosiaster, in commenting on Rom. iv. 5, uses the expression twice over, (*sola fide, per solam fidem*).

Such were some of the pleas that were put in, and appropriately and powerfully urged, in defence of Luther.

Bengel stands true to the German *Megalander*, and fell on an ingenious method of vindicating the *only*. He applies arithmetic to the case. Two things only are referred to,—

Faith and works, ...	2
Works are excluded, ...	1
Faith remains alone, ...	1

One being subtracted from *two*, there remains *but one*. It is, says Bengel, an *arithmetical demonstration.*

Tholuck says that Erasmus (*Liber Concion.* lib. iii.) remarks,—*vox* **sola**, *tot clamoribus lapidata hoc seculo in Luthero, reverenter in patribus auditur*,—"The word *alone*, which has been received with such a shower of stones when uttered in our times by Luther, is yet reverently listened to when spoken by the Fathers." Hodge repeats the quotation and the reference. We do not know where Tholuck picked it up. But while the observation seems to bespeak, by its peculiar felicity and piquancy, an Erasmian origin, it is certainly not to be found in that great repository of felicities, and wisdom, and wit, and semi-garrulities,—the *Liber Concionandi.*

Luther and his apologists were taunted as being *solifidians* (or rather, *solafidians*) and *fidesolarians.* They accepted the taunt, so far as the matter of justification is concerned, and gloried in it. But they ever contended that faith must not, and does not, remain *solitary* in the soul. (*Non* **sola est,** *etsi* **sola justificat.**) Their maxim was, that "faith never *exists* without works, although it *justifies* without works," (*fides, etsi nunquam* **sine operibus est,** *tamen* **sine**

operibus justificat). And now that the storm of the old controversy has subsided, Reithmayr himself allows that the little word *only*, which Luther introduced, is not, as considered in itself, to be blamed. The genius of the German language, he says, not only permits, but demands it, in order to give pointed expression to the opposition. (*Der erklärende Zusatz wäre an sich nicht zu tadeln, da der Genius der deutschen Sprache es zulässt, ja es fordert, um nur den Gegensatz scharf auszudrücken.*) This is going all the length that Luther himself went in his Self Defence: and it is a little too far. Yet the eloquent Mussus, in the midst of the "tragedies" that were enacted in connection with the controversy, went as far in his interpretation of the Apostle's words. He says:—"No works have place in the justification of man before God. Men are justified by faith alone, without works, moral, ceremonial, or judicial, of any law whatsoever, whether natural, mosaical, or evangelical," (*unica fide justificantur universi homines apud Deum, sine operibus moralibus, ceremonialibus, judicialibusque, cujusvis legis, vel naturae, vel mosaicae, vel evangelicae. Audis Paulinam sententiam?*–Com. in loc.). What Protestant could go farther? The language would have delighted Luther. But then the eloquent expositor had his theological back-door. He held that the reference is only to "the first justification, which is obtained in baptismal regeneration." Aquinas and Estius had another back-door. They held that the reference is to works preceding faith, and to them only. Many of their *confrères* coincide in this view. Abelard and Dionysius à Ryckel have another back-door. They say that the reference is to works external and corporeal,—such is the representation of Abelard, or to works ceremonial and judicial,—such is the representation of Dionysius. The back-door of Mac-Evilly, again, is this,—"The Apostle refers to the works performed by the sole aid of the law of Moses and the law of nature, without grace and faith, and he comes to the conclusion that these works have no share in justification." It is by one or other of these methods, or by a combination of several of them, that

Roman Catholic expositors and theologians in general, and others who in this matter side with Roman Catholics, back out of the natural import of the Apostle's phraseology. Cardinal Cajetan, however, rose in a great measure superior to the prejudices which surrounded him, and which too often, indeed, exerted a warping influence on his own judgement. He says that the Apostle does not intend to dissuade from performing the works of the law: he only intends "to exclude them from having any justificative power," (*non intendit, inquam, excludere ab executione sed a justificatione, hoc est,* **a virtute justificativa** *hominis absolute, quod est dicere* **a virtute remissiva peccatorum**). Nothing more than this idea of the great Cardinal is required to satisfy the requirements of enlightened Protestantism:—for even in the apophthegms of Gregory the Great, that "we get to works by faith, not to faith by works,"—"to virtue by faith, not to faith by virtue,"—(*non operibus venitur ad fidem, sed fide venitur ad opera,—non virtutibus venitur ad fidem, sed per fidem venitur ad virtutes*),—require to be interpreted as having reference to the highest element in virtue and good works,—*supreme love to God,* or else to be accepted with a grain of qualification. It is enough to say that *works of law* have,—in the case of transgressors of the law,—no justificative or remissive virtue or meritoriousness whatsoever. It is altogether uncalled for to deny that an unbeliever may be in some, or perhaps in many, respects a noble man,—noble in honesty, noble in honour, noble in patriotism, noble in philanthropy. Yet his nobility of character has no justificative element in it. Perfect nobility in all relations, God-ward and man-ward,—perfect or full-orbed righteousness from beginning to ending of the probationary career,—would be requisite, if man were to be justified by works of law.

VER. 29. Ἢ Ἰουδαίων ὁ θεὸς μόνον; Οὐχὶ δὲ καὶ ἐθνῶν; Ναὶ καὶ ἐθνῶν· VER. 30. ἐπείπερ εἷς ὁ θεὸς ὃς δικαιώσει περιτομὴν ἐκ πίστεως, καὶ ἀκροβυστίαν διὰ τῆς πίστεως.

Eng. Auth. Ver. Is he *the God of the Jews only?* is he *not also of the Gentiles? Yes, of the Gentiles also: Seeing* it is *one God, which shall justify the circumcision by faith, and uncircumcision through faith.*

Revised Version. *Is God (the God) of Jews only? Is he not, on the contrary, (the God) of Gentiles also? Yes, of Gentiles also; seeing it is one God who shall justify circumcision by faith, and uncircumcision through faith.*

§ 1. We shall consider the initial particle, ἤ, at the conclusion of the exposition of the two verses. The reason of this postponement will then become sufficiently evident. It is enough, in the meantime, to note that the interrogative nature of the clause to which ἤ is prefixed is not dependent on the presence of the particle. Indeed, the particle is omitted altogether in some few manuscripts, as also in Theodoret's text. Mill regarded it as spurious, (*praefixum haud dubito è marg. ob majorem emphasin*).

§ 2. *Is God (the God) of Jews only?* (Ἰουδαίων ὁ θεὸς μόνον;) We say *of Jews,* rather than *of the Jews;* for this is one of the cases in which our English idiom coincides so far with the Greek as to enable us to preserve the indefiniteness of the original. There is a fine and solemn significance in this indefiniteness: for there is an inner circle of the divine relationship within which God was peculiarly the God of such Jews (and Gentiles) as were believers of the Gospel.

The Apostle's query is exceedingly condensed; and has hence occasioned considerable difference of opinion regarding its construction. The Authors of our *Eng. Auth. Version,* following the English Geneva and Tyndale, have regarded the articulated word *God* (ὁ θεός) as belonging to the predicate of the preposition; and hence they have rendered the clause thus,—"Is he *the God of the Jews only?*" Tyndale's translation is the same. The English Geneva is similar in principle, but more awkward,—"God, is he *the God of the Jews only?*" The French Geneva is identical with the English,—(Dieu est il *seulement le Dieu des Juifs?*) The translation is almost identical with Calvin's French version,—"Dieu *est il seulement Dieu des Juifs?*" It is more natural, however, and more in harmony with the unfolded expression in Matt. xxii. 32, to regard the articulated noun as being the subject of the proposition:—"*Is God* (the God) *of Jews only?*" (If both the subject and the predicate had been expressed, the query would have run thus,—ὁ θεὸς θεὸς Ἰουδαίων μόνον; See Matt. xxii. 32.)

Fritzsche supposes that there is the ellipsis only of the substantive verb. He would render the expression thus,—"Is God of the Jews only?" that is, "Does God belong to the Jews only?" (*An ad Judaeos Deus pertinet tantummodo?*) His authority swayed the judgement and carried the concurrent votes of de Wette and Meyer, in their second and subsequent editions, as also of Maier, Oltramare, Philippi, &c. We rather think, however, that the view taken of the construction by Luther and Grotius, Baumgarten-Crusius, Krehl, van Hengel, and Matthias,—the view given in our translation,—is more correct. It assumes the ellipsis of the predicate *God*, as well as of the substantive verb;—*Is God the God of Jews only?* This view of the construction is favoured by a comparison of Luke xx. 38 with Matt. xxii. 32, as also by the expressions that occur in 1 Cor. xiv. 33, and in Rom. ii. 28, 29. Even although Fritzsche's interpretation were to be so far accepted, it would still be requisite, in order to unfold completely the Apostle's idea, to add, as a secondary supplement, the expression, "as their God:"—*Does God belong to the Jews only, viz., as their God?* Thus the ellipsis would be enlarged, instead of being contracted.

Tischendorf (1849 and 1859) supposes that, in the correct reading of the query, the adjective *alone* is used, instead of the adverb *only*, (Ἰουδαίων ὁ θεὸς μόνων; instead of Ἰουδαίων ὁ θεὸς μόνον). He is supported by the Vatican MS., and a few of the cursives. But the overwhelming majority of the cursives, as well as ℵ A C F G K L, sustain the reading of the *Received Text.* It is supported likewise by the Vulgate (*tantum*) and d. e. f. g. There can be little doubt that Lachmann, therefore, was right in abiding by the received text; and so Scholz, Griesbach, &c.

The Apostle does not query whether or not *God is the God of Jews.* He would be ready to acknowledge that God was *Abraham's God*, and *the God of Abraham's seed.* (Gen. xvii. 7, 8.) He was *the God of Abraham, and of Isaac, and of Jacob.* (Matt. xxii. 32.) He was the God of the Hebrews. (Lev. xxvi. 45.) The word *God* in such expressions is used relatively and appellatively. God was *the God* of the patriarchs and their seed, in the sense of being to them *the Lord God, merciful and gracious, long-suffering, and abundant in goodness and truth.* All that is involved in his Godhead was laid under contribution for the promotion of their weal, so far as promoting that weal was consistent with their moral state on the one hand, and his wide œcumenical relations on the other. But within the circle which embraced the divinely beneficent influences which were made to converge upon the Jews, there was an inner circle. And there was also a circle beyond. In the inner circle God was and is, in an emphatic sense, the God of Abraham and of Abraham's spiritual seed,—the God of believers of the Gospel,—the God of the good. These enjoyed and enjoy his selectest influences—his richest blessings. (*Want wat grooter, wat uitnemender goed kan 'er boven dit genoemt worden, als dat God hem tot een God zij: want dit moet van even soo veel kragt zijn, als dat God,* **al wat dat 'er is en zijn kan,** *tot voordeel en dienst des sondaars sal aanwenden.*–Vitringa.) In the circle beyond, God was and is the God of all flesh—of all mankind. He is "good unto all, and his tender mercies are over all his works." He is pouring out of the inexhaustible cornucopia of his fulness all the blessings that are needed to make all men blessed. If any lack, they are straitened in themselves, not in God. There is thus, in the moral administration of the human world, concentric circles of divine efflux and influence. In one of those circles the Jews were situated.

And hence the Apostle recognizes, as a fact, that *God was the God of the Jews.*

In asking whether "God be the God of the Jews *only,*" he makes reference to imaginations of spiritual monopoly that were too common among his Jewish brethren. They misunderstood the intention of God regarding their situation in the divine circle in which they lived, and moved, and had their being. They erroneously fancied that within the expanding sphere of blessings in which their lot had been cast, and in which they enjoyed the presence of God as their God, there was no room for any but themselves. Hence the Apostle's query. Hence, too, his next query.

§ 3. *Is he not, on the contrary, of Gentiles also?* (οὐχὶ δὲ καὶ ἐθνῶν;) that is, *Is he not, on the contrary,* (*the God*) *of Gentiles also?* Is it not the case that, as regards both the outer and the inner circles of blessings, God is the God of Gentiles also? Are not the resources of God thrown open to *all Gentiles,* and made available, so far as their own moral receptivity will admit? Are not these same resources lavished, without stint on the one hand or partiality on the other, upon *all such Gentiles as, through faith, have their moral receptivity enlarged?* Such is the expansion of idea contained in the Apostle's query, and suggested by the indefinite form of his expression;—*Gentiles,* not *the Gentiles.* The Apostle's eye swept, as we conceive, over *the outer zone* of gracious relationship, and took cognizance of it. But its aim was directed toward *the inner zone,* in which justification for everlasting life is realized.

The word which we translate *Gentiles,* though originally signifying *nations,* (ἔθνη), is here, as frequently elsewhere in the New Testament, employed to designate *individuals.* In other words, the collective force of the term is merged; and the units which constitute the collection or collections which it originally denoted rise into view. See Matt. xx. 19; Acts xiii. 48; xiv. 2, 5; xxi. 25; Rom. xi. 13; Gal. ii. 12; &c.

We freely translate δέ, *on the contrary:*—"Is he not, *on the contrary,* of Gentiles also?" (οὐχὶ δὲ καὶ ἐθνῶν;) The force of the expression, on the supposition that the δέ is genuine, might be thus represented:—"Is God the God of Jews only? *They are too apt to think so; but* is he not also the God of Gentiles?"

Almost all the critical editors have thrown out the δέ. Mill condemned it. He supposes it to have been spuriously intruded, (*elegantiae causa*). Griesbach ejected it from the text, and has been followed by Knapp, Tittmann, Schott, Lachmann, Tischendorf, Scholz, as also by Vater, Hahn, &c. The great body of Uncial MSS. omit it, viz., ℵ A B C D E F G K. It is also omitted in several quotations from the Greek fathers. And there is nothing to represent it in the Italic and Vulgate versions. Why, then, should it not be banished? Fritzsche would approve of its banishment; and so does Meyer, and Oltramare, and van Hengel. And yet we hesitate.

The matter is, indeed, of no significance, exegetical or doctrinal. And hence there need not be anxiety. Nevertheless, the overwhelming mass of cursive manuscripts are on the side of the Received Text; and there must doubtless have been older manuscripts from which these cursives copied their reading. L too has the particle. It is found also in the texts of Theodoret, Theophylact, and Œcumenius.

Tischendorf refers to Chrysostom as also supporting the particle: but incorrectly, we presume. So far, at least, as our edition (1723) is concerned, the authority of Chrysostom's text is in the other scale. The particle is omitted. And the omission was noticed by Bengel, Wetstein, Griesbach, Scholz, &c.

We incline, on the whole, to retain the particle,—just because we can scarcely conceive of its arbitrary introduction into the text, if it was originally absent. Its presence seems rather to cumber the liveliness of the interrogative phraseology. Its absence seems to leave the language tighter and more nervous. Had the Apostle been fastidious in his use of words:—had he aimed at that "wisdom of words" which consists of elegance, and neatness, we can suppose that he might not have inserted the δέ. Had a rhetorician been at his side, he might perhaps have suggested that the point of his query would be sharpened by the omission of the particle; and mayhap, too, the Apostle would have assented, and added that he was a stranger and foreigner in that whole region of things that pertains to the minutiæ of the "wisdom of words." We cannot, hence, conceive of any transcriber studiously importing the word into the text. We can easily conceive, on the other hand, of many a transcriber thinking it an intrusion and an encumbrance, and therefore cancelling it. We would hence apply, in this case, Bengel's maxim, *proclivi dictioni praestat ardua.*

Mill's idea, that the particle was surreptitiously introduced *for the sake of elegance,* seems to us to be, in its own little world of things, a turning upside down of the entire reality of the case. And hence, indeed, as well as on account of the difficulty of translation, it has happened, as a matter of fact, that many translators, who never doubted the canonicity of the particle, have nevertheless ignored it in their versions :—Erasmus, for instance, and Luther, and Calvin, and Beza, and Piscator; as also Tyndale, and our Authorized English Version, and the old Dutch; also Diodati; and the French Geneva, and Martin, Ostervald, le Cene, Beausobre et Lenfant, &c. In consequence of the omission of the particle in these translations, we put little weight upon the adduction, by Tischendorf and others, of the Vulgate, and Italic, and other versions, in support of the reading that omits it. Neither would we, on the other hand, attribute much significance, in defence of the particle, to the fact that the Peshito version runs thus,—"for is God of the Jews only, *and* not of the Gentiles?"

Fritzsche says that if the particle be inserted, then we have simply one interrogation, instead of two,—*Is God of the Jews only, but not of the Gentiles?* His idea on this matter has been received, and is echoed, by Meyer, Baumgarten-Crusius, Maier, Oltramare, and van Hengel. But we doubt its accuracy. For, *in the first place,* the *yes* (ναί) of the following clause would have been,—in the case supposed, and especially when the Apostle's use of the adverb is taken into account, and, indeed, its New Testament use in general,—somewhat inappropriate,—so inappropriate as to have prevented, we should suppose, the apocryphal intrusion of the connective δέ. And, on the assumption, again, that δέ is not apocryphal, it would be unlikely that the Apostle should have answered the one complex query,—which Fritzsche puts into his mouth, and which necessarily shades off into a merely secondary position the second member of the interrogation,—in such a manner as to suggest, so far as the affirmative *yea* or *yes* is concerned, that God *is* the God of Jews only. But, *in the second place*, Fritzsche has overlooked the fact that multitudes of editors of the text, as well as translators, who never entertained a suspicion of the spuriousness of δέ, have nevertheless recognized the duality of queries;—as Erasmus, for example, and Robert Stephens, in their various editions; and le Fèvre, in his *Intelligentia;* and Luther, and the other translators specified above. The same double query is also found in the texts that were issued from the presses of Henry Stephens (the great), of Robert Stephens (the second), and of Platter, and the Elzevirs, &c., &c.

We accept, then,—though hesitatingly,—the reading of the *Textus Receptus* in this case; and yet we would contend for the duality of queries.

§ 4. *yes, of Gentiles also,* (**ναὶ, καὶ ἐθνῶν**). The Apostle, instead of answering his first question,—*Is God the God of Jews only?* runs it on, as we have seen, into its obverse phase, *Is he not, on the contrary, the God of Gentiles too?* and then he contents himself with answering this second question:—*Yes, yea, certainly, assuredly,—he is the God of Gentiles also.* All that is implied in the Godhead of God is, according to the mind of the Apostle, on the side of Gentiles as really as of Jews, so far as they are morally susceptible of availing themselves of the fulness of his essential goodness. Zinzendorf translates the affirmative particle, *without doubt,* (*ohne zweiffel*). It is strongly affirmative, and turns up in the Latin *nae;* and yet it is interestingly connected with the English *nay,* and the Latin and Gothic *ne.* There is a point of things at which affirmation and negation shake hands, as it were. When we *deny* a question as a question,—when we *deny*, that is to say, that a question needs to be proposed, we *affirm* that the thing questioned is unquestionable.

§ 5. *seeing it is one God who will justify circumcision by faith, and uncircumcision through faith,* (ἐπείπερ εἷς ὁ θεὸς ὃς δικαιώσει περιτομὴν ἐκ πίστεως, καὶ ἀκροβυστίαν διὰ τῆς πίστεως). The literal translation would be,—*seeing the God who will justify circumcision by faith, and uncircumcision through faith, is one.* The numeral adjective *one* (εἷς) is the predicate of the proposition. The articulated noun *God* (ὁ θεός) is the subject. The clause, *who will justify circumcision by faith, and uncircumcision through faith,* is analytically illustrative or explicative of the subject.

The Apostle is rendering a reason for his strong affirmation at the conclusion of the preceding verse. But, in rendering it, he does not aim at a strict logical demonstration. There is, indeed, a genuine syllogistic filament running through his thoughts and words. But it is not stiff. It is free and easy. He is taking his breath, as it were, after his somewhat elaborate discussion, extending from chap. i. 16 to chap. iii. 26. He is pausing and looking back on what he has been exhibiting and establishing. Hence his corollary of verse 27. Hence, too, his corollary of verse 28; and hence, too, his corollary of verses 29, 30.

§ 6. It is remarkable that, in many editions of the New Testament, either a full point or a colon is interposed between verses 29th and 30th. Before the versicular division by Robert Stephens, a full point was inserted by Erasmus. It is found, too, in Platter's edition of 1540, and in Froben's of 1545. Robert Stephens contented himself with a colon in his 1549 and 1550 editions. But in his versiculated edition of 1551 he, too, inserts a full point, which is also found in Henry Stephens's edition of 1587; and in all Beza's editions; and in the Elzevirs; and in Maestricht's editions, too, of 1711 and 1735; and in the editions of Courcelles; in Mill also, and Wetstein, Bengel, Schoettgen; Griesbach too, and Matthaei; Knapp also, and Tittmann, Naebe, Goeschen, Vater, Hahn, Muralto, Ornsby, &c. But certainly there should be only a comma. And this is the point that Lachmann, Fritzsche, Tischendorf, Alford, Buttmann, have inserted, and of which Meyer approves.

§ 7. *seeing that*, (ἐπείπερ),—*since at all events*. We may in some such way represent the force of this compound conjunction. The Apostle's idea is substantially this, *since, as must be admitted;—since, as will be admitted, whatever else may be denied.*

There is some difficulty in determining the proper reading. Instead of ἐπείπερ, ℵ A B C read εἴπερ, (*if at all events*). Griesbach hesitated,—retaining, however, ἐπείπερ. Lachmann accepted εἴπερ, and it was ultimately approved of by de Wette. Alford, too, has accepted it. So did Tischendorf in his 1849 edition. In his 1859 edition, however, he has restored ἐπείπ ερ, which is the reading of the *Received Text*, and of the great body of the cursive manuscripts; as also of D E F G K L, and of Chrysostom, Theodoret, Theophylact, and Œcumenius; as likewise of the text from which the Vulgate was made, and its prae-Hieronymian precursors, (*quoniam quidem*). The great body of modern expositors—though Matthias is an exception—approve of retaining ἐπείπερ. They are right, we apprehend; as seems to be rendered the more apparent when we take into account that ἐπείπερ occurs nowhere else in the New Testament, whereas εἴπερ occurs repeatedly. Some transcribers might stumble at the unusual word. Others, who were copying at a common bench, from the dictation of a reader, might lose the slight initial sound ἐπ-,—made by the simple compression of the lips. And as that sound would be immediately followed by the full toned -είπερ—a familiar acquaintance to the ear of the New Testament copyist,—we can easily suppose that its indistinct echo might readily die away, or be altogether unnoticed.

§ 8. *God is one,* (εἷς ὁ θεός). It is in the admitted idea of monotheism that the Apostle finds the basis of his confident conviction that God is the God of Gentiles as well as of Jews. The Jews and Judaizers would not be disposed to challenge the idea. The very first principle of the Mosaic theocracy is thus expressed :—" Hear, O Israel, the Lord our God is one Lord." (Deut. vi. 4.) "Is there a God beside me?" asks God himself by the mouth of his prophet Isaiah; and he answers his own question thus;—" Yea, there is no God; I know not any." (Isai. xliv. 8.)

Koppe has the strange notion that a full point should be placed after the expression, *since God is one,* and that the relative pronoun which follows should be interpreted as meaning *He then.* (*Post θεός, punctum posui, ut argumentatio finiatur.*—ὅς *pro* οὗτος οὖν.) Tholuck, in his first edition, acquiesced in Koppe's notion. But such an interpretation of the relative is the extreme of arbitrariness; and the abscission of the whole relative clause is almost tantamount to cutting off a right hand. It involves the sacrifice of that peculiar aspect of the unity of God which stood out prominently to the eye of the Apostle. Some expositors imagine that, strictly speaking, there is no reference in the Apostle's expression, to the monotheistic idea. They think that the word *one* is "not numeral." So Sclater expresses it. It has reference, he says, either to the divine unchangeableness or to the divine impartiality. Such a notion, however, altogether fails to sound the depths of the Apostle's reasoning. If we do not go down to the unity of the divine substance, relatively at least to mankind, we shall find no real basis for the impartialities of providence and propitiation. And, so far as unchangeableness is concerned,—unchangeableness either of essence or of principles of procedure,—it has nothing to do with the Apostle's argumentation. The inspired man's thoughts draw deeper, and have reference to the area, or extent of sphere, within which the attribute of unchangeableness finds scope. Is this area bounded off by the limits of the Jews?—or does it comprehend the whole world of mankind?

§ 9. *the God who will justify circumcision by faith, and uncircumcision through faith,* (ὁ Θεὸς ὃς δικαιώσει περιτομὴν ἐκ πίστεως καὶ ἀκροβυστίαν διὰ τῆς πίστεως). The Apostle might have said, *who justifies.* And so, indeed, the Vulgate has rendered his expression, (*qui justificat*). Luther, too, has given the same rendering; and Tyndale; and the authors of our Authorized English Version; and many others besides. Grotius defends the translation on the principle that the future is put for the present, *after the Hebrew manner,* (*more Hebraeo*), when continuous acts are referred to;—the Hebrew language having no tense that quite corresponds with the present in Greek, Latin, English, German, &c. Rückert, in his 1st edition, rested in the same explanation. In his 2nd he interprets the future as denoting *the relation of sequence* that subsists logically between a conclusion and the premisses from which it is deduced, (*since God is one, it follows that he justifies all in one way*). Seb. Schmidt had long before him entertained the same idea, (**justificabit,** *ratione consequentiae*). Mehring substantially agrees. Beza, again, thought that the Apostle was referring to the justification that will be realized at the last day. Fritszche approved of this idea. Tholuck, in his 4th edition, adopted the same interpretation. In his first three editions he took no notice of the tense. In his 5th he shifts his ground, and supposes that the future is used *potentially,* (*God is morally able to justify by faith both Jews and Gentiles*). Hodge, again, says that the future expresses "a permanent purpose."

We question whether any of the explanations specified hit the nail on the head. That of S. Schmidt and Rückert is certainly out of the question,—as is more especially evident when we notice that the clause in question belongs to the subject of the proposition, and forms no part of the conclusion that is deduced from the unity of God. The interpretation of Beza, again, is utterly inadmissible,—and for this among other reasons, that justification on the last day is never represented in Scripture as being *by faith* or *through faith.* Men shall then be judged according to their deeds, "that every one may receive the things done in his body, according to that he hath done, whether it be good or bad." (2 Cor. v. 10; Matt. xxv. 31—46.) It is character that will then be taken into account. (Rom. ii. 5—10, 13, 16.) There is, however, a filament of truth in the idea of Grotius; and another and kindred filament in the idea of Hodge. But the real explanation of the peculiar tense,—the explanation into which the specified filaments enter, though only as filaments that from the nature of the case could not well be absent,—seems to be found in the fact that the Apostle realized that the grand evangelistic epoch of the world's history had just been initiated. The Propitiation had just been accomplished. The mystery that had been from of old had just been unfolded. The one true *crusade* had just been inaugurated. The middle wall of partition had just been broken down. The heralds of the Gospel, as bearers of good news to every creature, had just started from the evangelic centre in Jerusalem, and with their jubilee trumpets they were rushing forth, radiatingly, to the outlying world. In these circumstances it was natural for the Apostle to be looking to the future, rather than to the past or to the present, for the triumphs of the Gospel. All that was past was but preliminary to what was to come. And the present was to the Apostle but the transition-point between the former sowing-time and the reaping of those fields of the world that were already white unto the harvest, and ready for the sickle. The Apostle had a profound realization of his position in the ages. And this realization was vivid within his consciousness while he was penning the contents of this chapter. Compare the "now" of verse 21st, and "this time" in verse 26th. It is of course implied in the Apostle's expression that the series of God's justificative acts will be continuative; and thus Grotius's idea is realized. It is also implied that the series will be continuative, because of God's purpose; and thus Hodge's idea is realized. Nevertheless, if the triumphs of the Gospel had been mainly in the past, the Apostle would not have employed the future tense. It is in his conviction that they were to be mainly in the future that we find the real key to his expression. (*Respexit ad eos, qui adhuc essent in Judaismo, seu paganismo,*–Erasmus:—

Das futurum braucht Paulus in Absicht auf die Zeit des neuen Testaments, welche damals, zur Zeit Pauli, ihrem grössten Theil nach, noch zukünftig war.–Rambach.)

The Apostle says,—"who will justify *circumcision*" (περιτομήν) and "*uncircumcision*," (ἀκροβυστίαν). Conybeare seems to suppose that these nouns are used in their customary abstract sense. Hence he translates the whole clause thus: —"he will justify through faith *the circumcision of the Jews*, and by their faith will he justify also *the uncircumcision of the Gentiles*." So Heinfetter. But certainly the great body of expositors are right in regarding the terms as used concretely,—so that *circumcision* means *circumcised* (*Jews*) = περιτετμημένους, or περίτμητους, while *uncircumcision* denotes *uncircumcised* (*Gentiles*) = ἀκρόβυστους. (καλεῖ δὲ περιτομὴν μὲν τοὺς Ἰουδαίους, ἀκροβυστίαν δὲ τὰ ἔθνη,–Theodoret.) Comp. Rom. ii. 26; iv. 9; Gal. ii. 9; Eph. ii. 11; &c. It is probable that the abstract nouns are employed by the Apostle to give prominence to the condition of the individuals referred to. The circumcision of the one class would be no recommendation in the matter of justification. The uncircumcision of the other class would be no disqualification. In the sphere of things referred to, circumcision would be no help, and uncircumcision no hindrance. Comp. Col. iii. 11. The article is omitted because it is not the entire circle either of the circumcised on the one hand, or of the uncircumcised on the other, who are referred to.

In the expression, "who will justify circumcision *by faith*," (ἐκ πίστεως), the words *by faith* are evidently to be connected, not with the noun *circumcision*, but with the verb *will justify*. Wakefield, indeed, and Belsham, and Burton, take the other alternative,—supposing that the Apostle means "the circumcised that have faith" as Wakefield expresses it, or "the Jews who accompany circumcision with faith," as Burton explains it, (as if the Apostle's expression had been τὴν ἐκ πίστεως περιτομήν or περιτομὴν τὴν ἐκ πίστεως). Tyndale took the same view of the construction;—*circumcision which is off faith*. So the

English Geneva of 1557. Rosenmüller, too, originally held the same opinion; though he ultimately abandoned it. Basil Cooper espoused it, and so Glöckler, and Olshausen. Mehring, too, though hesitatingly, proposes it, (as *de novo*). Jowett, too, inclines toward it. Knight contends strenuously for it. But it is a violent and utterly improbable interpretation. The antithesis between the two clauses of the Apostle's expression caps the improbability. For such is the nature of the second clause, that it is scarcely possible to conceive of the expression *through faith* as adjectively qualifying the noun *uncircumcision.*

Our English phrase, *by faith,* is an exceedingly imperfect rendering of the original expression, (ἐκ πίστεως). And yet we can scarcely say *from faith* or *of faith,*—though the former version is given by Thomson, and the latter by the E. Geneva. If we were to say *in consequence of faith,* we should approximate very nearly to the force of the Apostle's preposition, which brings into view *outcome* or *result.* (Rilliet has, *en conséquence de la foi.*) But our phrase *by faith* has got fixed and idiomatized; and we may hence abide by it. The Apostle's idea is, that when God justifies circumcised Jews, his act of justification emerges into objective realization out of their condition of faith.

It is added—"and uncircumcision *through faith,*" (διὰ τῆς πίστεως). The article has puzzled many expositors. Vaughan and Knight suppose that it objectifies the word *faith;*—*the faith,* that is, *the Gospel.* Mehring supposes that it is not so much its presence in the expression before us, as its absence in the preceding expression, that requires to be accounted for; and he accounts for that absence in the manner already noticed;—thinking that the phrase *by faith* is to be construed not with the verb *will justify,* but with the noun *circumcision.* It is strange that he did not perceive that, on such a hypothesis, it is the absence of the article, in agreement with the noun *circumcision,* that would require to be wondered at. The reason of the presence of the article in the expression before us seems very evidently to be found in the writer's intentional reference to the faith particularized in the preceding expression. It is one of those delicate shades of inter-relationship which cannot be reproduced in English. Were we to translate the articulated phrase, as Beausobre et Lenfant, Michaelis, and Wakefield have done, *through the same faith,* we should, indeed, be running on the right line of thought, as Green has perceived (*Gram.* p. 300, ed. 1842), but we should also be greatly intensifying and exaggerating the article's force. The Apostle does no more, in his introduction of the article, than simply turn, as it were, his finger, for a moment, by a slight and elegant motion, in the direction of the foregoing *faith.* The Peshito translator not unhappily reproduces the same referential effect by a peculiar Syriac idiom,—the preliminary introduction of the pronoun, accompanied with the preposition that is to be repeated with the noun, (ܒܗ̇ ܒܗܝܡܢܘܬܐ).

Knight supposes that the phrase *through faith* qualifies the noun *uncircumcision,* instead of being attributed to the action of the verb *will justify.* He imagines that the phrase *uncircumcision through the faith* denotes those whose uncircumcision is "perpetuated by means of the faith,"—who are convinced by the Gospel that a change from a state of uncircumcision to a state of circumcision is unnecessary. The idea is good enough. But the construction is like the tearing up of a tree by the root, and then planting it again, with inverted head.

There has been great speculation among expositors in reference to the two prepositions employed in the respective clauses,—"*by* faith"—"*through* faith." The great body of commentators conclude that the diversity is a mere rhetorical variety. This was the opinion of Augustin, (*non ad aliquam differentiam dictum est, tanquam aliud sit* **ex fide,** *et aliud* **per fidem**; *sed ad varietatem locutionis,*–De Spir. et Litt. cap. xxix.). It was also the opinion of Pelagius, (*ipsum est* **ex fide** *et* **per fidem**). So Abelard, (*diversitas est locutionis, non sententiae*). So Beza, Melville, Grotius, Este, Day. So, too, in modern times, Klee, Rückert, Meyer, de Wette, Philippi, Krehl, Oltramare,

Maier, Turnbull. Hence Beausobre et Lenfant employ in their translation the same preposition in both clauses, (*la circoncision* **par** *la foi, et le prepuce* **par** *la meme foi*). Michaelis uses the same liberty, only he gives the preference to the Apostle's second preposition, whereas Beausobre et Lenfant give the preference to his first, (*die Juden* **durch** *den Glauben, und die Heiden* **durch** *eben denselbigen Glauben*). Conybeare uses a greater liberty still. He retains the two prepositions, but reverses their position:—*he will justify* **through** *faith the circumcision of the Jews, and* **by** *their faith will he justify also the uncircumcision of the Gentiles.* Mace, again, throws out altogether the first of the two:—*who will justify both the Jews and the Gentiles through faith.* These are unwarrantable liberties on the part of translators. They assume far too much. They assume that there must be no difference intended, since no difference is by them perceived. Calvin thought that the difference was in minutiae only,—and the minutiae of form, not of essence or of substantive thought. He imagined that there was a touch of irony in the Apostle's remark,—as if he had said:—*If any one will have a distinction between Gentile and Jew, let him have this,—that the former is justified* **through** *faith and the latter* **by** *faith.* (*Itaque subesse in verbis ironiam judico, acsi diceret, Si quis vult habere differentiam Gentilis a Judaeo, hanc habeat, quod ille* **per** *fidem, hic vero* **ex** *fide, justitiam consequitur.*) Tholuck, in his 2nd, 3rd, and 4th editions, approved of Calvin's idea. So Stengel; and so Philippi. Fritzsche too;—though he does not refer to Calvin,—as, indeed, neither did Stengel, nor Tholuck in his 2nd and 3rd editions. We rather think, however, that this notion of irony is out of harmony with the earnestness and solemnity of the feelings that were, at the time, in a state of tension within the Apostle's mind.

Is there, then, a distinction intended, in the variety of prepositions? Van Hengel is certain that there is, although he candidly confesses that he does not know how to draw the line. (*Quomodo vero utrumque distinguendum sit, candide me nescire fateor.*) Theodore of Mopsuestia was convinced that there was a difference. But he fails in his attempt to explain it, (ἐπὶ τῶν Ἰουδαίων τὸ ἐκ πίστεως τέθεικεν, ὡς ἂν ἐχόντων μὲν καὶ ἑτέρας ἀφορμὰς πρὸς δικαίωσιν, οὐ δυναμένων δὲ αὐτῆς μετέχειν πλὴν ἐκ τῆς πίστεως). Origen, too, made most ingeniously the attempt, but failed. Aquinas, too, made the attempt, and fails. So does Bisping, notwithstanding very considerable confidence. Matthias is very sure that there is a wide difference, and he toils, in page after page, to exhibit it;—establishing, with all his might, that "by faith" denotes, in some sense, the *ground* of justification, and "through faith" the *means;*—the former phrase being equivalent to *because they believe,* (*weil sie glauben*), and the latter to *when* or *if they believe,* (*wenn sie glauben*);—the former having reference to the reward of faithfulness to their peculiar covenant relationship, (*als Lohn ihrer Bundestreue*), the latter having no such reference; &c. The whole effort, so far as Matthias's treatment of the case is concerned, leads into nothing. Manifestly, he has not got hold of the cue. But Camerarius did get hold of it, and Wetstein, and Er. Schmid; and so, too, substantially, Heumann, Baumgarten-Crusius, and Reithmayr, and Webster and Wilkinson.

The cue is this, we apprehend:—In the first phrase,—the one that is used in relation to Jews,—there is a latent antithesis to the counter phrase, *by works,* (ἐξ ἔργων); while in the second phrase,—the one that is employed in relation to Gentiles,—the latent antithesis is not unnaturally dropped, so that room is left for a phrase which, in itself considered, is simpler and more philosophically appropriate. The distinction, indeed, is not to be too much made of. It is not to be very much made of. It must not be inflated on the one hand, or squeezed on the other. The idea must not be taken up that the Apostle could not have reversed the position of the prepositions. He evidently could, without committing any real phraseological or theological impropriety. Jews are justified *through faith* just as truly as Gentiles are. (See Gal. ii. 16.) And Gentiles are justified *by faith,* or *in consequence of faith,* or *out of faith,* just as truly as Jews are. (See Gal. iii. 8.) The denial of this reciprocity of possibility is fatal to Matthias's theory of explication, and to that of Bisping. Nevertheless, while it would be wrong to make a great deal of the distinction, or to fancy that important theological conclusions lie couching in it,—it is easy enough to see that there was propriety in the variation of phrase, and, in addition, a beautiful suggestiveness.

In speaking of the relation of works to justification, the Apostle never uses the expression—*through works*, (δι' ἔργων). His expression is invariably *by works, out of works*, (ἐξ ἔργων). Comp. Rom. iii. 20; iv. 2; Gal. ii. 16; iii. 10; &c. There is a reason for this fact. Works were regarded by the Jews as *the true meritorious cause* or *meritorious source* of salvation, and not merely as an adjunctive condition. So deeply was this prejudice rooted in their minds, that most of them, we presume, would have been ready to admit that faith in the Messiah might be necessary, as an adjunctive condition, provided always that their favourite works were allowed to be the true meritorious cause or source. It was, we apprehend, in direct antithesis to this notion that the Apostle said, *by faith, out of faith, in consequence of faith.* Not that he meant that *the act of faith* is the meritorious cause of justification. (Jaspis, Goeschen, Schott, Fritzsche, are unhappy in their translation, when they render the Apostle's phrase, *propter fidem, on account of faith.*) But he meant that the meritorious cause or source of justification was to be looked for in the direction of *faith* as distinguished from *works.* It was really in faith's object, —the propitiation of the Messiah. And it was when that object was apprehended by the act of faith, that the act of justification emerged into realization. When, therefore, no direct antithesis is intended to the idea that is expressed by the phrase *by works*, or *out of works*, it is simpler and more philosophical to say *through faith*, that is, *by the intermediacy, on the part of man, of the act of faith.* The Apostle, hence, having completed in the first clause of his expression his antithetic representation, drops it in his second clause, and employs the simpler and more philosophic expression.

It is easy to see the reason why the nouns *circumcision* and *uncircumcision* precede the phrases *by faith* and *through faith.* The emphasis of idea lies on them, and not *vice versa:* and hence it was befitting that they should be betoned.

§ 10. We are now in a position to turn back to the commencement of these two verses, and to consider the force of the initial ἤ. Luther, and, after him, the German translators, in general, translate it disjunctively, *or* (*oder*). So Piscator, Reitz, Heumann, Bengel, Michaelis, Brentano, Stolz, Schrader, &c. But not Zinzendorf. Cocceius and Vitringa coincide with Luther, (*aut, of*). So do the greater portion of the modern German critics; and, of the Dutch, Greve, Bosveld, van Hengel, Vinke. So, too, of the French, Oltramare and Rilliet, (*ou*). Our English translators, on the other hand, from Tyndale downward, almost unanimously, leave the particle untranslated. Worsley, however, and Dewes are exceptions. Conybeare too. Diodati left it untranslated. So, too, the French Geneva, following Calvin's French version. So Martin, Ostervald, Beausobre et Lenfant, and le Cene. So, too, the Dutch translators, old and new. The force of the particle seemed to these translators to be absorbed in the interrogatory essence of the expression. The same idea seems to have been entertained by the authors of the old Latin versions, inclusive of the Vulgate; for they render the particle by the Latin *an.* So, too, in modern times, le Fèvre, in his version; Erasmus, in his; Beza, in his; and Castellio, Arias Montanus, and Erasmus Schmid, in theirs, &c. Seb. Schmidt gives *num* in his. Theodoret, as we have already mentioned (§ 1), omits the particle from his text. And the other Greek expositors make no use of it as a disjunctive.

We think that the Greek fathers are right; and that the Vulgate is right in its translation: and that our English translators are right too, in allowing the particle's force to express and exhaust itself in the interrogation. Moses Stuart was of the same opinion; but when he said that "an interrogation made by ἤ supposes that the person who is addressed will agree in the answer with the person who puts the question; so nicely are the Greek interrogative signs adjusted,"—he lost sight entirely of the real function of the particle. The particle is ambidextrous,—and neither grasping you with the right hand nor repelling you with the left. It always implies an alternative: and to this extent the great body of the critics who follow Luther are justified in assigning to it a disjunctive import. But they are wrong, we apprehend, when they assume that, in the case before us, it is the *second* alternative that is referred to, and that hence the particle should be rendered *or*. When the two alternatives of thought are explicitly specified, they may be respectively introduced by the repeated particle, (ἤ—ἤ); and the particle may thus, in the first instance, be rendered *whether*, and in the second, *or*. Very often, however, the one or the other of the alternatives is implicit only, and not explicit. If it be the first that is unexpressed, we may then employ *or* to render the ἤ of the second. But if it be the second that is suppressed or metamorphosed, it would be leading ourselves astray to render the solitary ἤ by the disjunctive *or*, as Luther has done in the case before us. Its force in such cases is infused entirely into the interrogation as an interrogation,—which carries, nevertheless, more or less distinctly in its bosom the notion of an alternative.

The critics who have followed in the wake of Luther's version have perplexed themselves to discover the first and latent alternative in the case before us. Some think that it is wound up and concealed in the word *man* in verse 28th:—*Am I right in saying* **man,** *and not* **Jew? or** *is God the God of Jews only?* Others, and these in greater numbers, suppose that it is wound up and concealed in the 28th verse viewed as a whole:—*Is it the case that it is by faith, without works of law, that men are justified?* **or** *is God the God of Jews only? He is not the God of Jews only; and hence it cannot be the case that men are justified by works of law, for the law was given to Jews only: and thus it follows that it must be by faith that men are justified.* Such is the apagogic argument supposed. Oltramare, again, imagines that the first alternative is found in the 27th verse:—*Where is boasting then? It is excluded, is it not?* or *is God the God of the Jews only?*

But all of these attempts to bring to light the invisible alternative fail. For, as to the first, the word *man* in verse 28th is not the emphatic term of the proposition. As to the second, the idea that justification might be *by works of law,* if God were the God of Jews only, is not consistent with Pauline theology, or any true theology whatsoever. The Apostle has shown, most emphatically and convincingly, that "*no flesh* can be justified by works of law," (ver. 20). As to the third, Oltramare has to go too far back for his alternative; and he has, moreover, in addition to his too lengthened retrogression, to assume that we must read *for* (γάρ) instead of *then* (οὖν) in verse 28th.

The alternative in the Apostle's query looks, we apprehend, forward instead of backward for its complementary antithesis. It is found in the second clause of the verse:—*Is he not the God of Gentiles also?* Had the antithesis been stated in regular form, the two queries would have run thus:—*Is God the God of Jews only?* or *of Gentiles also?* (ἢ Ἰουδαίων ὁ θεὸς μόνον; ἢ καὶ ἐθνῶν;) But the impetuous Apostle, in handling a subject so very clear, seems, as it were, to have been impatient of remaining in the purely deliberative mood for so long a time as was required to complete the balance of competing alternatives. And hence, abandoning the merely deliberative appeal, he, in the second clause, assumes that all needful deliberation is ended, and that decision has been reached,—"*Is he not* the God of Gentiles also?"

In other circumstances still, there might have been no second query expressed at all. And then, as in Rom. vi. 2; vii. 1; &c., we should have been left to our own resources to supply the implied alternative; and it could always be easily supplied in some such way as the following:—*Is God the God of Jews only?* or *is he not?*

It does not fall within our scope to theorize regarding the primary force or radical import of the interrogative ἤ. The variety of ideas expressed in Greek by this particular vowel-sound, in isolation, is proof of a convergence of lines from a variety of points in that extended circumference of speech out of which arose the full and normal development of Greek. The ᾖ of the substantive verb seems to be far removed in origin from ἤ, the comparative conjunction. And the relation of ἤ, the comparative conjunction, to ἦ, the adverb, and ἤ, the interrogative conjunction, opens up a wide field for philological speculation on the inter-relation of the elements (the στοιχεῖα) of language. So far as the interrogative is concerned, we query with ourselves whether or not it be not a remnant of primitive and inarticulate speech, such as remains in our kindred English *eh?*—a wide-spread interrogative sound, found in its perfection among the barbarous tribes about Sierra Leone on the west coast of Africa.

It is more within our sphere to state, or rather to repeat, that we regard the Apostle to be uttering a succession of compacted apophthegms in the five concluding verses of the chapter. Verse 27th is one, and self-contained. The Apostle pauses when he completes it. He, as it were, takes his breath; and then he utters the corollary-apophthegm of verse 28th. He again takes his breath; and then he gives expression to the corollary-apophthegm of verses 29th and 30th. He pauses once more for a moment; and then gives utterance to the grand corollary-apophthegm of verse 31st. These corollary-apophthegms are all distinct. Yet they are all closely connected. They are strung, like beads, together. They form a finely beaded corolla, crowning the preceding discussion, and sparkling, as with the light of inestimably precious gems, upon the forehead of apostolic thought.

VER. 31. Νόμον οὖν καταργοῦμεν διὰ τῆς πίστεως; Μὴ γένοιτο· ἀλλὰ νόμον ἱστάνομεν.

Eng. Auth. Vers. *Do we then make void the law through faith? God forbid: yea, we establish the law.*

Revised Version. *Do we then abolish law through faith? Far be it. On the contrary we establish law.*

§ 1. This is the concluding corollary of the cluster. It has been all along a favourite with those students of Bible truth who have been desirous that the element of purity or sanctification should not be overlaid, in man's representations of God's evangelical scheme, by the element of pardon or justification. This passage, says Melancthon, teaches us how to interpret all other passages that speak of works and law. (*Hic locus docet nos interpretari omnia dicta de operibus et lege.* Comment. in loc.)

§ 2. The apophthegm is, as Melancthon and many other expositors remark, an *occupatio.* "The words have in them," says Sclater, "a preoccupation." They anticipate an objection which many might be ready to start. (*Ipse sibi, quod ab alio aliquo proponi posset, obtendit.*-Origen.) Jewish and Judaizing critics, especially, would, in many cases, be forward to insinuate or assert that the Apostle's doctrine regarding the method of justification amounted to the abrogation of law.

§ 3. Note the inferential *then,* (οὖν). It "glints" on the apophthegm in verse 28th,—"We reckon, then, that a man is justified by faith *without works of law;*" and thence it gleams backward on the general scope of the preceding discussion, alighting more particularly on those hill-tops of thought that rise conspicuous in verses 22nd and 20th. The Apostle, as it were, says, *Since it is the case that we do maintain that justification is through faith,* **without works of law,** *does it follow that we do away with law altogether?*

§ 4. *Do we abolish law?* (Νόμον καταργοῦμεν;) The verb employed by the Apostle,—a favourite with him, though with no other writer known,—is not easily reproduced in translation. This difficulty is evidenced by the remarkable multiplicity of renderings which the word has received in our *English Authorized Version.* It is rendered *to make without effect, to make of none effect, to make void, to bring to nought, to put down, to do away, to put away, to make to cease, to make to fail, to make to vanish away, to loose, to deliver, to abolish, to destroy.* In addition to the acknowledged epistles of Paul, it occurs once in Hebrews ii. 14, where it is translated *to destroy.* It occurs in one other passage of the New Testament, Luke xiii. 7, where it is rendered *to cumber.* It occurs in the Septuagint only four times, and all the four instances are found in one book, in Ezra, (iv. 21, 23; v. 5; vi. 8). In these Septuagintal passages the word has very nearly its primitive etymological meaning, *to throw idle.* It is used in reference to the rebuilders of Jerusalem. In Luke xiii. 7 the word has a corresponding meaning,—*Why cumbereth it* (καταργεῖ) *the ground?—Why should such a tree be allowed to make the ground idle* (*so far as fruit-bearing is concerned*)? In the *Phoenissae* of Euripides, 765,—one of the few classical passages in which the word occurs,—its etymological import is also preserved,—*But I go, that we may not be idle handed,* (ἀλλ' εἶμ', ὅπως ἂν μὴ καταργῶμεν χέρα),—*that we may not make the hand idle.* It is well, when considering the very various branches of application into which the word develops itself, as it grows and expands in the soil of the Apostle's mind, to keep in view their connection with the stem-idea. Even when he prophesies that the time will come when "prophecies *shall fail,*" the idea is that by and by prophecies shall have no more *work to perform.* They shall not require to utter themselves, in their own peculiar way, in the ears of men. When death is represented by him as *abolished* by Christ, the idea really is, that death is *thrown idle,*—having got no more *work to do.* When "the body of sin" is said by him to be *destroyed,* the meaning is, that it is rendered *inactive.* Even when believers are represented as *delivered from the law,* (κατηργήθημεν ἀπὸ τοῦ νόμου), the idea is, that, so far as concerns the right of the law to set them *to work for life,* they are thrown idle. The law has no more authority to say to them, *Do this, or die.* It does continue to say, *Do this;* but it does not say, *Do this, or die,—Do this, and live.*

When, in this 3rd chapter of Romans, verse 3rd, the question is put,—"shall their unbelief *make* the faithfulness of God *to fail?*" the meaning, at bottom, is, "shall their unbelief *throw idle* God's faithfulness,"—so that God's faithfulness to his promises *shall have nothing henceforth to do?* And so, in the passage before us, the question really is,—*Do we throw law idle? do we deprive it of its work?* that is, *do we make it a dead letter? do we nullify it? do we abolish it?* —*do we upset it?* The Vulgate has it rather too strongly, "Do we destroy?" (*destruimus?*), or as Wycliffe gives it, "distrien we?"

The Apostle does not refer to legislative action. His meaning is not,—*Do we, by legislative action, repeal law?* And when, in the 2nd member of the verse, he says, "*Far be it!—we establish law,*" his meaning is not, that law is established by some new legislative enactment. There was no occasion, in the divine moral government, for additional legislative action in the sphere of things referred to. And even though there had been, the Apostle would never, when speaking of such action, have said, "Do *we* abrogate law? Nay: but *we* establish it."

The reference of the Apostle's expressions is entirely to *moral influence,* as involved in evangelical teaching or doctrine. Hence it is that his interrogation is introduced as a corollary from the preceding discussion,—"Do we *then* throw law idle?"—"do we *then* upset law?" Hence, too, the self-consciousness that is expressed in the query,—self-consciousness in the direction of efficient agency,—"Do *we* then upset law?"—*we,* who preach and promote the Gospel of salvation,—the good news of propitiation, and of the consequent attainability of gratuitous justification by faith in the Great Propitiator? The force of the Apostle's query is this:—"Do we, preachers of the Gospel, introduce "a doctrine which involves a species of moral lawlessness?— "Do we take off the reins of moral restraint?—Do we para- "lyze the moral power of divine law?—Is it a legitimate "inference from our doctrine, that law is thrown idle, and has "got nothing more to do?—Is it involved in the glad tidings "which we preach, that licentiousness may be indulged in "with impunity?"—Such ideas were supposed by some to be inseparable from the doctrine of *justification by faith without works of law.* Hence the Apostle's subsequent query—"Shall we continue in sin, that grace may abound?" (Rom. vi. 1.) Hence, indeed, much of his profound and glorious discussion in chapters vi., vii., viii. Hence, too, the theory and the practice that characterized such communities of self-deceivers as sprang up sporadically toward the left hand of Christianity,—under the name of Nicolaitanes, &c. Hence, too, the protest which James, in the second chapter of his epistle, lifts up against the abuse of the evangelic doctrine,—a protest in which he reminds the church that there is another phase of justification besides that which is by faith alone,—a phase which Paul never intended to deny, or dispute, or ignore. His question here, indeed, looks entirely in the same direction with the representations of James:—*Do we then upset law* (*in its moral influence upon manners within, and manners without*)?

Law, (νόμον). What law? Expositors have differed; and many have felt perplexed. Theodoret seems to have supposed that the word denotes *the Old Testament Scriptures.* He explains it, at all events, as meaning *the law and the prophets.* Semler, in modern times, takes the same view, decidedly, (*ipsis Judaeorum libris*). Rosenmüller began by awarding the preference to the same view: and he got confirmed in it as he went on with his subsequent editions. Koppe, too, decided for it (*oracula V. T. quaelibet*), and Bolten (*die Schrift*), and Morus, and Flatt, and Moses Stuart. De Wette began his career with the same idea, (*das A. T.*); but he abandoned the interpretation in his 2nd edition, and persisted in the abandonment. Tholuck, on the other hand, started from a different standpoint, and with a different interpretation; but in his 2nd and 3rd, as also in his 4th and 5th, editions, he accorded the preference to this. These critics generally suppose that there is in the Apostle's query, or at all events in his answer to it, the echo of the statement that he makes in the 21st verse—"attested by *the law* and the prophets." And they suppose, too, that in the succeeding chapter the Apostle proceeds to unfold his idea, and to show in detail that his doctrine was really in harmony with the Old Testament Scriptures. The interpretation is,—in its sharply-outlined definitiveness at least,—untenable. For,—not to insist that, on the hypothesis of its correctness, we should have expected the word *law* to be articulated,—there is nothing in the preceding discourse which could give a handle to the objection that is anticipated. Everything the reverse. The Apostle everywhere grounds his doctrines on the Old Testament Scriptures, and nowhere uses any expression that could be construed into apparent opposition to the Word of God. And, again, he does not proceed in the 4th chapter to show that his doctrine *establishes* the Old Testament Scriptures. It is his aim, on the other hand, to prove that the Old Testament Scriptures *establish his doctrine*, —a very different idea,—the contrary, indeed, of the former.

Other interpreters suppose that the Apostle has in view what they call *the Jewish law, as such.* They mean by this Jewish law *that system of ordinances*—divinely revealed in the Old Testament Scriptures—*which was binding on the Jews as Jews, during the currency of their peculiar dispensation.* This was the opinion of Dionysius à Ryckel and de Lyra, who say that, as the Mosaic law culminated in the Gospel, it was not *abolished* or *destroyed*, but only developed, fulfilled, perfected, and thus *confirmed.* Erasmus took the same view, (*Neque enim id aboletur, quod in meliorem reparatur statum, non magis quam si defluentibus arborum floribus succedat fructus, aut umbrae succedat corpus*). So Michaelis, (*Vermuthlich ist seine Meinung, die Lehre vom Glauben ist nichts anders als der Sinn des Levitischen Gesetzes*). Cardinal Cajetan agreed in the interpretation, so far as regards the reference of the word *law*, though he took a different view of the aim of the Apostle. He thought that the Apostle was showing that the doctrine of justification by faith illuminates and commends the whole Mosaic Institute as a system really divine; seeing that the Jewish law *was based upon the Gospel.* The same view of the word *law* is taken by many modern expositors, although they differ widely as regards the Apostle's intention in his query; and although, too, it is with very varying degrees of definiteness or indefiniteness that the word is understood. Fritzsche thus interprets it, and de Wette ultimately, and Meyer, and Oltramare, and Alford. But it cannot be the case that the reference of the Apostle is, sharply, to *the law*, as *a system of peculiar ordinances, or commandments, for the Jews, as Jews, during the currency of their peculiar dispensation.* For, in the first place, it is not in this narrow sense that he uses the word *law* in the preceding context. (Verses 28th, 21st, 20th.) In the second place, the law, in this sense, was not *established* in its influence by the Apostle's teaching. In the third place, the law, in this sense, was *old, and ready to vanish away.* It was really *thrown idle,* having little or no farther *work to do.* And yet, in the fourth place, it was not by the doctrine of justification through faith that the law, in this sense, was thrown idle. It was not by this doctrine that it had become obsolete or obsolescent. The doctrine of justification by faith had been one and the same from the very commencement of the various dispensations of grace; for,—as Cajetan truly remarks,—"Every one who, in any age of the world, has received the forgiveness of sins, has been characterized either by explicit or by implicit faith in Christ," (*Fides Jesu Christi semper fuit explicite vel implicite in omnibus qui consecuti sunt remissionem peccatorum ab initio mundi*). Hence, as it was not by the doctrine of justification through faith that the Jewish law was thrown idle, but by the advent of Him who fulfilled the prefigurative peculiarities of the law, and who has always been, explicitly or implicitly, the Great Object of justifying faith, we should have expected that if the Apostle saw meet, on technical grounds, to deny that he and his compeers were throwing the law idle, he would nevertheless have pointed out what it was that was really effecting the law's obsolescence. At all events, we should not have expected that he would have proceeded, without any reference to this, to say:— "Far from that: *we establish* the law."

A very large proportion of expositors have had no definitely rounded conception at all of the reference of the word *law.* Origen, for instance, thought that it was well that the Apostle, instead of saying that the law is *not thrown idle,* contented himself with asseverating that it was not *he* who threw it idle. The law, he thinks, was thrown idle, but by a higher hand. Ere, however, he finishes his exposition, he views the law as *the Scriptures.* To the eye of Chrysostom, too, and of Theophylact, and Œcumenius, the word *law* was floating as in a mist. They did not distinguish what was evanescent from what was permanent. They did not observe, indeed,—at least for the time being,—that the law is, as law, many-sided; and hence they did not seek to find out the particular side of its reality at which the Apostle was looking. The same indeterminateness has prevailed down through the ages to modern times. We find it in Aquinas, for instance; and in Calvin too. And, coming down to our own era, we find Baumgarten-Crusius saying that the word *law* is here used in a double sense (*im Doppelsinne*), as denoting both *the Mosaic law* and *the Holy Scriptures.* Bengel, in his day, fancied also a double sense. De Wette, and Meyer too, while protesting that the word means *the Mosaic law,* and not *the Old Testament Scriptures,* yet terminate their expositions by running up to the virtual assumption that the word must, after all, mean *the Old Testament Revelation.* Böhme says that it means *Judaism:* Reiche, that it means, partly, *the moral and religious Revelation underlying the Old Testament writings,* and partly *the Economy founded thereon,* (*die, in der Urkunde des A. T. niedergelegte, sittlich-religiöse Offenbarung, und die darauf gegründete Verfassung*). We need not specify other phases of opinion.

The word must be viewed, we apprehend, from a somewhat different stand-point. It has reference, we suppose, to that particular phase of *the Divine Instruction,* (הַתּוֹרָה), *authoritatively vouchsafed to men,* (**νόμος**), which exhibits *the duty of man as man.* This is the fundamental element of the entire body of the various Revelations that God has made of Himself in connection with mankind. It is hence, and emphatically, the fundamental element of that verbal Revelation which God has made of Himself in the Holy Scriptures. It is hence, too, the fundamental element of that portion of the verbal Revelation that constitutes the Old Testament Revelation. It is hence, also, the fundamental element of the oldest portion of the Old Testament Revelation,—*the Law of Moses* in particular. It is, also, the fundamental element of all the divine Revelations that historically preceded the giving of the law of Moses. It is, likewise, the fundamental element of that inner law that is uttering its imperative in every man's reason and conscience. It is, in short, *the law of laws.* It is *the law,* by way of eminence. It is *law* "par excellence." Nothing else can be legitimated as law to man, that does not spring up from it, or lean down and rest upon it.

It is to *law,* viewed in this its fundamental element, that reference is made in verse 20th, verse 21st, and verse 28th. And it is doubtless to the same fundamental element of law that reference is here made. The Apostle, in short, looks to the innermost of the concentric rings of the whole complex body of divine Revelations. He looks past that mere external and circumferential sphere that exhibited *the duty of Jews as Jews;* and he fixes his attention on the sphere that exhibits *the duty of man as man.* This sphere of things he found in the Jewish Institutions and Books. But not there only. He found it likewise in all men's minds. He might have called it, *the law.* But he chooses to use the unarticulated expression, *law.* And, as our English idiom admits, equally with the Greek, of both phases of representation, there is no reason why we should, with Alford and others, render the word more definitive than we find it,—*the law.* Still less, however, is there good reason to introduce, with Vaughan, the indifferently indeterminate, yet individualizing article,—*a law.*

The reason why the Apostle makes reference to that fundamental element of all divine Revelation toward men, —*the moral law,*—is evident. His doctrine of "justification through faith, *without works of law,*" was liable to be misunderstood, as if it involved the idea of a virtual abrogation of the authority of moral law. It has, in fact,—as witness all the phases of antinomianism,—been frequently so misunderstood. Hence the *occupatio*:—"Do we then make law inoperative?"—Is moral law deprived of its proper sphere of operation?—May men, or, at all events, may believing men, live without regarding the injunctions of moral law?

Augustin takes this view of the word *law*, (*De Spir. et Litt. cap.* xxx.); and in full agreement with his view is the leading element of the interpretations of Melancthon, Melville, Este, Philippi, Krehl, Umbreit, &c. In some of these, as in the interpretation of Calvin and many others, there is a want of definiteness and fixity, resulting, we presume, from a feeling of uncertainty. But the main aim of all the expositors specified is in the direction stated. Bishop Middleton, too, aimed in the same direction, when he says that the word denotes *moral obedience*. For, though the form of his thought is, indeed, a strange inversion of the natural pyramid of idea represented by the term *law*, yet the substance of his meaning is theologically and exegetically correct.

§ 5. *through faith?* (διὰ τῆς πίστεως;)—through *the* faith already referred to: but not, as Vaughan would have it, *through the Gospel. Do we upset law by that peculiarity of our great evangelical doctrine which consists in the idea that justification is* **through faith, without works of law?** The expression *through faith* does not of itself mean *through the doctrine of faith;* and yet the Apostle is certainly referring to the place that *faith* holds *in his doctrine.*

§ 6. *Far be it*, (μὴ γένοιτο). *That be far from us!* (*A nobis tanta impietas procul!*-Mussus.) See on verse 3rd. He repels the idea with intensity of dislike. He, as it were, intimates that he could never be a party to the promulgation of any such doctrine. He could not for a moment engage in preaching and promoting any doctrine that had bound up in it, as a legitimate involution, the subversion of moral law.

§ 7. *On the contrary, we establish law,* (*ἀλλὰ νόμον ἱστάνομεν*). There is some diversity of reading, as regards the form of the verb. — In the Received Text its form is *ἱστῶμεν*,—a reading that has the support of E K L and the great body of cursive manuscripts. It occurs also in the texts, as we have them, of Chrysostom, Theodoret, Œcumenius, and Theophylact. *Ἱστάνομεν*, again, is the reading of ℵ A B C F. It is supported, too, by D, which has *περιστάνομεν*; and by G, which has *στάνομεν* at the beginning of a line. It is found, likewise, in Origen's *Commentary on John*, tom. xiii. 17; as also in Cyril of Alexandria, and Procopius, and Damascene. It is a matter of no exegetical significance which of the two readings should be preferred. Both of them are the indicative plural of unusual forms of the verb *ἵστημι*,—the one belonging to *ἱστάω*, the other to *ἱστάνω*. There is a preponderance of old diplomatic authority for *ἱστάνομεν*; and the employment of that form,—not in the current text,—so liable to be tinkered,—but in an incidental quotation, by Origen, lends very considerable weight to the probability of its canonicity. Fritzsche decides for *ἱστῶμεν*, on the ground of euphoniousness at the conclusion of the sentence, and of rhythmical relationship to *καταργοῦμεν* in the preceding member of the verse. Oltramare agrees with him. Philippi, too, acquiesces. And Wordsworth regards his opinion as "entitled to consideration." We rather think, however, that the obvious euphoniousness of *ἱστῶμεν* affords presumptive evidence that Readers and Transcribers would not readily have substituted *ἱστάνομεν* in its place, if they had found *ἱστῶμεν* in their codices. But if, on the other hand, they found *ἱστάνομεν*, we can easily conceive that some would have but little scruple in exchanging it for the full-toned *ἱστῶμεν*, more especially when they reflected that they did not thereby introduce a different word, but only a different and more melodious form of the word that was before them. Griesbach, Knapp, Schott, and Scholz, retain *ἱστῶμεν*. Lachmann and Tischendorf, Hahn and Alford, give *ἱστάνομεν*. Meyer and van Hengel approve.

Böhme,—reading, as he did, ἱστῶμεν,—throws out the conjecture that perhaps the word was the subjunctive of the common form of the verb;—*let us establish.* He adds, however, that he does not know of any author who had taken that view; and he does not press his conjecture. Fritzsche misrepresents him in this matter, (*Pelagius et Boehme* ἱστῶμεν *conjunctivum esse putant*). Baumgarten-Crusius misrepresents Paulus in the same matter. He says that Paulus regarded the verb as being in the subjunctive mood. But this is not the case. It is, however, the case that in *one* of the expositions given under the name of *Pelagius* this interpretation of the word is assumed, (*stare faciamus*). Of course, it is an untenable interpretation,—being inconsistent with the reading ἱστάνομεν on the one hand, and with the mood of mind on the other in which the Apostle was when composing the paragraph before us. He was not in the mood of an exhorter, but in that of a systematizer or system-builder.

What does he mean when he says,—*we establish law?* Tyndale translates the verb *we mayntayne.* It is too feeble a rendering; unless we were to suppose that the Apostle was simply discharging the function of an advocate. And this supposition would be far from the real state of the case. Matthias proposes to translate the word, *we let stand,* (*lassen wir stehen*). But this is feebler still, and quite aside, at once from the natural import of the verb and from the grand moral aim of the Apostle. Zinzendorf translates it, *we make to stand* (*wir machens stehen*),—a far better rendering, and quite in harmony with the naturally causative import of the word. It is not, however, sufficiently idiomatic. Luther renders it, *we set up* (*wir richten das Gezetz auf*),—also a just and good rendering; for, although it does imply, as Matthias objectingly remarks, that law had fallen, and was lying prostrate, yet the implication, when properly understood, is consonant at once with the matter of fact in the case assumed, and with the Apostle's representation of the case. Chrysostom long before had remarked that the Apostle's expression implies that the law was *not standing,* (αὐτὸ γὰρ τὸ εἰπεῖν, ἱστῶμεν, ἔδειξεν οὐχ' ἑστῶτα). It implies, says Theophylact, that the law was *lying*, (διὰ δὲ ταύτης τῆς λέξεως δείκνυσιν αὐτὸν κείμενον).

The law, indeed, had not *fallen*, and was not *lying prostrate*, so far as its legislative validity and authority were concerned. In the sphere of legislative validity and authority its position was the same that it had been from the beginning, and will be to the end. It was stable as the throne of God Himself. But when the law is contemplated in a lower sphere,—the sphere in which it comes into contact with human volition,—the sphere consequently of its actual or factual moral influence upon the inner and outer life of man, we see that there is a sense in which it has been, with awful impiety, not only pushed aside, but overturned and trampled under foot. It has been *upset*. It has been *overthrown*, and laid prostrate as in the dust. Nay, it has been *broken*. And men, in their infatuation, have danced deliriously over its fragments. . Such is sin. There is in*sult* in it, in reference to the law and the authority of the Lawgiver. This is solemn matter of fact. And the Apostle was thinking of it; as is evident from the scope of the entire preceding part of the Epistle.

Now, his doctrine of *justification by faith in the propitiation of Christ* not only meets the wants of men in the direction of pardon for the past; it also meets their wants in the direction of purity for the future. It involves provision for the establishment of the moral influence of moral law. Into whatever soul it finds an entrance,—in that soul it raises up, as from the dust, the prostrate law, and *makes it stand*. It *sets-up* that which was *up-set* by sin. It *establishes*, in the sphere of the soul's inner and outer activities, an ethical influence, which is really,—when we let down our line into the depths of the subject,—nothing more, nor less, nor else, than the native moral influence of the moral law. There is a point of unity whence both propitiation and legislation respectively start, and whither they return.

Luther's translation is thus perfectly legitimate. It has been accepted by Michaelis, and ultimately by Stolz. But *establish* — a kindred rendering — is still better. It is

Wycliffe's version, (*we stablischen*). It is given, too, by Erasmus, (*stabilimus*); and accepted by Calvin, Beza, Piscator (*bestätigen*); by the English Geneva too, and also the French Geneva (*establissons*); by Diodati, likewise, (*stabiliamo*); and by Felbinger, Reitz, Bengel, Struensee, Bolten, Brentano, van Ess, Kistemaker, &c., among the German translators; also by Er. Schmid, and Seb. Schmidt, and Schott (ultimately). The Dutch translations are equivalent, (old,—*verstercken:* new, *bevestigen*). And so Schrader, (*stelle ich fest*). The Apostle's doctrine of justification by faith *establishes* the ethical influence and authority of law, viz., in the souls of believers.

How? The Apostle explains the *how* at considerable length in chapters vi., vii., viii. Here he contents himself with simply asseverating, as in one intense flash of light, the fact that the influence of law is established by the influence of faith. He contents himself with this,—for he was touching off, in rapid succession, gleams of corollaries; and he was in haste, when done with them, to carry his readers into another part of his great discussion on the method of justification, (chap. iv.).

It is lawful, however, for the expositor to anticipate a little. How, then, does *the doctrine of justification by faith in Jesus Christ* involve *the establishment of a right ethical influence,—the influence of law,—within the believer's soul?* Commentators give manifold answers,—some in lines of thought that certainly run up to the centre of the reality, others in lines that diverge and lose themselves in surrounding chaos or nonentity. There is room for variety and complexity of representation. For the Apostle's idea on the subject does not confine itself to a single line. It expands into a sphere, filled with multitudinous lines,—but lines that, instead of running zigzag into tanglement and confusion, go in, from every point of the superficies, harmoniously and convergingly, to the centre of the believer's experience.

In that centre we find the realization of the fundamental principle of all stable society among moral beings,—**love.** It is love that binds man to man, and men to God,—and God to men. Love is the bond of the moral universe. It is in the possibility of the perfection of love, that there is the possibility of perfect union and communion. It is hence the case that love is the mightiest of all motive powers in the sphere of things moral. Remove love, and thought would be for ever inert for want of motive power. Suppose the non-existence of love, and in thought you have annihilated everything of the nature of motive, not only for activity in the moral creature, but also for creation by the Creator. You have done more:—you have annihilated, in thought, the very central element of infinite perfection in infinite being. You have thus undermined the idea of God. A being who is not moral,—a being who is not **love** in the centre of his morality,—is not an infinitely perfect being. Such a being is not, and could not be, God. It is no wonder, then, that in the word **love** we find the sum and substance of moral law. (Deut. vi. 5; Lev. xix. 18; Rom. xiii. 8—10; Jas. ii. 8; Matt. xxii. 37—40.) It is no wonder, too, that in the fact of God's love we find the secret of his moral power over the hearts of his moral creatures. And, in the case of sinful and prodigal and alienated moral creatures, such as men, it is still the case that it is love only that can win them. If they are to be *won* they must be *wooed.* It is love only that is the morally recuperative power,—love in the form of loving-kindness, benevolence, compassion, mercy, tender-mercy, tender-mercies. This only is the hammer that can break in pieces the hard heart. This only is the fire that can fuse its inductility and obduracy. Love is the power of powers. And it is simply because **the object of justifying faith comprehends in its bosom the most astonishing manifestation of divine love,** that it has power, when believed in, to subdue the rebellion of the heart, that is, *to re-establish the authority of moral law within the soul.* **God overcomes men's evil by his good—his love.** That is the secret of the wonderful involution of sanctification in justification,—of purity in pardon. Therein, too, we see the reason of the precedence of justification and pardon in relation to sanctification and purity. "We love him, because he first loved us," (1 John iv. 19); and "loving Him," we love all who bear his image, and we "keep his commandments," (1 John iv. 20; v. 2, 3; John

xiv. 15). John Staupitz,—Luther's early spiritual adviser, —though enveloped, like his pupil, in no little darkness, yet saw so far as to notice this ethical sequence of things. Hence the 10th and 19th chapters of his little book on *Love to God*, which are respectively entitled :—" Our love to God is born out of the revelation of God's love to us." —" He who loves God will undoubtedly keep his commandments." (*Das Liebe in uns zu Gott wird geboren aus der Offenbarung der Liebe Gottes zu uns.—Der die wahre Liebe hat zu Gott, der vollbringt unzweifenlich alle seine Gebote.*) God is in Christ. And hence in Christ's love we have God's love; and thus it is that "the love of Christ *constraineth us to live not unto ourselves, but unto him who died for us, and who rose again.*" (2 Cor. v. 14, 15.) The divine love constraineth us to love in return, and to live in love. It constraineth us, that is to say, to aim continually at the fulfilment of the law. There is no power in the universe equal to love for *constraining* on the one side, and *restraining* on the other, heart and head and hands. Hence the experience of all Christians. Hence, too, the marvellous power with which such words as the following are instinct :—" God **so loved** the world, that he gave his only begotten Son, that whosoever believeth in him should not perish, but have everlasting life." (John iii. 16.) Hence, too, the key to the amazing devotedness of Paul :—" The life which I now live in the flesh I live by the faith of the Son of God, **who loved me, and gave himself for me."** (Gal. ii. 20.) It is **love** which is "the fulfilling of the law." And this love is begotten within us by the love of God, which is exhibited in the object of justifying faith. Thus are we to account for the Apostle's statement,—*We establish law by faith.* Obedience to law, on our part, may be set aside, and is set aside, in the matter of justification,—but it never can be set aside in the matter of sanctification. It is, indeed,—to speak scholastically,—the form, or formal cause, of sanctification.

Augustin caught the Apostle's idea,—though he gave it a peculiar shape,—and that not the best possible,—in reproducing it. "The law," he says, "is established by faith, because faith obtains grace whereby the law is fulfilled," (*Lex statuitur per fidem, quia fides impetrat gratiam, qua lex impleatur.*)–De Spiritu *et Litt.* cap. xxx. See also his Enarrat. in Psal. cxviii. 66; and his Sermo clvi. cap. iv. Zuingli, too, caught the Apostle's idea,—"He," says he, "who has faith in God through Christ will study the will of God, and righteousness, though he will not trust to his works for salvation." (*Qui fidit deo per Christum, is voluntati Dei et innocentiae studebit, sed non fidet suis operibus, nec salutem aut justitium ex operibus sperabit.*) Luther was not so successful as Augustin or Zuingli. His gloss is the following:—"Faith fulfils all law; works fulfil no fraction of law," (*Der Glaube erfüllet alle Gesetze; die Werke erfüllen kein Titul des Gesetzes*). His meaning,—if we may judge of it at once from the gloss itself, and from his observation on the 3rd Chapter of Romans in his *Golden Preface*, and from the expositions of some of his followers,—amounts to this,—*Faith finds in Christ the fulfilment of all law, and it thus, by accepting Christ, honours and magnifies and establishes the law.* "By the righteousness of faith," says the Lutheran Hunnius, "is the law fulfilled,—for it involves in itself the perfect fulfilment of the *whole* law by Christ," (*Hac ipsa justitia fidei impletur lex; cum includat totius legis impletionem perfectam a Christo praestitam*). "How," says Hemming, "is the law established? Christ so heals the corruption of our nature, that by his righteousness imputed to us through faith, we obtain the end of the law; and because he hath fulfilled the law for us, he is made righteousness to us." (*Quomodo igitur stabilitur lex? Vitiositati carnis nostrae et communi corruptioni ita medetur Christus, ut ejus justitia nobis imputata per fidem, finem legis consequamur, propterea quod Christus pro nobis legem implevit, factus sit nobis justitia.*) "I therefore judge," says Sclater, "with the best modern interpreters, that the law is thus far established by the doctrine of faith,—that the righteousness which it requireth, *quod ad materiam,* is not abolished, but rather stablished, inasmuch as what it requires, *Do this, and live,* we have it in Christ by believing;—Faith finding in him what man cannot find in himself,—the perfect obedience which the law enjoineth." So, too, Seb. Schmidt, and Christian Schmid, &c. We do not wonder that such an interpretation of the passage was not quite satisfactory to the finer exegetical tact of Melancthon. In his first work on the Epistle, his *Annotations* of 1522, he saw in the passage a reference to the yearning of the believing soul after newness of heart, so that the law might be obeyed. (*Est ergo Christianismus assiduus gemitus postulantis per Christum, non imputari delictum, sed adjuvari et innovari cor ita ut fiat Lex.*) In his *Commentary* of 1540, he laid down the two principles, (1), that without faith obedience to the law is an impossibility; (2), that with faith obedience to the law begins. (*Teneantur ergo hae duae regulae;—sine fide impossibile est legem fieri;—item, fide fit et placet lex, fide inchoatur obedientia et placet.*) In his *Enarratio* of 1556 he has a long dissertation on the verse, in which, after making some irrelevant reference to the ceremonial law, he comes to the moral law as what is chiefly referred to by the Apostle. That law he regards as running itself up ultimately into identity with the eternal wisdom of God. It is the eternal rule of righteousness that is inherent in the nature of God. It has been revealed to rational creatures in such a way as to demand their conformity in character to God, and to consign to destruction all such as will not be conformed. This eternal wisdom of God, he says, is by no means abolished in the Gospel. How could it? It is "established" through faith. How? He somewhat wavers in his answer. But he specifies the three ways following:—(1.) By the acknowledgement which faith accords of the justice of the condemnation which the law pronounces on sinners. (2.) By the acknowledgement, which faith accords, that it is only through the perfect obedience of the Mediator to the law that the remission of sins is obtained; thus the law, in its threatenings, is recognized as something very different from an empty murmur, (*inane murmur*). (3.) By the hope which faith inspires of perfect personal obedience to law in heaven,—the beginnings of which perfect personal obedience are realized on earth. It is in the third of these ideas that his exposition culminates. It is on it that he dwells. And the good old man waxes eloquent on the subject. He deplores the imperfections characteristic of believers on earth, (their *obedientia* is *valde languida et squalida*); he rejoices in the prospect of perfection in the future, (in that *aeterna Academia* in which believers shall be employed for ever in studying the love of God and of Christ); and he bursts out into direct prayer to the Saviour to kindle in us his own light, and to destroy all the sins and blasphemies of monks and cynics and ungodly men.

§ 8. In consequence of not understanding the Apostle's aim in this corollary-apophthegm, a considerable number of critics have supposed that the 31st verse of chapter iii. should have been the 1st of chapter iv. So, more or less decidedly, Rosenmüller, Bahrdt, Koppe, Oertel, Böhme, Morus; Reiche too, and de Wette, Meyer, Oltramare, Cooper, Krehl, Maier, Matthias, Ewald. The mode, however, in which the 1st verse of chapter iv. starts (Τί οὖν ἐροῦμεν κ.τ.λ.) affords abundant evidence that there was a considerable pause in the progress of the Apostle's thoughts just at the point that intervenes between the two chapters. It is fortunate, therefore, that the capitular division is as it is.

OMNIPOTENS atque Misericors Deus, Gratias tibi dehinc habeo, quas possum maximas, pro singulari et paterno tuo auxilio, quo me in Epistolæ hujus Illustratione hactenùs tam clementer direxisti, adjuvisti, sublevasti. Inprimis quod telam hanc antehac cœptam potuerim tuâ fretus et adjutus gratiâ pertexere, nonnisi inter catenatos multiplices labores alios, et morbi sævi ac pertinacis varios impetus atque remoras.—Affunde è cœlesti tuo Sanctuario benedictionem huic labori meo, ut redundare possit ad Gloriam Nominis tui, ad Veritatis æternæ illustrationem et propagationem, errorum, quibus Ecclesiæ hoc seculo ab hominibus contentiosis, ambitionis typho inflatis, perturbari solent, dispulsionem, ad Juventutis studiosæ multiplicem ædificationem, ad patientiæ in variis tentationibus atque ærumnis consolidationem, vitæ denique nostræ totius quotidianam emendationem et reformationem.

Da DOMINE, *ut nos, quamdiu in hoc seculo peregrinamur, intentos semper oculos et animos habeamus in Cynosuram et lumen Verbi tui, quod nobis per Sanctos Prophetas et Apostolos tuos reliquisti, ut Lumen hoc nobis quotidie prælucens, diligamus, dilectum sequamur, et totos nos in reliquo vitæ nostræ curriculo ad ipsius splendorem et ductum conformemus; donec suo tempore à via ad metam nobis propositam feliciter progressi, Te non ampliùs in speculo aut ænigmate cognoscamus, sed de facie ad faciem in cœlesti Patriâ contemplemur, et cum Filio tuo unigenito Domino Nostro* JESU CHRISTO ET SPIRITU SANCTO *Paracleto celebremus, sine fine accinentes myriadum myriadibus sanctorum Angelorum:—Amen, benedictio, et gloria, et sapientia, et gratiarum actio, et honor, et potentia, et robur* DEO *nostro, in secula seculorum.* AMEN.

(THEODORUS ZUINGERUS,

In fin. suae Analyt. Recensionis Epist. ad Romanos.)